Contents

Contents

VOLUME II

Śāstrīya Saṅgīta and Music Culture of Bengal Through the Ages

Vol. II

CHHAYA CHATTERJEE

Sharada Publishing House
Delhi - 110035
1996

First Published 1996

This book is published with financial assistance of
SANGEET NATAK AKADEMI
New Delhi.

Rs. 1500 (2 Vols. Set)
ISBN: 81-85616-34-5

Published by B.L. Bansal
SHARADA PUBLISHING HOUSE
(Publishers on India's Past and Present)
40, Anand Nagar, Inderlok, Delhi - 110035
Phones: 5117390, 5116763
Typeset by Neographics
1811 Gyani Bazar, Kotla, New Delhi - 110003
and Printed at Santosh Offset,
Delhi - 110035

Styles of Music in various Centres of Bengal at a glance — Periodwise

Centre	1750-1775	1775-1800	1800-1825	1825-1850	1850-1875	1875-1900	1900-1947
Krishnanagar	Pakhāvaj & Dhrupad	Same	Khayāl also	Same as before-	—	—	—
Bishnupur	Kīrtana	Pakhāvaj, Dhrupada & Kathakatā also.	Same as before, also Khayāl, Bīn & Tablā	Same as before, Sitār. Esrāj & . Thumrī	Same as before	Same as before	Same as before
Murshidabad	Bāīnac, Pakhavaj, Dhrupada	śāstrīya saṅgīta	Śāstrīya Saṅgīta of all styles.	Same as before	Same as before, also tablā	Same as before	—
Burdwan	—	Khayāl, Ṭappā	Ṭappā, Khayāl	Dhrupada also	Same as before	Same as before	—
Calcutta & its various "bāḍis"	Kavigāna, Bāināc	Ṭappā, Pā̃cālī, Ākhḍāi, Pakṣīdalergāna, Half-akhḍāi	Dhrupada, Pakhāvaj, Ṭappā Brahma Saṅgīta	Jātrā, Sitār, Dhrupada, Khayāl, Tappa, Brahma Saṅgita	Nātya Saṅgita, Swadesi-sangita, Thumri, all instruments and all Sastriya vocal Styles.	Same as before, also Rabindra & Kavya Saṅgita	Same as before.
Chinsura	Ākhḍāi - (1700) Kavigāna	—	Dhrupada, Pakhavaj	Same as before, also Khayāl & Tablā	Same as before	Samde as before	—
(Vikrampur) Dhākā	Dhrupada, Śāstrīya all styles.	Same as before	Same as before, also Sitar Pakhāvaj & Tablā	Same as before	Same as before	Same as before	Same as before, also Kāvya & Swadesi gāna
Rānāghāṭ	—	—	Kathakatā, Ṭappā	Dhrupada	Khayāl	—	—
Chandrakona	—	Dhrupada, Pakhāvaj	Dhrupada	Dhrupada	Dhrupadā	—	—
Guptipāṛā	—	Ṭappa	Same as before	Same as before	Same as before	—	—
Tripurā	—	—	—	—	Dhrupada, Sitār, Pakhāvaj, Tablā.	Same as before, also Khayāl.	Same as before.

Styles of Music in various Centres of Bengal at a glance — Periodwise

Centre	1750-1775	1775-1800	1800-1825	1825-1850	1850-1875	1875-1900	1900-1947
Coochbihar	—	—	—	—	—	Dhrupada, Khayāl. Sitār	—
Majilpur	—	—	—	—	Dhrupada & Pakhāvaj	—	—
Muktāgāchā	—	—	—	—	—	Dhrupada, Pakhavaj, Sarod. Sitar	—
Tālanda-Rajshahi	—	—	—	—	—	Saroḍ, Sitār,	Saroḍ, Tablā.
Śhāntipur	Ākhḍāi (1680-1700)	—	—	—	Pakhāvaj	—	—
Gaurīpur	—	—	—	—	—	Pakhāvaj, Tablā, Esrāj, Jātrā, Nātya Saṅgīta	All vocal Style & all instrument-viz-Rabāb Bin, Sarod, Sitar etc.
Śrīrāmpur	—	—	—	Dhrupada	—	—	—
Pharāsdāṅga	—	Kavigāna	—	—	—	—	—
Chandarnagar	—	Kavigāna, Ṭappā	—	—	—	—	—
Chandannagar	—						
Hugli	Kavigāna, Ṭappā Akhdai - (1700)	—	—	—	—	—	—

MUSICIAL STYLES PRACTISED IN BENGAL

Prācīna Kaviwālār Gāna

The origin of *Prācīna Kaviwālār Gāna,* perhaps evolved out of a number of musical styles that were prevalent at the end of 17th century and early 18th century. The pundits and researchers however differ in their opinion, and they consider one of the following styles as the source of this art form:

(a) *Kheuḍ,* (b) *Pā̃cālī,* (c) *Jhumur,* (d) *Jātrā gāna,* (e) *Mālasī,* and (f) *Viṣama-dhruva Pā̃cālī.*

When the subject matter of *Kavi gāna* is analysed, it becomes evident that it embraces in its compass, Purāṇas, Upapurāṇas, *Maṅgala-kāvyas, Vaiṣṇava-padāvalīs, Āgamanī-Bijayā,* riddle songs and vulgar episodes of *Kheuḍ.*

Some scholars also believe that *Kaviyāl / Kaviwālār gāna* had some influence of *Kavvālī,* which was practised in Bengal at the houses of the *Āmīrs,* after the Muslims had settled down in Bengal. It will be seen that there is some resemblance between the names *Kaviyāl* and *Kavvāl.* The techniqes of *Citen-Parciten* also has some resemblance with the high pitched presentations of the *Kavvāls* in *Kavvālī.*

Kavi gāna was originated in the early 18th century perhaps by a person named Gonjla Guin. At that period of time, Bengal was comparatively peaceful and this style became popular not only in the rural areas but also in big cities like Calcutta, Pharasdanga / Chandannagar, Chinsura, Hugli, Saptagram, and Birbhum -Siudi, where the *Kaviwālās* thrived under the patronage of the wealthy rajas, zamindars, and businessmen. The *Kaviwālās* used to have the busiest session during the festival of *Durgāpujā, Dol* (Holi), *Rās-bāroāri,* etc., when the sponsor devoted more time and spent huge sums of money in these functions. The fun and festivities used to take precedence over other things and *kavi gāna / Kaviwālār gāna* used to be performed all through the festival periods starting at night and lasting through the wee hours.

The *Kaviyāls* or *Kaviwālās,* as the performers were called, were first encouraged by the Zamindar Indranarayan Chaudhuri of Chandannagar. It is known that Lalu Nandalal, the disciple of Gonjla Guin was patronised by him. After the emergence of Calcutta as the capital and main business centre, the elites of the nouveau riche class, sponsored the different groups of *Kaviyāls* during various festivals all the year round. Raja Nabakrishna Deb of Shobhabazar was the first to introduce and popularise *Kavi-gāna* in Calcutta. Other patrons who followed the Debs, were the successors of Ramdulal Sarkar, Sils of Kalutola, Basus of Bagbazar, Dattas of Hatkhola, Mitras of Darjipara, zamindars of Paikpara and Kashimbazar, and some others.

Kavi-gāna was a verbal duel composed of lyrics set in music between two teams of poets or *kaviyāls* who composed and presented their *gānas* on the spot in the form of questions and answers. It was called '*Kavir-laḍāi*', meaning fight between poets. The team which performed better used to be cheered and rewarded and declared the winner. The questions were called *cāpān* and were put forward by one team. The other team had to give an appropriate reply to it called *kāṭān* or *khanḍan* or *utor*. This *cāpān* and *kāṭān* used to go on for hours, till one team became victorious. Sometimes the two teams used to secretly plan the *cāpān* and *kāṭāns* beforehand. The predetermined compositions used to be called *bā̃dhuṭi* while the songs of *cāpān-utor* that were composed on the spot were called *Upasthiti-gāna*. The peak period of popularity of this style was between 1760 and 1830, although it was very much in practice till the first decade of 20th century.

Kavi-gāna has been mentioned as *Dā̃ḍā Kavigāna, Dā̃ḍā* meaning, *rīti* or style of singing. The *Pā̃cālī-gāna* was much older than this style, and its singers were termed as *pāye-calī kavis* by the rural people, who made out the meaning of *Dā̃ḍā-Kavi* as those poets who sang while standing, *dā̃ḍā*, also meaning to stand.

Although there is no apparent difference between *Kavigāna* and *Dā̃ḍā-kavigāna*, researchers opine that the original type of professional *Kavigāna*, which was not bound by *Śāstrīya rāgas* and *tālas* and used to be composed both lyrically and musically on the spot by the creative *kaviyāls* was *Kavigāna*, while *Dā̃ḍā-kavigāna* became formalised having its own *dā̃ḍā* or a set pattern based on *rāgas* and *tālas* of proper *śāstrīya* standard. A team of singers and composers of high calibre who were sometimes non professionals, termed in Bengali as '*Saukhīn*' used to take part in *Dā̃ḍā-kavigāna*. As mentioned earlier, *Kavigāna* emerged as a popular style at the beginning of 18th century, when *Maṅgala-kāvya* was on its way out. This new style borrowed its theme and technique from the previous styles, e.g.

1. *Sakhīsamvāda- goṣṭha- gauracandrīkā* of *Padāvalī Kīrtana*,
2. *Mālasī- Ḍākmālasī- Laharmālasī* of *Āgamanī-Bijayā* or *Śyamā-saṅgīta*
3. *Tarjā*,
4. *Kheuḍ*,
5. *Ākhḍāi*, and
6. various other contemporary social topics. The first five topics only, had been used by the *Kaviyāls* of the earlier days, while the last came in later.

In *Kavigāna*, the popular episodes of *Sakhīsamvāda, Goṣṭha* and *Gauracandrīkā* were adopted in a suitable manner from the *Padāvalī kīrtana*. The themes of this style of music included:

1. *Mān, Kalaṅka, Kalahāntaritā, Kalaṅka-bhañjana, Khaṇḍitā, Viraha*, and *Viccheda* as part of *Sakhīsamvāda*; love and affection of *Goṣṭha;* and some poets added prayer

to Gauranga at the beginning of the performance to seek the blessings of the Lord for success.

2. During the *Pujā* festivals, the poets composed and sang *Āgamanī-Bijayā* episodes of Goddess *Dūrgā*. These songs were written specially for the goddess who came to visit her parents for four days only, depicting the happy and tender moments of union and then the sad emotions of parting. These songs were composed and sung in a different way from Rāmprasada's compositions, although the theme was the same. These songs were: a) *Āgamanī* — composed for the welcoming of the goddess, b) *Saptamī* - depicting the happy mood of Girirāja and Menakā for having their daughter Durgā or Umā amidst them, c) *Navamī* - expressing the setting in of depression of the parents on the eve of departure of their beloved daughter, and d) *Bijayā* — the pangs of separation as the daughter leaves.

3. *Tarjā* meaning riddle or puzzle, termed in Bengali as *Heyā̃lī* or *Prahelikā,* used to be an important part of *Kavigāna* and this part of the *gāna* was called *Cāpān* which used to be duly answered back by the opponent party in *Utor* or *Kāṭān.* Previously, *Tarjā* used to be *Vākovākya* meaning arguments and counter arguments between two parties which used to end up in taunt, jeer and quibbles. From ancient days, this sort of wranglings between poets or pundits very often used to be a part of court entertainment. Raghunath Das brought in elements of vulgarity and jeer into *Tarjā* to gain cheap popularity.

After the various episodes of *Sakhīsamvāda, Bhavānī-viṣaya* or *Āgamanī-Bijayā, Viraha,* stories from the Purāṇas were sung, the *Kaviyāls* would end the performance with *Kheuḍ* or *Cuṭkilahar,* attacking each other by making personal remarks.

Gradually the better portions of the *Kavigāna* like *Sakhīsamvāda,* episodes from the Purāṇas, etc. were eliminated and were substituted by *Cuṭkilahar* or *Kheuḍ* portions of vulgarity which earned more popular appeal. The two teams of *Kaviwālās* used to attack each other by word contest composed of personal insult and jeering, often amounting to vulgarity. Sometimes *Tarjā* and *Kheuḍ* used to get mixed up. *Kheuḍ* was '*Aślīla-rasagāna*', that is, the *gāna* embodying vulgarity, while *Tarjā* was more witty consisting of a battle of word - compositions between the two parties of *Kaviyāls*. *Kheuḍ* used to be of two types: a) composed with plenty of similies and parables, and b) with allegorical expressions. Both the types had taunting strains. Unfortunately, *Kavigāna* ended up with too much of *Aślīla-rasagāna* of *Kheuḍ.*

Kavigāna composed on social, national or any other contemporary events were free of vulgarity and were called *Bhaṇitā* by the *Kaviyāls.* These were short compositions.

In the 19th century, there used to be four successive themes that were followed, viz. *Gurudever gīta, Sakhīsamvāda, Viraha* and *Kheuḍ*.

Kavigāna consisted of the following divisions, viz - 1) *Citen (Udgrāha)*, 2) *Par-citen* (the *Ābhoga* part after *Citen*), 3) *Dhuyā*, 4) *Meltā* (*Melāpaka*), 5) *Khād*, and 6) *Phukā* (used in place of *Antarā)*, and also *Paḍan, Dolan* and *Sawārī*. *Kaviyāls* presented their *gānas* sometimes with just a few of them. There was however no uniformity regarding the *tuks* or divisions presented. The *Kaviwālās* of East Bengal (present Bangladesh) followed different patterns of *tuks*. This can be understood from the examples quoted later in the article.

The presentation of *Kavigāna* was done in the following manner: The team of a *Kavigāna* consisted of one or two *mūl-gāyen* (main singer) and two or four *dohārs* (assisting singers). The *mūl-gāyen* used to be called the *Kavi* or *Kaviyāl* and the *dohārs* as *dohārkā*. Also there used to be composers who were called *bā̃dhandārs*. Their duty was to compose suitable *padas* on various subjects of *Kavigāna* and also for the particular occasion. The *mūl-gāyen* would commence a *pālāgāna* with *citen* or *mahaḍā (udgrāha)* and then compose and sing the *padas* of *parciten*. The next portions of *pada* and *tena* were composed with *dolan, paḍan* and *sawārī* (the *sambhoga* portion of music). Upto the *khād* and *phukā* portions were sung by both the *mūl-gāyen* and the *dohārs*. Only the *dhuyā* used to be sung by the *dohārs*, when the *mūl-gāyen* took rest. Regarding the *tuk* of *Kavigāna* there used to be different approaches by different *kavis*, e.g. *Kavi* Ishwarchandra Gupta mentioned three tuks in *Samvāda Prabhākara* (1854 - 1855) viz. *Mahaḍā, Citen* and *Antarā;* Gopal Bandopadhyay in *Prācīna Kavisaṃgraha* (1877-1878) mentioned the *tuks* as *Citān, mahaḍā, antarā,* and second *vitāna*. Each *tuk* was further subdivided as:

1. *Citān* into *Prathama Citān, Prathama Parcitān, Prathama Phukā, Prathama Meltā.*
2. *Mahaḍā* into *mahaḍā, Khād, Dvitiya Phukā, Dvitiya Meltā.*
3. *Antarā.*
4. *Citān* into *Dvitīya Citān, Dvitīya Parcitān, Tṛtiya Phukā, Tṛtiya Meltā,* etc.

The mention of *Prathma, Dvitīya Citān* etc. were to mean repititions.

In East Bengal, the *tuks* were as follows:

Citān, Parcitān, Paḍtā, Prathama Fukar, Mukh, Pẽj, Khõj, Dvitīya Fukar, Par-fukar, Par-khõj and *Antarā.*

Though originally *Kavigāna* started in West Bengal and spread to East Bengal, the style and sequence of *tuks* gradually took different shape in the East and even from district to district. The comparative study is given below:

	From Jessore to Khulna	*From Mymensing to Bikrampur*
1.	*Citān / Mahaḍā & paḍan / Pārānī*	*Citān & Parcitān*
2.	*Prathama Fukar & Par-Fukar*	*Mil & Mahaḍā.*
3.	*Mukh, Pẽj & Khõj*	*Dhuyā & Khād*
4.	*Antarā*	*Lahar*
5.	*Dvitīya Fukar, Par-Khõj, Parcitān*	*Jhumur*

The famous *Kaviyāls* and their usual counterparts were:

a.	Haru Thakur	versus	Ram Basu.
b.	Ram Basu	versus	Nilu - Ramprasad.
c.	Ram Basu	versus	Antony Kaviyal.
d.	Antony Kaviyal	versus	Baku Nede.
e.	Antony Kaviyal	versus	Thakur Singh.
f.	Antony kaviyal	versus	Bhola Moyra.
g.	Bhola Moyra	versus	Balai Sarkar.
h.	Bhola Moyra	versus	Yajneswari.
i.	Moti Pasari	versus	Hosain.
j.	Nitai	versus	Bhavani Bene.
k.	Ramu	versus	Ramgati.

Originally, the professional *Kaviyāls* did not follow any strict *Śāstrīya* norms and used to compose and sing on the spot, in *rāgas* and *tālas* prevalent at that time that came into their mind as suitable for the *padas.* While in *Dāḍākavigāna,* the composers were more of non professionals, '*Saukhīn*' types, who were also proficient in music and hence all *Śāstrīya rāgas* and *tālas* that were appropriate for the compositions, were made use of.

During the early period, the two teams participating in '*Kavir Laḍāi*' used to dress up in a red material covering from waist to the knee only, donning a triangular cap decorated with feathers and with jingle bells at their ankles. The singers used to dance also while singing. The participants in each team numbered around fourteen. The *Ḍhuli* or the *Ḍhol*-players used to announce the commencement of the programme by playing the *Ḍhol.* The first team would start by offering their prayers to the gods and godesses and the senior members were greeted with respect. They would begin their performance which was then presented phase by phase and the rival team furnishing their answers to the questions put forward by the first team. When the answers were appropriate, the team would be congratulated or else they would receive jeer and taunt from the audience.

An example of ***Kavigāna*:**

First Group—Candrāvalīr Sakhīr-dal
Second Group—Kāmkalār Sakhīr-dal
1st phase: Gurudev-gīta: Candrāvalīr Sakhīr-dal
Raga & *tāla* as per the choice of the *Kavi* .

धुया ॥ मन मजिल नारे केने गुरुर चरणे
चितान ॥ दश शतदल कमलेते यार बसंति अति गोपने ।
जनम सफल कर एकबार निरख श्रीनाथ ज्ञाननयने ॥
अज्ञान अन्धेर शुज्ञान अंजन के हेन ए तिन भुवने ।
प्रभु दयामय करे वराभय बितरे करुणा कातर जने ॥
भवजलनिधि निस्तारेण विधि गुरु कृपा निधि आपने ।
चतुर्वर्ग फले फले श्रीचरणे बाञ्छा कस्या लओ मोर येमने ॥
बाम उरुस्थित शक्ति सुशेभित बल्याछेन मुक्ति प्रदाने ।
खेद कर दूर मानसतिमिर विनासे मायेर ओ रूप ध्याने ॥.....
टप्पा ॥
धुया ॥ दिन गेलरे असाधने ॥
टप्पा साङ्ग ॥ आर मूढ़मन भ्रमिछ कि कारणे शरण मनन
ना करिले ध्यान श्रीनाथेर श्रीचरणे ॥

Kāmkalār Sakhīr-dal:
Utor (reply): *Rāga* & *tāla* as per the choice of the Kavi
धुया ॥ ओइ देख गुरु बसियाछे रमणी बामे करिया ।
चितान ॥ पञ्च पञ्च शत कमल आसन वृन्दावन अति विपिने
ये कृष्ण से राधा पुराय मनेर साधा देख हे युगलनयन भरिया ॥
अबला अक्षम तारे ज्ञानदान करे देख ओइ बसिया ।
छाड़िया मुरसी वराभय धरि दिते करुणा करिया हासिया ॥
प्रेम भक्ति फल फलिबे ये पदे आशा फुरि लओ याचिया ॥
टप्पा ॥ धुचिल सकल मनेर ज्वाला अभयपद हेरिया ।
आमार हरि कल्पतरु गुरु रूप धरिया ॥

(2nd Phase): Sakhī Saṃvāda: Candrāvalīr Sakhīr-dal:
Rāga & *Tāla* as per the choice of the poet.
धुया - ॥ देश देख सखि केमन साजाइयाछि युगले निकुंजे आनिया ॥
चितान ॥ जगत महिमा वासन्ती प्रतिमा सेरूप देखना चिनिते पार किना पार भाविया ॥

आर सखी कहे चिना नाहि याय हर गौरी देखि बसिया ।
जया सखि कय बहुरुपी हय आमि जानि भाल करिया ॥
हइले दशमी चिने लओ तुमि छाड़िबे ए-बेश मुरली लागिया ।
लुकाब राधाय देखाब तोमाय राधा राधा बलि बेड़ाइबे श्यामे डाकिया ।

टप्पा ॥ बदाबदे काम नाइ ओइ व्रजेर कानाइ ओ धरिते पारे अनेक रुप बलिहारी याइ ।

Kāmkalār Sakhīr-dal: *Rāga & tāla* as per the choice of the poet.

धुया ॥ सखिरे ओ लुकाइते नारे बाँका नयन ॥

चितान ॥ कोथा योगी हर लम्पट नागर देख ना चाहनि खानि
भुरु कामान कषिया गोपिनीर प्राण बधिछे नयनबाण ॥
नील अंग छटा नाहि याय ढाका कि करे आर चन्दन ।
पदतल चिह्न देख भिन्न भिन्न आगे देख्याछ केमन ॥
श्यामा सखि कय श्याम इच्छामय निति निति रूप नूतन ।
नित्य वृन्दावने युगल लइया सदा कर कालयापन ॥

टप्पा ॥ यत रूप पारुक धरुक नाहि तारे भावना ।
त्रिभंग भंगिमा खानि कभु मने छेड़ोना ॥

(3rd Phase): Viraha: Candrāvalīr Sakhīr-dal:
Rāgiṇī-Bihāga, tāla as per the choice of the poet.

धुया ॥ गोपिनीर प्राण ममेर समान गलाइल सइ विरह आगुन ॥

चितान ॥ कोथा वातिकर अन्वेषण कर मनसुत दिया करिबे गठन ॥
द्वितीय विरह देह करे दाह ना माने शीतल कि नीर कि चन्दन ।
आर दिते दिते हय द्विगुण ॥

टप्पा ॥ Rāgiṇī-Bihāga, Tāla Paśto
बुझि कामकला सती हइल बाँशेर मोति
लागिल याइया घोड़ा हइया सतीर पति ।

Kāmkalā Sakhīr-dal: *Rāgiṇī-Jhinjhiṭ, Tāla* as per the choice of the poet.

धुया ॥ परधन पाइया से धन हाराइया केने कर एत खेद ॥

चितेन ॥ ओहे चन्द्रावली परधने केलि ।
इहार निश्चय हय एके दिने से धनेते विच्छेद ॥
तपे निज धन कर उपार्ज्जन से धने वंचित नहिबे किन्तु
मधुकर यदि हओ आसक कलिर आसवे दिवानिशि यत भृंग
यातायात विरह मिलने ए भेद ॥

टप्पा ॥ *Rāgiṇī-Jhinjhiṭ, Tāla* as per the choice of the poet.
सब कमलिनी प्रफुल्ल धैबये थाक ।
एके एके मधु भ्रमर खाइबे गुंजरिया आसितेछे ओइ चाय्या देख ॥

4th Phase: *Kheuḍ:* Candrāvalīr Sakhīr-dal: *Rāga & tāla-Dakṣiṇī*
धुया ॥ चन्द्रवंशे जन्म यार कलंके कि करे तार भोजन
गोयाला घरे जाति पाति अति ॥
चितान ॥ कुमारी सहित पुन ये करे पिरीत कामकला करे तारे पति ।
साबास साबास ओलो सति ॥
प्रति अंगे कुटिलता कुटिल बरण धाता हारे अष्टावक्र मुनि यबे करे गति
कागा बगा पाखी मारि भुलाय परेर नारी तार सने बिहार करे कामुकी युवती ॥
टप्पा ॥ *Rāga & tāla-Dakṣiṇī*
कामेर कामिनी काछे मानीर मान थाकेना ।
जगत् मालिक हय तबु तारे करे जय ब्रजेर सेइ तामासा देखना ॥

Kāmkalā Sakhīr-dal: *Rāga and tāla* as per the choice of the poet.
धुया ॥ गरजे सकलि सहिते हय कुलटार वाणी ॥
चितान ॥ यावत् ना जाने लोके सती बले ताके केबा जाने छिनाल काहिनी ॥
आधोदेश बाकी कार राखियाछे ब्रजेर नीलमणि एके एके बल देखि
सत्य कथा धनी । याचिया यौबन दिया एखन कर टेम्बा खानि ॥

[This song is incomplete without the end *ṭappā*]

In each phase or episode it has been mentioned over the song "Rāga o tāla Kavir" — which means, the *rāga* and *tāla* are as per the choice of the *kavi* (poet). In a few however, specific *rāgas* and *tālas* have been mentioned. This song specimen given above, is not an example set in the rural areas but perhaps composed by urban poets, who have used polished language. Though incomplete, it gives an idea about the various episodes depicted in a *Kavi gāna.*

Short Biographies of Kaviyāls:

Gonjla Guin

The first *kaviyāl* about whom information is available is Gonjla Guin. In *Saṃvāda-prabhākara,* Ishwarchandra Gupta writes that Gonjla was a professional singer who formed a team of his own and used to sing on contract at various well-to-do people's houses. The name of the leader of his rival team is however not known.

Gonjla was born perhaps at the end of 17th. century A.D. and became well known as a singer in the first part of 18th. century. Famous among his disciples were: Lalu-Nandalal, Raghunath Das, and Ramji Das.

Raghunath Das

Raghunath Das was one of the disciples of Gonjla Guin and was the *guru* of Rasu-Nrisimha and Haru Thakur. It is not known when he was born, but it is surmised that he was living at least till the mid 18th. century. He hailed from Pharasdanga and was born in a family of weavers. There is a controversy regarding his birth place. Some opine that it is Salikha, while others say that it is Guptipara. In one of his songs he says that he was a "*Śimle-bāsī adhyāpaka*" meaning a professor who resided at "*Śimle*". It is possible that he lived in a place called Shimulia in Calcutta.

Raghunath was a composer whose compositions excelled in sentiments of incitement and devotion. He composed high quality songs of *Bhavānītattva, deha-tattva* and philosophies of life, but certain strains or elements of vulgarity had penetrated in some of his compositions. He helped and corrected Haru Thakur during his probation period and Haru Thakur acknowledged this favour in the *bhaṇitā* of certain songs composed by him.

Lalu - Nandalal

The two poets were patronised by Zamindar Indranarayan Chaudhuri of Chandannagar. According to Ishwarchandra Gupta, Lalu Nandalal was the name of one person as has been mentioned by him in *Saṃvāda-prabhākara,* but the *bhaṇitā* part of various compositions by Lalu-Nandalal indicate clearly that Lalu and Nandalal were two different persons, e.g.

लाल चन्द्र कहे ए बेशे कोथाय चलेछो लो विनोदिनी ।
नन्दलाल भणे चेया आमापाने हेसे कथा कह शुनि ॥

(Suniti Kumar Chatterjee's article - "*British Museume , Bāṅglā Kāgaj patra*").

It is opined by scholars that probably, one was the singer while the other was the composer. There is also difference of opinion regarding their place of origin. According to some researchers, they hailed from Chinsura while others maintain that they were born in Birbhum and later came to Chinsura. They were contemporaries of Bharatchandra and Ramprasad, around the 2nd. or 3rd. part of 18th. century.

Some of their disciples were: Balahari Ray of Barul and Kalo Pal / Haradhan Pal of Birbhum.

Lalu-Nandalal's compositions, were full of *Karuṇa* and *madhura rasa* particularly in *Sakhī-saṃvāda* and *Viraha* compositions. The *padas* on *Rūpāvisāra* and

Kṛṣṇakāli - saṃvāda were influenced by Vaiṣṇava style. The '*Kavir-lahar*' compositions of Lalu-Nandalal were predominantly of *Kheuḍ* style.

Kavi Ramji Das

Ramji Das was the disciple of Gojla Guin and was a resident of Hugli. He excelled in composing '*Kavir Lahar*', which was based on themes from *Rāmāyaṇa, Maṅgala-kāvyas, Śivāyana, Kālikā-maṅgala,* etc. He composed *Sakhī-saṃvāda* in Vaiṣṇava style. Other topics on *Bhavānī, Viraha,* birth of Sītā, Hanumān, etc. were richly composed.

Kavi Rasu-Nrisimha

These two were brothers and were born in a well-to-do family of Gondalpara in 1734 and 1738 respectively in Pharasdanga. Their father Anadinath Ray sent them to a missionary school in Chinsura after completing primary education. But they came back to Gondalpara as they were not interested in higher studies. Soon after, their father died and the two brothers started learning *kavigāna* under Raghunath Das to earn a living. They formed their own group and became very famous in Pharasdanga and were in great demand.

Out of the two, one was a good singer and the other a great poet. Their songs on various subjects were excellent in literary and aesthetic quality. They were also pioneers in introducing shorter songs in place of long ones, at the same time richer in thoughts and literary beauty. These compositions helped the later poets to develop *gīti-kavitās.*

Rasu-Nrisimha were patronised by Dewan Indranarayan Chaudhuri of Pharasdanga (Chandannagar).

Kavi Haru Thakur / Harekrisha Dirghangi

Born in 1145 B.S. (1738-39 AD), Haru Thakur was the true follower of Rasu-Nrisimha's style. His father Kalyanchandra Dirghangi was a poor Brahmin who lived in Shimulia, Calcutta, and was unable to educate Haru very much, except for some initial studies in a local *pāṭhaśālā* (primary school). After the death of his father, Haru joined the team of Raghunath Das as a singer. Sometimes, he composed songs which were corrected by Raghunath. Once, when he had visited Shobhabazar palace and took part in the *kavigāna,* Raja Nabakrishna was very much attracted by his singing and excellent compositions and encouraged him to form his own professional group. Haru Thakur was patronised by Raja Nabakrishna and enjoyed the privileges offered by the raja. Haru Thakur soon became famous as a *kaviyāl.* He composed many devotional songs full of *bhaktirasa* and philosophy, for Raja Nabakrishna and used to solve riddles for the raja in witty poems. He used to be in great demand to perform at places like the palaces of Burdwan, Krishnanagar, and at the houses of other wealthy people of Bengal and earned a lot of wealth and fame. Lesser *kaviyāls* of his time such as Bhavani Bene, Nilu Thakur, Bhola Moyra had joined his team as probationers and later formed their own groups. They even collected songs from Haru Thakur for their performances and became famous as *kaviwālās.* Haru Thakur was particularly fond of Bhola Moyra and trained him with all his affection.

Raja Nabakrishna appointed Haru Thakur as the judge for the *kavi-gāna* performances that were held at his palace. After the death of the raja, Haru Thakur gave up both his profession of *kaviyāl* and acting as judge. He died in 1219 B.S. (1812 A.D.)

Poet Satu / Satkadi Ray

He was born in a Brahmin family of Bechi village near Shantipur. He earned a name as a composer of *kavi-gāna,* but never formed a professional group, neither acted as *kaviwālā.* He used to compose songs for other *kaviyāls* free of any charges.

He used to be an employee of the zamindars of Shantipur, and composed songs for the *kaviyāls* who came to perform at the court of zamindar Sivachandra. Even Bhola Moyra used to obtain songs for his team from Satu Ray. He was well known for his compositions on *Sakhī-samvāda.*

Towards the later part of his life, he worked as a *Moktār* in Barasat under the zamindars of Ranaghat.

Poet Balahari Ray

Balahari Ray's ancestors were Rajput soldiers who came to Bengal with Raja Mansingh to fight with Raja Pratapaditya. Afterwards, these families settled down in Bengal and merged with the local Bengalis. Balahari Ray was born in Barul village in 1743. His father was Alamchand Ray.

Balahari was a disciple of Lalu-Nandalal and became so famous as a *kaviyāl* that he earned the name - "*Kabir Guru*". Among his disciples, Nitai Das and Raicharan Ray, became famous.

Balahari composed some beautiful *mālasī* and *padāvalīs* on *Sakhī-samvāda.*

Poet Nityananda Vairagi

More well known as Nite or Nitai, Nityananda was born in 1751 in Chandannagar in a Vaiṣṇava family. He became famous both as a singer and composer , although he employed two composers called *bā̃dhandār,* for his group. They were: Nabai Thakur and Gaur Kaviraj who excelled in composing *Sakhī-samvāda, Viraha* and *Kheuḍ.* Nitai's victory in the "*Kavir laḍāi*" over his rival teams often used to be attributed to the excellent *padas* of the above mentioned two *bā̃dhandārs.* Nitai became so affluent in his profession that he built a temple at Chandannagar and an *ākhḍā* (place for musical rehearsal) in Chinsura.

Nitai was not only a very good singer, but also an excellent *ḍhol* player. Although he had employed a *ḍhol*-player named Mohan, son of famous *ḍhuli* Ram Baiti, but very often while singing in great ecstacy, he would snatch the instrument from Mohan and play it himself. His popularity made him one of the topmost favourites to be invited for special occasions at the various zamindars' and affluent households. Normally, his rival used to be Bhavani Bene, another famous *kaviyāl.* During that period, three *kaviyāls* were most sought after, and they were: Nitai Das, Haru Thakur, and Bhavani Bene. When they performed, people flocked to hear them from far off localities, trekking miles. Nitai's immense popularity was evident from his fans and followers, who elevated him to the same pedestal as a *Vaiṣṇava mahājan* and called him *Prabhu.* His popularity reigned supreme over a large area like Kumarhatta, Bhatpara, Triveni, Bali, Pharasdanga, Chinsura, etc.

Poet Bhavani Bene

Bhavani was born in a family of *Gandha Vaṇik* in a village called Satgeche in Burdwan district. He later shifted to Barahanagar for his profession. Before he started his own team of *Kavi-gāna,* he used to be an assistant in Haru Thakur's team and also sang as a *dohār.* He left Haru Ṭhakur and joined Ramji for songs and later got the *kavi-gāṅas* composed by Ram Basu.

He became famous as a rival *kaviyāl* of Nitai Vairagi and earned a lot of money. His own compositions were more predominant with *tattva-guṇa* and some compositions in *Sakhī-saṃvāda* were of high standard.

Poet Ram Basu

Ram Basu was one of the best *kaviwālās,* who excelled in both singing and composing *kavi-gāna.* His expertise lay mostly in *mālasī, viraha* and *Sakhī-saṃvāda* in which no other *kaviyāl* could equal him.

Ram Basu or Rammohan Basu was born in 1193 B.S. (1786-87 A.D.) in a village called Salikha in the district of Howrah. His father Ramlochan Basu and mother Nistarinidevi enrolled him in the local school when he was only five. From that tender age Ram used to compose poems and show these to his friends. He was then sent to Calcutta for higher studies. He studied as well as he composed poems. Accidentally, Bhavani Bene discovered Ram Basu's extraordinary poetic talents and engaged him as *bā̃dhandār* for his *kavirdal.* Equally accidentally, he joined this group as a singer. His father was upset because of these activities, and Ram Basu gave up all connections with the *kaviyāls.* But soon after, his father died and Ram

Basu had to join *kavirdal* to earn a living. He composed *kavi-gāna* for Bhavani Bene, Nilu Thakur, Mohan Sarkar and others. In due course, he formed his own group, first as an amateur and then as a professional. Soon, he was able to establish himself as a much sought after *kaviyāl* and earned enough. Unfortunately, he died when he was only forty-two years old.

Ram Basu not only excelled in composing *Sakhī-saṃvāda, Mālasī,* etc., but his compositions on various other topics of *kavi-gāna* were unique in their literary value and *rasa.* As an educated *Kaviyāl,* his knowledge of Śāstras, Purāṇas and *Maṅgala-kāvyas* helped him to compose his *gānas* in rare quality, beauty and depth of thought. *Kavir-Lahar* composed by him represented deep knowledge, though written on the pattern of *Tarjā.* In his compositions of *kavi-gāna,* influence of Rasu Nrisimha and Ramprasad Sen is evident, although his own creative genius is supreme.

Poetess Yajneswari

A contemporary of Bhola Moyra, Nilu Thakur and Ram Basu, Yajneswari was a lady-*Kaviyāl* who formed her own *kavirdal.* She used to take part in *kavir-laḍāi* against giant *kaviyāls* such as Bhola Moyra and others. Unfortunately, Bhola Moyra introduced some vulgar type of compositions in *kheuḍ* while competing against her.

Poet Nilu Thakur

Nilu Thakur and Ramprasad were two brothers, who formed their group called "Nilu-Rāmprasad" *kavirdal.* Nilu Thakur started his professional life as a *dohār* under Haru Thakur and used to collect songs from Haru Thakur even when he formed his own group. Later, Krishnamohan Bhattacharya used to compose *kavigānas* for him.

Nilu himself was a good composer. After his death, his brother owned the group.

Antony Phiringi

Henseman Antony, a European, became a famous *kaviyāl.* He and his brother Kolisaheb were wealthy businessmen and used to stay in Chandannagar. Antony came into bad company during his youth and went to a place called Gariti with a Brahmin girl. Gariti at that time was under French rule. Antony became almost a Hindu under the influence of the Brahmin girl and left his western habits, dresses etc. He became very fond of *kavir gān* and used to invite groups at his place during *Durgā-pūjā.* Soon he formed a group of his own with amateur artistes. This was an expensive hobby and soon his savings dwindled. He therefore turned his amateur group into a professional one of which he was the director. He employed one *bā̃dhandār* named Gorakshanath for his team. Once during *Durgā-pūjā*, Gorakshanath let him down, and Antony then composed himself for his team. He became a great success and took part in competitions of *kavir-laḍāi* against Bhola Moyra, Thakurdas Singh, Ram Basu and others.

Antony's success was due to his knowledge of Hindu Purāṇas and his unbiased outlook on various religions. His presence of mind and literary competence in Bengali was amazing. To quote an example:

> खृष्टे आर कृष्टे किछु प्रभेद नाइ रे भाइ
> शुधु नामेर फेरे मानुषे फेरे एओ कोथा शुनि नाइ ।
> आमार खोदा ये हिन्दुर हरि से, ओइ देख श्याम दाँड़िये रयेछे,
> आमार मानव जनम सफल हबे यदि गंगा चरण पाइ ।

This was his answer to a taunt inflicted by Ram Basu at him during *Kavirlaḍāi*. His compositions were full of *śṛṅgāra* and at the same time *vātsalya* and *prati-vātsalya rasa*. Although a foreigner, he absorbed the true sentiments of *kavirgāna* and became one of the most successful *kaviyāls*.

Bhola Moyra

Bhola Moyra was one of the most successful *kaviyāls* who particularly excelled in replying during a *kavir laḍāi*. People flocked from far to attend Bhola Moyra's *kavir-laḍāi*. A Vaiṣṇava, Bhola was born in Guptipara village. His father was Kriparam and mother Gangamani. They had a sweet shop in Bagbazar of Calcutta. According to some sources, he was born in Calcutta and his father was Ramgopal Modak, a confectioner.

Bhola did not have much formal education apart from some basic studies at a local village *pāṭhśālā*. His real training was at Calcutta, by listening to *kathaks* intently when they recited *Rāmāyaṇa*, *Mahābhārata*, and other Purāṇas, and also by joining the *saṅkīrtanas*. This acquired knowledge and experience was reflected in his *Kavir-gāṇa*. He had joined the *Kavir-dal* under Haru Thakur and became his favourite disciple.

Bhola Moyra's main competitors in *kavir-laḍāi* were: Antony Kaviyal, Ram Basu, Balai Sarkar, and Husein Khan of Murshidabad. Mostly, Bhola used to come out victorious because of his superior wit and superb talent for composing the right answer at the right time, all extempore.

After Raghunath Das, he was the *kaviyāl*, who used cheap vulgarity in his *gāna*, which brought him popularity. He knew reasonable amount of Hindi, Sanskrit and Persian.

Apart from these early *kaviyāls*, there were many others who carried on this art form till the beginning of 20th. century. Some of the well known names are: Sitanath Mukhopadhyay, Gurudayal Chaudhuri, Gurodumba, Madhav Moyra, Krishnalal, Krishnamohan Bhattacharya, Gadadhar Mukhopadhyay, Thakurdas Chakravarti, Ramapati Thakur, Jainarayan Bandopadhyay, Darpanarayan Kaviraj, Parbaticharan Bandopadhyay, Krishnamohan Bandopadhyay, Rajkishore Bandopadhyay, Ramkamal, Nabai Thakur, Chintamani Moyra, Mohan Sarkar, Ramsundar Ray and some others.

There were some other places, where this art form thrived, viz. Jessore, Mymensingh, Birbhum, Siudi, Dhaka,-Bikrampur, etc. *Kaviyāls* from Jessore were: Rasmohan Das, Kalicharan Das, Raicharan Mal, Suryakumar Chakravarti, Akshayadas Vairagi, Panchanan Dutta, Mahesh Kana and others. *Kaviyāls* from Birbhum and Siudi were: Balahari Ray, Kailas Ghatak, Chandikali Ghatak, Sristidhar, Vishnuchandra Chattaraj, Nitai Das, Rajaram Ganak, Ramananda Chakravarti (Ramai Thakur), Chakar Jugi, Banwari Chakravarti, Sarada Bhandari, Radhanath, Raicharan Ray and others. The poets who hailed from Mymensingh area were: Lochan Karmakar, Harail Biswas, Chandiprasad Ghosh, Harekrishna Nath, Kanai-Balai, Lal Mamud (a muslim), Ramgati, Ramu and Ramkanai, Tarachand, Mahesh Chakravarti, Mahesh Bandopadhyay and others. Dhaka-Bikrampur area had been famous for music. *Kaviyāls* of this area were: Harimohan Acarya, Rasikchandra Acarya, Kailashchandra, Paranchandra and others.

Apart from these *kaviyāls*, it is essential to give a short account of two poets who were much involved with *Kavir-gāna*. These two poets are: Ishwarchandra Gupta and Manomohan Basu.

Poet Ishwarchandra Gupta

It is due to the effort and research of Ishwarchandra that one is able to know about so many *kaviyāls* and their works.

Ishwarchandra, also known as 'Gupta Kavi', was a genius who used to compose *kavi-gāna* for different groups from the tender age of twelve. He was born on 25th Phalgun, 1213 B.S. (1806 A.D.) in Kachrapara village of 24 Parganas. He lost his father at the age of ten and could not pursue higher studies, but kept up his hobby of composing poems.

In 1237 B.S, he published and edited a journal called *Saṃvāda Prabhākar* under the patronage of Jnanendramohan Thakur of Pathuriaghata, for two years only as Jnanendramohan died in 1239 B.S and with his death the paper also stopped. He started another journal in the same year called *Samvāda-ratnāvalī* under Zamindar Jagannathprasad Mullick of Andul, but this paper also did not last. From 1243 Śrāvaṇa, *Saṃvāda Prabhākar* was restarted by the poet. From 1246' B.S it became a daily journal. He published two weeklies: *Pāṣaṇḍa-pīḍan* in 1253 B.S and *Sādhurañjana* in 1254 B.S. He composed many songs for the *kavirgāna* and *Half-ākhḍāi* groups during this period, and realised the necessity to compile the biographies of the different *kaviwālās* and their works. The first issue of *Saṃvāda Prabhākar* of every month carried some valuable biographies and works of different ancient *kaviyāls*. He is pioneer in this field, and due to his efforts, it has been possible to know about them and also details about Ramprasad Sen, Bharatchandra and their works. Through this journal, three of his books, viz . *Probodh Prabhākar, Hitakar,* and *Bodhendu-vikāśa* were published.

Ishwarchandra excelled in composing *kavigānas* on the themes of *Sakhī-samvāda* and expressing pathos in *Viraha* uniquely .

He expired on 10th. Magh 1265 B.S.(1858).

Manomohan Basu

Manomohan Basu was born in Jagulia village of 24 Parganas in 1845 A.D. Since childhood, he could compose poems and verses extempore. He wrote excellent *padas* for various styles of *gānas*, viz. *Jātrā, Half-ākhḍāi, Kavigāna, Bāul, Saṃkīrtana,* etc. He published a journal called *Madhyastha,* and wrote plays such as : *Rāmābhiśeka, Satīnāṭaka, Hariścandra, Praṇayalīlā,* etc.

Rajkishore Bandopadhyay, Gopalchandra Bandopadhyay, and Jaynarayan Bandopadhyay were also famous poets who wrote *gānas* for the *kaviyāls*.

BIBLIOGRAPHY

1. Bandopadhyay, Gopal Chandra. *Prācīna Kavi Saṃgraha.* Calcutta, 1284. B.S. (Beng.).
2. Bandopadhyay, Kedarnath. (Compiled & Pub.). *Prācīna Kavi Saṅgraha (Gupta Ratnoddhāra).* Calcutta, 1301. B.S. (Beng.).
3. Goswami, Utpala. *Kolkātāye Saṅgīta Carcā.* Calcutta, 1991. (Beng.).
4. Gupta, Iswarchandra. (Ed.) *Saṃvād Prabhākar.* Calcutta, 1261. B.S. Ashwin to Phalgun issues. (Beng.).
5. Lahiri, Durgadas. *Bāṅgālīr-gāna.* Calcutta, 1312 B.S. (Beng.).
6. Mitra, Rajyeshwar. "*Uniś Śatake Bāṅglā-gāna*", in *Deshbinodan* (Bengali Journal). Calcutta, 1391. B.S. (Beng.).
7. Mukherji. D.K. *Bāngālīr Rāga-Saṅgīta Carcā.* Calcutta, 1976. (Beng.).
8. Mukhopadhyay. *Gītaratnamālā.* Calcutta, 1303. B.S. (Beng.).
9. Pal, Profulla Chandra. *Prācīna Kaviwālār Gāna.* Calcutta University, 1958. (Beng.).
10. Sen, Sukumar. *Bāṅglā Sāhityer Itihās.* Part I. Calcutta.
11. Thakur, Rabindranath. *Sādhan Kavi Saṅgīta.* Calcutta, 1302. B.S. (Beng.).

Example of Kavi - gāna:
1. Composer - Gonjla Guin: Milan - Bhāva Sanmelana.

एसो एसो चाँद वदनि, ए रसे नीरस कोरोना धनि ॥
तोमाते आमाते एकइ अंग, तुमि कमलिनी आमि से भृंग,
अनुमाने बुझि आमि से भुजंग, तुमि आमार ताय रतनमणि ॥
तोमाते आमाते एकइ काया, आमि देह प्राण, तुमि लो छाया,
आमि महाप्राणी तुमि लो माया, मने मने भेवे देख आपनि ॥

2. Composer - Lalu-Nandalal:

डाक दुर्गा दुर्गा बले मनेर कुतुहले
दुर्गा नाम दुख हरे ।
चितान : दुर्गा नामत भवेर तरणी मुक्तिदायिनी, नरक दुस्तर वारिणी ॥
आमि तो मा तोमारि दासी, मनेते एइ अभिलाषी ।
बासना पुराओ यदि, आमि अनुगत हइये रइ तोमार दासी
तुमि मनोबाञ्छापूर्णकारिणी बलि गो मा से कारण ।
धुयाः चतुर्भुज कुकुरमुखो हलो गो बल मा कोन् मुनिर नन्दन ।
केन हलो कुकुरेर माथा, बल गो मा सेइ कथा,
किबा नामटी ताहार ।
किबा नाम धरे तार पिता,
ब्रह्म अंशे जनम हये कुकुर मुख तार कि कारण ॥
हस्तपद मानुषेर लक्षण
गले यज्ञसूत्र धरे, जिज्ञासि तेँइ तोमारे,
सत्य करे आमाय बल मा एखन ॥
कार गर्भेते जनम हलो कि जन्ये कुकुर वदन ॥
लहर : सत्य करे बल गो मा, सभार साक्षाते मिथ्या बलोना,
प्रवंचना कर यदि, तुमि, आमि से कथा तो मानब ना ॥
चितान : सत्य कथा कओ जननी, मागो त्रिलोक तारिणी,
आमाके मिथ्या बल ना ।
आमि तोमार पदेर दासी, एइ अभिलाषी,
आमाके कपट करो ना ॥
के जाने मा तोमार महिमे ।
ब्रह्मादि देवतागणे, देखा पायना गो ध्याने,
आमि किगो जानि तोमार महिमे ॥
तुमि त्रिलोक तारिणी माता त्रिलोकेर शरण ॥

3. Composer - Haru Thakur.

महड़ा : ओ सखिरे ! कइ विपिनविहारी विनोद आमार एलोना ।
मनेते करिते ए विधुवयाने,
सखि ए ये पापी प्राणे धैर्य ना माने,
प्रवोधि केमने ता बलो ना ॥

चितेन : सइ हेरि धारापथो, याकये येमतो, तृषितो चातकजना ।
आमि सेइमतो होये, आछि पथ चेये,
मानसे करि से रूपो भावना ॥

अन्तरा : हाय कि हबे सजनि, याय ये रजनी
केन चक्रपाणि एखनो ।
ना एलो कुंजे, कोथा सुख भुंजे रहिल ना जानि कारणो ॥

चितेन : बिगलित पत्रे, चमकित चित्ते, होतेछे स्थिर मानेना
येन एलो एलो हरि, हेन ज्ञान करि,
ना एलो मुरारि, पाइ यातना ॥

अन्तरा : सइ रबि किरणेरो प्राय हिमकरो ए तनु आमारो दहिछे ।
शिखि पिकि रबो, अंगे मोर सबो बज्राधात सम बाजिछे ॥

चितेन : सइ, करिये संगतो, हरि केन एतो, करिलेको बंचना ।
आमि बंरच गरलो, सखि सेओ भालो,
कि फलो विफले काल् यापना ॥

अन्तरा : सखि देख निजकरे, प्राणपणो कोरे,
गाँथिलाम ए कुसुम हार ।
एकि निरानन्द, बिने से गोबिन्द,
हेन माला गले दिब कार ॥

चितेन : सइ, खेदे फाटे हिया, कारो मुख चेये,
रहिब अबला जना ।
आमि श्याम अन्वेषणे, पाठालाम मने,
तारो संगे केन प्राणो गेलना ॥

4. Composer - Kanai, Lahar Mālasī (लहर मालसी)

चितान : तुमि त्रिगुण धारिणी तारा, वेदे शुनते पाइ ।
पाराण : तोमार नामेर गुण, तोमार चरणेर ये गुण

	मागो, से गुणेर संख्या किछु नाइ ।
लहर :	तुमि आद्याशक्ति तारा, तोमाय धरते देओना धरा,
	जीवके सारा, करले माया जाले
	तोमार मायाते, मा, हये मुग्ध
	विषय - विषे हलेम दग्ध
	सार पदार्थ सकलि याइ भुले ।
मिल :	पाप पूण्य मा तोमार कार्य
	दोषेर भागी आमि, - ठिक बाजीकरेर मेयेर मत,
	देखाओ भोजेर बाजी भूमण्डले ॥

5. Composer - Ram Basu: Māthur (माथुर)

महड़ा :	द्वारी एकबार् बल् तोदेर कृष्ण राजार साक्षाते
	गोपिनी, कृष्ण तापे तापिनी,
	तोमाय देखबे बोले आछे बोसे राजपथे ॥
	एसेछि आमरा अनेक दुःखेते ॥
	तोदेर राजा नाकि दयामय ।
	दुःखिनीर दुःख देखले, देखबो केमन दया हय ॥
	इथे हबे तोमार पुण्य, कर आशा पूर्ण,
	प्रसन्न होये गोपीर साक्षाते ॥
चितेन :	वृन्दे विरह कातरा, हइये सत्वरा,
	राजद्वारे दाँड़ाये कय ।
	मधुर राज्येर अधिपति कृष्ण,
	शुने ताइते एलेम् कंसालय ॥
	मने अन्य अभिलाषो नाइ ।
	राखाल राजार बेश केमन शोभा देखे याइ ॥
	कोथा भूपति जानाओ शीघ्र गति
	विनति करि धरि करेते ॥
अन्तरा :	ताइ एत तोये विनति कोरे बलि ।
	बड़ तापित होये एसेछि द्वारी ॥
	ताइ एत तोय विनति कोरे बलि ।
	दंशिये पलायेछे कालिये कालो वरण फणी,
	आमरा सेइ ज्वालाय ज्वलि ॥
चितेन :	बिषे ना माने जलसार, होयेछे ये राधार,

आर तो ना देखि उपाय ।
फणिमन्त्र जाने तोदेर् राजा द्वारी,
ताइते एलेम मथुराय ॥
एइ आमरा शुनेछि निश्चय ।
राजार दृष्टि मात्रेइ, से बिषे निर्बिषो हय ॥
कृष्ण प्रेमेर बिषे, कृष्ण बिच्छेद बिषे
ब्रह्माण्डे औषध नाइ जुड़ाते

[In some books this song has been attributed to Krishnamohan Bhattacharya]

5. Composer - Rasu-Nrisimha: Māthur (माथुर)

महड़ा : कुब्जागो, तोदेर राज्ये किगो,
श्याम शुकपाखी एसेछे ।
ब्रजे आमादेर राइ चन्द्रमुखी, पुषेछिल श्याम शुकपाखी,
प्रेम पिंजरेर से पाखी अक्रूर एनेछे हरे ।
आमरा तार पाइने देखा, पाखीर माथाय पाखीर पाखा,
सेइ पाखाय श्रीराधार नाम लेखा आछे ॥
खाद : यथार्थ बल आमार काछे ॥
फुँका : से ये श्याम शुकपाखी, राधार प्रियपाखी,
छिल कुंज धामे कुब्जागो ।
तार भंगी सुठाम थाकतो राइ-प्रेम-पिंजरे,
मुरली करे, बलित से चन्द्राधरे, श्रीराधार नाम ॥
मेलता : तारे देखले चिनते पारि, भंगी देखे नयन देखेगो,
भृगु पद चिह्न तार बक्षे रयेछे ॥
प्रथम चितेन : अष्ट सखिगणे कंसेर भवने हइये उदय ।
पाड़ेन : कुब्जार अन्तःपुरे, बले भंगी करे,
कौशले परिचय जानाय ॥
फुँका : आमरा ब्रजवासी, राइ दुःखिनीर दासी,
छिलाम स्वदेशे एलेम एदेशे ।
श्याम नामे श्यामशुकपाखी, आमरा तारे हारिये सखि,
अन्वेषण करि पाखी, देशे देशे ॥
मेलता : हलो अनेक दिन पाइने कोनो देशे, कुब्जागो
अबशेषे जानते एलेम तोमार काछे ॥
अन्तरा : से ये सुठाम शुकपाखी,

अक्रुर आनले राधाय दिये फाँकि ।
पाखीर बरण चिकन कालो,
तार रूपे करे भुवन आलो,
एमन रूप आर कोथाओ नाइ ।
आमरा ब्रज गोपीकाय, ठेकेछि ए दाय,
ताय झोरे आँखि ॥

द्वितीय चितेन : से ये श्याम-शुक-पाखी, प्रेम सुखेर पाखी, सामान्य से नय ॥

पाड़ेन : तार ये भंगि बाँका, दुटी नयन बाँका,
सर्ब अंग केबल बाँकामय ॥

फुँका : शुन गो कुब्जा सखि, श्याम केमन शुकपाखी,
जानना मर्म कुब्जागो,
से पूर्ण ब्रह्मनाम निले जीबेर निस्तार,
अनायासे हय भवपार, दक्षिण चरणेते याँर गंगार जन्म ॥

मेलता : त्यजे वैकुण्ठ ब्रजमाझे हलेन उदय ।
राइ प्रेमेर दाय गो ।
पाखी हये पाखीर व्याभार धरेछे ॥

Pā̃cālī Gāna

Pā̃cālī gāna originated from pure folk music and was limited in the Eastern region of India. In course of time *Pā̃cālī* acquired a few characteristics of *prabandha-gīti* and was raised to the level of *Saṅkīrṇa prabandha-gīti.* Harināyaka of Orissa called it a *Kṣudragīta* in his *Saṅgītasāra.* The *śāstrakārs* of Bengal and Orissa placed *Pā̃cālī* under *Saṅkīrṇa* or *Kṣudra prabandha.* Out of the fourteen *Kṣudragītas* four were considered to be important. These were: *Druvapadā, Citrapadā, Citrakalā* and *Pā̃cālī.*

In *pā̃cālī* there used to be अन्त्य-अनुप्रास, '*antya*' meaning last or end and '*anuprāsa*' meaning alliteration. *Pā̃cālī* were sung in Bengali language also and were called *pā̃cālī / pā̃ncālī gāna.*

Ghanaśyāmdāsa / Narahari Cakravartī mentioned, that *pā̃cālī* was a style in which the Vaiṣṇavas of East India sang songs of *Kṛṣṇalīlā.* Around the 15th-16th century *pā̃cālī* was furthger shaped and improved upon with *śāstrīya* norms by learned Vaiṣṇavas. They composed these songs in simple *rāgas* and *tālas.* Later, with the advent of *śāstrīya kīrtana, pā̃cālī* could not maintain its popularity and position in the field of pure *śāstrīya saṅgīta* and remained as a rural style. Around 18th century, *pā̃cālī* came to towns, particularly to Calcutta, as a mixture of song, recitation and acting, composed on themes from *Kṛṣṇalīlā, Rāmāyaṇa, Mahābhārata,* and *Maṅgala-kāvyas.* Around mid 19th century *pā̃cālī* used to be performed with five *upāṅgas,* viz - 1) *sāj-vādya,* 2) *padas,* on *Bhavānī* or *Śyāmā-viṣayaka,* 3) *Sakhī-saṃvāda,* 4) *viraha,* and 5) *chaḍā-kāṭā.*

Pā̃cālī used to be presented in the following sequence: at the beginning, the *mūl-gāyen* sang a part from each *pada* which was repeated by the *dohārs,* followed by the instrumentalists who played the same tune. The *mūl-gāyen* then recited and enacted a portion of the *pada.* Thus, *pā̃cālī* used to be presented by singing and reciting alternately. Originally, *pā̃cālī* was more of a style like *kathakatā* or monotonous recitation in tune but later, it acquired some traits of *kavi-gāna.*

Laksmikanta Biswas and Ganganarayana Naskar moulded *pā̃cālī* further in *śāstrīya* style. Laksmikanta, popularly known as Lake Kana was a trained musician in *dhrupada* and *khayāl* styles. He composed *pā̃cālī* songs in *rāgas* and *tālas* and was patronised by Gopimohan Thakur of Pathuriaghata. The duel competition between Lake Kana and Ganganarayana was very popular during that time. Both were born around mid 18th Century, and Laksmikanta expired around 1820. *Pācālī* was finally revitalised by Dasarathi Ray who composed aesthetically beautiful *padas* for the style. (See Maṇgalagīti and Pā̃cālī - pp. 72-75)

Pā̃cālī - gāna . Composer—Dasarathi Ray

धनि, आमि केबल निदाने ।
विद्या ये प्रकार वैद्यनाथ आमार विशेषगुण से जाने ।
ओहे ब्रजांगना कर कि कौतुक ? आमार सृष्टिकरा चतुर्मुख,
हरि वैद्य आमि हरिबारे दुख भ्रमि एइ त्रिभुवने ॥

स्थायी

+			२			०			३		
			रा	रगा	-मपा	पा	पा	मा	मा	-गरा	सा
			ध	नि०	००	आ	मि	के	ब	००	ल्
सा	रा	रा	-ा	-ा	-ा	रा	रमा	पा	पा	पा	धमा
नि	दा	ने	०	०	०	वि	द्या०	ये	प्र	का	र०
मा	पा	ना	र्सा	र्सा	र्सर्सा	ना	नर्सा	र्रा	णा	धा	पा
वै	द्य	ना	थ्	आ	मार्	वि	शे०	ष	गु	ण	से
मपा	मगा	-रा									
जा०	ने०	०									

अन्तरा

						०			३		
						मा	पा	पा	ना	ना	ना
						ओ	हे	ब्र	जां	ग	ना
र्सा	र्सा	र्सा	र्सना	र्सा	र्सा	ना	र्सा	र्री	र्री	-ा	र्री
क	र	कि	कौ०	तु	क	आ	मा	र	सृ	०	ष्टि
र्री	र्रर्गर्मा	र्मा	र्मर्गा	र्गर्री	र्सर्सा	पा	ना	ना	ना	ना	र्सा
क	रा००	च	तु०	०र्	मुख्	ह	रि	वै	द्य	आ	मि
ना	सरा	वा	वा	धा	पा	पा	धा	ममा	-मा	मा	मा
ह	रि०	बा	रे	दु	ख्	भ्र	मि	एइ	०	त्रि	भु
मा	गा	-रा									
व	न	०									

[This example is from "Kalaṅka Bhañjana" *pālā* of Dasarathi Ray]

Dasarathi Ray

Born in 1804 in the village called Bandmura, in the district of Burdwan, Dasarathi Ray became a renowned singer-composer of *pā̃cālī*. He belonged to the *Rāḍhī* Brahmin caste and was a gifted poet and a musician. He was brought up by his maternal uncle in the village of Pila and had studied Bengali and English. He took up a job in one of the Indigo companies run by the British.

Dasarathi had joined initially a group of *kaviyāls* led by a lady, named Aksaya Patani who belonged to a low caste, but soon he left this group and formed his own. Because of his extraordinary talent as a composer-singer and his melodious renditions, Dasarathi, popularly known as Dasu earned great fame as a *pā̃cālī*-singer. He composed about sixty *pālā-gānas*.

He died in 1857.

BIBLIOGRAPHY

1. Cakravartī, Narahari. *Bhaktiratnākara*. Pub. by Gaudiya Mission. Calcutta, 1940. (Beng.).
2. Das Sharma, Amal. *Saṅgīta Maṇīṣā*. Part I. Calcutta, 1979. (Beng.).
3. Goswami, Utpala. *Kolkataye Saṅgīta Carā*. Calcutta, 1991. (Beng.).
4. Roy, Bimal. (Suchanda Dattagupta) "*Pā̃cālī*", in *Surachanda* (Bengali Journal). Calcutta, 1982, October Issue.

Ṭappā

Ṭappā came into Bengal around the end of 18th century A.D. The pioneer from Bengal in this style was Kali Mirza / Kalidas Chattopadhyay (1750-1826), although the credit for popularising *Ṭappā* in Bengal is attributed to Nidhubabu or Ramnidhi Gupta (1741-1839).

There is however some controversy over the question, whether Nidhubabu's compositions were of the true nature of Hindusthani *ṭappa* or not. In his own anthology of song compositions named '*Gītaratna*', 1st ed. 1837-38, he himself says in the introductory chapter that:

> - - - "एइ गीत सकले आलापचारिर द्वारा ये सकल तान बसियाछे ताहा कोन हिन्दुस्थानी ख्याल ओ टप्पार सुरे गीत रचना करिए देओया एमत नहे, अथच गानकरण मात्र राग रागिणीर रूप अविकल बुझाइतेछे"।
> meaning that - 'the *tānas* set by *ālāpcāri* in my compositions are not as per any *Hindusthānī khayāl* or *ṭappā* style, yet these express exact *rāga-rūpas*'. He himself says that his compositions are neither *khayāl* nor *ṭappā*. The list of heavy *rāgas* and *tālas* enlisted in this book also point to the fact that *ṭappās* could never be set on such serious *rāgas* as: *Dhāneśrī - puriā, Malkauṅs, Multānī, Kānaḍā-lalit, Lalit-bhairav, Toḍī, Darbārī-toḍī, Paraj, Purvī*, etc. *Tālas* mentioned are: *Āḍācautāla, Dhīmā-tritāla, Dhāmār, Ektāla, Madhyamāna*, etc. and also *Jalad-tritāla*.

The other fact is that when Nidhubabu went to Chapra, he received his *tālim* in Hindusthani *śāstrīya-saṅgīta* from 'one *ustād*'. This *ustād* perhaps could not have been a *ṭappa* maestro from Shori Miya's *khāndān*, because Nidhubabu was in Chapra from 1776-1794 A.D. and Shori Miya flourished in the court of Nawab Suja-ud-Daula of Lucknow, who ruled between 1753-1775. Considering the short gap of time span, it seems improbable that Shori Miya's disciples reached Chapra so fast in those days when travelling was misererably slow and besides, proper patronage was necessary. However, it is known that there used to live a few musician families in Chapra during that time and used to sing old style of *ṭappās* which were in vogue long before Shori Miya. This style was prevalent even during Shahjahan's reign. Shori Miya later formulated his own style from the old style. Therefore, it is probable that Nidhubabu learnt that old style, which might have some trends of *khayāl* and *ṭappā*, not necessarily of Shori Miya's style. It is also known from Kavi Ishwarchandra's biographical accounts of ancient *kavis*, that 'this *ustād*' did not teach his *gharānā* specialities to his disciples and so Nidhubabu left his *guru* and composed songs on his own and in his own style. This style of his was devoid of any fast *tānkāri* of *ṭappā* style which abounds in *khaṭkā, murak, rerak, khaḍḍā, fandā, zamzamā*—the essential qualities of *ṭappā* of Shori Miya's style. Instead, his compositions were of *madhyalaya*, with slow undulated patterns that unveiled the exquisite mood of the lyrics. *Madhyamāna-tāla* dominated his songs.

It is a well known fact that in Bihar and Bengal, the ancient musical styles were often composed in *miśra-rāgas* which abounded in the compositions of Vidyāpati, as has been recorded by Locana Kavi in his *Rāgataraṅgiṇī*. Nidhubabu's compositions also were predominantly based on *miśrarāgas*.

When Nidhubabu and Kali Mirza went out of Bengal, they were already proficient in the *śāstra*-based *prācina* (old) Bengali style of music. Then they learnt from out side of Bengal but their compositions have the predominant characteristics of old style of Bengali songs.

Very probably, Nidhubabu first emerged as an *ākhḍāi* exponent and artiste-composer. His *kheuḍ* and *prabhātī* songs included in *ākhḍāi*, were structurally similar to his *ṭappā* compositions. Judging from the dates when reformed and polished *ākhḍāi* was started (1805-1806), it may be said that Nidhubabu was the earliest composer of *rāga* based *ṭappā* style *kheuḍ* and *ṭappā* style *prabhātī* in Bengal. His technique of *ṭappā* was special and unique and was different from Hindusthani *ṭappā* style. It is also probable that other singers of *Dāḍā-kavi-gāna*, who were proficient in singing *ṭappā*, called Ndhubabu's *ākhḍāi* compositions as '*Nidhubābur ṭappā*'.

Whatever the case may be, Nidhubabu's songs famous as '*Nidhubābur ṭappā*' were most suitable for expressing pathos of love songs, and his style brought in a real change in Bengal's music style, which lasted for a whole century. His style even influenced religious music, *svadeśī-saṅgīta*, and other styles of *kāvya-saṅgīta*. This achievement would not have been possible through Hindusthani style of *ṭappā*, which is fast in laya and the short compositions are love songs only. 'Nidhubabu's *ṭappā* was totally *śāstra* oriented and elevated '*baiṭhakī-gāna*' or chamber music to a connoisseur's delight.

Kali Mirza was younger than Nidhubabu. He went to Banaras, Delhi and Lucknow, particularly to study Hindusthani *śāstrīya-saṅgīta* in *khayāl* and *ṭappā* styles. He came back to his native place Guptipara in 1780-81 and started his professional career in music. Real *ṭappā* style was started in Bengal by him from then. Chronologically however, Kali Mirza preceded Nīdhubabu in composing *ṭappā* style of songs both in Hindi and Bengali twelve years ahead, as he learnt the style earlier than Nidhubabu, and started his career as a musician by 1780-81, while Nidhubabu learnt music in Chapra between 1776 to 1794 and started his proper musical activities after returning to Calcutta.

Kali Mirza's style was slightly different from Nidhubabu's and he built up his professional career in Hoogly and Burdwan area by composing and singing *ṭappā* both in Hindi and Bengali and also training disciples in the art. He had learnt *ṭappā* style at Banaras, Lucknow and Delhi and became well known as a singer-composer of this style both in Bengali and Hindi. He composed love lyrics of two *tuks* in tasteful language with alliteration and he set these in pure *rāgas*. His Bengali *ṭappās*, about 400 in number, were also slower in laya than the Hindusthani ones. The *dānās* used were also much softer, to express the true sentiments of Bengali lyrics.

Radhamohan Sen Das was another contemporary *ṭappā* composer, who wrote *Saṅgīta-taraṅga* in 1818. Radhamohan learnt *ṭappā* from Kali Mirza.

After Nidhubabu and Kali Mirza, the person who elevated *Ṭappā* to one of the most favourite styles of Bengal was Sridhar Kathak (b. 1816). Born in a Brahmin family, he was initially a *kathak* and was endowed with a melodious voice. He composed excellent *ṭappās* both lyrically and musically, and was perhaps the most meritorious composer of the first half of 19th century His copositions have become immortal and were often mistaken as Nidhubabu's. Some of his compositions were even put erroneously under the authorship of Nidhubabu. His compositions were characterised by poetic sensibility, alliteration, excellent rhyming and linguistic refinement. Many of his compositions have been compiled in '*Bāṅgālīr Gāna*' (Calcutta 1905), by Durgadas Lahiri. Being an excellent artiste of *kathakatā* and *ṭappā*, he linked the two styles in his performances. Between 19th and 20th centuries, there were many singers and composers who elevated Bengal's *ṭappā* to a great height of popularity. Important among them are: Ashutosh Deb (Satubabu - 1809-49), Amritalal Basu (1853-1929), Atulkrishna Mitra (1857-1912), Dasharathi Ray (1804-1857), Dayalchand Mitra, Durgadas Dey, Gopal Ude (b. 1835), Govinda Adhikari (1798-1876), Girishchandra Ghosh (1843-1911), Harimohan Roy, Jagannath Prasad Basumallick, Jadunath Ghosh, Kalidas Chattopadhyay, Kalidas Gangopadhyay, Kasi Prasad Ghosh, Munsi Vilayat Husein, Manamohan Basu, (1831-1912), Ramchand Bandopadhyay, Ramapati Bandopadhyay, and Shivchandra Sarkar.

Zamindar Jagannath Prasad Mallick of Andul (Howrah) was not only a *ṭappā* composer, but was the author of '*Saṅgīta-rasa-madhura*' (Calcutta 1844). Jagannath Ghosh of Belur, another *ṭappā* composer, wrote *Saṅgīta-Manorañjana*' (Cal 1861). The two, made *ṭappā* light and lively by composing with a less poignant language and theme, although the previous undulated *calan* or movement set by Nidhubabu, Kali Mirza and their followers was retained.

Kaliprasad Ghosh was one of the most educated *ṭappā* composers, who was a brilliant student of erstwhile Hindu College. He composed his *ṭappās* on the lines of Nidhubabu and these were compiled in *Gītāvalī*. Kalipada Pathak of 20th century is another musician who gave a special touch to this style.

Ṭappā had influenced considerably all styles of music of Bengal, viz. *Rabīndra-saṅgīta, Brahma-saṅgīta, Nātya-saṅgīta, Svadeśīgāna, Atulprasādī, Dwijendragīti, Nazrulgīti,* and devotional songs. But gradually, popularity of *ṭappā* waned because of its retarted growth and deteriorating cultural value, due to some third rate compositions of erotic verses set to *ṭappā*-tunes indiscriminately by nondescript poets. This trend was partly reverted by some *jātrā-kavis*, playwrights and dramatists like Gopal Ude, Manamohan Basu, Girishchandra Ghosh, Ramapati Bandopadhyay and Amritalal Basu through stage. But Nidhubabu was forgotten and *ṭappā* was considered to be a musical obscenity by the highly placed socialites and intellectuals of Bengal. But for the efforts of Krishnananda Vyas,a Marwari who was a musician-musicologist and a great collector and compiler, these valuable lyrics of *ṭappā* would have been lost. He compiled song compositions of various poets from all over India, including compositions of Nidhubabu, Kali Mirza, Ashutosh Deb and many others of Bengal. Later, Ishwarchandra Gupta, Rangalal Bandopadhyay, Rev. James Long, Durgadas Lahiri, Sisirkumar Ghosh, Anathkrishna Deb, Harimohan Mukhopadhyay and some others compiled these lyrics in their anthologies.

Nidhubabu and Kali Mirza adopted *ṭappā* style to develop Bengali songs in a unique style of its own, which was not strictly Hindusthani *ṭappā* of Shori Miya's style, as has been explained earlier. The uncorrupted form of original Hindusthani *ṭappā* was introduced to Bengal much later in the mid 19th century by the Misras of Banaras and Ramzan Khan, when they settled down in Calcutta. Maheshchandra Mukhopadhyay (1838-1905) was more well known as '*Mahesh Ostād*' for his mastery over *khayāl* and *ṭappā* style, although he was adept in Bengali *ṭappās* as well, and composed many. Maheshchandra had his proper *tālīm* in *śāstrīya saṅgīta* from the covetted *Prasadu-Manohar gharānā* of the Misras of Kasi. Ramkumar and Shivsahay Misra, the two sons of Manohar and Prasaddu respectively, taught Mahesh the art of *khayāl, ṭappā* and *ṭap-khayāl*, in which he excelled, particularly in *ṭappā* which was of Shori Miya's style.

The Misras of Banaras had influenced the music of Bengal, particularly in Calcutta, in a very major way. Many Bengali aspirants in music took *tālīm* from them. Ramkumar Misra particularly was a *great ācārya* and trained not only Mahesh Ostād but also others like Madhusudan Banerji, Kiranmayee, Surama, Kaliprasanna Ghosh, Surendranath Majumdar, Laxminarayan Babaji, Tulsidas Chattopadhyay, Nibaran Kathak, Jogindranath Ghosh, Shambhucharan Mukhopadhyay. The *māhol* or atmosphere of Hindusthani *ṭappā* was created by members of this *gharānā*.

Ramzan Khan, son of Imam Badi, the famous *ṭappā* singer of Kasi was an excellent performer of *ṭappā* and *ṭap-khayāl*. He settled down in Calcutta permanently after the fall of Metiaburuj music *durbār*, and trained Kalipada Pathak, Jitendranath Bandopadhyay, Nikunjabihari Datta, Phanishankar Mukhopadhyay, and Ramchandra Chattopadhyay. Imam Badi herself taught Nagendranath Bhattacharya of Ranaghat.

Kalipada Pathak trained Gopal Chattopadhyay, Chandidas Mal, Dilip Mukhopadhyay, Tusharkanti Pathak (nephew), Rajyeshwar Mitra.

Ramnidhi Gupta

More well known as Nidhubabu, Ramnidhi Gupta was a great singer-composer of *ṭappā* style of songs and created a special type of *ṭappā* in Bengali. His lyrical compositions were of great poetical value as *gīti-kavitās*. He was perhaps one of the pioneers in composing songs in Bengali language, set to pure classical *rāgas* and *tālas*. May be, that is why he wrote:

"नानान देशेर नानान भाषा
बिना स्वदेशीय भाषा, पुरे कि आशा"

meaning, there are many languages of different countries but unless it is your own mother tongue, you do not get the satisfaction.

Ramnidhi was born in Capta village, in 1741 in a *kavirāj* family. Originally he hailed from Kumartuli area of Calcutta but due to the atrocities of the Maratha *Borgies,* his father Harinarayan Gupta moved to Hoogly with his family for a short while. After his formal education at Calcutta in Persian, Sanskrit and also English under a missionary, he got the job of a second clerk in Chapra collectorate in 1776 and later as head clerk. Here he found an opportunity to learn Hindusthani *śāstrīya-saṅgīta,* as Chapra was then a small centre of music, with a few musician families settled down there. Ramnidhi had no formal training earlier except perhaps the essential rudiments at Calcutta. But as he was keen on music he started learning methodically at Chapra under a Muslim musician, whose name is not known. As the *ustād* was not keen to part with the best of his *gharānā* techniques Nidhubabu parted company and started composing songs in Bengali in the format of Hindi songs, set them to tune in *rāgas* and *tālas* of his choice and sang them in his own creative style. This art of his reached its perfection when he came back to Calcutta in 1794 at the age of fiftythree, retiring prematurely from his job.

Nidhubabu was married and was a responsible family man although he was attracted towards a well known lady named Srimati. He composed many songs on her. One of them is: *Bhālobāsibe bole bhālobāsine.* There is however slight controversy about the composer of this song. Some place it under the authorship of Nidhubabu while others, under Sridhar Kathak. Nidhubabu mostly composed on the spot extempore and these were not written down always. Thus very often many of his lyrics were lost or misplaced.

Nidhubabu introduced light topics of love in place of heavy religious and philosophical themes but he composed his songs in such a language that there was no vulgarity. He designed his *ṭappā* in a unique manner to express the deep pathos of his love-lyrics, suitably through *rāgas* and *rāgiṇīs* and also *miśra-rāgas.* His style of *ṭappā* was very different from Hindusthani *ṭappā style which is predominated by murak, rerak, zamzamās, khaṭakā-tānas,* very fast tempo and short lyrics, mentioned earlier. Instead, Nidhubabu adopted slower tempo, with elongated, undulated wave like *tānas,* fit to express the longing and poignancy of his lyrics. His choice of serious *rāgas* and heavy *tālas* are also contrary to the Hindusthani *ṭappās.* He created a great impact for a whole century on the people and music composers of Bengal, by his *ṭappā* style.

Being an excellent singer with a melodious voice he fascinated his listeners. His admirers include *ustāds* like Rasul Bakhs, Abubaras Khan, connoisseurs like Maharaj Tejashchandra of Burdwan, Mahananda Ray of Murshidabad and many others.

Nidhubabu spent his early and retired life in his family abode of Kumartuli in Calcutta. It was here where he composed his innumerable songs and published his book '*Gītaratna*' in 1837-38 when he was around ninety-seven years of age.

Nidhubabu's knowledge of *rāgas* and *tālas* was so deep that he could compose a song on the spot and set it to an appropriate *rāga* and *tāla* condusive to the *padas.*

Apart from *ṭappā* style, his contribution in *Ākhḍāi* style of music is commendable. He composed excellent *padas* in place of cheap compositions, introduced *rāgas* and discipline of *śāstrīya-saṅgīta* and also elaborate orchestration.

Nidhubabu organised two amateur groups in *ākhḍāi* in aristrocratic circles. These groups were of Bagbazar / Shobhabazar and Pathuriaghata. He led the Bagbazar group. These groups became so popular that all other *ākhḍāi* groups had to withdraw. He polished *ākhḍāi* to a high classical standard which was extremely complex and difficult.

Nidhubabu composed a *Brahma-saṅgīta* on the spot at the temple of Brahmo Samaj, when he was around eighty-eight years of age:

Rāga - Bihāga Tāla - Āḍāṭhekā

परमब्रह्म तत्परात्पर परमेश्वर
निरञ्जन निरामय निर्विशेष सदाशय,
आपना आपनि हेतु विभु विश्वधर ॥
समुदय पंचबोध ज्ञानाज्ञान यथावास
प्रपंच भूताधिकार ॥
अन्नमय, प्राणमय, मानस विज्ञानमय
शेषेते आनन्दमय प्राप्त सिद्धनर ॥

Nidhubabu had a long and healthy life. He kept up his musical activities till the end. During his long life Nidhubabu experienced the turmoil that Bengal passed through, such as: the notorious atrocities of the Marathas (*Borgies*), the Battle of Plassey, the new English regime after the Muslim rule and the shifting of the capital of Bengal from Murshidabad to Calcutta in 1773. Calcutta was then more like a village than a prosperous city and there were no patrons of music at that time of early stage. The centres of music were Murshidabad, Krishnanagar, Dhaka, etc. Calcutta grew gradually after 1794, with the various zamindar families moving in and sponsoring musicians from various places. But Nidhubabu was a non-professional musician who would not go to others to perform; on the contrary his musical soirees were held at his own place of choice. His favoutite place was the *āṭcālā* (shed) of Babu Ramchandra Mitra of Shobhabazar where people used to come to listen to him.

Nidhubabu published his book '*Gītaratna*' towards the end of his life when he found out that many of his compositions were misused, mishandled and misinterpreted. In this book he has given a list of *rāgas* with their time for singing, and also ninetysix songs. The *rāgas* along with their time, enlisted in this book are as follows:

Rāgas	***Time***
Āḍānā-bāhār	after one and half *prahar* of noon.
Āḍānā	same as above.
Āsā-bhairavī	after one *prahar* in the morning.
Yaman	soon after evening.
Yaman-puriyā	after four *danḍas* of night.
Yaman-bhūpālī	soon after evening.
Yaman-kalyāṇa	same as above.
Yaman-Jhījhiṭ	same as above.
Elāyā (Alhaiyā)	morning.
Elāyā-jhījhiṭ	morning.
Kāliṅgḍā	early morning

There are many other *miśra-rāgas* mentioned in this book used for his songs. These are: *Lum-kāfi, Bāgeśrī-toḍī, Bāgeśrī-āḍānā, Bāgeśrī-kānāḍā, Bāgeśrī-multānī, Bāgeśrī-bāhār, Bhūpālī-jhījhiṭ, Dhāneśrī-puriyā, Gārā-jhījhiṭ, Hindola-bihāga, Hamīr-khamāja, Kāmod-gauḍa, Kāmod-khamāja, Kāfi-kaukav, Kāfi-jayjayantī, Kāfi-palāsa, Kedār-kāmoda, Kāliṅgḍā-khāmāja, Kāfi-jhījhiṭ, Kedāra-khāmāja, Khāmāja-bāhār, Lalita-bhairava, Lalita-bibhāsa, Hamīr-khāmāja, Hindola-bihāga, Gārā-jhījhiṭ, Mālkauṅs-bhairava, Mālkauṅs-bāhār, Mālkauṅs-basanta, Multānī-bāhār, Multānī-palās, Rāmkeli-lalita, Sohinī-kānaḍā, Sohinī-mālkauṅs, Śyāma-purvī, Sughrāi-bāhār, Sāhānā-āḍānā, Sindhukāfi, Sarpardā-kālingḍā, Jogiā-lalita, Jogiā-gāndhāra.*

Tālas mentioned are: *Āḍācautāla, Dhīmā-tintāla, Dhāmār, Ektāla, Hari-tāla, Jalad-tintāla, Kavvālī,* etc.

Nidhubabu's distinctive pattern of love poetry and style of music influenced his contemporary and also next generation poet-composers. Notable among them are: Rabindranath, Dwijendralal and Sridhar Kathak.

Nidhubabu composed a great number of songs but many of these are lost today. However, some of his songs are available in his own book - *Gītaratna,* 1st ed. published in 1837-38 by him. It is an anthology of his *ākhḍāi* and *ṭappā* songs, ninetysix in number. Other books are:

1. *Saṅgīta-rāga-kalpadruma.* Pub. in 1849 by Krishnananda Vyas containing about 150 songs.
2. *Saṅgīta-sāra-saṅgraha* - Part II. Pub. by Harimohan Mukhopadhyay containing over 400 songs.
3. *Prītigītī.* Pub. by Avinash Chandra Ghosh — containing a number of songs in different chapters, divided according to the themes of the songs.
4. *Bāṅgālīr-gāna.* Pub. by Durgadas Lahiri. It has a huge collection of his songs numbering more than 400. Besides these major compilations, there are many other minor ones having *Nidubābur-ṭappā* or *ākhḍāi* songs.

Nidhubabu's ṭappā examples:

१. Rāga Multān - Tāla Āḍātheka
नयनेरे दोष केन ।
मनेरे बुझाय बल, नयनेरे दोष केन ।
आँखि कि मजाते पारेना, हले मनो मलिन ॥
आँखिते बदन हेरे, सकलइ कि मने धरे,
येइ थाके मने करे, सेइ तार मनोरंजन ॥

२. विच्छेदे ये क्षति तार अधिक मिलने ।
आँखि कि आशा पूरे क्षण दरशने ॥
प्रवल आनन्द देख किंचित जीवने ।
निर्वान हइते केह देखेछ कखने ॥

३. की यातना यतने मने मने मनइ जाने ।
पाछे लोके हासे शुने
आमि लाजे प्रकाशिते पारिने ॥
प्रथम मिलनावधि येन कतो अपराधी

निरबधि साधि प्राणपणे ॥
तबु तो से नाहि तोषे, आरो दोषे अकारणे ।
की यातना यतने मने मनइ जाने ॥

४. Rāga Kedārā - Jalad tetāla
मनपुर हते आमार हारायेछ मन
काहारे कहिब कार दोषदिब निले कोन जन,
ना बले केमने रब बले बल कि करिव
तोमा बिने आर सेखाने काहार गमना गमन ।
अन्येर अगमनीय, जान से स्थान निश्चय
इथे अनुमान हय एइ प्राण तुमि से कारण,
यदि ताहे थाके फल, लयेछ करेछ भाल
नाहि चाहि आमि, यदि प्राण तुमि करह यतन ॥
(Written, after the demise of his first wife *c.* 1771)

५. नानान देशे नानान भाषा
बिने स्वदेशीय भाषा पूरे कि आशा
कत नदी सरोबर
किबा फल चातकीर
धाराजल बिने कभु घुचे कि तृषा ?

६. कत भालवासि तारे, सइ ! केमने बुझाब
दरशने पुलकित मम अंग सब ।
यतक्षण नाहि देखि रोदन करये आँखि
देखिले कि निधि पाइ, कोथाय राखिब ।

७. Rāga Sindhu-bhairavī - Tāla Madhyamāna.
भालबासिबे बले भालबासिने,
आमार स्वभाव एइ तोमा बइ आर जानिने ।
बिधु मुखे मधुरहासि, आमि बड़ भालबासि
ताइ तोमारे देखते आसि देखा दिते आसिने ॥

Sthāyī

३ +

सा सा ‖ रा मज्ञा -ज्ञा -मज्ञा -मा मा -पा मा | पा -पदा -णदणा -दपा ज्ञा -मज्ञा मा पा |

भा ल ‖ बा सि० ० ०० ० बे ० ब | ले ०० ००० ०० भा ०० ल बा |

२ o

| पा -णणा -दा पा -पदा -णदा -पमा -पा | -दपा -मज्ञा -मा -पमा -ज्ञरा -सा णा णा |

| सि ०० ० ने ०० ०० ०० ० | ०० ०० ० ०० ०० ० आ मा |

३ +

| धा णा धा णा -ा -ा धा णा | -ा र्सणा -ा -धप -ा पा दा पपा |

| र स्व भा व ० ० ए इ | ० ०० ० ०० ० तो मा बइ |

२ o

| पपा मा पा पा -पदा -णदा पमा -पा | -दपा -मज्ञा -मा -पमा -ज्ञरा -सा सा सा ‖

| आर जा नि ने ०० ०० ०० ० | ०० ०० ० ०० ०० ० "भा ल' ‖

Antarā

३ +

पा पा | पा -ा -ा -धपा धा णा र्सर्सा र्सर्सा | र्सा -ा ज्ञॅा -री -र्सा -री र्सा णा |

बि धु | मु ० ० ०० खे म धुर हा० | सि ० ० ० ० ० आ मि |

२ o

| धा णा -ा -ा र्सा णा -ा धा | पधा -णर्सणा -दणा दा पा -ा णणा णा |

| ब ड़ ० ० भा ल ० ० | ०० ००० ०० बा सि ० ताइ तो |

३ +

| धा णा णणा णा -ा -ा धा णा | णा -ा -धा -पा -ा पा धा पा |

| मा रे देख ते ० ० आ सि | ० ० ० ० ० दे खा दि |

२ o

| पा मा पा पा -पदा -णदा -पमा -पा | -दपा -मज्ञा -मा -पमा -ज्ञा -रा सा सा ‖

| ते आ सि ने ०० ०० ०० ० | ०० ०० ० ०० ० ० "भा ल" ‖

Kalidas Chattopadhyay

In *c.* 1750, a few years before Battle of Plassey, Kalidas was born in a village called Guptipara which was then well known for its intellectual and musical activities. Kalidas was not only a musician and composer of *ṭappās* and an *ācārya* of *saṅgīta* but he was a pundit of *śāstras* and *Vedānta*. He was a meritorious student of Sanskrit and was very sharp and intelligent. After completing his studies in Guptipara, he went to Banaras for further studies in *Vednāta* and also in music, around 1770. After a few years of studies at Banaras, he went to Delhi and Lucknow for further training in music. He learnt Persian also at these two places. After completing his studies and *tālīm* in music he returned to Guptipara around 1780 /81 and got married.

Kalidas, though a Brahmin and a pundit of *śāstras*, embraced music as his profession. He taught in Guptipara and its surrounding areas, where he formed his group of disciples who learnt *ṭappā* from him. Out of these disciples, Ambikacharan became an *ācārya* and trained Umanath Bhattacharya (1829-1894), who became one of the top *kathaks* and *ṭappā* singers of his time. Umanath taught his eldest son Nagendranath Bhattacharya (Ranaghat) in this art. Later, Nagendranath became an *ācārya* of *saṅgīta*. Nirmalchandra Chattopadhyay and Nagendranath Datta were his disciples who became top *ṭappā* singers and trained many students till the mid 20th century. Thus, Kalidasa's style of *ṭappās* was maintained through generations of his disciples.

Kalidas, famously known as Kali Mirza, joined the *durbār* of Kumar Pratapchand of Burdwan for a few years around 1805. Then he shifted to Calcutta and joined the *durbār* of Gopimohan Thakur of Pathuriaghata. But Pratapchand was so fond of him that he kept sending his remuneration regularly, although Kalidas was no longer under his employment.

The Calcutta phase of his life was the best part of his career. Gopimohan was an ardent admirer of Kalidas. He not only enjoyed listening to his music at his *durbār* but used to take Kalidas with him to the temple of *Kālī-Brahmamayī* at Mulajod where Kalidas used to compose songs on the great attributes of the Goddess. Probably it is due to this fact that a chunk of his compositions are *Śyāmā-saṅgīta*. Kali Mirza remained at Gopimohan's *durbār* for about eight years and used to attend all music performances held in different places of Calcutta, as a much sought after artiste and also as an invitee. Raja Rammohun Ray was one of his disciples. He was witty, intelligent, amiable and a pleasant person. He was tall, fair and handsome and used to dress like a noble. He used to attend music mehfils riding on his horse and was more famous as Kali Mirza than Chattopadhyay.

Kalidas's last few years were full of grief as he lost his wife, children and his younger brother. He spent the last few years of his life in Kasi where he breathed his last in *c.* 1820. But even during his stay in Kasi he was hailed as a musician and performed at the *durbār* of Raja Uditanarayana Singh (1795-1835) of Kasi, who was himself a musician and his *durbār* boasted of such greats as Nirmal Shah Senī; the three Senī brothers - Zafar Khan, Pyar Khan and Basat Khan; Shadi Khan - a *ṭappā* expert of Shori Miya's tradition, and many others.

Kali Mirza became famous for his musical abilities as a composer of *ṭappā, mālasī* and *Śyāmā-saṅgīta.* Like Nidhubabu he was also one of the pioneers in composing songs of light themes of love in Bengali. The language he used was chaste, rich in poetic value and aesthetic beauty. His *tappās* were short compositions of two *tuks* only and full of alliteration. He set these lyrics on pure as well as *miśra-rāgas* and used *tālas* like *Āḍāṭhekā, Madhyamāna, Teoṭ,* etc. but he perhaps gave preference to *Āḍā ṭhekā.* His compositions are available in *Saṅgīta-rāga-kalpadruma* of Krishnananda Vyas, *Gītalaharī, Gītaratnamālā, Prītigīti, Saṅgītakoṣ, Saṅgīta-sāra-saṅgraha* and *Bāṅgālīr-gāna.*

1. A few example of his compositions: Rāga Sohinī, Āḍāṭhekā , Ṭappā
   चाहि चाँदेर पाने तोरे हय मने ।
   तुल ना हइले दोँहि तुलना हबे केमने ॥
   यदि समतुल करि नयने नयने
   मृगाङ्क हइये शशी लुकाय तब बदने॥

2. Rāga Sāhānā , Āḍātheka , Ṭappā
   कब तारे कत भेबेछिलाम अन्तरे,
   सकल भुलिये गेलाम देखिया तोमारे ॥
   मुखे ना सरे वचन नयन पलक हीन,
   आमि ये आमार नइ, कि हल आमारे ॥

3. Bhakti - saṅgīta, Rāga - Kāfi, Āḍāṭhekā
   भीष्म जननी भागीरथी गंगे
   तारण कारण भव भय वारण
   स्थावर जंगम कीट पतंगे ।
   हरिद्वारवती अति द्रुत गति
   जह्नुमुनि ध्यान भंगे ।
   सागर सन्तति, तादेर मा दितेगति
   मिलित सागर संगे ।
   कारण वारिणी पतित उद्धारिणी
   नारायणी द्रव अंगे ।
   कलुष कातर काली कलेबर
   पड़ेछे पाप तरंगे ॥

Purātanī: Composer - Kali Mirza. Surchanda - Sept. 1981

Rāga - Sindhu-Bhairavī Tāla - Āḍā ṭhekā

अनेकेरे मने करे मने ना धरे
याहारे नियेछे मने कदाच तारे ना पाशरे ।

येइ जन प्रियजन कहे अप्रिय बचन
तबु तारे कखन भुलिते ना पारे ॥

Sthāyī —

+	२	०	३
		‖{ सा	रा ज्ञमा ज्ञरा -ज्ञा
		अ	ने के० ०० ०रे
मा पा -ा पा	-दा -पदा -णदा पा	मा -ा ज्ञा मा	पा पदा -णदा दा
म ने ० ०	० ०० ०० क	रे ० ० म	ने ना० ०० ध
पा दा -णदा -पमा	-मपा -दपा -मज्ञा -ज्ञमा	-पमा -ज्ञरा -सा णा	-ा धा णा -ा
रे ० ०० ००	०० ०० ०० ००	०० ०० ० जा	० हा रे ०
णर्सा र्सा -ा णर्सा	-र्रसा -णधा -धणा -ा	धा पा -ा पा	पदा -णदा पा मा
नि० ये ० छे०	०० ०० ०००	म ने ० क	दा० ०० च ता
पपा पदा -णदा -पमा	-मपा -दपा -मज्ञा-ज्ञमा	-पमा -ज्ञरा -सा }‖	
रेना पाश रे० ००	०० ०० ०० ०	०० ०० ०	

Antarā

		पा	पा पा धा -णा
		जे	इ ज न ०
र्सा र्सा -णर्सा -र्रज्ञा	-री -ज्ञी -ा री	र्सा -णा -ा धा	णा णा -ा र्सा
प्रि य ०० ००	० ० ० ज	न ० ० क	हे अ ० प्रि
णा -दा -ा पदा	-णर्सा -णदा -दा णा	दा -पा -ा णा	-ा धा णा -ा
य ० ० ब०	०० ०० ० च	न ० ० तबु	० ता रे ०
-णर्सा -र्सा -ा णर्सा	-र्रसा णधा -णा -धा	-ा पा -ा पा	णा णा -धा णा
०० ० ० क०	०० ख० ० ०	० न ० भु	लि ते ० ना
पा दा -नदा -पमा	-मपा -दपा -मज्ञा -ज्ञमा	-पमा -ज्ञरा -सा ‖	
पा रे ०० ००	०० ०० ०० ००	०० ०० ०	

Composer - Kali Mirza

Rāga - Sarfardā Tāla - Āḍāṭhekā

बासनार कि बासना तबु तारे भालबासे ।
भानु लक्षान्तरे थाके कमल सलिले भासे ॥
चक्रवाक चक्रवाकी, कि सुखे ताहारा सुखी,
निशिते विच्छेद देखि केह नाहि कारो पाशे ॥

Ṭappā Rāga-Kalingdā Tāla Madhyamāna.

मिलन हइये ना हल मिलन ए केमन मिलन ।
समुखे मुखे मुखे नाहिक बचन ॥
बहु यतनेते आसि मानेते पोहाय निशि
साधिते आर बिषाद निषेध ना माने ॥

Composer - Kali Mirza

Rāga - Sindhuḍā Bhairavi Tāla - Āḍā-ṭhekā

एमन नयनवाण के तोमाय करेछे दान ?
हेरो ना दर्पणे मुख आपनि हाराबे प्राण ।
नयन अक्षय तूण ताहे कटाक्ष निपुण
यदि विधि दित गुण बधिते आमार प्राण ॥

Sridhar Kathak

Born in 1223 B.S. (1816 A.D.) in a Brahmin family of Bansbedia village, his family was reputed for its intellectual abilities and music. They were *kathaks* and his grandfather Lalchand Vidyabhushana was well known as a *kathak* singer. Sridhar had learnt *kathakatā* under Kalicharan Bhattacharya of Behrampur and was associated with the groups of *pā̃cālī* and *kavi-dal,* but all his compositions were of *ṭappā* style. His lyrics have been compiled in '*Bāṅgālīr-gāna*'. Sridhar Kathak was perhaps the most outstanding composer of *ṭappā* in the first half of 19th century.

Sridhar was a singer of great repute and blended the styles of *kathakatā* and *ṭappā.* His compositions were of the same standard as those of Nidhubabu and were often mistaken as the latters. The famous song *Bhālobāsibe bole bhālobāsine* which is attributed to Nidhubabu is also found in the composition book of Sridhar in a slightly different version. As Nidhubabu's songs were mostly extempore it is probable that Sridhar sang this song with a few changes which were unintentional. However, the song that Nidhubabu composed is normally rendered by exponents of *ṭappā.* Both the versions are given below.

Nidhubabu's composition:

भालबासिबे बले भालबासिने,
आमार स्वभाव एइ तोमा बइ आर जानिने ।
बिधु मुखे मधुर हासि, आमि बड़ भालबासि,
ताइ तोमारे देखते आसि देखा दिते आसिने ॥

Sridhar Kathak's composition:

भालबासिबे बले भालबासिने,
आमार से भालबासा तोमाबइ आर जानिने ।
बिधु मुखेर मधुर हासि देखिले सुखेते भासि,
ताइ देखते आसि – देखा दिते आसिने ॥

Composer - Sridhar Kathak
(Surchanda - Sept. 1981)

Purātanī Rāga-Sindhu Tāla - Āḍāṭhekā

यावत जीवन रबे कारे भालबासिबना,
भालबेसे एइ हलो भालबासार कि लांछना ।
आमि भालबासि यारे से कभु भाबेना मोरे
तबे केन तारि तरे नियत पाइ ए यन्त्रणा ॥
भालबासा भुले याब मनेरे बुझाइब
पृथिवीते आर येन केउ कारे भालबासेना ॥

Sthāyī

+				२				०					३			
												मा	मा	पपमपा	-धणा	णधपा-
												या	ब	त०००		०० ००जी०
मा	ज्ञा	-ा	-ा	-रज्ञमा	-ज्ञमा	ज्ञा	रा	-ा	-ा	-ा	सा		रा	सा	-सणृ	सा
व	न	०	०	०००	००	र	बे	०	०	०	का		रे	भा	००	ल
रा	मा	-मप	-मपधणा	-णधा	पमा	-ज्ञा	-रा	-सा	-ा	-सरा	पा		र्सना	र्सा	र्सा	-ा
बा	सि	० ०	००००	००	बना	०	०	०	०	००	भा		ल०	बे	से	०
ना	-र्सा	-नर्सर्रर्सा	णा	-ा	धा	पा	-ा	-धपा	-मा	-ा	पा		धा	णा	र्सा	-ा
ए	०	००००	इ	०	ह	लो	०	००	०	०	भा		ल	बा	सार	०

+				२				०				३			
णा	-णधा	पा	-मपधणा	-णधा	पमा	-मज्ञा	-ज्ञरा	-सा	-ा	-रा					
कि	००	लां	००००	००	छला	००	००	०	०	०					

Antarā 1sṭ & 2ṇḍ

											मा	मा	पा	-ा	धा
											आ	मि	भा	०	ल
											भा	ल	बा	०	सा

ना	र्सा	-ा	-ा	-ा	र्सा	र्सा	-ा	-ा	-ा	-ा	र्सा	-ना	र्सा	री	री
बा	सि	०	०	०	जा	रे	०	०	०	०	से	०	क	भु	ना
भु	लि	०	०	०	जा	ब	०	०	०	०	म	०	ने	रे	बु

री	-र्सरी	-र्मज्ञी	-ा	र्रसा	-ा	नर्सर्रसा	-णा	-धणर्सणा	-धपमा-	मा	पा	र्सना	र्सा	र्सा	-ा
बे	००	००	०	ना०	०	मो०००	०	००००	००००	रे	त	बे०	के	न	०
झा	००	००	०	इब	०	००००	०	००००	००००	०	पृ	थि०	वी	ते	०

ना	र्सा	-नर्सर्रसा	-णा	-ा	धा	पा	-ा	-धपा	-मा	-ा	पा	धा	णा	र्सा	-ा
ता	रि	००००	०	०	त	रे	०	००	०	०	नि	य	त	पाइ	०
आ	रि	००००	०	०	जे	न	०	००	०	०	केउ	का	रे	भा	०

णा	-णधा	पा	-मपधणा	-णधा	पमा	-ज्ञा	-रा	सा	-ा	सरा					
ए	००	जन्	००००	००	त्रणा	००	००	०	०	००					
ल	००	वा०	००००	००	सेना	००	००	०	०	००					

(There are three types of tunes available for this song)

Rāga-khamāja   Tāla - Madhyamāna

एमन ये हबे प्रेम याबे ए कभु मने छिलना ।
ए चिते निश्चित छिल बिपरीते बिच्छेद हबेना ॥
भेवेछिलाम निरन्तर, हये रब एकान्तर,
यदि हय कथान्तर, मतान्तर ताय हबेना ॥
एमन हल अन्तर, पिरिति हल अन्तर,
आँखि झरे निरन्तर प्राणान्तर ताय हबेना ॥

Maheshchandra Mukherji

Born around 1838, Maheshchandra belonged to a well established and respected family of Maheshpur village in the district of Jessore. Mahesh's ancestor Haladhar Mukhopadhyay received the title of 'Chakavarti' and was the raj-priest of Jessore temple. Mahesh's step-brother Shridhar Śiromaṇi was a pundit of Sanskrit and used to run a school in Bowbazar area of Calcutta, where Mahesh often resided. Shridar's grandson Harinarayana Mukhopadhyay, the famous *dhrupadīyā* has mentioned that Maheshchandra and Madhusudan Bandopadhyay used to visit his *guru* Ramdas Goswami. However, Madhusudan and Mahesh were the two most famous disciples of Ramkumar Misra of Banaras *gharānā.*

Maheshchandra was an inborn artiste and used to sing on his own from his childhood. He got the opportunity to learn under Ramkumar Misra of *Prasaddu - Manohar gharānā,* and imbibed from his *guru,* the authentic *ṭappā* style of Shori Miya. He also received *tālīm* in *ṭappā* and *ṭap-khayāl* from Shiv Sahay and became successful in *ṭappā-gāyakī.*

Some sources believe that Maheshchandra travelled to Gwalior to learn music, but it is learnt from other sources that he learnt *ṭappā* and *ṭap-khayāl* under Ramkumar Misra and Shiv Sahay in Calcutta. Though he was an established singer of Hindusthani style of *ṭappā* he composed many Bengali *ṭappās* and rendered them in *mehfils.*

Maheshchandra was patronised by Jotindramohan Thakur initially and later, by Taracharan Guha of Masjidbari Street where he stayed from around 1881 and breathed his last there in *c.* 1905.

He had many admirers in the music circles of Calcutta and participated in the *mehfils* of Pathuriaghata Thakurbari, Guha-bari of Masjidbari Street, Pathuriaghata Banga Natyalaya, Belgachia Villa, and Kalikrishna Thakur's *sabhā.*

He was also an *ācārya* and trained Harishchandra Bandopadhyay, Rajani Chattopadhyay, Mati Chattopadhyay, Bholanath Das, Bihari Basu, Satishchandra Chattopadhyay, Birendrakumar Mukhopadhyay, and many others. Satishchandra became a *sabhā-gāyaka* of Saurindramohan Thakur.

For his expertise in *ṭappā* and *ṭap-khayāl* Maheshchandra became famous as 'Mahesh Ostād'.

Composer - Mahesh Chandra Mukherji

Rāga - Sindhu Tāla - Jat.

छाड़ अंचल चंचल श्याम ।
ओहे गुणधाम, दधि बेचिबारे याइ ।
पथ माझे मरि लाजे, एकि त्रिभंग कानाइ ?
तुमि हे निष्ठुर हरि,
क्षमा दाओ मिनति करि,
तब पदे धरि तबु दया नाइ ?

शिरेर पशरा टले, पाछे पड़े भूमितले,
गंजना दिबे सकले, ए बड़ भय पाइ ॥

Rāga Bihāga Tāla-Kavvālī

कि बुझिबे जीबे तब लीलार कौशल ?
ओहे नित्य निरमल,
महा मोह मद्यपाने जगत बिह्वल ॥
श्रुतिस्मृति मीमांसाय, चतुर्वेदे बिधाताय,
अन्त नाहि पाय सांख्य पातञ्जल ।
अंकुश आघात करि - मानुषे चालाय करी;
बिषधर करे धरि खेले मालदल ॥
दिबाकर निशाकर भूलोके आलोक कर,
बाहु भये थरथर कम्पित दुर्वल ।
देब दानब मानव आर जीव जन्तु सब,
भवे उद्भव पवने एक बिन्दु जल ।
तोमार लीलार लेश योग ना पेये,
उद्देश महेश पागल ॥

BIBLIOGRAPHY

1. Bandopadhyay, Amritalal. *Gītalaharī*. Calcutta, 1904. (Beng.).
2. Chakravarty, Ramakanta. "*Nidhubābu and his Tappā*; in *The Music of Bengal.* Ed. by Jayashri Banerji. Baroda, 1988.
3. Das Sharma, Amal. *Saṅgīta Maṇīṣā*. Part I. Calcutta, 1979. (Beng.).
4. Datta, Narendranath. & Basak Vaishnav Charan. *Saṅgīta-Kalpataru*. Calcutta, 1887. (Beng.).
5. Datta, Pranakrishna. *Kolkātār Itivṛtta*. Calcutta, 1981. (Beng.).
6. Ghosh, Abinash Chandra. *Prīti-gīti*. Calcutta, 1981. (Beng.).
7. Ghosh. L.N. *Gītavādyam*. Calcutta, 1975. (Beng.).
8. Goswami, Utpala. *Kolkatāye Saṅgīta Carcā*. Calcutta, 1991. (Beng.).
9. Gupta, Ishwar Chandra. *Kavi Jīvanī*. Ed. by Bhabatosh Datta. Calcutta, 1958. (Beng.).
10. Gupta, Ramnidhi. *Gītaratna*. 2ṇḍ ed. Ed. by Ramakanta Chakravarty. Calcutta, 1971. (Beng.).
11. Lahiri, Durgadasa. *Bāṅgālīr-gāna*. Calcutta, 1312. B.S. (Beng.).
12. Mitra, Rajyeshwar. *Bāṅglār Gītikār O Bāṅglā Gāner Nānādik*. Calcutta, 1973. (Beng.).
13. Mukherji, D.K. *Bāṅgālīr Rāga-Saṅgīta Carcā*. Calcutta, 1976. (Beng.).
14. ———. "*Bāṅglāy Hindusthānī Ṭappār Dhārā*", in *Bishwa Beena* (Bengali Journal). Calcutta, 1372. B.S. Feb-March issues.

15. Mukhopadhyay, Aghornath. (Ed.) *Gītaratnamālā*. Calcutta. (Beng.).
16. Mukhopadhyay, Upendranath. (Ed.) *Saṅgītakoṣa*. Calcutta, 1896.
17. Ray, Sukumar. "*Classical Musical Activities in Bengal during the 19th century and later*", in *The Music of Bengal*. Ed. by Baroda Jayashri Banerji. 1988.
18. Ray, Sukumar. *Music of Eastern India*. Calcutta, 1973.
19. Raychaudhury, Bimalakanta. *Bharatīya Sangitkoṣa*. 2nd ed. Calcutta, 1954. (Beng.).
20. Raychaudhury, Harendra Kishore. *Musicians of Bengal*. Calcutta.
21. *Surachanda* (Bengali Journal). Calcutta, 1986 May & September issues.

Ākhḍāi

Ākhḍāi is an old musical tradition that was practised in Bengal around the later part of 17th century A.D. The earliest centres of *Ākhḍāi* were in Shantipur in Nadia district. According to poet Ishwarchandra Gupta, this style originated in Shantipur and was innovated by the gentlemen class of people.

The word '*ākhaḍā*' means a club, where classical music used to be practised. Abul Fazal has mentioned a type of love song named *Ākhārā.* This was based on pure *rāgas* and *tālas* and was prevalent in North India during 15th - 16th century A.D.

Ākhḍāi of Bengal initially used to be love songs based on the themes of *Rādhā-Kṛṣṇalīlā.* Later, it was of two parts consisting of *Kheuḍ* and *Prabhātī. Kheuḍ* or *Kheḍu* songs were obscene love episodes composed of vulgar language, while *Prabhātī* songs, *prabhāt* meaning dawn, were based on themes when a lover is awakened in the dawn. Around the beginning of 18th century, *Akhḍai* reached Chinsura (Hoogly) where it shed off some of its pristine vulgarity. It was then given a new sophistication by introducing an introductory part of *padas* composed on *Bhavānī* —the goddess, with a proper musical structure and orchestral preludes. *Ākhḍāi* had reached Calcutta via Chinsura towards the end of 18th century. The *ākhḍāi* artistes of Chinsura and Calcutta, such as : Vaishnavadasa who was a professional *ustād,* and Rajmoy Sen who was a famous singer, added to this style a symphonic prelude with orchestral ensemble (साजवाद्य) which included instruments from *sitār* to earthen pots. The *ākhḍāi* group was called '*Bāiśerā*', '*Bāiś*' meaning twentytwo. Perhaps the group consisted of twentytwo orchestral ensemble and hence the name. Some more professional groups came up in Halsibagan, Nimtala, and other areas of Calcutta. Raja Nabakrishna Deb Bahadur of Shobhabazar was the chief patron of this style in Calcutta. His *durbār* musician Kaluichandra Sen was a relative of Nidhubabu, who was also associated with the court of Shobhabazar, but non-professionally. Kaluichandra introduced classical *rāgas* and *tālas* in *Ākhḍāi* with polished language, good theme and *śāstrīya* musical structure. But it was Nidhubabu who raised *ākhḍāi* to the high standard of *Baiṭhakī-gāna* which used to be of the highest standard of Bengali classical chamber music of the then Bengal. Nidhubabu further polished the style by reorienting and reorganising the whole repertoire. He discontinued with the vulgarity in the composition and instead, gave it an aesthetic touch along with classical norms. He modelled it on the *khayāl* style with light *dānā* of *ṭappās* but without any *tānas.* The following measures were introduced by him:

1. The introductory part of *Bhavānī-viṣayaka* consisted of passages on the glory of Goddess *Bhavānī* and were made aesthetically beautiful with good lyrical compositions.

2. The second part of *Kheuḍ* consisted of sophisticated love episodes.
3. The third part of *Prabhātī* was made artistic with excellent *gītikavitās* expressing pangs of separation (आक्षेप) at early hours of dawn.
4. He added *rāgālāpa* like *dhrupada* and *khayāl* styles.
5. In *ākhḍāi,* orchestration also occupied a very important place. In orchestral symphony, specialities were introduced in laya or tempo. These were of four types, viz. (a) *Piḍe-bandī* (overture), (b) *Dolan* (swing), (c) *Sab-dauḍ* (full swing) and (d) *Moḍ* (climax).
6. In *akhḍāi* there was no *sawāl-javāb* between rival groups as in *Kavi-gāna.* On the contrary, compositions were short, and *rāgālāpa* and *rāga* intricacies exhibited by the groups in vocal and instrumental music portion of *ākhḍāi* gave more credence to the performers.

Artistes of *ākhḍāi,*both vocalists and instrumentalists, had to have proper training in *śāstrīya-saṅgīta,* to achieve perfection. A group of *ākhḍāi* artistes usually consisted of more than thirty vocalists and instrumentalists. Rehearsals for a performance some times used to take even a full year. The instruments used by Nidhubabu as accompaniments, were: violin, *sitār, tānpurā, jaltaraṅga, vīṇā, mandirā, mocaṅg, saptasvarā,* flute, *ḍhol, karatāla,* etc. These instruments were used according to the *rāgas* used in the performance. Nidhubabu used *rāgas* such as: *Bhairavī, Khaṭ, Khamāja, Kāliṅgḍā, Bihāga, Lalita, Kāmoda, Paraja, Soraṭ, Lalita-bhairava* etc.

The structure or pattern of *ākhḍāi* used to be as follows:

1. The song composition used to consist of three stages, viz. *Bhavānīviṣayaka, Kheuḍ* and *Prabhātī.* The prelude and interlude consisted of orchestral pieces of high quality called: '*Sājer bājnā*' characterised by ingenious *tālas* and *rāgas* mixed in a unique manner.

2. Each of these song compositions had sequences or *tuks / dhātuvinyāsa* like *śāstrīya saṅgīta.* These were: (a) *mahaḍā* (महड़ा) or *sthāyī* or preparatory stanza, (b) *citen* (चितेन) or *melāpaka / mānjhā* or presentation, (c) *Prathama padaṅg* (प्रथम पड़ं) or first *antarā,* and (d) *dvitīya paḍaṅg* (द्वितीय पड़ं) or second antarā or the concluding para. Each *tuk* was preceded and followed by orchestral music in all the three song compositions. The vocalists rested after *mahaḍā* was sung, and the instrumentalists took over to play *piḍe-bandī.* Similarly, after *citen* was sung *dolan* was played. *Sab-dauḍ* was presented after *prathama-padaṅg* and *moḍ* was played by the orchestra after *dvitīya-padaṅg* was sung. The last piece used to be played in very fast tempo resembling somewhat like *jhālā* of *sitār.* Often, whole night used to be required for presenting the *ākhḍāi* fully. Nidhubabu's refined *ākhḍāi* was extremely complex and difficult.

His *ākhḍāi* was first presented in 1804 and became so popular that other earlier professional groups could not stand the competition, whether in musical score or in aesthetic presentation. Nidhubabu formed two amateur groups for its propagation in aristocratic circles, one in Bagbazar-Shobhabazar area and the other in Pathuriaghata. He used to direct the first group while the second was under the direction of Sridam Das and Gokul Das, sons of Kaluichandra Sen.

Some of the renowned performers of *ākhḍāi* were:

Govinda Mal (who became the principal singer of Brahmo Samaj), Rasikchand Goswami, Nyata Balai, Nabu Adhya, Raju Adhya, Radhanath Sarkar and Parvaticharan Basu. The orchestration used to be dominated by *dholak* players, viz - Rasikchandra Goswami and Nyata Balai, Nabu and Raju who were masters of the art. The most famous violinists were Radhanath Sarkar and Parvaticharan, and the leading *sitār* player was Madhabendra Ghosh.

Mohanchand Basu was the best disciple of Nidhubabu and was a talented singer of classical songs. He innovated the style of *Half-ākhḍāi*. Unfortunately, Nidhubabu's *ākhḍāi* lasted only for two decades. The reasons were: (a) its large number of performers, (b) long time required for rehearsals, which cost a lot of money and (c) the strict *rāga* disciplines which were too difficult for the ordinary listeners to appreciate.

An example of Ākhḍāi Song : Composer - Nidhubabu

Bhavānī Viṣayaka: (Passage on the glory of Goddess Bhavānī)

त्वमेका भुवनेश्वरी सदाशिवे शुभंकरी
निरानन्दे आनन्द दायिनी ।
निश्चित त्वं निराकारा अज्ञानबोधे साकारा
तत्वज्ञाने चैतन्यरूपिणी ।
प्रणते प्रसन्न भव, भीमतर भवार्णव
भये भीत भवामि भवानी ।
कृपावलोकन करि तरिबारे भवबारि
पद तरी देह गो तारिणी ।

Kheuḍ:

मनेर ये साध मनेते रहिल,
तोमाय साधना करि साध ना पुरिल ।
साधिये आपन काज, एखन बाड़िल लाज,
आमार गेल से लाज, बिषाद हइल ॥

Prabhātī:

यामिनी कामिनी बश हय कि कखन ?
नलिनी हासिबे केन, कुमुदी बिरसानन,
ए सुखे असुख तबे करे कि अरुण ॥
हले कि बिधुमुख हेरिये मलिन ?

BIBLIOGRAPHY

1. Chakravarti, Ramakanta. "*Nidhubābu and his Ṭappā*", in *The Music of Bengal*". Ed. by Jayashri Banerji. Baroda, 1988.
2. Goswami, Utpala. *Kolkātāye Saṅgīta Carcā.* Calcutta, 1991. (Beng.).
3. Mukherji, D.K. *Bāṅgālīr Rāga Saṅgīta Carcā.* Calcutta, 1976. (Beng.).

Half-ākhḍāi

Ākhḍāi style of music dominated the scene for about a century. Towards the end, of 18th century, this style was reoriented and polished by Kaluichandra Sen of Shobhabazar *durbār* and further systematised by Ramnidhi Gupta. This new reoriented style was immensely popular from 1804 to around 1825. Because of its strict *rāga* discipline and elaborate orchestration with a great number of artistes, *ākhḍāi* was becoming expensive to maintain. Soon *ākhḍāi* was replaced by another style called *Half-ākhḍāi* with lighter compositions both in language and music, innovated by Nidhubabu's main disciple Mohanchand Basu. Though Nidhubabu did not approve of this style at first, he later relented and gave his approval and blessings to his disciple.

Half-ākhḍāi was first performed in 1831, on 23-24th January at Ramsevak Mallick's place at Barabazar. This style was a combination of *ākhḍāi* and *Dā̃ḍā-kavigāna* and gained in popularity among the lower social order and also among the sycophants of the '*Bābus*' of Calcutta.

Half-ākhḍāi generally consisted of *tuks* more like *kavigāna*, such as:

1. *Bhavānī-viṣayaka padas*—having, *citen, parciten, fukā, second fukā* and *meltā.*
2. *Sakhī-saṃvāda* — having, *mahaḍā, khād, fukā, second fukā, second meltā*
3. *Kheuḍ* - having - *second citen, parciten, fukā,* second *fukā* and third *meltā.* The style being a cross between *ākhḍāi* and *kavigāna,* the *tuk-vinyāsa* or arrangements of stanzas were also a mixture of the two styles and did not adhere to the same pattern always.

Half-ākhḍāi used to have competition between two groups, same as '*Kavir-laḍāi*', where questions and answers called '*utor-cāpān*' took place. *Cāpān* was termed as '*dhartā*' and *utor* remained as *utor,* in *Half-ākhḍāi.* Simple *rāgas* and *tālas* were used and even orchestration was simplified with lesser number of instruments. The preferred *tālas* were: *Āḍā, Teoṭ, Khemṭā,* etc.

Half-ākhḍāi used to be on themes of love, but later, contemporary themes on social reforms, such as re-marriage of widows, etc. were introduced. The last authentic composer of *Half-ākhḍāi* was Manomohan Basu a disciple of Kavi Ishwarchandra Gupta.

This style was last staged in November 1918 at the palace of Shobhabazar, sponsored by Anath Krishna Deb and the songs were composed by Rasaraj Amritalal Basu.

Mohanchand Basu

Born in *c.* 1790, Mohanchand was the grandson of Dewan Ramcharan Basu of Bagbazar. His father was Jaynarayana Basu. Mohanchand was brought up amidst luxury and was reasonably educated. He was gifted with a melodious voice and creative ability. Young Mohanchand used to provide '*jil*' (vocal support) in the *ākhḍāi* group of Nidhubabu who soon became attracted to this artiste of great promise. He trained Mohanchand with particular care and became very fond of him. According to Ishwarchandra Gupta, Mohanchand could perform every composition of his *guru* with perfection whether it was a *ṭappā* or an *ākhḍāi.* He became known as '*khās-bhāṇḍār*' (meaning, the store house) of Nidhubabu's songs.

Mohanchand was attracted towards *Dā̃ḍā-kavigāna* and had realised that with the change in the cultural scene and taste of the then '*Bābu*' society of Calcutta, *ākhḍāi* would not last for long. Hence he innovated *Half-ākhḍāi* on the basis of

Dāḍā-Kavigāna and *ākhḍāi*. But even *Half-ākhḍāi* went down in popularity during the life time of Mohanchand who died in *c.* 1860.

Mohanchand stopped performing towards the end of his life, but used to compose the music. In November, 1854, *Half-ākhḍāi* was performed at the Jorasanko house of Nabakumar and Shyamacharan Mallick. Ishwarchandra Gupta himself composed the lyrics, which Mohanchand set to tune.

BIBLIOGRAPHY

1. Chakravarty, Ramakanta. "*Nidhubabu and his Ṭappā*", in *The Music of Bengal.* Ed. by JayashriBanerji. Baroda, 1988.
2. Goswami, Utpala. *Kokātāye Saṅgīta Carcā.* Calcutta. 1991. (Beng.).
3. Sen, Sukumar. *Bāṅglā Sāhityer Itihās.* Part I. Calcutta, 1948. (Beng.).
4. Vidya Sagar, Gangacharan Vedaratna. *Half-ākhḍāi Saṅgīta Saṅgrāmer Itihās.* Calcutta, 1326. B.S. (Beng.).

Pakṣī-daler Gāna

This style was innovated by Narayana Mishra of Calcutta, a resident of Nimatala. Actually, this style was introduced by some idle youths who had ample money and were addicted to gānja. Most of them were sycophants and tried to please their patrons by introducing some novelty in the existing styles of music. They were allotted certain names of *pakṣī, meaning* birds, according to their ability of consuming the quantity of *gānjā.* Originally this was an eccentric game of the adults, but later got associated with music. The members of a group used to dress up like birds (hence the name) and sang songs which were a combination of serenity and sorrowfulness but most often full of fun and jeer. These songs were based on *rāgas* and *tālas,* and were sung in a semi-classical fashion or *baiṭhakī* style.

Narayana Mishra started his *Pakṣīr-dal* around 1794. He belonged to a well to do Brahmin family and used to have his group of *pakṣīs* assembled at the famous Baṭtalā of Shobabazar where there was a structure called *Āṭcālā* (Shed). Ramnidhi Gupta also used to have his music sessions here every evening, after his return from Chapra. The members of this *dal* were great admirers of Nidhubabu who became associated with them and taught them music.

These *dals* or groups were patronised by the then rajas and zamindars. Maharaja Gopimohan Thakur and Raja Nabakrishna Deb Bahadur of Shobhabazar were such patrons. Under Nabakrishna Deb's patronisation the *Pakṣīr-dal* of Bagbazar was started by his baffoon Shivchandra Thakur (Mukhopadhyay). The most famous *pakṣī* of this group was Rupchand Das Mahapatra, an Oriya, born in Calcutta in 1815. Rupchand became the leader of the Bagbazar group and soon became famously known as Rupchand Paksi. He used to dress up like a bird and go around the town in a specially made carriage which was done up like a bird's cage.

Though an Oriya by birth, Rupchand was very much a Bengali every way and he also knew English. He spent most of his life in Bowbazar and learnt music in traditional way from Ramchandra Bandopadhyay, Chote Miya, Chuti Khan, Gammu Khan, Kanai Das, Ghulam Abbas, (*pakhāvaj*), Pannu Miya (*sitār*), and others. Thus he had a thorough grooming in *śāstrīya saṅgīta* and was an excellent composer. He also knew *kīrtana* and *Bāul* well. In his younger days he was interested in *Ghēṭu* and *pā̃cālī gāna* and composed some songs for *Ghēṭu-pūjā.* He also led a group of non-professional *pācālī* singers. He was blessed with a melodious voice and poetic ability. He composed lyrics which were full of fun and jeer and also songs which were devotional. He composed his songs on the foundation of *śāstrīya-saṅgīta* and sometimes on *kīrtana* and *bāul.* Many of his songs became so popular that some were used for the famous drama '*Kulīn-Kula-sarvasva*' of Ramnarayana Tarkaratna. He died towards the end of 19th century.

Dhiraj was another famous name in *Pakṣī-dal*, but this style was very short lived and by arround 1860 died a natural death.

An example of a *Pakṣī-dalergāna*: Composer - Rupchand Pakshi. Sparrow's song:

Rāga-Bihāga, Tāla - Addhā

दूर समीरे डरि
निज मुखे निजे बिहरि ॥
प्रेम नाहि मानि भय, साधे सतत उदय ।
प्राणे प्राणे प्राण विनिमय ।
लोक लाज कभुना करि ॥
पंच शर सदा स्मरि, नाहि प्रणये चातुरि ।
पोड़ा लोके नाहि बुझे, पारि कि हारि ॥

BIBLIOGRAPHY

1. a) Chakravarty, Ramakanta. "*Nidhubabu and his Ṭappā*",
b) Kundu, Pranay Kumar. "*Development of Stage and Theatre Music of Bengal*", in *The Music of Bengal.* Ed. by Jayashri Banerji. Baroda, 1988.
2. Goswami, Utpala. *Kolkātāye Saṅgīta Carcā.* Calcutta, 1991. (Beng.).

Dhrupada in Bengal

Dhrupada and *Dhāmār* styles of music came to Bengal during the time of the Mughals, probably as early as Akbar's reign. During Shahjahan's time his son Shah Suja who was the governor of Bengal, brought along with him two musicians around 1650 A.D. They were: Mishir Khan Dhadi, trained in *Senī-gharānā* and Guna Khan Kalavant. The latter stayed on in Bengal till his death but nothing is known about their disciples in Bengal. Although *dhrupada* and *dhāmār* became the most major styles in North India between 15th to 17th century, their proper impact was felt in Bengal only during the second quarter of 18th century between 1725-1750.

Raja Rajballabha's *durbār* of Bikrampur (Dhaka) was famous, where masters of *dhrupada*, such as Kalandar Khan, Visram Khan, Abubaras and some others were employed. Murshidabad, the then capital of Bengal, was also a centre of music, though all the names of *dhrupadīyas* are not known, except Bade Miya.

Krishnanagar was another pioneer centre where *dhrupada* and *dhāmār* used to be cultivated. Maharaj Krishnachandra's *durbār* boasted of Visram Khan, while during Raja Girishchandra's reign (1801-1841), Hasnu Khan and Dilawar Khan, the *dhrupada ustāds* of Delhi joined his court. These two *ustāds* were the sons of Kayem Khan of Delhi. Hasnu Khan served at the Delhi *durbār* before coming to Bengal. Hasnu and Dilawar trained three Chakravarti brothers—Krishnaprasad, Bishnuchandra and Dayaram, under the patronage of Raja Girishchandra. Krishna and Bishnu then came to Calcutta invited by Raja Rammohun Roy in 1830, to take up the appointment of '*saṅgītācārya*' of 'Brahmo Samaj'. Krishna died early but Bishnu (1804-1900) propagated the *dhrupada* style of his *gurus* in Calcutta. He was also the *acārya* of Jorasanko Thakurbari. His influence on *Brahma-saṅgīta*, *Rabīndra-saṅgīta* and *Svadeśī-saṅgīta* was very important.

Towards the end of 18th century *dhrupada* was learnt by Ramshankar Bhattacharya (1761-1853) of Bishnupur from a *saṅgīta-ācārya* of Mathura-Brindavan area. As mentioned earlier, this *dhrupada* maestro stayed at Bishnupur for some length of time and trained Ramshankar. Thus the foundation of *Bishnupur gharānā* of *dhrupada-dhāmār* was laid. The style of *dhrupada* practised in Bishnupur was simple in style, deep and serene in thought and presentation - more akin to *Bishnupadas* of *Havelī-saṅgīta*. Ramshankar trained a number of talented disciples who carried forth this *gharānā* style all over Bengal. (See *Bishnupur gharānā*). Many of these musicians left Bishnupur after their training and joined different *durbārs*. Some came to Calcutta and received further training under other maestros, who came from North India. Ramkeshab Bhattacharya was the first from Bishnupur to propagate their *gharānā* style of *dhrupada* at other places of Bengal including

Calcutta, around 1825. Others who carried forward this style were — Ramprasanna Banerji, Gopeshwar Banerji, Surendranath Banerji, Rameshchandra and Satyakinkar Banerji. The Thakur families of Pathuriaghata and Jorasanko had engaged maestros of this *gharāna*, viz. Kshetramohan Goswami, and Jadu Bhatta.

Chuchura or Chinsura was another centre where Man Khan of Gwalior came in 1806 and taught *dhrupada* and *khayal* to Ramchandra Sil, a wealthy resident of Chinsura. Ramchandra had connections with Murshidabad and was fortunate to have Baḍe Miya, the court singer of Murshidabad visiting his own place to teach him music. Ramchandra trained three disciples, viz. Gopalchandra Pathak, Paran Mukhopadhyay and Jaladhar Mukhopadhyay.

Another important branch of *dhrupada* was propagated by Ganganarayan Chattopadhyay who was born in 1808 in a village in Nadia and was the first Bengali to have gone to Delhi and Banaras to study *Khāṇḍār Bāṇī* style of *dhrupada*. He learnt under Mir Nasiram and some other *ustāds* and was responsible in creating an environment of proper stylish *dhrupada* in Calcutta. His best disciple was Jadu Bhatta who had his initial *tālīm* for a short while in Bishnupur *gharānā* style under Ramshankar, who was then in his nineties. Ganganarayan's other famous disciples were — Haraprasad Bandopadhyay, Shriram Shiormani, Shrichandra Gupta and Rajnarayan Mukhopadhyay. Jadu Bhatta inspired the Tagores (Thakurs) of Jorasanko, particularly Rabindranath and Jyotirindranath.

Haraprasad Bandopadhyay (b. 1830) was an outstanding singer and teacher. He was also trained by Maula Bakhs of Baroda. He trained his own son Kaliprasad and others such as: Krishnadhan Bhattacharya, and Uday Bhattacharya.

Another branch of *dhrupada* was that of Ramapati Bandopadhyay (early 19th century-1872) of Chandrakona. He learnt *dhrupada* from his father Gangabishnu, Muhammad Bakhs, Asmatulla, Vaidyanath Dube and Ramshankar Bhattacharya.

From mid 19th century onwards *dhrupada* was being nurtured at many centres of Bengal, the compositions being both in Hindi and Bengali. Other later stalwarts of *dhrupada* were Jadunath Ray, Gopalchandra Chakravarti, Laxminarayan Babaji, Ramdas Goswami, Aghor Chandra Chakravarti, Radhika Prasad Goswami and others.

Murad Ali Khan of *Tilmandi-gharānā*, who was a *durbār* musician of Wajid Ali Shah at Metiaburuj, trained Jadunath Ray, Ramdas Goswami, and AghorChandra Chakravarti.

Gopalchandra Chakravarti, more well known as Nulo Gopal (1832 - 1903) was a great *ācārya* and an excellent *dhrupadīyā* who trained Alauddin Khan, Lalchand Boral, Ramprasanna Banerji, and Satkadi Malakar. Nulo Gopal's knowledge of music was very deep. He had learnt *dhrupada* and *khayāl* from Gopalaprasad Misra of Kasi and at Gwalior under Haddu and Hassu Khan.

Dhrupada was also brought into Calcutta by Guru Prasad, Shivnarayana and Bishwanath Rao (of *Betia-gharānā*) who groomed - Radhika Prasad Goswami, Madan Mohan Burman, Binod Goswami, Gopeshwar Bandopadhyay, Jadumoni and Shashibhushan De. Radhika Prasad trained his own brother Nakud, nephew Jnanendra Prasad and others outside the family such as - Mahindranath Mukherji, Girija Shankar Chakravarti, Jogindranath Bandopadhyay, Bhutnath Bandopadhyay, Dhirendranath Bhattacharya, and many others. Mahindranath taught his son Lalitmohan.

Banaras gharānā of the Misras came through Gopala Prasad, Lachmi Prasad and Sarada Sahay. This *gharānā* recipients were Gopal Chandra Chakravarti, Ksetramohan Goswami, and Jadumoni.

Thus *dhrupada* became an established style in Bengal, and Calcutta became the biggest centre by the late 19th century.

Dhrupada bandiśes were composed both in Hindi and Bengali by most of the established musicians starting from Ramshankar Bhattacharya of Bishnupur to all most all the maestros of this *gharānā*, e.g. Bishnu Chakravarti, and Jadu Bhatta. Maharshi Debendranath and his sons composed *Brahma-saṅgīta* on the format of *Dhrupada*.

The seats of *dhrupada* in Calcutta were many, but the main ones were: Metiaburuj, Thakurbaris of Pathuriaghata and Jorasanko, Raj-baris of Shobhabazar and Kashipur and aristocratic houses of Ashutosh Deb, Lahas of Thanthania and Sinhas of Jorasanko.

Short biographies of a few eminent dhrupada singers:

Aghor Chandra Chakravarti

Born in *c.* 1851, in a village called Rajpur in 24 Parganas, Aghor Chandra was a famous musician endowed with a melodious voice. He used to visit Calcutta often on business and kept himself abreast with the musical activities of the city.

Aghor Chandra learnt under Ali Bakhs of *Senī gharānā* for several years. His other *gurus* were *dhrupadīyā* Murad Ali and Daulat Khan. He then learnt *Ṭappā* from Srijan Bai, and *bhajan* from Bholanath Das. He used to have a unique *gāyakī* style which kept his listeners spell bound.

Although Aghor Babu was averse to recording his voice, there are four songs which were recorded at Jotindramohan Thakur's residence without any rehearsal or musical accompaniment. These songs are: *Biphala Janama, Ānanda bana girijā, Najra dilbāhār,* and *Govinda mukhāravinda,* but from the poor quality of recording, it is difficult to ascertain the greatness of the musician.

Aghor Chandra was an *ācārya* and trained several aspirants who became successful vocalists, viz. Gopal Chandra Bandopadhyay, Amarnath Bhattacharya, Nantu Chakravarti, Nikunja Bihari Datta, Prankrishna Chattopadhyay, Bamacharan Bandopadhyay, Srikumar Bandopadhyay, and Shachindranath Mitra. From among his disciples, several became *ācāryas,* such as:

(a) Gopal Chandra who trained Jaikrishna Sanyal,
(b) Nikunja Bihari Datta, who groomed Swami Prajnanananda,
(c) Bamacaran Bandopadhyay, who taught Dilip Kumar Ray.

Aghor Chandra spent his last days in Kasi where he died in early 20th century.

Anantalal Bandopadhyay

Born in 1832, Anantalal was one of the most successful disciples of Ramshankar Bhattacharya, the founder of Bishnupur *gharāna.* He succeeded his *guru* as the *saṅgītācārya* of Bishnupur, apointed by Maharaja Gopal Singh. The Maharaja also conferred upon him the title of 'Saṅgīta Keśarī'. Anantalal is more well known as an *ācārya* although he was a renowned musician, musicologist and a composer. Unlike other successful disciples of Ramshankar, he stayed on in Bishnupur all his life, training aspirants who later became famous musicians adorning various courts of Bengal. They were: Radhika Prasad Goswami, Uday Chandra Goswami, Bipin Chandra Chakravarti, the sons of the Maharaja of Bishnupur and his own sons - Ramprasanna, Gopeshwar, Surendranath, and Ramkrishna. Ramprasanna, Gopeshwar and Surendranath attained national fame as musicians and musicologists. Anantalāl died at Bishnupur in 1896.

A song composition by Anantalal:

नाद विद्या सबसे सेरा, कोइ न पावे पार,
ऋद्धि सिद्धि दायिनी सकल विद्या किसार ।
चतुर्मुख पञ्चानन नारद मुनि भकत प्रधान,
तान मान धरत होय सब मतवार ।
संगीत सुखदायी जो जन करत चरचा ये
ताको छुटत दुख अँधियार ।
कहत द्विज अनन्त कोइ न पाये इह अन्त,
अनन्त सुख निदान, नाद सिन्धु अपरम्पार ॥

Rāga Darbāri Kānaḍā, Cautāla

+		०		२		०		३		४	
सा	ण्सा	द्	ण्	-सा	सा	रा	रा	सा	रण्	-सा	सा
ना	००	द	वि	०	द्या	स	ब	से	से०	०	रा
						स	स				
सा	ण्	सा	रा	-सा	रा	ज्ञा	-ज्ञा	-मा	रा	-ा	सा
स	क	ल	वि	०	द्या	की	०	०	सा	०	र
{मा	पा	पा	णदा	-णा	णा	र्सा	-ा	र्सा	-ा	र्सा	र्सा
{च	तु	र	मु०	०	ख	प	०	ञ्चा	०	न	न
						र्म	र्म				
र्सा	णा	र्रा	र्रा	र्सा	र्रा	र्ज्ञा	र्ज्ञा	र्ज्ञर्मा	र्रा	-ा	र्सा}
ना	र	द	मु	नि	भ	क	त	प्र०	धा	०	न}
र्सणा	-र्रा	र्सा	णदा	-णा	पा	पा	-मा	-पा	-णदा	णा	पा
ता०	०	न	मा०	०	न	ध	०	०	००	र	त
		म									
मा	-पा	ज्ञा	मा	-णा	पा	मपा	मज्ञा	-मा	रा	-ा	सा
हो	०	य	स	०	ब	म०	त०	०	वा	०	र
मज्ञा	-मरा	मा	-ा	-पा	पा	पा	मा	-पा	णदा	-णा	पा
सं०	००	गी	०	०	त	सु	ख	०	दा०	०	इ

+		०		२		०		३		४	
		ण						म			
मा	पा	दा	णा	पा	पा	मा	पदा	ज्ञा	-मा	रा	·सा
जो	ज	न	क	र	त	च	र०	चा	०	ये	०
	ण्										
सा	दा्	-रा	रा	-रा	रा	रा	-ा	-सा	णा्	-सा	सा
ता	को	०	छु	०	ट	त	०	०	दु	०	ख
	म			ण		द					
सा	-ज्ञा	-मरा	पमा	-दा	-णपा	-मा	-पज्ञा	मरा	-ा	-रा	सा ‖
अँ	०	००	धि०	०	००	०	००	या०	०	०	र ‖
{मा	पा	णदा	णा	-र्सा	र्सा	र्सा	-ा	-ा	र्सा	-ा	र्सा
{क	ह	त०	द्वि	०	ज	अ	०	०	न	०	न्त
						र्म	र्म	र्म			
र्सा	णा	र्रा	र्रा	-र्सा	र्रा	र्ज्ञा	र्ज्ञा	-र्रा	र्रा	-ा	र्सा}
को	इ	न	पा	०	य	इ	ह	०	अ	०	न्त}
						ण					
णा	र्सा	र्रा	णा	र्सा	र्सा	दा	-णदा	णा	पा	-मा	पा
अ	न	न्त	सु	ख	नि	दा	००	न	ना	०	द
णदा	-णदा	-णा	पा	मा	पा	-णा	मज्ञा	-मा	रा	-रा	सा ‖‖
सि०	००	०	न्धु	अ	प	०	र०	०	म्पा	०	र ‖‖

Anantalal Bandyopadhyay.

Ganganarayan Chattopadhyay

Born in c. 1808, Ganganarayan was one of the pioneers who popularised *dhrupada* style in Bengal. He was the first to travel to upper India to different centres and learn the proper styles of *dhrupada* specialising in *khāndārbānī* style. He became a well known *ācārya* and imparted his expertise in Bengal by training a number of worthy disciples already mentioned earlier, who in turn kept up this *gharānā* style in Bengal through their disciples.

Ganganarayan learnt all the four *bāṇīs* of *dhrupada* but *Khāṇḍārbāṇī* was his forte. The names of all his *gurus* in the different *bāṇīs* are not known. The only name that in known, is of Mir Nasiram, a Hindu who used Mīr as a title only. He was both a *dhrupadīya* and a *bīnkar*.

Ganganarayan was born in a village called Bilvapushkarini in Nadia district and his father was Nakud Chandra, a pundit in Sanskrit. Ganganarayan was more interested in music than Sanskrit and came away to Calcutta to learn the art. It is said that because of his powerful and melodious voice, he was encouraged by Prasaddu and Manohar Misra to learn *dhrupada* from great masters. He left Calcutta at the age of 17 or 18 and travelled to North India in search of a proper guru and proper *tālīm*. He came back to Calcutta around 1836 and took up music as his profession.

It is said that he used to practise voice culture with the sound of two conch shells.

Ganganarayan became famous as a *dhrupadiya* in Calcutta and near around places . He was patronised by Ashutosh Deb, Harakumar Thakur of Pathuriaghata, Syamacharan Mallick, Raja Sukhamoy Ray and others. He used to participate regularly in the *Saṅgīta durbārs* of the above mentioned patrons and also at Maharaja Mahatapchand of Burdwan, Maharaj Birchandra Manikya of Tripura, Nawab Faridun Jha of Murshidabad, Zamindars of Gobardanga, etc. The Nawab gave him the title of "Dhrupada Bāhādur". *Bhairava-rāga* was his favourite.

He was the first in his family to become a professional musician and his two sons-Amarnath and Panchanan followed his path, trained under their father. Panchanan also learnt *ṭappā* and *khayāl.* Tulsidasa, the third son became the disciple of Kesablal Misra and learnt vocal as well as violin and wrote a few books, viz. *Ektigat, Saral Svaralipi Śikṣā* in four parts. His son Haripada was also a *dhrupadīya, ṭappā - singer* and violinist.

Ganganarayan had close ties with the two brothers—Prasaddu and Manohar Misra and their families.

He lived a very successful life as a musician and died in 1874 at his residence at No. 59, Balaram De Street, at Calcutta.

Gopalchandra Chakravarti:

Born in c. 1832, handsome Gopalchandra was more well known as Nulo Gopal, a name that stuck to him due to his slightly short arms. He was one of the greatest *dhrupadiyās* and *ācāryas* of music Bengal ever had.

As mentioned earlier, Gopalchandra learnt *dhrupada* from Gopala Prasad Misra of Banaras and was an exponent of this style in Calcutta. He became the *durbār* musician of Maharaja Jotindramohan Thakur who sponsored him to learn *dhrupada* from Gopala Prasad at Banaras and *khayāl* from Haddu Khan at Gwalior. In Banaras he earned great fame as a *dhrupadīyā* and took part in all prestigious *mehfils* including Dighapatiya palace of Kasi, where top-ranking musicians from all over India participated.

Gopalchandra was an extraordinarily gifted and creative musician with a melodious voice. He had mastered *dhrupada, khayāl,* and *ṭappā* and presented these styles in his own distinctive way, with different *alaṅkāras.* He also presented *tarānās* and *sargams.*

Among his many pupils, the following were famous: Radhika Prasad Goswami, Lalchand Boral, Ramprasanna Bandopadhyay, Satkadi Malakar, Alauddin Khan, Ramtaran Sanyal, Sashi Karmakar, Brajendra Narayan Deb, (an aristocrat of Entally), Binodkrishna Mitra of Shobhabazar, Barendranath Thakur, Rajmohan Bandopadhyay and many others. Harinarayan Mukhopadhyay of Kasi learnt *Rāga-mālā* of *Kalyāṇa* and *Darbāri-kānaḍā* from him.

Gopalchandra lost his voice towards the end of his life due to some mishap. He was a strict teacher and from Alauddin Khan's description in '*Āmār-kathā*', it is known that he insisted on thorough grooming in *rāgas* by practising *sargam* or *Svara -sādhanā, palṭās* and *tālas* all at the same time, by playing the *tānpurā* and keeping *tāla* with the foot.

Nothing however is known about his personal life. He died in *c.* 1903.

Jadu Bhatta:

Jadunath Bhattacharya, more wellknown as Jadu Bhaṭṭa, was born in 1840 in Bhattapara of Bishnupur. His father Madhusudan Bhattacharya was also a famous musician who was an expert in *Sitar, Surbahar* and *pakhavaj.* He was a *durbār* musician and teacher of Raja Nilmani Sinha of Panchakot. It is probable that Madhusudan had received his *tālīm* from Ramshankar Bhattacharya of Bishnupur. Jadu was a '*Śrutidhar*' (one, who picks up by listening only once), a poet, a composer and a creative musician having a melodious voice.

It happened once in the *durbār* of Tripura - raj Birchandra Manikya, that a visiting *ustād* from Northern India sang a *bandiś* in *Rāga Naṭanārāyaṇa* and challenged Jadu to sing one. Jadu did not know the *rāga* but he listened to the *ustād* intently and next day presented a *bandiś* of *Naṭanarayaṇa in Cautāla,* which he composed himself.

Jadunath was very keen on music, particularly vocal styles. Initially, his father trained him in *sitār* and *pakhāvaj* but observing Jadu's keen interest in vocal music, he sent his son to Ramshankar at Bishnupur. Ramshankar at that time was almost ninety years old and Jadu was a boy of ten or eleven and had received guidance for no more than two to three years., Ramshankar died in 1853. Jadu Bhatta left his village in 1855 after finishing his elementary education in a Sanskrit *ṭol.* He went to Calcutta in search of a *guru* and had to go through a lot of hardship till he found Ganganarayan Chattopadhyay who was charmed with his voice and singing style, and took him home to teach him in the art of *Khāṇḍār-bānī dhrupada.* Jadu received precious *tālīm* from his *guru* for sixteen years, from 1855 to 1871. Jadu Bhatta was fortunate to have his initial training in *Biṣṇupur - dhrupada* style which was simple yet serious in depicting *rāgas,* and *khāṇḍārbānī* style which was rich in *gamaka* and *reraka.*

Jadu Bhatta then went to various centres of North India to get more *tālīm.* He participated at many centres and assimilated more knowledge while listening to many *ustāds.* Thus he developed a style of his own and earned a lot of fame. In 1873 he was engaged by Debendranath Thakur as the family teacher and in 1874 as the singer of Adi Brahmo Samaj and teacher of the music school attached to it. Rabindranath and Jyotirindranath benefitted much in *rāga* music due to the presence of Jadu Bhatta at their house, and Rabindranath acknowledges his immense qualities as an "*ustad*". Jadu Bhatta became famous as a *dhrupadīya* while at Jorasanko Thakurbari. In 1877 he joined the *durbār* of Birchandra Manikya, the maharaja of Tripura. Here he came in contact with *Senī* Kasim Ali, the famous *Rabāb* player and enhanced his knowledge of *rāgas* by listening to Kasim Ali's recitals at the *durbār.*

Jadu Bhatta performed at various prestigious music centres of Bengal, viz. Thakurbari of Pathuriaghata, House of Keshab chandra Mitra—the famous *pakhāvajī* at Bhavanipur, Metiaburuj *durbār* of Nawab Wajid Ali Shah, House of Raja Digamber Mitra of Jhamapukur, Burdwan *durbār, durbār* of Panchakot, *durbār* of Pal - Chaudhuris of Ranaghat and many more. He used to be accompanied by Keshabchandra Mitra and Jagatchand Goswami, who were renowned *pakhāvaj* players of his time.

Jadu Bhatta married around the age of twenty-six. While at Tripura *durbār,* he took ill and came back to Calcutta but did not stay for long. He went back to Bishnupur where he died in 1883 at the age of 43 only.

Jadu Bhatta was a creative musician with a great sense of aesthetics, and a composer of very high order. His disciples were Radhika Prasad Goswami, Bankim Chandra Chattopadhyay, Nagendranath Bhattacharya of Ranaghat, Sasibhushan Karmakar and members of Jorasanko Thakur family. The Tripura - rāj honoured him with the title of 'Tānrāj' and Raja of Panchakot with "*Raṅganātha*". Jadu used these titles as his *bhaṇitā* in many of his compositions. A few examples:

Composer - Jadu Bhatta

Rāga - Lacchāśākha   Tāla - Jhāptāla

जयति जय दुर्गे जग-तारिणि ज्वालामुखि,

जगन-मयि योगेशि जग-पालिनि नाशिनि,

जग-मन-मोहिनि योगेन्द्र गतिदायिनि ।
जीव-शिव-कारिणि ज्योति स्वरूपिणि,
तिजग-अघ नाशिनि जयन्ति यदु-नन्दिनि ॥

+	२	०	३	+	२	०	३
गा गा	गा रा सा	गा -ा	रा सा न्ा	सा -ा	गा गा गा	मा -ा	पा पा -ा
ज य	ति ज य	दु र्	गे ज ग	ता ०	रि णि ज्वा	ला ०	मु खि ०
मा गा	सा गा मा	पा पा	पा पा पा	पा -ा	ना ना -ना	र्सा -र्सा	धा पा -ा
ज ग	न म यि	यो गे	शि ज ग	पा ०	लि नि ०	ना ०	शि नि ०
मा गा	मा रा -ा	गा -पा	धा ना ना	र्सा -ना	धा पा णा	धा -पा	धा मा -ा
ज ग	म न ०	मो ०	हि नि यो	गे न्	द्र ग ति	दा ०	यि नि ०
पा -ा	पा नधा ना	र्सा -ा	र्सा र्सा -ा	र्सा -धा	ना -र्सा री	र्सा: र्स:	धा पा -ा
जी ०	व शि० व	का ०	रि णि ०	ज्यो ०	ति ० स्व	रू ०	पि णि ०
मा गा	गा मा रा	गा -पा	धा ना ना	र्सा -ना	धा पा णा	धा -पा	धा मा -ा
त्रि ज	ग अ घ	ना ०	शि नि ज	य न्	ति य दु	न न्	दि नि ०

[*Jadu Bhaṭṭa O Tā̃r Gāna* - Itu Banerji]

Composer: Jadu Bhatta (*Saṅgīta-candrikā*. Gopeshvar Banerji)
Rāga - Bhairava   Tāla - Jhāptāla (madhyalaya)

शशधर तिलक भाल, गंगा जटा व्याल,
करधर त्रिशूल रुद्राक्ष राजे ।
भस्म अंग छाये, गरे रुण्डनकी माल,
भैरव त्रिनयन हर योगी साजे ।
बृषभ वाहन आसन वसन मृगछाल,
कालकूट कण्ठ पर तिमिर लाजे ।
करत हरिनाम नित, श्रवण सोहे कुण्डल,
ध्यावत ''तानराज'', नितही हिय माझे ॥

+	२	०	३	+	२	०	३
सा सा	दा दा ना	दा दा	पा -ा मा	गा -ऋ	गा -मा पा	मा -गा	ऋ -ा सा
श श	ध र ति	ल क	भा ० ल	ग ङ	गा ० ज	टा ०	व्या ० ल

+	२	०	३	+	२	०	३
सा सा	सा (न)द्रा -ा	द्रा सा	-न्रा -ऋा सा	सा ऋा	गा -मा पा	मा -गा	ऋा -ा सा ‖
क र	ध र ०	त्रि शू	० ० ल	रु द्	रा ० क्ष	रा ०	० ० जे ‖
‖{मा मा	(न)दा -ा दा	र्सा -ा	र्सा र्सा र्सा	र्सा र्ऋा	र्गा र्मा र्पा	र्मा -र्गा	-र्ऋा -ा र्सा}‖
‖{भस् म	अ ङ ग	छा ०	ये ग रे	रु ण्	ड न की	मा ०	० ० ल}‖
र्सा -ा	ना दा पा	ना दा	पा मा गा	गमा -ना	-दा -ा पा	मा -गा	-ऋा -ा सा ‖
भै ०	र व त्रि	न य	न ह र	यो० ०	० ० गी	सा ०	० ० जे ‖
‖सा सा	सा दा -ा	दा दा	ना दा पा	दा मा	पा गा मा	गा -ा	-ऋा -ा सा
‖बृ ष	भ वा ०	ह न	आ स म	व स	न मृ ग	छा ०	० ० ल
सा -ा	सा सा -ा	(न्)द्रा -ा	न्रा सा सा	सा ऋा	गा मा पा	मा -गा	-ऋा -ा सा
का ०	ल कू ०	ट ०	क ण् ठ	प र	ति मि र	ला ०	० ० जे
{मा मा	दा दा दा	र्सा -ा	र्सा र्सा र्सा	र्सा र्ऋा	र्गा र्मा र्पा	र्मा र्गा	र्ऋा र्सा -ा}‖
{क र	त ह रि	ना ०	म नि त	श्र व	ण सो हे	कु ण्	ड ल ०}‖
र्सा -ा	ना दा पा	-ना दा	पा -मा गा	मा ना	ना दा पा	मा -गा	-ऋा -ा सा ‖‖
ध्या ०	व त "ता	० न	रा ० ज"	नि त	ही हि य	मा ०	० ० झे ‖‖

Laxminarayan Babaji

Born between 1830-35, Laxminarayan was an extremely accomplished musician of the 19th century Bengal. He was a master of *dhrupada, khayāl, ṭappā, ṭhumrī, pakhavaj, tablā, bīn, sitār* and *esrāj* and learnt all these different vocal styles and instruments under different *gurus,* for which he had to travel to other parts of India extensively. Though he was such an expert in many branches of music, he was most well known as a *dhrupadīyā* and *bīnkār.*

Nothing much is known about his private life not even his surname, as he was a true Vaiṣṇava. Babaji suffix was attached to his name because of his saintly life style. He also dressed like a *sanyāsī.* Like most Bengali musicians he was non - professional. Many patrons like Raja Jotindramohan, Saurindramohan Thakur, Purnachandra Singh of Paikpara supported him.

Laxminarayan learnt under famous *gurus,* such as:

1. Ramkumar Misra of *Prasaddu-Manohar gharānā—Dhrupada* and *Khayāl,*
2. Hyder Khan of *Haddu-Hassu Gharānā of Gwalior—Khayāl* and *Dhrupada,*
3. Thadidasa—*a sanyāsī pakhāvajī and dhrupadiya—Pakhāvaj* and *Dhrupadc,*

4. Babu Khan of *Lucknow gharānā—Tablā,*
5. Ramzan Khan—*Tappā,*
6. Srijan Bai—*Thumrī*

Laxminarayan's main *guru* was Thadidasa who was all the time on the move from one pilgrimage to another. He roamed around with his *guru* to learn music. Most of his training in music was achieved outside of Bengal. He learnt *sitār, bīn* and *esrāj* in Kasi, but the names of the *gurus* are not known.

In most of the prestigious *mehfils* of Calcutta he used to sing *dhrupada* and play *bīn,* and used to be accompanied by such *pakhāvajīs* as Keshabchandra Mitra, Basanta Hazra, Murari mohan Gupta, Nagendranath Mukhopadhyay and others. He himself once accomapnied *dhrupadīyā* Murad Ali on *pakhāvaj.* Keshab Mitrā arranged *mehfils* many times at his residence, specially to accompany Laxminarayan.

The most wellknown disciples of Laxminarayan were: Rajendranath Ghosh, Nagendranath Bhattacharya, Jogendranath Ray, Lalmohan Basu, Brajajivan Mukhopadhyay. Satkadi Malakar and Sharat Chandra Mitra also learnt under him for some time.

This great musician died in the early part of 20th century at Calcutta.

Mahindranath Mukhopadhyay

Born in 1873, Mahindranath was gifted with a highly melodious voice and a natural talent to pick up any kind of music that he heard. When he was young he used to be boisterous and would not concentrate in studies. Radhikaprasad Goswami at that time was Mahindranath's neighbour, who had just come from Bishnupur and was learning vocal music under Guruprasad and Shivnarayan Misra of *Betiā gharānā.* It was a chance incident by which Mahindranath became the disciple of Radhikaprasad. One day, Radhikaprasad was singing a Bengali song which influenced and attracted Mahindra very much, and he started learning from him. He was then about thirteen or fourteen years old. Since then he became Radhika's most devoted and one of the most successful disciples. Soon he became proficient in *dhrupada* style and earned fame in the music circle of Calcutta. He never left his *guru* for another and neither did he go out of Calcutta to learn elsewhere.

Mahindranath came from a well to do family. His uncle Lalmadhav Mukherji was a physician who helped Dr. R. G. Kar to establish the Carmaichael Medical College of Calcutta.

Mahindranath played an important role to establish his *guru* in Calcutta as a top ranking musician. He himself also participated in most of the prestigious music conferences and particularly in the *mehfils* held at Pathuriaghata's "Harakuṭīr" and at the residence of Pradyumna Mullick. He used to arrange, organise and also participate in the *mehfils* sponsored by Manmatha Chattopadhyay. "*Murārī Sanmelana*" and "*Śaṅkar utsava*", the two annual music festivals used to be graced by all top ranking musicians and Mahindranath was one of them. Mahindranath mostly used to be accompanied by Nagendra Mukhopadhyay and Durlav Chandra Bhattacharya on *pakhāvaj*.

Mahindranath's voice was his asset, besides being thorough in the delineation of a *rāga*. He was an *ācārya* who groomed many disciples at the school established by Radhikaprasad at Brajadulal Street and also at his own residence. The most famous among them was his own son Lalit Chandra who became a great *dhrupadīya* like him and took part in many music festivals. He became a star artiste of All India Radio. Like his father he also died early at the age of forty six in 1944. Mahindranath's other disciples were Bhutnath Bandopadhyay, Jogindranath Bandopadhyay, Dhirendranath Bhattacharya, Kartik Chandra Sen, Nanilal Chattopadhyay and Satyendranath Datta. All his disciples were taken care of by his *guru* Radhika prasad when Mahindranath died in 1918 at an early age of forty five only.

Mahindranath turned down the offers of the gramophone companies as he was not in favour of singing a *dhrupada* in three minutes which used to be the time limit those days. His favourite *rāgas* were *Darbārī-Kānāḍā, Basant, Yaman-kalyāṇa, Kauśikī-Kānaḍa, Bageśrī* and *Kedār.*

Radhikaprasad Goswami

Born in 1863 in Bishnupur, Radhikaprasad was an outstanding musician during the last part of 19th century and begining of 20ṭḥ century. His father Jagat Chand Goswami was a renowned *pakhāvajī* who accompanied Jadu Bhatta during the latter's stay in Bishnupur.

Radhika's initial grooming in music was in *Bishnupur gharānā* tutored by Anantalal Bandopadhyay, the *ācārya* of Bishnupur. He stayed there learning music till he was around fifteen years of age. Then he spent about ten years doing *riāz* and compiling compositions of various masters. He was also groomed by Jadu Bhatta for a year. He then moved to Calcutta and with the help of Kshetramohan Gosvami learnt *dhrupada* under Shivnarayan and Guruprasad Misra of *Betia gharana.* He was also fortunate to receive training under Jadu Bhatta in Calcutta for sometime and lessons in *Khayal* from Gopal Chandra Chakravarty. But Radhika's real *gnrus* were the Misra brothers of *Betia gharānā,* who moulded his style.

Radhikaprasad became famous for his *dhrupada* and *khayāl* styles. He was employed as an *ācārya* at Jorasanko Thakurbari and Brahmo Samaj. His influence over the members of Thakurbari particularly on Jyotirindranath and Rabindranath was very deep. Rabindranath was an ardent admirer of Jadu Bhatta and Radhikaprasad in whom he found absolute music and not mere *rāgas* and *tālas*. Radhikababu inspired Rabindranath in composing Bengali songs on the basis of Hindi *Śāstrīya* compositions and from 1305 to 1311 B.S. many were composed. In 1304 B.S. Radhikaprasad was engaged as the *ācārya* of Bharat Sangita Samaj established by Jyotirindranath, for six years, and of Adi Brahmo Samaj till 1316-17 B.S. In 1312 B.S. Radhikababu joined the *durbār* and music school of Maharaja Manindrachandra Nandi of Kasim Bazar and stayed there for eighteen years. He had also become the *durbār guru* of Zamindar Bhupendranath Ghosh at Pathuriaghata.

Radhikaprasad was much revered in the then music circle of Bengal and India as well. He participated in all prestigious musical soirees as a veteran *dhrupada* and *khayāl* singer.

Radhikaprasad also edited *Sangīt Vijñān Praveśikā*, a journal of *Śāstrīya Saṅgīta*, and wrote valuable articles for the journal.

Radhikaprasad's father and eldest brother Krittichand, were renowned *mṛdaṅga* players while his youngest brother Nakuleshvar or Nakud specialised in *sitār* and taught in Shantiniketan as a vocalist and instrumentalist.

Radhikababu died in 1331 B.S. in the month of *Māgh* (1924).

His famous disciples were: Mahindranath Mukhopadhyay, Kader Bakhs, (Murshidabad), Girija Shankar Chakravarti, Jnanendraprasad Gosvami, Jogindranath Ray (Nator), Mahimchandra Mukhopadhyay. Manmathanath Ghosh, Gurudas Chattopadhyay—grandson of Raja Saurindramohan, Bhutnath Bandopadhyay, Dhirendranath Bhattacharya, Lalit Chandra Mukhopadhyay, and Kishorimohan Bhaskar.

Composer - Radhikaprasad Goswami—a song example :

Rāga - Chāyanaṭa Tāla - Jhāptāla.

नव धन वरण जाके झलक अति सुन्दर,
निरख मन भाव लगी ऐसे नही जगत पर ।
मूरली जब कर धून वस होय सकल जन,
तेज प्रगट कियो गोवरधन धारण कर ।
ऐसे निये त्रिभुवन पूजे तुआ चरण ।
धन धन तुँ राज नन्दकुमार वर ।
राधिका प्रसाद कैसे चरण में शरण पावे,
नित नाम भावे हो नररूप ईश्वर ॥

Sthāyī

+	२	०	३	+	२	०	३
सीं सीं	सीं सीं ना	सीं धा	पा -रा रा	रा गा	मा धा पा	मगा -मा	रा सा -ा
न व	ध न व	र ण	जा ० के	झ ल	क अ ति	सु० ०	न्द र ०
मा गा	मा ा सा	(न)सा -ध्ा	पा रा रा	रा -गरा	गा मा पा	मा गा	रा सा -ा
नि र	ख म न	भा ०	व ल गी	ऐ ००	से न ही	ज ग	प र ०

Antarā

पा पा	सीं सीं सीं	सीं सीं	सींना -सीं सीं	ना धा	ना -सीं रीं	सीं ना	सीं धा पा
मु र	ली ज ब	क र	धू० ० न	व स	हो ० य	स क	ल ज न
पा -रीं	रीं सीं सीं	सीं -ना	सीं धा -पा	रा गा	मा धा पा	मा गा	मा रा सा
ते ०	ज प्र ग	ट ०	कि यो ०	गो व	र ध न	धा र	ण क र

Sañcārī

मा -ा	गा मा रा	गा मा	धा पा -ा	पा -ा	ना -धा ना	सीं -ना	सीं धा पा
ऐ ०	से नि ये	त्रि भु	व न ०	पू ०	जे ० तु	आ ०	च र ण
धा धा	पा पा पा	धा -पपा	रा -ा रा	रा -गा	गा -मधा पा	मा गा	मा रा सा
ध न	ध न तुँ	रा ००	० ० ज	न ०	न्द ०० कु	मा ०	र व र

Ābhoga

पा पा	सीं -ा सीं	सीं सीं	सीं -ा सीं	ना धा	ना सीं सीं	सीं ना	(न)सीं -धा पा
रा धि	का ० प्र	सा द	कै ० से	च र	ण मैं श	र ण	पा ० वे
पा रीं	सीं -ा ना	सीं -धा	धा -पा रा	रा गा	गा -मधा पा	मा -गा	-मा रा सा
नि त	ना ० म	भा ०	वे ० हो	न र	रू ०० प	ई ०	० श्व र

BIBLIOGRAPHY

1. Banerji, Itu. *Jadu Bhatta - Tā̃r gāna.* Calcutta, 1990. (Beng.).
2. Banerji, Rameshchandra. *Dvitīya Dillī-Biṣṇupur.* Calcutta, 1941. (Beng.).
3. Das Sharma, Amal. *Saṅgīta Maṇīṣā* - part I. Calcutta, 1979. (Beng.).
4. Ghosh, Shantideb. *Rabīndra Saṅgīta Bicitrā.* Calcutta, 1972. (Beng.).
5. Goswami, Utpala. *Kolkātāye Saṅgīta Carcā.* Calcutta, 1991. (Beng.).
6. Mukherji, Dilipkumar. *Bāṅgālīr Rāga Saṅgīta Carcā.* Calcutta, 1976. (Beng.).
7. Mukherji, Dilipkumar. *Bhārater Saṅgīta Guṇī* – Part I. Calcutta, 1384. B.S. (Beng.).
8. Mukherji, Dilipkumar. *Bhāratīya Saṅgīte Gharānār Itihās.* Calcutta, 1977. (Beng.).
9. Prajnanananda, Swami. *Bhāratīya Saṅgīter Itihās.* Calcutta, 1961. (Beng.).
10. Raychaudhuri, Bimalakanta. *Bhāratīya Saṅgītkoṣa.* 1ṣṭ ed. Calcutta, 1372. B.S. (Beng.).

Khayāl in Bengal

Khayāl style developed in Bengal during the latter part of 18th century at Burdwan, Krishnanagar, Bishnupur and then in Calcutta and other places. It was not as popular as *dhrupada* or *ṭappā* at the beginning, but by the mid 19th century it gained ground among the connoisseurs of music.

Khayāl was first cultivated by Raghunath Ray (1750-1836) of Chupi village. He became the *dewān* of Maharaja Tejashchandra of Burdwan. The Maharaja had employed *kalāvants* of *Kavvāl-bacchā gharānā* from Lucknow and Delhi in his *durbār*. Raghunath had the opportunity to learn the style of *khayāl* under them. Although the *khayāl bandiśes* consist of two *tuks* only, Raghunath composed many *khayāls* of four *tuks* in Bengali on the themes of Śyāmā and Kṛṣṇa. This type of *khayāls* consisting of four *tuks* were called '*Olār*'.

During the first half of 19th century, some Bengali musicians learnt *khayāl* methodically under *gurus* who came to Bengal from North India. At Krishnanagar, *Kavvāl* Miya Miran of Girishchandra's court taught *Khayāl* to Krishna and Bishnu Chakravarti while they were at the court of the raja. Later, the brothers went to Calcutta as the '*saṅgītācāryas*' of Brahmo Samaj and Jorasanko Thakurbari and propagated the art of *khayāl* singing in Calcutta, although they were primarily *dhrupada* singers.

Little before this, Kanailal and Madhavlal Chakravartis of Bishnupur became well known for *khayāl*. Their *guru* was Muhammad of Bundelkhand. They had also learnt *khayāl* under Miya Miran at Krishnanagar *durbār* and from Bade Muhammad.

During mid 19th century Kartikeya Chandra Ray (1820-1825), the *dewān* of Nadia-Krishnanagar became well known as a *khayāl* singer. His *gurus* were Madhavchandra Mukhopadhyay and Maheshchandra Khajanchi, both Bengali maestros.

After mid 19th century, Bengal was exposed to *ustāds* of many *gharānās* who came to Bengal for sponsorship, and trained many Bengali aspirants in this art form. These *ustāds* were from *Senī-khāndān*, Banaras, Gwalior, Rampur, Agra, Gaya, Kirana, etc and influenced the music culture in a major way. They were:

(a) Taj Khan of *Senī-gharānā* of Metiaburuj *durbār*, who trained Bamacharan Bandopadhyay and Gopalchandra Bandopadhyay.

(b) Ali Bakhs of Gwalior settled down in Barabazar, after the fall of Metiaburuj and groomed Bamacharan Bandopadhyay in *khayāl gāyakī*.

(c) Ahmad Khan of Lucknow, also of Metiaburuj *durbār* trained many disciples - principal among them were Beni Madhav Adhikari, better known as '*Beni Ostād*' and Bamacharan Bandopadhyay. Beni Ostad also groomed Amritalal Datta and

Swami Vivekananda and was the music director-composer of the dramas staged by Girishchandra Ghosh.

(d) Chote Miya of Metiaburuj *durbār* was a *khayāl* singer who stayed in Calcutta.

(e) The Misra musicians of Banaras had great expertise over *khayāl, ṭappā, ṭhumrī, tablā* and stringed instruments. Ramkumar Misra of *Prasaddu-Manohar* line of Banaras, trained a number of talented disciples in Bengal in different spheres of music. Prominent among them in *khayāl* were Laxminarayan Babaji, Surendranath Majumdar and Kaliprasanna Ghosh.

Lakshmiprasad of this *gharānā* groomed many, in different styles of vocal and instrumental music, but in *khayāl*, the following were famous: Anathnath Basu, Jogesh Chandra Ghosh, Madanmohan Mishra, Shyamacharan Basu, Kshemendramohan Thakur, Maniklal Haldar, and Satish Chandra Arnav.

Shivsevak and Pashupatisevak Misra taught *khayāl* and vocal styles to Sudhindranath Majumdar, Abhayapada Chattopadhyay, Lalitmohan Das, Anil Krishna Ray, Sudhamoy Basu, Satish Chandra De, and many others.

(f) Shivnarayana and Guruprasad of *Betia-gharānā* gave *tālīm* in *dhrupada, dhāmār*, and *khayāl* but more in *dhrupada* and *dhamār*. It was Guruprasad who gave *tālīm* in *khayāl* more than Shivnarayana. Radhika Prasad Goswami, Binod Goswāmi, Shashibhushan De, Surendranath Majumdar, Gopeshwar Banerji, Ashutosh Chattopadhyay and many other veterans were groomed by them.

Radhika Prasad became an *ācārya* and trained many, among whom were: Girija Shankar Chakravarti, Mahindranath Mukhopadhyay, Bhutnath Bandopadhyay, Jogindranath Bandyopadhyay, Jnanendra Prasad Goswami and others.

(g) Wazir Khan *Senī* from *Rampur-gharānā* came to stay in Calcutta for seven years. He had trained many in vocal and instrumental music. His most prominent disciple in *khayāl* was Pramathanath Bandopadhyay. Wazir Khan's son Sagir Khan and particularly grandson Dabir Khan who made Calcutta his home, imparted *tālīm* in *khayāl* to—Jnanprakash Ghosh, Shailendranath Bandopadhyay, Dolly De, Binapani Mukhopadhyay, and Kalidas Sanyal.

Mehdi Husein and Khadim Husein of this *gharānā* were particularly famous for their *khayāl-gāyakī* and groomed many musicians, such as: Satyendranath Ghosh, Birendrakishore Raychaudhuri, Amulyacharan Raychaudhuri, Chandranath Basu, Jnanprakash Ghosh, Anil Bagchi, Dr. Bimal Roy, Dolly De, Bijan Basu, Kalidas Sanyal, Nidanbandhu Banerji, Ratneshwar Mukherji, and others.

(h) *Khayāl-gāyakī* of *Agra-gharānā* came to Bengal through Faiyaz Khan, and his disciple and brother-in-law Atta Husein Khan. Faiyaz gave *tālīm* to Rathindranath Chattopadhyay, and Dipali Nag. Atta Husein trained Arun Bhattacharya, Kalpana Mukherji, Purnima Sen, and others.

Bashir Khan of this g*harānā* groomed Dipali Nag and Aparna Chakravarti,

(i) Hanumandasji of *Gaya-gharānā* groomed Dhirendra Chandra Mitra in *khayāl.*

(j) Bengal did not receive *tālīm* directly from the stalwarts of *Kiranagharānā.* However, Niyaz Ahmed Faiyaz taught Dilshad Dasgupta.

(k) Amir Khan of Indore, the famous *khayāl* singer trained a few Bengalis, such as: Usharanjan Mukherji, Kamal Banerji, Kamal Bose, Krishna Dasgupta, Pradyumna Mukherji, Purabi Mukherji, Dilip Chakravarti and Kankana Banerji.

(l) Bade Ghulam Ali of *Patiala* - (Alia - Fattu) *gharānā* trained Prasun Banerji, Mira Banerji, Sailendra Banerji, Prabhati Mukherji, and Sandhya Mukherji. Ghulam Ali's uncle Kale Khan had trained Tarapada Ghosh.

(m) Families of Krishnadas Karmakar and Jitram Ray of Dhaka specialised in vocal and instrumental music, *khayāl* being one of them.

(n) In Calcutta, Gopal Chandra Chakravarti, Laxminarayana Babaji, Girija Shankar Chakravarti were famous for their *khayāl-gāyakī* and as *ācāryas.* They brought in the Gwalior style of Haddu and Hassu Khan; Muzaffar Khan of Delhi; Inayat Husein Khan of *Sahaswān-gharānā* ; and also of *Khalifā* Badal Khan. (see Music Culture)

(o) The other two khayālīyās who need mention, are: Bhismadeb Chattopadhyay and Chinmoy Lahiri who were great *ācāryas* also.

BIBLIOGRAPHY

1. Goswami, Utpala. *Kolkātāye Saṅgita Carcā.* Calcutta, 1991. (Beng.).
2. Mukherji, D.K. *Bāṅgālīr Rāga Saṅgita Carcā.* Calcutta, 1976. (Beng.).
3. Ray, Sukumar. "*Classical musical activities in Bengal during the 19th Century and later*", in *The Music of Bengal.* Ed. by Jayashri Banerji. Baroda,1988.
4. Raychaudhury, Bimalakanta. *Bhāratiya Saṅgītkoṣa.* 1st ed. Calcutta, 1372. B.S. (Beng.).

Ṭhumrī in Bengal

When *dhrupada* and *khayāl* were established firmly, *ṭhumrī* did not create a niche for itself among the orthodox music connoisseurs of Bengal. Although some texts of *ṭhumrī* are available in *Saṅgīta-rāga-kalpadruma* (1842), its form and nature are not known. At the outset, this style was looked down upon, as *ṭhumrī* was cultivated and presented by the *Bāijīs* or nautch girls, although they were extremely talented and trained musicians. The serious minded pundits of music considered *ṭhumri* as semi-*śāstrīya* and the styles of *dhrupada* and *khayāl* predominated the scene.

As mentioned by Karam Imam in his *Madnul Mausiqi*, Dhaman and Lajjat Bakhs were exponents of *ṭhumrī* long before Nawab Wajid Ali Shah. Their style made its way to the eastern provinces of India upto Bengal. Around mid 19th century, *ṭhumrī* started becoming popular with the arrival of Wajid Ali Shah in Calcutta with his troupe of musicians. He himself was a highly qualified musician and singer - composer of *ṭhumrīs*. His court used to be adorned with *Bāijīs* who performed *ṭhumrīs* in a style called '*Bol-bhāo-ki-ṭhumrī*' or '*Kahan ṭhumrī*', in which a performer had to act the subtle emotional nuances expressed through the different *bol-banāo* of this style. The Nawab himself often presented such *ṭhumrīs* dressed up as a woman singer-dancer.

Later, during the first few decades of the 20th century *ṭhumrī* became so popular that it was a status symbol for the *rajas* and aristocrats to invite and engage musicians and *bāijīs* from Western India at one's own *durbār*. Through the *bāijīs*, *Ghanāksharī* and *Khaḍī* varieties of *ṭhumrī* were propagated.

Ṭhumrī culture gained ground in earnest when Bhaiya Ganpatrao and the Misra musicians of Banaras came to Bengal. Others who contributed towards the popularity and propagation of this style were: Jagadip Misra, Badal Khan, Mehdi Husein Khan, and various *baijis* from Banaras and Lucknow who made Calcutta their home, such as: Gauharjan, Malkajan and others.

Gaurishankar Misra who belonged to the line of Buddhu Misra was a musician of great knowledge though primarily a *sāraṅgī* player. He was an *ācārya* and trained many in the art of vocal music, particularly in *ṭhumrī*. His stay in Calcutta for fifty years made a mark in the music society. The personalities he trained were: Kiranamayi, Surama, K.C. De, Shvetangini, Krishnabhamini, Indubala, and Anathnath Basu.

But the contribution of Bhaiya Ganpatrao and his disciples is perhaps the greatest to popularise this art form. Bhaiya Saheb came to Calcutta through the good offices of Shyamlal Kshetri who was not only his disciple but a '*rais*' — a wealthy citizen of Calcutta and a connoisseur of music. Bhaiya Saheb had trained a host of great talents in '*lacāo*' and '*Kahan*' *ṭhumrī* which became extremely popular in Bengal. His disciple Maujuddin Khan became an instant hit in Calcutta's music circles, and spent twenty years of his best professional life there. His brother Rahimuddin also came to Calcutta which was then the most lucrative centre for artistes. Maujuddin took part in almost all *mehfils* and was also under the patronage of Seth Dulichand who was a patron of music. The best benificiary of his style of *ṭhumrī* was Girijashankar Chakravarti. Maujuddin had trained Amulyadhan Pal, Anathnath Basu, and Jamiruddin Khan of Patna besides some famous *bāijīs* of Calcutta.

Shyamlal Kshetri trained Amiyanath Sanyal. Girijashankar became one of the most outstanding musicians of Bengal in vocal styles. He excelled in *Khayāl* and *ṭhumrī* and had received *tālīm* from Bhaiya Saheb, Badal Khan and had benifitted a great deal by listening to Maujuddin Khan. Girijashankar trained many aspirants, viz. Anil Hom, Arati Das, Iva Guha, Uma Mitra, A. Kanan, Gita Das, Jaykrishna Sanyal, Jnanprakash Ghosh, Tarapada Chakravarti, Debiprasad Bhattacharya, Jamini Ganguli, Sukhendu Goswami, Sudhirlal Chakravarti, Sunil Kumar Bose, and others. Jamini Ganguli trained Prasun Banerji, Binodkishore Raychaudhuri, Rani Ray and Sandhya Mukherji. Sukhendu Goswami's successful disciples were Chabi Banerji, Tandra Moitra, Hiranmayee Pandit, and Hena Burman.

Another line of exponents of *ṭhumrī* from Patna flourished through Jamiruddin Khan, who trained Nagendranath Datta, Angurbala, Indubala, Kamal Dasgupta, Krishnachandra De, Satyendranath Ghosh, Subal Dasgupta, Bhishmadeb Chattopadhyay, Kaji Nazrul Islam and Harimati.

Mehdi Husein Khan and Khadim Husein Khan, the two brothers from Rampur trained many successful disciples in *Ghanākṣari*, *Pachāvā* and *Lacāo* varieties. The famous among them are: Anil Bagchi, Amulyacharan Raychaudhuri, Kalidas Sanyal, Girijashankar Chakravarti, Chandranath Basu, Jnanprakash Ghosh, Dolly De, Nidan Bandhu Banerji, Dr. Bimal Roy, Satyendranath Ghosh, and Sunil Kumar Basu. Most of them became *ācāryas,* who trained others in the above mentioned styles of *ṭhumrī.*

Gradually *ṭhumrī* curved its own niche in the domain of *śāstrīya saṅgīta* and it became the norm to present one, after an elaborate presentation of a *khayāl*, to bring a performance to a grand finale.

Like *dhrupada* and *khayāl*, *ṭhumrī* also had influenced Bengali songs, particularly *rāga-pradhān gāna* and some of the *kāvya-saṅgītas.*

BIBLIOGRAPHY

1. Goswami, Utpala. *Kolkātāye Saṅgīta Carcā.* Calcutta, 1991. (Beng.).
2. Mukherji, D.K. *Bhāraler Saṅgīta Guṇī.* Part II. Calcutta, 1386. B.S. (Beng.).

3. Ray, Sukumar. *Bāṅgla Saṅgīter Rūp.* Calcutta, 1969. (Beng.).
4. ———. "*Classical musical activities in Bengal during the 19th century and later*", in *The Music of Bengal.* Ed. by Jayashri Banerji. 1988.
5. Raychaudhury, Bimalakanta. *Bhāratīya, Saṅgītkoṣa.* 1st ed. Calcutta, 1372. B.S. (Beng.).
6. Roy, Bimal. "*Thumri*", in *Surachanda* (Bengali Journal) Puja special issue. Calcutta, 1985 October. (Beng.).

Girija Shankar Chakravarti

Born in Bahrampur, in Murshidabad district, Girija Shankar popularly known as Girijababu was one of the most outstanding musicians of Bengal. He showed keen interest in music from his early boyhood and was encouraged by his father Bhavani Shankar to learn this art. He mastered almost all the styles of vocal music.

He learnt from Radhika Prasad Goswami from 1904-1912. Around 1912, he was introduced to Shyamlal Kshetri and stayed with him to learn *ṭhumrī*. Here, he met *ustād* Maujuddin Khan and Bhaiya Ganpat Rao and picked up the finer aspects of *ṭhumrī*. Later, he came to be regarded as the master of *ṭhumrī* in India.

The Maharaja of Kasimbazar took him to Delhi *durbār* where he became the disciple of Muzaffar Khan (*Khayāliyā*). He then went to Rampur and learnt some special techniques of *dhrupada* and *horī* from the aged master Muhammad Ali Khan, a descendant of Tansen. He also learnt varieties of *dhrupada* and *dhāmār* from Chamman Sahib (Rampur) and styles and techniques of *Khayāl* from Inayat Husein Khan (Sahaswan).

After returning to Calcutta he worked as a stock exchange broker for sometime, but soon became a disciple of Khalifā Badal Khan (Sāraṅgi nawāz) and learnt further techniques of *Khayāl gāyakī*.

He became a renowned exponent of *dhrupada, khayāl* and *ṭhumrī*. His *dhrupada* and *dhamār* styles belonged to Rampur and Betia *gharānā*, *ṭhumrī* to Banaras and Lucknow *gharānā*, while *khayāl* was a style of his own built up on various *gharānā* styles, laying special stress on the *bandiś, rāga* elaboration and their aesthetic aspects. He assimilated, combined and blended all the outstanding qualities of Agra, Rampur, Gwalior, Sahaswan and Betia *gharānās* in his *gāyakī*.

In 1930, he started an institution named "Saṅgita Kalā Bhavan". He also headed the classical section of "Saṅgīta Bhārati" in "Gītabitān" from 1943-48. As an able and imaginative *ācārya* he groomed such renowned disciples as-Jnanendra prasad Goswami, Jogendra Banerji, Tarapada Chakravarti, Pannalal Ghosh, Sudhirlal Chakravarti, Jnanprakash Ghosh, Jamini Ganguli, Chinmoy Lahiri, A.T. Kanan, Sunil Bose, Jaykrishna Sanyal, Debiprasad Bhattacharya, Binod Kishore Raychaudhuri, Rathindranath Chattopadhyay, Sukhendu Goswami, Smt. Naina devi, Anil Hom, Arati Das, Iva Guha, Shiela Sen, Gita Das (Mitra), Uma Mitra (De), Smt. Dipali Nag and others. He promoted and popularised Indian classical music, particularly *khayāl* among educated middle class of Bengal.

He had participated in music conferences all over India, gaining rare appreciation from the then stalwarts of music and the common audience alike.

Girija Shankar was also an eminent painter, studying at Govt. School of Arts, Calcutta and also acted in dramas.

The great musician died on 25th April 1948.

BIBLIOGRAPHY

1. Das Sharma, Amal. *Saṅgita Maṇiṣā*. Calcutta, 1979. (Beng.).
2. Raychaudhury, Bimalakanta. *Bhāratīya Saṅgītkoṣa*. 1st ed. Calcutta, 1372. B.S. (Beng.).

Brahma Saṅgīta & Raja Rammohun Roy

Raja Rammohun Roy's contribution of *Brahma-saṅgīta* in the field of music, is very important. Though very modern and progressive in his ideas and outlook, he was a great believer in his ancient heritage and tradition and that is why he believed in *Upaniṣads* and *śāstrīya-saṅgīta.*

When Rammohun came to stay in Calcutta after leaving his job at Rangpur, from 1815 to 1830, he became a disciple of Kali Mirza. He did not learn music to be a musician but to acquire indepth knowledge about *rāga-saṅgīta.* During his early life when he visited different places, he had observed that different religious sects such as *Daśanāma-sanyāsī, Dādupantha, Kabīr* and *Nānaka sampradāyas* meditated through deep devotional music, and so did the Christians and Muslims. Rammohun had not only studied the Hindu scriptures but also other religions such as Buddhism, Islam and Christianity. The solemn hymns of the church had inspired him and these hymns sung in chorus as community singing appealed to him. He got his cue from Yājñavalkya's Ṛṣi-vākya that - *'Ṛkgāthāpāṇikā dakṣavihitā Brahmagītikāḥ. Geyametat tadabhyāsāt paraṃBrahmādhigacchati'* (ऋक्गाथापाणिका दक्षविहिता ब्रह्मगीतिकाः । गेयमेतत् तदभ्यासात् परंब्रह्माधिगच्छति) i.e. one may ạchieve the Ultimate through *Śāstrīya saṅgīta* .

Rammohun was a connoisseur and patron of music. Apart from Kali Mirza, he had engaged Rahim Khan at his house to listen to his music. Nikki Bāījī, a famous songstress also took part in one of the soirees arranged by him in his garden party in 1823. Besides these, he used to have regular music sessions every week from 1815 to 1819 in a *sabhā* (get together), called 'Ātmīya-sabhā' where vocalist Govinda Mal used to present *Brahma-saṅgīta* and Shivprasad Misra chanted Vedic hymns. *Brahma-saṅgīta* started from Ātmīya Sabhā. Rammohun's first composition was '*Ke bhulālo hāy*' and was sung in 1816. After the abolition of this *sabhā* in 1819 and before Brahmo Samaj was started in 1828, Rammohun composed a number of *Brahma-saṅgītas* which he published along with compositions of others as '*Brahma-Saṅgīta*', in 1828.

Brahma-saṅgītas were songs composed on the themes of Brahma — the Ultimate, *adhyātmatattva*—meaning spiritualism or Vedānta philosophy, and *bhakti* or devotion to the Lord. The musical scores for these songs were based on *śāstrīya rāgas* and *tālas.*

Rammohun had engaged musicians of high calibre to perform in Brahmo Samāj, such as : *dhrupadīyā* Krishnaprasad and Bishnuchandra Chakravarti as vocalists and Ghulam Abbas as the accompanist on *pakhāvaj.* All three of them were well known in their own spheres of expertise. Rammohun had set a high standard of classical music in Brahmo Samaj and this was kept up by Maharsi

Debendranath Thakur who took over. He also engaged top ranking musicians such as Bishnu Chakravarti, Jadu Bhatta, Radhikaprasad Goswami and others. Many devotees were attracted by this music and even well known musicians used to visit Brahmo Samaj because of its pure musical atmosphere. Initially, when Brahmo Samaj had started, both *śāstrīya-saṅgīta* and *Brahma-saṅgīta* were presented at the prayer meetings.

Rammohun composed his last song '*Ki svadeśe ki bideśe jakhan jethāy thāki*' in England in 1832, a year before his death. This song was set in *rāga Bāgeśrī* and *Āḍāthekā tāla.* It is not known how many songs he composed but it is estimated that about forty songs were composed by him. It is difficult to make out which were composed by him as he did not use any pen-name. Rammohun used to encourage his friends to compose *Brahma-saṅgīta.* The well known composers were: Krishnamohan Majumdar, Becharam Chattopadhyay, Bishnuram Chattopadhyay, Trailokyanath Sanayal, Nimaicharan Mitra, Bhairavchandra Datta, Kalinath Ray, Gaurmohan Sarkar, Nilratan Haldar and others. Even Ramnidhi Gupta (Nidhubabu) composed one, although he was a *ṭappā* exponent. When Maharṣi Debendranath took over, he himself and his whole family became involved in composing *Brahma-saṅgīta.* They were: Girindranath, Dwijendranath, Ganendranath, Satyendranath, Jyotirindranath, and Rabindranath.

It is commonly believed that Rammohun's *Brahma-saṅgīta* was *dhrupada* based and that he was the originator of *dhrupadas* in Bengali. But when his book '*Brahma-saṅgīta*' is analysed, it becomes evident that these compositions though were set on pure *rāgas* and *tālas,* were not *dhrupadas.* The *tālas* that are prescribed for *dhrupadas* are: *Cautāla, Sur-fāktā, Teorā,* and *Jhaptāla,* while Rammohun used tālas like *Āḍāṭhekā, Ektāla, Kavvālī, Teoṭ, Ṭhumrī, Jhaptāla* and *Dhāmār* for his songs. The songs composed by Rammohun were perhaps in *khayāl-aṅg,* judging from the *tālas, chandas* and *tuk-bibhāgas.* Out of the thirty two songs in *Brahma-Saṅgīta,* twentyfour were in *Āḍāṭhekā,* two in *Jhaptāla,* two in *Ektāla,* one in *Ṭhumrī* one in *Kavvālī,* one in *Teoṭ* and one in *Dhāmār.* Since his songs were sung with the accompaniment of *pakhāvaj,* it is probable that these songs were taken as *dhrupadas.* Besides, his *guru* Kali Mirza was a *ṭappā* exponent and hence he was groomed not in *dhrupada* style.

Dhrupada culture came into *Brahma-saṅgīta* after the Chakravarti brothers — Krishnaprasad and Bishnuchandra were engaged as *saṅgītācāryas* of Brahmo Samaj. Whatever the case may be, *Brahma-saṅgīta* innovated by Rammohun was deeply devotional, and set in pure *rāgas* and *tālas.* These songs were sung with the accompaniment of *tānpurā, behālā* (violin), *mandirā* and *pakhāvaj* which gave this style serinity and depth like those of *dhrupada.*

Brahma-saṅgīta may be divided into three phases:

(a) during Rammohun's time—compositions based on *Jñāna mārga/dharma*

(b) during Debendranath's time—compositions based on *yoga dharma/mārga.*

(c) during Keshab Sen's time—compositions based on *bhakti dharma/mārga.*

The song compositions during the first phase were of *advaita-vāda,* i.e. to know the unknown self. During the second phase, these were based on the subject of *Paramātmā,* the Ultimate. The last phase was based on *Īśvara* and the devotee, *bhakti* being the predominant factor.

During the life time of Rammohun it was Govinda Mal who was the singer of Ātmīya-sabhā, but later when he formed Brahmo Samaj in 1828, the two Chakravarti brothers were employed by him in 1830 and Ghulam Abbas was the percussionist. But, by then it was time for him to go to England in 1831. The two brothers Krishnaprasad and Bishnuchandra, as has been mentioned earlier, were talented musicians groomed in Krishnanagar under musicians of Western India and were adept in *dhrupada* and *khayāl.* Krishna died early but Bishnu stayed on for more than fifty years as the *saṅgītācārya* of Brahmo Samaj and Jorasanko Thakurbari. He was gifted with a melodious voice and sang with tonal and accentual clarity. The *padas* were given full attention by him. Ādi Brahmo Samaj published six volumes of *Brahma-saṅgīta,* of which most of the songs were tuned by him.

Ghulam Abbas, the *pakhāvaj* accompanist in Brahmo Samaj was a famous percussionist and he established a school of music in Calcutta in 1838.

The style of *Brahma-saṅgīta* changed during Debendranath's time more towards *dhrupadāṅga,* because of his own knowledge in *śāstrīya* music and association with musicians such as Bishnu Chakravarti, musicians from *Bishnupur-gharānā,* viz. Jadu Bhatta and Radhikaprasad Goswami, Shyamsundar Misra, Rajchandra Ray, Ramapati Bandopadhyay, and Maula Bakhs. His sons were also involved in *Brahma-saṅgīta* both in the composition of the lyric and music. Songs composed during this period were mostly in *Cautāla, Jhaptāla, Sūltāla, (Surfaktā), Rūpak, Dhāmār,* etc. and in *dhrupada* style, based on Hindusthani *saṅgīta. Pakhāvaj* became the main percussion accompaniment while *tānpurā,* accordian and later, harmonium came in for vocal support. The number of song compositions also increased tremendously and varieties of *rāgas* used were many. These songs were valued much and became popular due to their classical nature. Some of these were presented in the *mehfils* of classical music side by side with *dhrupada* or *khayāl.*

During the third phase, Keshabchandra used to be surrounded by youths aspiring for a spiritual uplift. These aspirants composed *Brahma-saṅgīta* in a variety of styles. Trailokyanath Sanyal composed more than two thousand songs while Rabindranath composed many songs in a wealth of *rāgas, tālas* and deep philosophical thought. After Rabindranath, some songs were composed by Atulprasad,

Rajanikanta and others. Also, there are compositions where the composers have remained unknown.

Being secular in its outlook, Brāhma dharma embraced all faiths and also the songs composed by saints belonging to different sects. These saints are: Kabir, Nanaka, Dadu, Mirabai, and others. Their compositions have been placed together with other *Brahma saṅgītas* in the compilation book of *Brahma Saṅgita.*

Rammohun Roy

Son of Ramkanta Roy, Rammohun was born in 1774 in Radhanagar village of Burdwan. He had his initial schooling at home and then went to Patna and Varanasi where he learnt Persian, Arabic and Sanskrit. From Varanasi he travelled to Tibet to study Bauddha religion in detail from the Lamas. He returned to Calcutta at the age of twenty-two and began learning English thoroughly. After the death of his father in 1803, he took up the job of a clerk under the collector of Rangpur and was soon promoted to the rank of 'd*ewan*'. Gradually, he bought some landed property and became one of the affluent citizens of Bengal. But his pursuit for knowledge was never ending. He learnt Latin, Greek, Hebrew and higher subjects of mathematics.

At the age of sixteen he wrote a booklet against idol worship and later when he settled down in Calcutta permanently in 1814-15, he wrote many articles on this subject in different languages. He wrote a book named '*The Precepts of Jesus, the Guide to Peace and Happiness*' in English. He also wrote in Bengali and Sanskrit - '*Jīśukhrishter Upadeśāvalī*', '*Śānti o Sukher Pathapradarśaka*'. At the beginning, he faced lot of criticism from everyone including his mother, but he kept fighting against multi-marriage, '*satī* ' (Suttee)and other social nuisances.

In 1815 he established Ātmaya Sabha and in 1828 Brahmo Samaj, giving stress on *Brahmaṇyavāda* — the knowledge of the Supreme Being or the Absolute and no idol worship. He started the custom of prayer at the *sabhā* and *samāj* through *Brahma-saṅgīta* which were excellent devotional compositions both lyrically and musically, based on *Upaniṣads* and *śāstrīya-saṅgīta.*

Out of the many religious and social reforms and progressive welfare activities, Rammohun's memorable achievements were;

(a) establishing Brahmo Samaj,
(b) introducing *Brahma-saṅgīta,*
(c) abolishing *'Suttee',* and other social evils,
(d) fighting for women's education by establishing schools, etc.for them.

Rammohun was sent to England in 1831 through a 'farmān' received from the Mughal Emperor who honoured him with the title of 'Rājā' in 1830, to plead for the financial problems of the Emperor. Rammohun made an immediate impact on the British by his personality and intellect. He then went to France in 1832 and Louis Philip, the French monarch, received him with great honour. He learnt French and went back to England. He fulfilled his mission for which he was sent, but took ill soon after and died in Bristol on 27th September 1833.

BIBLIOGRAPHY

1. Bandopadhyay, Amritalal. *Gītalaharī*. Calcutta, 1904. (Beng.).
2. Biswas, Dilipkumar. "*Brahma Saṅgīta*", in *Deshbinodan* (Bengali Journal). Calcutta, 1391. B.S. (Beng.).
3. Goswami, Utpala. *Kolkātāye Saṅgīta Carcā*. Calcutta, 1991. (Beng.).
4. Ghosh, Loknath, *Kolkātār Bābu-vṛttānta*. Tr. by Shuddhodhan Sen. Calcutta, 1983. (Beng.).
5. Mitra, Rajyeshwar. *Bāṅglār Gītikār O Bāṅglā-gāner Nānādik*. 2nd ed. Calcutta, 1973. (Beng.).
6. Mukherji. D.K. *Bāṅgālīr Rāga Saṅgīta Carcā*. Calcutta, 1976. (Beng.).
7. *Rāmmohun Gītāvalī*. Printed by Kalidas Chakravarty, Adi Brahmo Samaj. Calcutta, 1888. (Beng.).

Rammohun's first composition:
Rāga-Sindhu-bhairavī Tāla-Ṭhumrī.

के भुलालो हाय, कल्पनारे सत्य करि जान;
ए कि दाय ।
आपनि गड़ह याके,
ये तोमार बशे ताँके
केमने ईश्वर डाके कर अभिप्राय ?
कखनो भूषण देओ कखनो आहार;
क्षणेके स्थापह, क्षणे के करह संहार ।
प्रभु बलि मान यारे,
सम्मुखे नाचाओ तारे,
हेन भुल ए संसारे देखेछ कोथाओ ?

Rammohun's last composition:
Rāga-Bāgeśrī Tāla-Āḍāṭhekā.

कि स्वदेशे कि बिदेशे यथाय तथाय थाकि ।
तोमार रचना मध्ये तोमाके देखिया डाकि ॥
देशभेदे काल भेदे रचना असीमा,
प्रतिक्षणे साक्ष्य देय तोमार महिमा,
तोमार प्रभावे देखि ना थाकि एकाकी ॥

Brahma Saṅgīta - Composer Rammohun Roy.
Rāga - Bāgeśrī Tāla - Ektāla.

स्मर परमेंश्वरे अनादिकारणे ।
बिबेक बैराग्य दुइ सहाय साधने ।
बिषयेर दुख नाना, बिषयीर उपासना,
त्यज मन ए यन्त्रणा, सत्य भाव मने ॥

+			२			०			३		
								ससा	-मा	-ज्ञमपा	ममा
								स्मर	०	०००	पर
मपा	-मा	-ज्ञा	रज्ञमा	-ज्ञमा	-रा	-सरा	-नसा	ससा	-मा	-ज्ञमपा	ममा
मे	०	०	श्वरे०	००	०	००	००	स्मर	०	०००	पर

+			२			०			३		
मपा	-मा	-ज्ञा	रज्ञमा	-ा	ममा	पा	-धा	-णा	र्सा	-ा	-णा
मे	०	०	श्वरे०	०	अना	दि	०	०	का	०	०
(ण)र्सा	-ा	-णा	-धपा	-पधा	-णर्सणा	र्सणा	णा	-धा	-णा	-पमा	ममा
रणे	०	०	००	००	०००	"स्म०	र	०	०	००	पर"
								ममा	मा	-ज्ञा	ज्ञा
								बिबे	क	०	बै
मा	-णधा	णधा	र्सना	-र्सा	र्सा	र्सा	र्सर्सा	-र्मज्ञी	-र्मा	-र्रसा	(र्स)र्रसा
रा	००	ग्य०	दु०	०	इ	स	हा०	००	०	०य	सा०
र्सा	-णा	-धा	-णपा	पधा	-णर्सणा	र्सणा	णा	-धा	-णा	-पमा	मपा
ध	०	०	००	ने०	०००	"स्म०	र	०	०	००	पर"
								ममा	णा	-धणा	-धर्सर्सा
								विष	ये	००	००र
र्सा	र्सा	-ा	-ा	र्सा	-नर्सा	र्सा	-ा	र्सर्सा	र्सना	(न)री	-ा
दु	ख	०	०	ना	००	ना	०	विष	यी०	र	०
-र्सा	-ना	नर्सा	-ा	ना	(न)र्रसा	र्सा	-णधा	णा	पमा	(म)णणा	पा
०	०	उपा	०	०	स०	ना	००	त्य	ज०	म०	न
-मा	-ज्ञा	मणधा	र्सा	-नर्सा	र्सा	र्सा	र्सर्सा	-र्मज्ञी	-र्मा	-र्रसा	(र्स)र्रसा
०	०	ए्०	त्र	००	णा	स	त्य०	००	०	००	भाव
र्सा	-णा	-धा	-णपा	पधा	-णर्सणा	र्सणा	णा	-धा	-णा	-पमा	ममा
म	०	०	००	ने०	०००	"स्मर	र	०	०	००	पर"

[*Brahma Sangita,* Part III Calcutta 1362 B.S]

Brahma Saṅgīta - Composer - Manomohan Chakravarti
Rāga - Miśra Jayjayanti Tāla - Jhaptāla.

प्राणाराम, प्राणाराम, प्राणाराम ।
कि येन लुकानो नामे ताइ मिष्ट एत तब नाम ।
नाम रसे डुबे थाकि, ब्रह्माण्ड सुन्दर देखि,
बिश्वे बहे प्रेमनदी, सुधार धारा अबिराम ।
नामे भुलायेछ यारे, से कि येते पारे दूरे,
नाम रसे ये मजेछे से बुझेछे कि आराम ।
आमारे भुलाये राख, हृदि आलो करे थाक,
जीबने मरणे मम तुमि चिर सुख धाम ॥

+		२			०		३		
		[गमा	-पधपधपा	-मगा	मा	गा	रगा	-मगमगा	रसा]
॥{ ग मा	मा	मा	-ा	-ा	रा	गा	रसा	-ा	-ा
प्रा	णा	रा	०	म्	प्रा	णा	रा०	०	म्
रा	मा	पा	-ा	-ा	-ा	-ा	-ा	-ा	॥ -ा
प्रा	णा	रा	०	०	०	म्	०	०	० }
पा	ना	ना	-र्सा	र्सा	र्सना	र्रर्सा	र्सणाः	णः	धा
कि	ये	न	०	लु	का०	नो०	प्रा०	णे	ताइ
पा	धा	पा	माः	-गः	रा	रमा	मा	-ा	-ा ॥
मिष्	ट	ए	त	०	त	व०	ना	०	म् ॥
[ना	ना]								
॥{ मा	पा	ना	-ा	ना	र्सा	र्सा	र्सा	र्सा	-ा
ना	म	र	०	से	डु	बे	था	कि	०
									[-र्ज्ञा]
णा	णा	णधा	-पा	पा	पा	परी	री	र्सा	(-ा) }
ब्र	ह्मान्	ड०	०	सुन्	द	र०	दे	खि	० }
र् ना	ना	ना	-ा	र्सा	र्सना	री	र्सा	णा	-धा
विश्	शे	ब	०	हे	प्रे०	म	न	दी	०

+		२			०		३		
पा	धा	पा	मा:	–ग:	रा	मा	मा	–ा	–ा
सु	धार	धा	रा	०	अ	वि	रा	०	म्
					ग				
सा	सा	रगा	–मपा	मगा	रा	रा	रा	–ा	रा
ना	मे	भु०	००	ला०	ये	छ	या	०	रे
			ग				र		
रा	गा	मा	–मपा	पमा	मा	मगा	गा	–ा	रसा
से	कि	जे	००	ते०	पा	रे०	दू	०	रे०
रा	रा	मा	–ा	मा	पा	पा	धा	पध:ण:	–धपा
ना	म	र	०	से	ये	म	जे	छे००	००
पा	धा	पा	मगा	–रगा	मा	पा	पा	–ा	धपा
से	बु	झे	छे०	००	कि	आ	रा	०	म्
[र्ना	ना]								
मा	पा	ना	–ा	र्सा	र्सा	र्सा	र्सा	र्सा	–ा
आ	मा	रे	०	भु	ला	ये	रा	ख	०
									[र्ज्ञा]
णा	णा	णधा	पा	–ा	पा	पर्रा	र्स	र्रा	(–ा)
ह	दि	आ०	लो	०	क	रे०	था	क	०
ना	ना	ना	–ा	र्सा	र्सर्ना	र्सर्रा	र्स	णा	–धा
जी	व	ने	०	म	रा०	णे:	म	म	०
पा	धा	पा	मा:	–ग:	रा	मा	मा	–ा	–ा
तु	मि	चि	र	०	सु	धा	धा	०	म

Jātrā and Nāṭya Saṅgīta of Bengal

The origin of *nāṭya - saṅgīta* may be traced back to the music of *jātrā*, which was the most popular mode of entertainment of rural Bengal consisting of music and acting based on episodes from the Epics and Purāṇas. These *jātrās* were performed on open-air stages, and music used to be the life of them.

These ancient *jātrās* were initially musical narration plus acting of devotional and philosophical themes such as *Kṛṣṇa-jātrā, Rāmajātra, Kālīyadamaṇa-jātrā, Caṇḍī-jātrā,* etc.. From 19th century onwards, more stress was given on acting the roles of the different characters but without neglecting the musical side. Gradually these *jātrās* became popular in the newly developed urban areas under the foreign powers. Though the themes enacted in rural areas remained more or less the same, these had to be altered to suit the tastes of the urban elites who hired them for various festivals and festivities.

The owner-director of a *jātrā-party* was called the '*adhikārī*' on whom the success of the *jātrā* much depended. He had to be a musician, director, producer, actor — all rolled into one. Three *adhikārīs* who moulded this art form during the 19th century are well known in the history of the evolution of *jātrā*. They are Govinda Adhikari, Krishna Kamal Goswami, and Nilkantha Mukherji.

Govinda Adhikari was born in a Vaiṣṇava family in 1798 at Jangipara in Hoogly district. He learnt *kīrtana* under Golakchandra Das Adhkari of Dhurkhali village, in the district of Howrah. Golakchandra employed him as a *dohār* in his *kīrtana* group after training him. Govinda was gifted with a melodious voice and a keen sense of music. There is a difference of opinion regarding the name of his *guru*. Some say, he learnt music under Badana Adhikari while others maintain that Paramananda was his *guru*. Govinda later left the *kīrtana* group of his *guru* and formed his own. He organised a *jātrā* party or group and evolved a *Kṛṣṇa-jātrā* according to his own idea. Previously, *Kṛṣṇa-jātrā* consisted of more music than dialogue in prose form and the *adhikārī* of a *jātrā* party usually explained the whole episode in short, in *kathakatā* style. He enacted this part in the role of a '*dūtī*' meaning a female messenger. Recitation in *payār* and *catuṣpadī chanda* inbetween, were presented with music. There used to be short interludes in prose form to maintain the flow of the story or as a connection or link between two songs. Govinda Adhikari did away with the role of the *adhikārī* and instead, introduced proper acting in play form, setting the songs in proper coordinated manner, and adding *saṃlāpa* - meaning conversation in prose form. He himself used to be the play-wright, director, character-actor in the main role and composer of the lyrics and music. He became so successful and popular that the various zamindars of Rāḍha area patronised him. His *jātrā* party performed several times in Calcutta. He died in *c.* 1870 in Salkia.

One of his compositions is as follows:
Rāga Khamāja Tāla-Yat (Jat) m*adhyalaya.*

आर माला गाँथ कि कारण ।
राजनन्दिनी गो ।
यार तरे गाँथ माला से गेछे मधुभवन ।
मालती कुसुमेरमाला, माला हबे जपमाला,
से माला भुजंग हये,
तोमार श्री अंगे करबे दंशन ॥

Krishnakamal Goswami was born in *c.* 1810 in a Vaiṣṇava family. His parents Muralidhar and Yamunadevi belonged to the family of Sadashiva Kavirāj, who was a close associate of Caitanya Mahāprabhu. He studied Sanskrit and Vaiṣṇava literature in Nabadvipa and wrote '*Nimāi-sanyāsa*' *pālā* while still a student.

Krishnakamal moved to Dhaka after marriage. He also taught Sanskrit in the Sanskrit College of Calcutta, but his real profession was *kathakatā.* He became famous as a *kathak, kirtanīyā* and also for his *Kṛṣṇa-jātrā.* His *jātrā* was predominated by *kīrtana* and *kathakatā* styles because of his expertise in these two art forms. Another special feature of his style was that he did not allow music to over power the main story. He followed the principles of ancient *nāṭgīti* and polished it to a sophisticated style with no vulgarism, but with a devotional fervour. These songs became so popular that even people on the streets of Calcutta used to hum and sing them.

One of his most popular compositions:
Rāga Miśra Khamāja Tāla - Ektāla.

शोनो ब्रजराज स्वपनेते आज देखादिये
गोपाल कोथाय लुकाले ।
येन से चंचल चाँदे अंचल धरे काँदे,
जननी दे ननी दे ननी बले ।
नील कलेबर धुलाय धूसर
विधुमुखे येन कत मधुर सुर,
संचारिये डाके 'मा' बले । - - - -

Nilkantha Mukherji was born in *c.* 1841, in a village called Dhwani in Burdwan district. His parents were Bamacharan and Saraswatidevi who believed in Śāktaism. Nilkantha came to Calcutta in search of a job at an early age as he lost his father. He worked with a Marwari businessman of Barabazar area. Nilkantha was gifted with a melodious voice and a natural talent in music. He was trained by an expert songstress who was the lady-love of the businessman. Soon Nilkantha became a good singer and came back to his village to join a *jātrā* party. He changed parties twice and eventually joined the group of Govinda Adhikari and became his most favourite disciple. He learnt the art under Govinda and started his own *jātrā* group around 1864. He polished some of the *pālās* of *Kṛṣṇa-jātrā*, composed new songs for them and then presented them. He received a lot of popularity in Burdwan area and became a regular performer in the palaces of Burdwan and Hetampur. He was called '*Gīta-ratna*' by the connoisseurs of Nabadvipa. His popularity brought him to perform in Calcutta regularly at the prestigious music *durbār* of Maharaja Jotindramohan Thakur of Pathuriaghata. Among his many admirers were Thakur Ramakrishna Paramahamsa and Rabindranath Thakur who invited him to sing in Shantiniketan.

Nilkantha died in 1911 and was ably succeeded by his youngest son Ramkamal.

One of his popular song example:

Rāga - Miśra Bihāga   Tāla - Khemṭā.

दिन याय दीनबन्धु बले डाकरे रसना ।
एत साधेर मानब जनम हेलाते हारायोना ॥
ओ़ मन तुइ कार केइ बा तोमार,
देख भेबे एकटिबार सकलि असार ।
नयन मुदले सब अन्धकार, देखेओ कि ता देखना ॥
तुमि बल आमार आमार
किन्तु बल के बा काहार ये यार आपनार,
प्राणान्त हले थाकबे कोथा, ता कि एकबार भाबना ।
एखन मन हओ सचेतन, देख ह्रदे सेइ निरंजन, अखिलेर धन ।
नील कण्ठ बले, ताय, ना भाबिले तरिबारे पथ पाबिना ।

Along with this phase of *jātrā* of devotional themes, came another style in Calcutta called '*Sakher-jātrā*' or '*Notun-jātrā*' which was evolved by the elites, more for entertainment purposes than devotional. The themes of these *jātrās* were light and jocular. Initially these were based on some social episodes of contemporary life, and actors used to dress up in fancy dresses called '*saṅg-sājā*'. *Sakher-jātrās* were full of songs and dances and the dialogues used to be in prose, called *gadyāsaṃlāpa.*

Sakher-jātrā was innovated by a group of well to do youths of Bhavanipur area and they staged *Nala-Damayantī* in 1822. In 1823, Raja Vikramāditya was staged in this new technique.

In 1849 *jātrā* songs were fashioned after *ākhḍāi* and *half-ākhḍāi* styles by Ramchand Mukhopadhyay of Jorasanko, in place of straight forward *rāga-saṅgītas* or *kīrtanāṅga* based songs. He staged *Nanda Bidāy* with the help of eminent musicians such as Rajnarayan Bandyopadhyay, Tituram Boral and others who also took part in the play. Through *Nanda Bidāy*, female actresses were introduced for the first time. A young girl of thirteen named *Śrīdām* (nick name Pūṭi), sang with extraordinary melodiousness. This *jātrā* became so popular that eminent singers like *dhrupadīyā* Chotulal, Hira Bulbul, Umeshbabu of Burdwan *durbār* attended. The songs of *Nanda Bidāy* became hits and were sung even in the music *mehefils* of the '*bābus*' of Calcutta. From now on female roles were enacted mostly by ladies from humble walks of life.

Madanmohan Chattopadhyay of Chandannagar brought in further changes by introducing *juḍi-gāna,* set on *rāgas,* improved acting, and good stage decor. *Juḍis* were a pair of singers providing interludes between scenes. Their songs were composed of good lyrics set on intricate *rāgas* and *tālas.*

During the twenties and thirties of 19th century, *Vidyāsundara-jātrā* was performed as *sakher-jātrā* in Barahanagar area by the *adhikārī* Thakurdas Mukhopadhyay. There used to be characters called *Nandī* in *jātrās* who rendered high quality songs as interludes. These *Nandīs* had to be trained musicians and excellent singers. Thakurdas's team consisted of musicians such as Tarachand Bandopadhyay, Kalidas Bhattacharya, and others who enacted the roles of *Nandīs.* Other famous singers were Nimai Mitra, Prankrishna Tarkālaṅkāra, Radhamohan Chattopadhyay, and others. After the demise of Thakurdas, the group broke up. One of the instrumentalists named Ramdhan, formed a new group and revived the old style of narrating the whole story tunefully before the commencement of the *jātrā.* Even *dhrupadīyā* Bishwanath used to sing for this *jātrā* group.

Vidyāsundara-jātrā used to be performed by various other groups such as - Thakuro and Shibe Jugi, Pyarimohan, etc.. By and by, the songs of *Vidyāsundara* lost the pure classical touch and instead, cheap compositions for the taste of the masses replaced the *rāga*-based songs which used to be performed even in prestigious *mehfils.*

Gopal Ude, born in *c.* 1819 hailed from Orissa and came to Calcutta in search of a job when he was eighteen or nineteen years old. He became a fruit vendor and one afternoon as he was passing by Radhamohan Sarkar's villa selling bananas, his utterings of "bananas! who wants bananas" was so melodious that immediately Radhamohan sent for him, not for his bananas but for his melodious voice. Since then Gopal never looked back. He was just the character Radhamohan was looking for his fashionable *jātrā.* Gopal was trained under Harikishan Misra in music and other teachers were also appointed to teach him Bengali. Soon he became a polished and accomplished singer-actor-composer. His *ṭappā* and *ṭhumrī* style of singing were extremely popular and so was his acting. After the death of his patron - Radhamohan Sarkar, Gopal inherited the *jātrā* - party with all its assets and formed his own group. He made several changes by getting the *pālā* of *Vidyāsundara* rewritten and new songs composed by others and he himself set these to music in a lighter vein with simple and catchy tunes. *Āḍ Khemṭā tāla* was profusely used by him in a variety of songs and it is he who popularised this style. He also introduced *khemṭā* dance. Although his songs were not strictly classical or semi-classical types as was the trend before, but because of the light, simple and catchy tunes, Gopal Ude's *jātrās* became very popular throughout Calcutta, and he set a new trend in *jātrā* songs. He died in 1859-60.

After Gopal Ude, the person who brought further changes in *Jātrā* was Motilal Ray. As he was not a singer, his *jātrās* used to be predominated by acting and dialogues in prose. Songs used to be less in number.

Born in 1843, in the village of Bhatshala, Motilal studied till Entrance. He had his schooling in Nabadvipa, Barasat and Calcutta. For sometime he worked in the post office. At Bhatshala, he used to act in the main role in the *jātrā* party of Harinarayan Chaudhuri because of his ability in superior acting. Motilal's first *pālā 'Tarani Sen vadh'* was staged in Calcutta. In 1874 he organised a group called Nabadvīpa Baṅga Gītābhinaya Sampradāya', and from 1874 to 1904 he reigned supreme in the world of *jātrā* because of his progressive methods applied in the techniques of *jātrā*. At that time the European plays had become well established in Calcutta and Chinsura. Bengali plays were staged on the models of these European ones. Motilal also adopted some of the techniques of the stage acting in his *jātrā*. Although he kept the number of songs to the minimum, he composed more than a thousand songs for his various *pālās* .

Motilal died in 1908 in Kasi and his *jātrā* company was ably directed by his two sons Dharmadas and Bhupendranarayan.

To sum up, a *jātrā* used to be a *gīta-pradhān* (dominated by songs) narrative. The songs of the *jātrās* were *rāga* and *tāla* based and sometimes *kīrtaṇa* based, as the situation demanded. The performers had to be trained in *śāstrīya-saṅgīta* and the *adhikārī* himself used to be a musician, both a vocalist and an instrumentalist. These *rāga* based songs were rendered with adequate emotional fervour and as such, specific *rāgas* were chosen to bring forth the sentiments of the songs. Sometimes slight *ālāpacārī* used to be rendered also.

The transition to theatre culture and operas came about with the Europeans settling down in Calcutta and around, from the mid 18th century. They built theatres for their own entertainment in the Fort William, at Chowringhee and Dumdum. They even invited European troupes to India to perform at these theatres. Thus Calcutta was experiencing a new cultural atmosphere and the rich zamindars were inspired to establish their own theatres. Initially these theatres were entirely private and amateur, sponsored and patronised by the rich elites.

In 1795, Lebedeff a Russian, staged some English plays translated into Bengali. He set up a theatre hall in Domtala area of Calcutta and not only got the plays translated by a Bengali named Goloknath Das but took Bengali actors and actresses to play the roles. Thus he initiated the Bengalis into the culture of theatre acting.

The first Bengali theatre hall established by a Bengali was in 1835 by Nabinchandra Basu of Shyambazar, at his own residence. It was a private enterprise. *Vidyasundara* was staged with some songs, and orchestra was played by some Brahmin musicians who played *sitār, sāraṅgī, pakhāvaj,* etc. Another play in Bengali was enacted in 1857 at the residence of Ashutosh Deb. This play was the Bengali version of Kālidāsa's *Śakuntalam.* The first social drama named '*Kulīna-kula-sarvasva*', written by Ramnarayan Tarkaratna was staged in 1857 at the residence of Ramjaya Basak of Natun Bazar. The play was also staged at different parts of Calcutta. Rupchand Paksi composed the music for this drama, based on folk tunes, when it was staged in Chinsura. The song - "*Adhinīre guṇamaṇi paḍeche ki mane he*" became an instant hit. This was the period of private-amateur theatre.

In 1858, Belgachia Natyashala was established by the efforts of Raja Pratapchandra and Ishwarchandra Sinha of Paikpara and Raja Jotindramohan Thakur of Pathuriaghata. In this *nāṭyaśālā, Ratnāvalī,* translated by Ramnarayan Tarkaratna was produced with special musical scores. Orchestra was first introduced by Kshetramohan Goswami and Jadunath Pal who were encouraged by Jotindramohan. Because of the necessity of keeping the music score in front of the players of various instruments, notation system was evolved by Kshetramohan, who polished it further with Saurindramohan Thakur for notating Hindusthani *śāstrīya saṅgīta.* This system of notation became known as *Daṇḍamātrik Paddhati.*

Michael Madhusudan Datta's *Śarmiṣṭhā* was specially written and staged in 1859. Some of the songs were written and scored by Raja Jotindramohan and the invocation song was by Madhusudan Datta himself. This song was tuned in *rāga Bāhār* and set on *druta Tritāla.* Krishnadhan Bandopadhyay the famous musician of later years enacted the role of '*Śarmiṣṭhā*'. The art of play-back music was introduced in this play when the heroine imitated playing the *vīṇā* on the stage.

The two Thakur brothers of Pathuriaghata, established a small theatre in their own house called—'Pathuriaghata Banga Natyalaya', where many plays were staged and special attention used to be given to music and orchestration. Music set to songs and orchestra, was based on *śāstrīya-saṅgīta,* as Kshetramohan Goswami, Maharaja Jotindramohan and Saurindramohan were experts of classical music. These private theatres used to be sponsored and patronised by rich zamindars and elites, and unfortunately, the common man had no access to these fashionable modes of entertainment.

The first professional theatre for the people was established in 1872 in Chitpur Road in the house of Madhusudan Sanyal, under the name 'Calcutta National Theatrical Society' and staged *Nīladarpaṇa* of Dinabandhu Mitra. This theatre was remamed 'National Theatre' and was managed by such personalities as Girishchandra Ghosh, Nagendranath Bandopadhyay, Radha Madhav Kar, Ardhendu Shekhar Mustafi, Amritalal Basu, Amritalal Mukhopadhyay, Sureshchandra Mitra, Shivchandra Chattopadhyay, Jogendranath Mitra, Mahendralal Basu and others. Many more plays were staged at this theatre. This was the second phase of theatre culture when commercialism took over. During this time Dinabadhu Mitra's '*Līlāvatī*' was also staged with many songs. This play gained popularity in Calcutta, Chinsura and other places. The songs of this play were based on *rāgas* and *Manoharshāhī-kirtana*. '*Āge jodi jāntām*' was on *raga Pīlu* and '*Ke bale Gokule āmār Kānāi nāi*' on *Manoharshāhī* style.

The other independent professional theatres were: 'Bengal Theatre' and 'the Great National Theatre' set up in 1873. Later, many more theatres came up all over Calcutta and other towns of Bengal.

At that time, a play without songs was unthinkable, and the success of a play depended on its songs, particularly for its lyrical and musical merit, which was realised by the then playwrights.

After Dinabandhu, it was Manomohan Basu who built the bridge between old *jātrā* form and new Western style theatre. He wrote song-oriented plays which were categorised as *gītinātyas* or operas because of their number of songs. His *Rāmābhiṣeka* and *Hariścandra* were very popular and were staged both as *jātrā* and theatre. His songs reached the peak in popularity.

Jyotirindranath Thakur established a theatre at their Jorasanko residence, where many plays were staged. Jyotirindranath himself was a litterateur and musician, and staged such plays which were based on social or national themes. He composed songs for these plays which became famous as '*svadeśī-saṅgīta*', eg - '*Jval jval citā dviguṇ dviguṇ*', '*Mile sabe Bhārata santān*', etc.

Around 1863, proper *Gītināṭyas* were staged. The first of its kind was Annadaprasad Bandopadhyay's *Śakuntala*, staged in 1865, followed by *Ratnāvalī* of Harimohan (Ray) Karmakar. In 1874 '*Satī-ki-kalaṅkinī*' was staged, which was the first *gītināṭya* with songs only and it became an all time hit.

The three stage arts, i.e. *Jātrā, Nāṭakas* and *Gītināṭyas* or *Gītābhinayas* were closely linked with each other. While *jātrā* was a rural art form the other two were more sophisticated and recent, built up on Western influence. But songs and music predominated all the three and sometimes it was difficult to differentiate one from the other. When the intellectuals started staging plays disgusted by the crudity of the *jātrās,* they still maintained the importance of songs and music.

Gītināṭyas evolved out of *jātrā* and *nāṭaka* and on the model of Italian opera. The *gītināṭyas* were written by many eminent playwrights and poet-lyricists such as Girishchandra Ghosh, Manomohan Basu, Amritalal Mukhopadhyay, Swarnakumari Devi, Jyotirindranath, Rabindranath, and others.

Girishchandra excelled in acting, directing, writing plays and operas and composing songs. His '*Sadhabār ekādaśī*' play (1865) and '*Āgamanī*' opera were popular hits. He used to write the plays, and according to the situations arising from the drama, tunes were composed, to which suitable lyrics were written to fit in perfectly. Ramtaran Sanyal used to be his music composer in most of the plays. Other musicians who also composed music for some of his plays were: Janakinath Basu, Debkantha Bagchi, Radhamadhab Kar, Madanmohan Barman, Benimadhav Adhikari, and Baikunthanath Basu. Girishchandra, though not a performing musician, was knowledgeable in *rāga-saṅgīta* and got the songs tuned according to his taste by the above mentioned musicians and often composed the tunes himself. Girishchandra will be remembered for his unique contribution in stage and theatre music which is known as *nāṭya-saṅgīta.* He used not only classical and semi-classical melodies, but *kīrtana,* folk tunes, as well as tunes of Hindusthani songs.

Previous to commercial or public theatre, it was the age of the amateur and fashionable, when tunes were set on pure classical *rāgas* or traditional folk tunes. These being private enterprises there was no standardisation and stage music remained largely traditional or conventional. Standardisation came about only after 1872 when public theatres came up. Starting with 'National Theatre', a number of other prestigious theatres came up, such as - Hindoo National Theatre, Great National Theatre, Classic Theatre, Star Theatre, Bengal Theatre, Emerald Theatre, Minerva Theatre and Kohinoor Theatre. With so many commercial theatres coming up, activities in the dramatic circles became brisk. There were playwrights, actors, actresses, composers, musicians - who all flocked together. Actresses had to be experts in music, dancing and acting and played a big role in popularising stage music. Those who excelled in this art were: Krishnakumari, Binodini, Banabiharini, Gangamani, Manadasundari, Narisundari, Sushilabala, Ashcharyamayee No. 1 and 2, Tinkadi, Tarasundari, Kiranbala, Subasini, Jadumoni, and others. These actresses were trained singers and could render classical, semi-classical, *kirtana,* folk, *Rabindra -sangita, bhajan,* etc. in any *rasa* that was required for a particular scene, with perfection. It was due to the expertise of these singers that a play would be a box-office hit. Sometimes a particular actress would be responsible for the success of a particular role and the audience would not accept anyone else enacting the same character.

The period from 1872 to 1911 is ascribed to Girishchandra Ghosh as 'Girish-era'. During this period *nāṭya-saṅgīta* reached its climax in everyway. Girish himself was a good composer, and the stage singers both male and female particularly the latter, made theatre music memorable under his direction.

During the second half of 19th century, Bengal's social, cultural, literary, religious and other activities were greatly influenced as a result of the renaissance. Music was one of them. Many music establishments were established. 'Saṅgīta-samāj' was one of them, founded by Jyotirindranath. Music and acting both were taught. Rabindranath was also involved in the activities of this institution. Radhamadhav Kar was the *nāṭyācārya.* Madhusudan Datta's '*Meghnād-vadh*', Bankimchandra's '*Ānandamaṭh', Mṛṇālinī*' and many more plays, and operas penned by the Tagores were enacted here.

During this period some plays and operas were written with plots based on stories from foreignlands, such as — *Alibaba, Abu Hasan, Pārasya-prasūn / Pārisānā* etc. in which music was based on indigenous styles like *Kālu-bhulu, Gheserā-gheserāni,* and also *Khemṭā* and *Āḍkhemṭā.* Nidhubabu's *ṭappā* style was very popular at that time and in return influenced *nāṭya-saṅgīta.* Suitable *rāgas* were used to express an emotional situation or sense of pathos or happiness.

When the music of *nāṭya-saṅgīta* is studied carefully it is found that about twenty seven *rāga-rāgiṇīs* were used, viz. *Yaman-kalyāṇa Jhīnjhiṭ, Pīlu, Khamāja, Barvā, Bāhār, Lum, Bibhāsa, Jogiyā, Sindhu-bhairavī, Bhairavī, Āḍanā-bāhār, Sāraṅga, Paraja, Kakubha, Kāliṅgḍā, Lalita, Sāhānā, Jayjayantī, Hamīra, Paraja-bāhār, Multāna-khamāja* etc. The *tālas* mostly used were: *Tritāla, Cautāla, Kavvālī, Ṭhumrī, Āḍā-ṭhekā, Jat, Madhyamāna, Jalada-madyamāna, Jhapāla, Ektāla, Khemṭā* and *Āḍ-khemṭā.*

At the initial stage, *gītināṭyas* or operas that were staged were not operas in the real sense; they were more of a polished *jātrābhinaya* or *nāṭyas* with ample songs. It took some time to evolve *gītināṭyas* in the true sense and came about with Rabindranatha's *Vālmīki pratibhā,* staged in Star Theatre in 1886. He was the first to combine *kāvya, nāṭaka, nṛtya,* and *gāna* in a perfect blend.

After 1911, i. e. soon after the death of Girish Ghosh, Bengali theatre departed from the traditional and commercial mode and entered into a new phase. Playwrights of Girish-era catered for the stage and the public and their target was to achieve commercial success. In the new phase, the fresh batch of dramatists were both dramatists and music composers besides being litterateurs. They did not feel obligated to the stage audience for the sake of money. Their aim was to create artistic literary works with new theme, form, content and classy songs of poetic value. This new group consisted of such luminaries as Jyotirindranath, Rabindranath, D. L. Roy and others. They moulded the music of the stage in a new artistic form - more like *kāvya-saṅgīta.*

Musical forms, or any other art forms, are dependent on the contemporary conditions of life and evolve through these conditions. Constant experimentation goes on to produce the product. Similarly, *nātya-saṅgīta* of Bengal evolved through these experiments and culminated by the end of Girish-era, into a standardised pattern that had its great appeal for the audience of that time. Rabindranath gave it a further artistic maturity which had universal appeal.

To sum up, *jātrās,* plays, dramas and operas written on episodes from the Purāṇas and the Epics and also on social, devotional and nationalistic themes, propagated *nātya-saṅgīta, svadeśī-saṅgīta* and *kāvya-saṅgīta,* which were based on *śāstrīya-saṅgīta, kīrtana* and folk music.

Some Examples of Jātrā gāna
Composer - Gopal Ude [Vidyasundara Jātrā]
RāgāBhairavī Tāla Āḍāṭhekā

ऐ देखा याय बाड़ी आमार, चाद्दिके मालंचेर बेड़ा,
भमराते गुण् गुण् करे कोकिलेते दिच्छे साड़ा ॥
मयूर मयूरी सने, आनन्दित कुसुम बने;
आमार एइ फुल बागाने तिलेक नाइक बसन्त छाड़ा ॥
यदि अनुग्रह करे, एस ए अधिनीर घरे,
यत्नकरे राखि तोरे, बारेक ना करि छाड़ा ॥

Sthāyī

+			२			०			३		
		{सा	पा	-ा	पा	पा	णदा	-पा	मपा	मा	मा
		ऐ	दे	खा	जाय	बा	ड़ी०	०	आ०	मा	र
सा	-सा	ऋ	ज्ञा	मा	-मा	ज्ञऋ	मज्ञा	ऋ	सा	-ा	-ा
चा	०	द्दि	के	मा	०	लन्	चेर्	बे	ड़ा	०	०
-ा	-ा}	णा	सा	ज्ञा	मा	पा	पा	दणा	धा	पा	-ा
०	०}	भ्र	म	रा	ते	गुण	गु	०ण्	क	रे	०
ज्ञा	ज्ञा	-ज्ञा	मा	ह्मा	-मा	ज्ञरा	मज्ञा	ऋ	सा	-ा	-ा
को	कि	०	ले	ते	०	दि०	च्छे०	सा	ड़ा	०	०

Antarā

+			२			०			३		
-ा	-ा	ज्ञा	मा	दा	णा	र्सा	र्सा	-णा	र्ऋा	र्सा	-र्सा
०	०	म	यू	र	म	यू	री	०	स	ने	०
		य	दि	अ	नु	ग्र	ह	०	क	रे	०
-ा	-ा	णा	णा	र्सा	-ा	णा	र्ऋर्ऋा	र्सणा	दा	पा	-ा
०	०	आ	नन्	दि	त	कु	सु०	म०	ब	ने	०
०	०	ए	स	ए	अ	धि	नी०	०र्	घ	रे	०
-ा	-ा	पा	र्ज्ञा	र्ऋा	र्ज्ञा	र्सा	-ा	र्ऋा	णा	र्सा	-र्सा
०	०	आ	मार्	ए	इ	फु	ल	बा	गा	ने	०
०	०	य	ल	क	रे	रा	खि	०	तो	रे	०
पा	णधा	र्सणा	दा	दा	पा	ज्ञा	ज्ञा	रा	ज्ञा	-ा	-ा
ति	ले०	०क	ना	इ	ब	सन्	त	छा	ड़ा	०	०
बा	रे०	०क	ना	०	क	रि	०	छा	ड़ा	०	०

Prācīna Jātrār gāna. Composer: unknown. Tuned by Gopal Ude[1830-1870]
RāgāKhamāj Tāla-Āḍātheka

अबिचार कोरोना,
केन बिना दोषे दाओ यन्त्रणा ।
कोथाकार एक सर्बनेशे बासार आशे
सुरीत कुरीत कार केमन रीत
जानबो किसे;
महाराजा तत्त जले घर पोड़ेना ॥

+			२			०			३		
						सा	गमगा-	रगा-	मा	पा	-धपा
						अ	बि०००	०००	चार	क	००
मा	पा	-ा	-ा	गा	गा	गा	मा	-मगा	मा	पधा	-णधा
रो	ना	०	०	के	न	बि	ना	००	दो	षे०	००

+			२			०			३		
पा	धपा	मा	गा	रसा	-ा }‖						
दा	०ओ	-न्	त्र	णा०	०						
					गा	गा	गा	मा	पा	-ा	ना
					को	था	कार	एक	स	र्	ब
र्सा	र्सा	-ा	-ा	-ा	धा	ना	र्सा	र्रा	र्सा	ना	-ा
ने	शे	०	०	०	ए	से	छि	ल	बा	सा	र
धा	र्सा	-नर्सर्रर्सा	-नधा	-पा	पा	पा	धा	धा	धा	-ा	णा
आ	शे	००००	००	०	सु	रीत्	कु	रीत्	का	र्	के
धा	सणा	णधा	पा	धपा	-मगा	-रगा	-ा	मा	पा	-ा	-ा
मन्	री०	०त्	जान्	बो०	००	००	०	कि	से	०	०
-ा	-ा	गा	मा	पा	धा	मा	-ा	धा	पा	पा	-ा
०	०	म	हा	रा	जा	त	प्	त	ज	ले	०
ग	मपा	मा	गा	रसा	-ा ‖‖						
घ	०र	पो	ड़े	ना०	०						

Jātrā gāna Composer - Nilkantha Mukhopadhyay

स्थायी : ओ मन भावले बल कि आर हबे,
ओरे या आछे कपाले फलबे काले काले
कर्मसूत्रेर फल आपनि फलिबे ॥

अन्तरा : विधि या लिखेछेन कपाल उपरे,
कार साध्य ताहा खण्डाइते पारे,
बल, बुद्धि, विद्या, पौरुषे कि करे,
जाहा घटिबार ता घटिबे ॥

संचारी : बनवासी हये योगी ऋषि गण,
जाँर ध्याने ताँरा सतत मगन,
तथापि अन्त पायना यखन,
अन्ये केमने बुझिबे ॥

आभोगः कण्ठ कय एकबार भाबरे अदृष्ट,
अदृष्टेर फल मिलाइबेन कृष्ण,
कर ऐ पदे मन इष्ट निष्ट
ए सब यन्त्रणा याबे ॥

Rāga-Suraṭ Tāla-Ektāla
Sthāyī

+			२			०			३		
			{रा	रगा	-मपा	मा	मा	मंगा	रा	णा्	सा
			{ओ	म०	०न	भाव	ले	ब०	ल	कि	आर
गा	-रा	-ा}	-ा	मा	मा	मा	मा	मा	पा	पा	पा
ह	०	बे}	०	ओ	रे	या	आ	छे	क	पा	ले
मा	पा	ना	नर्सा	र्सा	र्सा	पा	पनर्सरी	र्सा	णा	धा	पा
फल	बे	का	ले०	का	ले	क	र्म०००	सू	त्रेर	फ	ल
मा	मा	गरा	गा	मा	मा	मा	मा	मगा	रा	णा	सा
आ	प	नि०	फ	लि	बे	"भाव	ले	ब०	ल	कि	आर"

Antarā

						{मा	पा	पा	ना	ना	ना
						{बि	धि	या	लि	खे	छेन
ना	र्सा	र्सा	र्सा	र्सा	र्सा}	{णा	णा	णा	धा	पा	धा
क	पा	ल	उ	प	रे}	{का	र	सा	ध्य	ता	हा
णा	र्सा	र्सा	णा	धा	पा}	{मा	मा	मा	मा	मा	मा
खन्	डा	इ	ते	पा	रे}	{व	ल	बु	द्धि	वि	द्या
मा	पा	ना	ना	र्सा	र्सा}	पा	पनर्सरी	र्सा	णा	धा	पा
पौ	रु	षे	कि	क	रे}	या	हा०००	घ	टि	बा	र
मा	गा	-रा	गा	मा	-मा	मा	मा	मगा	रा	णा्	सा
ता	घ	०	टि	बे	०	"भाव	ले	ब०	ल	कि	आर"

Sañcārī

+			२			०			३		
						सा	सा	सा	रा	रा	गा
						ब	न	बा	सी	ह	ये
मा	पा	पा	पा	पा	–ा	मा	मा	मा	मा	मा	गा
यो	गी	ऋ	षि	ग	ण	याँ	र	ध्या	ने	ताँ	रा
गा	गा	गमा	रगा	रसा	–सा	मा	मा	मपा	पा	पा	पा
स	त	त०	म०	गन	०	त	था	पि०	अ	न्	त
मा	पा	नसा	सा	सा	सा	धा	ना	धा	पा	मगा	मा
पा	य	ना०	ज	ख	न्	अ	न्ये	के	म	ने०	बु
-पा	पा	–ा	–ा	–ा	–पा						
झि	बे	०	०	०	०						

Ābhoga

						मा	पा	पा	ना	ना	ना
						क	ण्ठ	कय	एक	बा	र
न	र्सा	र्सा	र्सा	र्सा	र्सा	णा	णा	णा	धा	पा	धा
भा	ब	रे	अ	दृ	ष्ट	अ	दृ	ष्टे	र	फ	ल
णा	र्सा	र्सा	णा	धा	पा	मा	मा	मा	–मा	मा	मा
मि	ला	इ	बेन	कृ	ष्णा	क	र	ऐ	०	प	दे
मा	पा	ना	ना	र्सा	र्सा	पा	पनर्सरी	र्सा	णा	धा	पा
म	न	इ	ष्ट	नि	ष्ट	ए	भ०००	न	य	न्त्र	णा
मा	–गा	–रगा	मा	–ा	–ा	मा	मा	मगा	रा	णा्	सा
या	०	००	बे	०	०	"भाव	ले	ब०	ल	कि	आर"

BIBLIOGRAPHY

1. Bandopadhyay, Brajendranath. *Baṅgīya Nāṭyaśālār Itihās*. Calcutta. (Beng.).
2. Goswami, Utpala. *Kolkātāye Saṅgīta Carcā*. Calcutta, 1991. (Beng.).
3. Kundu, Pranay Kumar. *"Development of Stage and theatre music in Bengal"*, in *"The Music of Bengal"*. Ed. by Jayashri Banerji. Baroda, 1988.
4. a)——.*"Bāṅglā Gīti-nāṭya"*, &

   b) Sen, Gita. *"Bāṅglā theaterer gāna"*, in *Deshbinodan* (Bengali Journal), Calcutta, 1984. (Beng.)

Girishchandra Ghosh

Famous as a playwright, composer of *nāṭya saṅgīta* and actor, Girishchandra Ghosh was born in 1844 in Calcutta. His father Nilkamal Ghosh was a resident of Bagbazar in Calcutta. Girish lost his parents in his childhood and could not complete his education. But later when he grew up, he studied on his own, which reflected in his plays and lyrics composed for the dramas.

He formed a small theatre group with his friends at a young age and this amateur group staged '*Sadhabār-ekādaśī*' in which he acted as Nimchand and earned fame as an actor. Gradually this group became professional and formed National Theatre. Somehow, Girishchandra was averse to the idea of making money by commercialising this art and joined Great National Theatre as an honorary actor. He was then offered the post of manager. He started writing dramas at this time and acted as the manager, director, actor, and playwright - all rolled into one. Soon he became famous for his talents and used to direct plays even in other theatres, such as Star, Minerva, Emerald, etc.

Girishchandra wrote about seventy plays and operas on varied subjects. These were: *Prafulla, Bilvamaṅgala, Gṛhalaksmī, Āgamanī, Dol-līlā, Prahlād-caritra, Caitanya-līlā, Sītārāma, Janā, Mohinī Pratimā*, etc. and each one was rich in music. The period from 1872 to 1911 was ascribed to Girishchandra as Girish-*yuga* or era in the history of theatre of Bengal, and he was called the '*Naṭya Samrāṭa*'.

Girish had a unique way of writing his plays and composing music for the songs specially written for the various situations arising in the play, one after the other as it came to his mind. These were written down by his assistants immediately, and he used to edit these later.

Regarding music and dance in the drama, he would guide his music and dance directors by explaining in detail, just the way he wanted them. Although he was not a performing musician or dancer but he had acquired enough knowledge in these arts. He was trained by Brajanath Deb and other musicians who came close to him. His music directors were such well known musicians as: Ramtaran Sanyal, Debkantha Bagchi, Beni Ostad/Benimadhav Adhikari, Janakinath Basu, Baikunthanath Basu, and others.

Girishchandra started composing songs from an early age and brought in a style which was free of vulgarism. He tuned the songs of his plays in classical *rāgas* and *tālas* and also in *kīrtanāṅga, ṭappā* and folk styles, as per the subject of the play or the demand of the situation. To express the right mood and emotion of the scene or situation, tunes were composed first and then the *padas* were written accordingly. His other contribution was '*Gairiśī - chanda*' which was an adaptation of '*amitrākṣara /amitākṣara - chanda*' (blank - verse) but moulded to suit *nāṭya*.

Girishchandra made use of many *rāgas, miśra-rāgas* and *tālas* to bring in variety and appropriate emotion in his songs. *Khāmāja* alone was used in more than fifteen *miśra* varieties apart from complicated *rāgas,* while *tālas* like *Āḍ-khemṭā, Āḍā-ṭhekā, Yat / Jat, Ektāla, Tritāla, Kaharvā, Postā, Paṭ-tāla, Khāmsā, Dhāmār, Teorā, Madhyamāna* were used. He applied *Dādrā* in 2/4 *chanda* to enhance the dramatic effect. With *Āḍ-khemṭā,* he brought out not only emotions of pathos, but devotion, as well as gaiety:

A few examples:

1. Pathos:

याइ गो ओइ बाजाय बाँशी प्राण केमन करे
काला एकला ऐसे कदम तलाय
दाँड़ियेछे आमार तरे ।
जत बाँशरी बाजाय तत पथ पाने चाय
पागल बाँशी डाके उभराय
ना गेले से कैंदे कैंदे
चले याबे मान करे ।

2. Devotion:

रांगाजबा के दिले तोर पाय मुटो मुटो
देना मा साध हयेछे, परिये दे ना माथाय दुटो ।
मा बले डाकब तोरे,
हाततालि दे नाचब घुरे
देखे मा नाचबि कत
आबार वेंधे दिबि झुटो ॥

3. Gaiety:

देखि आज नतुन दुनिया
नतुन ताने नतुन प्राणे गेये याय हाओया
नतुन शशी उठेछे, शशी घेरे नतुन
नतुन तारा फुटछे
नतुन फुले आजके नतुन सौरभ फुटेछे
प्राण मन नतुन जीबन पेयेछि नतुन हिया
उथले उठे नतुन रसेर दरिया ॥

Girishchandra's style of *nāṭya-saṅgīta* not only influenced the music of the stage but music in general. Many of his songs were sung by *ustāds* as these were based on *śāstrīya-saṅgīta*. Girish's devotional songs had a great appeal over the audience. These were not highly philosophical, yet had a *rasa* of deep devotion like *bhajans*, e.g. '*Banaphul bhūṣaṇa śyāma muralīdhara*' - from *Janā*, set in *Deś-miśra, Ṭhumrītāla*, or '*Mūḍa candracūḍa Hara Bholā*' - from *Pūrṇacandra*, set in *Bhairavī, Ṭhumrītāla.*

Girish staged many of Bankimchandra's novels and set to music the songs of *Mṛṇāliṇī* penned by Bankim, viz. '*Sādher taraṇī āmār ke dilo taraṅge; 'E janamer saṅge ki soi janamer sādh puribe*', which became instant hits.

Girishchandra's contribution in stage craft, lighting, presentation, direction, combined with his extraordinary talent of writing plays, acting and composing *nāṭya-saṅgīta* will be ever remembered in the world of *nāṭya*. He expired in 1911.

BIBLIOGRAPHY

1. Das Sharma, Amal. *Saṅgīta Maṇīṣā.* Part I. Calcutta, 1979. (Beng.).
2. Dutt, Utpal. *Girish Chandra Ghosh.* Sahitya Academi, New Delhi. 1992.
3. Ghosh, Girish Chandra. *Girīśracanāvalī.* Calcutta. (Beng.).
4. ———. *Girīś-racana Sambhār.* Ed. by Pramathanath Bishi . Calcutta, 1963. (Beng.).
5. Goswami, Utpala. *Kolkātāy Saṅgīta Carcā.* Calcutta, 1991. (Beng.).
6. Kundu. Pranay Kumar. "*Development of stage and theatre music in Bengali*", in *The Music of Bengal.* Ed. by Jayashri Banerji.Baroda, 1988.
7. Mitra, Rajyeshwar, *Bāṅglār Gītikār O Bāṅglā gāner Nānādik.* Calcutta,1973.(Beng.).

Example of Nāṭya-Saṅgīta
Composer: Girishchandra Ghosh.
1. Rāga-Sahānā Tāla-Yat.

तुमि तो मा छिले भुले,
आमि पागल निये सारा हइ।
हासे काँदे सदाइ भोला,
जाने ना मा आमा बइ ।
भांग खेये मा सदाइ आछे
थाकते हय मा काछे काछे,
भालो मन्द हय गो पाछे
सदाइ मने भाबि ओइ ।
दिते हय मा मुखे तुले,
नय तो खेते याय गो भुले
खेपार दशा भावते गेले
आमाते आर आमि नइ ।
भुलिये यखन एलेम छले,
ओमा भेसे गेल नयन जले,
एकला पाछे जाय गो चले,
आपन छाया एमन कइ ?

2. Rāga-Surat-miśra Tāla-Yat.

कइ कृष्ण एलो कुंजे प्राण सइ,
देरे कृष्ण, दे कृष्ण एने दे
राधा जाने कि गो कृष्ण बइ ।
छिछि करे मान सखि मरि मरि,
एलो, कोथा गेल एने देलो
हरि आमार कालाचाँद प्राणे,
प्राणेर साध सइ कि जानना कृष्ण आनना,
बोलो बोलो तारे राधा प्राणे मरे,
काला विने रइते पारि कइ ?

Sthāyī

+		२		०		३	
-रा	-ा	पा	प-धपा	मा	ग-मगा	रा	सा
०	कइ	कृ	ष्ण०००	ए	ल०००	कुं	जे
धणा	-णा	धा	-णर्सा	-णा	-ध-णधा	प-धपा	मगरा
प्रा०	०	ण	००	०	० ०००	स०००	००इ
मा	मा	धणा	-णा	धा	-धा	णा	णा
दे	रे	कृष्ण	०	दे	०	कृ	ष्ण
धणर्सा	-र्सा	णा	-धणधा	पा	-ा	-पा	-ा
ए ००	०	ने	०००	दे	०	०	०
ना	ना	ना	नर्सा	र्सा	-र्सना	र्सा	-र्सा
रा	धा	जा	ने०	कि	००	गो	०
णा	-णा	धणसा-	-र्स-णधा	पा	-ा	-प--धपा	मगरा
कृ-	०	ष्ण०००	० ०००	ब	०	० ०००	इ००

Antarā

ना	ना	ना	नर्सा	र्सा	-ा	र्सा	र्सना
छि	छि	क	रे०	मा	न	स	खि०
घा	र्सा	ना	घा	घणा	-धा	-पा	-ा
म	रि	म	रि	० ०	०	०	०
घा	धणा	पा	धणा	धा	-पा	मा	-ा
ए	ल०	को	था०	गे	०	ल	०
मा	गा	रा	गा	मा	-गा	रा	सा
ए	ने	दे	लो	ह	०	रि	०

+		२		०		३	
मा	मा	मा	मपा	पा	धा	धा	-णधा
आ	मार	का	ला०	चाँद	प्रा	णे	० ०
पा	धर्सा	र्सा	-ना	-धा	-णधा	पा	-ा
प्रा	णेर	सा	०	०	००	ध	०
रा	रा	मा	मपधा-	पा	-मा	मा	गा
सइ	कि	जा	न०००	ना	०	कृ	ष्ण
रा	गमा	गा	-ा	-रा	-ा	रा	गा
आ	न०	ना	०	०	०	बो	लो
मा	पधा	पा	-ा	मा	-ा	मा	गा
बो	लो०	ता	०	रे	०	रा	धा
रा	गमा	गा	-ा	रा	-रज्ञा	-रा	-सा
प्रा	णे०	म	०	रे	००	०	०
ना	ना	ना	ना	र्सा	र्सना	र्सा	-ा
का	ला	बि	ने	र	इ०	ते	०
णा	-णा	धणर्सा-	र्स-णधा	पा	-ा	-प-धपा	-मगरा-
पा	०	रि०००	००००	क	०	० ०००	०००इ

Composer - Girish Ghosh [Janā nāṭaka] Tuned by - Debkantha Bagchi.
Rāga - Miśra Kānaḍā Tāla - Dādrā.

ओलो सइ, देखलो कत कान!
कथाय कथाय प्राण राखे पाय, शुधु कथार प्राण!
कथाय कथाय जे जन धरे पाय,
केउ येन ना भोले तार कथाय,
कथाय कथाय प्राण राखे पाय,
मजिये चले याय!
मन-मजानेर मजले कथाय थाके ना लो मान;
येमन आदर तेमनि अपमान ।

+			०			+			०		
		सा	सा	सरा	-ा	रा	रा	रा	-ा	रसा	रा
		ओ	लो	स०	इ	दे	ख	लो	०	क०	त
मज्ञा	-ा	मा	रा	सा	-ा	सा	-ा	रा	-ा	मा	पा
का	न	"ओ	लो	स	इ"	दे	ख	लो	०	क	त
मज्ञा	-ा	-ा	-ा	-ा	-ा	मा	मा	-ा	पा	पा	-ा
का०	०	न्	०	०	०	क	था	य	क	था	य
मा	-ा	पा	पा	पा	दा	मा	पा	-ा	दा	दा	पा
प्रा	ण्	रा	खे	पा	य	शु	धु	०	क	था	र्
र्सा	-ा	ज्ञा	रा	सा	-ा						
प्रा	ण्	"ओ	लो	स	इ"						
मा	पा	-ा	ना	ना	-ा	ना	र्सा	पा	-ा	ना	ना
क	था	य	क	था	य	जे	ज	न्	०	ध	रे
र्सा	-ा	-ा	-ा	-ा	-ा	पा	र्सा	र्सा	ना	र्सा	-ा
पा	य	०	०	०	०	के	उ	जे	न	ना	०
ना	र्सा	-ा	नर्सा	रा	णर्सा	णा	दा	-ा	-ा	-दणा	-पा
भो	ले	०	ता०	र्	क	था	य	०	०	००	०
-ा	-ा	-ा	-ा	-ा	-ा	मा	मा	-ा	पा	पा	-ा
०	०	०	०	०	०	क	था	य	क	था	य
मा	-ा	पा	पा	पा	दा	मा	मा	पा	मपा	-दा	मपा
प्रा	ण	रा	खे	पा	ये	म	जि	ये	च०	०	ले०
मा	ज्ञा	-ा	-ा	-ा	-ा	र्ज्ञा	र्ज्ञा	र्ज्ञा	र्रा	र्सा	-ा
या	य	०	०	०	०	म	न्	म	जा	ने	र्

+			०			+			०		
णा	र्सा	णा	दा	पा	-ा	मा	पा	-ा	मपा	-दा	मपा
म	ज	ले	क	था	य	था	के	०	ना०	०	लो०
						[सा	सा	रा	रा	रा	रा]
मा	ज्ञा	-ा	-ा	-ा	-ा	ज्ञमा	मा	मा	रा	सा	-ा
मा	न्	०	०	०	०	ये०	म	न	आ	द	र
		म									
रा	रा	ज्ञा	-ा	मा	मा	पा	-ा	ज्ञा	रा	सा	-ा |||
ते	म	नि	०	अ	प	मा	न्	"ओ	लो	स	इ"

Nāṭya Saṅgīta - "Satī ki kalaṅkiṇi" - Staged in 1847 in National Theatre. Notated by Kaliprasanna Banerji. Tuned by - Madanmohan Barman.

Rāga - Khāmāja Tāla - Khemṭā

धर हे राजबाला एनेछि माला
सुचिकन पर गले जुड़ाक जीवन ।
सुरभी फुले गेँथेछि माला
देखि टले किना कालार मन ॥

Sthāyī

+			२			+			२		
				गा	मा	पा	-ा	-धा	-पधर्सा	णा	धा
				ध	र	हे	०	०	०००	रा	ज
धपा	-मा	-पमा	गा	-मपमपा	-मगा	-रा	-सा	सा	गा	-रगा	गा
बा०	०	००	ला	००००	००	०	०	ए	ने	००	छि
गा	मा	-गमा	पा	-धा	मा	पा	-ा	-ा	-ा	-ा	-ा
मा	ला	००	खु	०	चि	क	०	०	०	०	०
पधा	-पधा	-पमा	-गमा	गा	मा	पा	-ा	ना	-ा	-ा	ना
न०	००	००	००	प	र	ग	०	ले	०	०	जु
ना	-ा	र्सा	-ा	-ा	र्सा	र्स:	-णा	-धा:	-पधा	-णा	-धा
ड़ा	०	क	०	०	जी	ब०	०	००	००	०	०
पा	-ा	-पधपधा	-पमा	गा	मा ||						
न	०	००००	००	"धा	र"						

Antarā

+			२			+			२		
-ा	-ा	पा	ना	पा	-ना	र्सा	-ना	-र्री	र्सा	-ा	-ा
०	०	सु	र	भी	०	फु	०	०	ले	०	०
-ा	-ा	र्सा	र्सा	-ा	ना	र्सा	-ा	ना	गा	मा	-ा
०	०	गैं	थे	०	छि	मा	०	ला	दे	खि	०
पा	-ा	ना	-ा	-ा	ना	ना	-ा	र्सा	-ा	-ा	र्सर्सा
ट	०	ले	०	०	कि	ना	०	का	०	०	लार्
र्स:	-णा	-धा:	-पधा	-णा	-धा	पा	-ा	-पधपध	-मा	गा	मा
म	०	०	००	०	०	न	०	००००	००	"ध	र"

Surchanda - Śāradīyā No, September - 1983

Rabindranath Thakur/Tagore and Rabīndrāsaṅgīta

Rabindranath was born on 25th Baiśākh, 1268 B.S. (7th May 1861) at Jorasanko. He was the fourteenth child of Maharsi Debendranath and Saradadevi. His own autobiography, and biographies written by various authors give an insight into the poet's highly sensitive and creative genius. His own deep knowledge in philosophy and humanity was proverbial. To sum up the contribution of this great personality in the sphere of music, that is - as a musician and music composer, out of his manifold talents and creative faculties, needs a short biographical sketch with the main events of his life.

As a gifted and imaginative child, Rabindranath did not like formal stereotyped education system of schools, although he attended Calcutta Training Academy (1865-66) at the age of five, Oriental Seminary, Normal School and Bengal Academy occasionally till the age of eleven. His real alround education was received at home under his elder brother Hemendranath, who was a disciplinarian and saw to the education of both Jyotirindranath and Rabindranath. This alround training included even wrestling as one of the musts along with literature, scriptures, science, geography, history, languages, art and music. In his later life he was much concerned about the whole system of education and the fruition of Shantiniketan and Vishwabharati were the outcome, because, Gurudev Rabindranath believed in the ancient '*gurukula*' education conducted in the '*tapovanas*', where nature also played a very big role for the upbringing of the young body and mind. He also believed in having art and music as essential subjects of a curriculum along with all other subjects.

From the early age of eight, his talent in composing poems was noticed. Child Rabi was much influenced by the simple verses such as — '*Bṛṣṭi paḍe ṭāpur ṭupur*' or '*Jal paḍe pāta naḍe*' , etc.

At the age of twelve, his '*upanayana*' or sacred thread ceremony was performed. In 1875 he lost his mother when he was only fourteen. In the same year he composed his first *gīti-kavitā* — '*Jval jval citā dvigun dvigun*' for Jyotirindranath's *Sarojinī nāṭaka* in a few hours time. He wrote *Karuṇā, Bhikhāriṇī, Kavi Kāhinī* and *Bhānu Siṃher-padāvalī* between the age of sixteen and seventeen. These were published in *Bhāratī* journal of which he became one of the editors. Incidentally, till the identity of *Bhānu Siṃha* was disclosed, the *padas* composed in Brajabuli, were acclaimed as superior to even Vidyapati's — a feat to achieve at the tender age of sixteen.

Rabindranath went to England for the first time in 1878. At home he was much exposed to Western and Indian classical music, as almost all the Tagores were knowledgeable in both Indian and Western art forms. While in England he learnt as well as rendered vocal Western music and Irish melodies. After his return from England in 1880, Rabindranath was inducted by Jyotirindranath into his own literary group to compose lyrics and tunes. Jyoti inspired him to write operas and the result was '*Valmīki Pratibhā*' and *Kālmṛgayā*'. Jyoti also helped to compose the musical score initially for *Vālmīki Pratibhā.* Rabindranath owed much to his brother who moulded his talents in literature and music in the right direction. The two brothers were very closely associated, although the age difference between them was twelve years. Jyotirindranath was his guide and mentor in all spheres. It was his inspiration through which Rabindranath used Western melodies in the *gīti-nātyas,* composed *dhrupada* oriented *Brahma-saṅgīta* and based *kāvya-saṅgītas* on *rāgas* by composing appropriate lyrics. He introduced new *chandas,* new *tālas,* and his immense contribution of *Rabīndra-saṅgīta* could be preserved for posterity through Jyoti's '*Ākār-mātrik svaralipi*'.

Rabindranath's first song '*Jval jval citā*' composed for Jyoti's *nāṭaka* was tuned by Jyotirindranath himself and so was the song - *Eka sūtre bāndhiyāchi sahasra jīvan.*

Rabindranath's *Vālimīki-pratibhā* was staged in 1881 and the poet himself took part as *Vālmīki.* This was not an ordinary *gītināṭya* or opera but an experimentation in which *padas* were set to tune on *rāga-rāgiṇīs* and Western melodies and not in strict *śāstrīya* principles of *tāla, laya, mātrā* etc. The main aim was to deliver the dialogues of different characters through such melodies which would convey the exact meaning and mood of the *padas.* For the purpose he used both *śāstrīya saṅgīta* and Irish melodies, but more of Indian, and giving more importance to tune than *tāla*. His *Kālmṛgayā* was also influenced by Western melodies.

Other works such as '*Bhagna-hṛday*' (*gīti-nāṭya*), *Rudra-caṇḍa* and '*Europe-Pravāsīr-Patra*' were published in 1881. *Sandhyā-saṅgīta* was published in 1882 and the poet considered this work as his first important work on music.

Rabindranath got married to Mrinalinidevi, a quiet partner to see the success of her wonderful husband. His most favourite sister-in-law Kadambaridevi, wife of Jyotirindranath, inspired him in all his initial compositions. She died in 1884.

Between 1885 and 1891 Rabi composed *Rabichāyā, Kaḍi-o-Komal, Rājarṣi, Māyār-khelā,* etc. The next most important event was the inaugaration of Shantiniketan, the dream child of Kaviguru, on 7th Pauṣa, 1308 B.S., that is 1901. During this time he wrote many books such as *Citrāṅgadā, Goḍāy-galad, Sonār-tarī,* etc. and spent a lot of time in editing and writing in *Bhāratī* journal, besides writing many other books. Important among them were *Kṣudhita-pāṣān, Lakṣmīr-pārīkṣā, Vicitra-galpa* and *Bidāy-abhiśāp*.

Rabindranath was a true nationalist. He read an article in the Town Hall resenting Sedition Act and joined Dhaka Pradesik Sanmelan. He helped Sister Nivedita in the great selfless task of nursing the patients of plague, during the epidemic in Calcutta. He also led the movement against Baṅga-bhaṅga, i.e. partition of Bengal in 1905.

On 23rd November 1902 he lost his wife Mrinalinidevi and in 1905 his father Maharsi Debendranath Thakur. Besides, he lost three of his children - Samindranath, Renuka, and Madhurilata. The death of Jyotirindranath in 1925 and Dwijendranath in 1926 gave him a great blow.

In 1909, Rabindranath composed the immortal *Gītāñjali* besides *Rājā, Jīvansmṛti,* and some national songs. Prior to this, he wrote and composed *Kanikā, Kathā O Kāhinī, Galpaguccha* and many more novels, collection of short stories and poems.

On 12th Jan. 1912 he was honoured by Baṅgīya Sāhitya Parishad. He visited Europe for the third time when he translated *Gītāñjali* in English and showed it to Rothenstein. *Gītāñjali* was recited by poet Yeats in an informal gathering of intellectuals and was hailed by everyone. *Gītāñjali* was then published by India Society and Rabindranath became the recipient of Nobel Prize for his extraordinary literary work, on 13th Nov. 1913. He was also honoured with D. Litt by Calcutta University.

Between the age of 53 and 57, Kaviguru had a busy schedule as series of important visitors came to his *āśrama* of Shantiniketan, he received Knighthood, visited Japan and America to deliver important lectures, met Sadler Commission and Lord Montegue.

In 1919, Rabindranath visited South India and delivered a lecture in Adyar National University as the Chancellor. In the same year he returned the Knighthood to the British Government in protest against Jalianwala massacre.

He established Vishwabharati University in 1919 with three branches: *Sāhitya, Lalitkalā,* and *Saṅgīta.* Sriniketan was another establishement where agriculture, cottage industries and village welfare were the main activities. In Saṅgīta-bhavan, the music *āchāryas* were Bhimrao Hasulkar Śāstrī (1914-1928/29) who taught *Vīṇā, mṛdaṅga* and Hindusthani *śāstrīya-saṅgīta;* Dinendranath taught Bengali songs and Nakuleshwar Goswami taught *esrāj* and vocal music.

In 1920-21, Rabindranath toured Western India and then sailed on a trip to Europe and America. After his return, he gifted away all his property of Shantiniketan to Vishwabharati.

Throughout these years, his pen worked non-stop. Innumerable proses and poetries, articles and his autobiography were written.

The years 1925-26 were extremely busy for the poet. He was invited by the Dhaka University and the Maharaja of Tripura. Soon after, on 11th June 1926, he visited Italy by invitation from King Victor Manuel, who accorded him royal reception. *Citrāṅgadā* was staged in Italian language. He then visited several European countries each of which received him most cordially. In 1927, he toured Malaya, Bali, Java, and Siam (Thailand). Even with all his hectic tours and appointments, he wrote many books.

In 1928, he met Sri Arobindo at Pondichery. In 1929, he was invited by the Canadian Government to deliver speeches. He returned from this visit via Japan and Indo-China. In 1930, he visited France and England again. His lectures at Oxford were published as - '*Religion of Man*'.

In 1931 he received the title of '*Sārva-bhauma*' from Sanskrit College and he delivered a lecture in protest against shooting in the camp of Hijli on Ist, October of the same year. His sensitive mind and deep love for the country could not tolerate any injustice against his country or countrymen. That is how he did not hesitate for a second, to return his knighthood when Jalianwala massacre took place in 1919. When Gandhiji was sent to jail in 1932, he wrote a letter to the British Prime Minister in protest. He felt extremely concerned when Gandhiji started his fast.

He visited Persia (Iran) at the invitation of Reza Shah Pahlavi in 1932, when he visited Iraq also. The Japanese poet Neguchi came to Shantiniketan in 1935 to meet the poet.

Kaviguru received D. Litt. from various universities apart from Calcutta University, viz.

(a) Benaras Hindu University in 1935
(b) Dhaka University in 1936
(c) Osmania University in 1937
(d) Oxford University in 1940 (7th August).

All leaders of the country like Gandhiji, Kasturba, Jawaharal Nehru, Madan Mohan Malaviya, Subhas Chandra Bose and others regarded Rabindranath as '*Gurudeva*'.

The poet led a very busy life even at the age of 79 and 80. He laid the foundation stone of Mahājāti Sadan on 19th August 1939, inaugurated Hindi Bhavan of Vishwabharati on 31st January, and Vidyasagar Smriti Mandir at Midnapore on 16th December of the same year. He received the title—'*Bharat Bhaskar*' from the Maharaja of Tripura.

His innumerable new compositions were published in the mean time, viz. *Bhānu Siṃher patrāvalī, The Child, The Golden Book of Tagore, Gītabitān, Sañcayitā, Tāserdeś, Mālañca, Śeṣ-saptak, Bithikā,* Citrāṅgadā *(Nṛtya-nātya), Śyāmalī, Śyāmā, (Nṛtya-nātya), Naba-jātaka, Chelebelā, Tinsaṅgī, Citralipi, Citrālī* (his drawings and paintings) and many more.

The Nobel Laureate was also hailed as one of the greatest artistes. Exhibition of his paintings and sketches were held in various places of Europe, like London, Paris, Germany, Copenhagen, etc.

His eightieth birthday was celebrated on 25th Baiśākh 1348 B.S. (7th May 1941). He composed his last poem '*Tomār sṛṣṭir path rekhecho ākīrṇa kari*' on 30th July 1941 just prior to his operation. He expired on 7th August 1941 (22nd Srāvaṇa 1348 B.S.) in his ancestral home of Jorasanko. The immortal song composed by Kaviguru '*Samukhe śānti pārābār*' was sung after his demise, as per his wish.

Rabindranath as a musician, music composer

The Jorasanko Thakurbari was a place where both Indian *śāstrīya-saṅgīta* and Western classical music were nurtured side by side. The *saṅgīta-gurus* of Rabindranath were all great masters. Out of them, the ones that influenced him the most from his childhood onwards were: Bishnu Chakravarti, Srikantha Sinha, Maula Bakhs, Jadu Bhatta, Radhikaprasad Goswami and Shyamsundar Misra. Bishnu was his first guru who was a famous pundit of *dhrupada* and *khayāl* and composed specially attractive simple rhymes into *rāgas* and *tālas* to teach the young Tagore children, not to bore them with mechanical *palṭās* of *sargam.* It is his sublime style of renditions that influenced the sensitive mind of Rabindranath, who always rebelled against any formality or compulsion. He was also an admirer of Shrikantha Sinha, whose spontaneous singing in great joy, and singing and dancing in ecstacy, influenced young Rabindranath who picked up the tunes and songs effortlessly. He held Jadu Bhatta in great esteem. Although Rabindranath resented the insistence of Jadu Bhatta to teach him music formally, for which he did not attend his classes, but he learnt from behind the door. He used to grasp many *rāgas* and *bandiśes* from the next room or outisde the room, and composed many songs on the frames of the Hindi *bandiśes* rendered by the *guru* as well as compositions of the maestro's own. The *bandiś* '*Rum jhum barase āju bādaravā*' in *Kāfi*, influenced many of the poet's monsoon compositions. His last two *gurus* were Radhikaprasad Goswami and Shyamsundar Misra. Apart from the deep knowledge of music of Radhikaprasad, Rabindranath appreciated the unique capacity to infuse subtle *rasa* in his *gāyakī*. Other visiting *ustāds* left an indelible mark of pure *śāstrīya saṅgīta* on the mind of the young poet.

Apart from this, the other influences were his own family members, particularly Jyotirindranath, Dwijendranath, his own father, his sister Svarnakumari, eldest brother-in-law Saradaprasanna Bandyopadhyay who was a very fine *sitār* player (learnt from Jwalaprasad Sitari), Dinendranath, his nieces - Pratibhadevi, Saraladevi, and Indiradevi who were always keen and alert to bring some new tunes for their '*Rabi kākā*', as they themselves were experts in Western and Indian music.

Rabindranath, though had limited formal training of Indian classical music in *guru-śisya parampara*, his constant exposure to the *ācāryas* and his own inborn talent made him a success in establishing a new style of music, i.e. '*Rabīndra-saṅgīta*', based on classical music, yet independent of the strict bondage of the *śāstrīya* norms.

Rabindranath gave uppermost importance to *vāṇī* or the *sāhitya* of the composition. He believed that the tune of a song is the vehicle to express the correct and innermost emotions of the lyric and vice versa. Rabindranath considered that the *kāvya* should not be throttled by the burden of *śāstrīya* norms, and on the contrary, should beautify the *padas* of the *kāvya* by being complementary. *Rabīndra-saṅgīta* is essentially *kāvya-pradhān* or *vāṇī-pradhān*, i.e. the lyric plays the most important role. The entire beauty of the song depends on its lyrical value combined with the proper melody and rhythm that are suitable with the composition.

Rabindranath composed his songs in two different ways:

(a) Compose the tune first and then the lyric and
(b) compose the lyric first and then the tune. He preferred the first.

The poet himself has narrated in '*Jīvan Smṛti*' how his Jyotidada used to play different *rāgas* and *rāgiṇīs* on the piano in various ways giving various colours to the same *rāga* and producing unique melodies, and how he started off composing *padas* on these melodies. That was his initial stage of composing songs, i.e.

composing appropriate *padas* for a tune already composed. The *bhāva* or mood of the tune had to be complimentary to the *padas.*

The *padas* of *Rabīndra-saṅgīta* are long, consisting of four *tuks* or stanzas mostly, like the *bandiśes* of *dhrupada,* but there is no scope for *ālāpcāri, baḍhat* or *tāna,* as the songs are complete by themselves. The songs are so beautifully blended with '*Kathā*' (words) and '*sur*' (melody) that there is no necessity to apply *tānas* or *baḍhats.* His best contribution to Bengali music is the role of *sañcāri,* the part between *antarā* and *ābhoga* creating unique beauty in the song, furnishing all the ethical requirements of *tānas.* Each part of the song expresses full musical beauty and the full song is complete by itself creating the satisfaction that is expected. This was possible only by a person of his talent and calibre.

The span of *Rabīndra-saṅgīta* is so vast that it is like the ocean—a confluence of different streams or currents of styles, such as *dhrupada, khayāl, ṭappā, ṭhumrī, bāul, kīrtana,* folk melodies, Western dance tunes, Church music, Irish melodies and even regional traditional songs of Punjab, Gujarat, Maharashtra, Kannad and Tamilnadu.

In the first phase, Rabindranath used mostly *śāstrīya rāgas* and *rāgiṇīs* for the compositions. In the second phase, his experimentations started. He chose different *rāgas* and Western melodies to express the emotional contents of his lyrics to utmost extent. For this purpose, he used different *layas* and *chandas* also. This trend is evident in '*Vālmīki -pratibhā*' and '*Kālmṛgayā*'. In the third phase, along with *rāgas* and *rāgiṇīs,* he used tunes outside *rāga-saṅgīta.* Folk tunes, *bāul, kīrtana* styles, etc. featured in his compositions. In the fourth phase, he composed and established his own style, free from any inhibitions.

The style of Rabindranath is also very special, because it needs a thorough knowledge of *svaras, rāgas, tālas, laya, chanda* and *kāvya,* to be able to express the subtle *bhāva* of the lyrics of *Rabīndra-saṅgīta.* This style also needs a special voice throw, modulation, proper and clear pronunciation and also some knowledge about the various other styles amalgamated in it, such as - *bāul, kīrtana,* Western melodies, *dhrupada, khayāl, ṭappā,* etc.

Rabindranath's keen sense of aesthetic beauty made him a firm believer in composing songs according to the *bhāva* of the lyric. He knew the vast wealth of *rāga-rāgiṇīs* and *chanda* variety in Indian music, which he amply and appropriately used in his exquisite lyrics of innumerable variety. He composed many songs in *dhrupada* style and original *khayāl* style using calm and serious *rāgas* and *tālas.* He used *Jhāptāla* and *Teorā* in songs of comparatively happy mood, while he used *Tintāla* for songs which were more *khayāl* oriented.

Rabindranath's *dhrupada* based songs could be termed as '*dhrupadāṅga*', because he never followed blindly the rules and regulations but maintained the ideals of *śāstrīya-saṅgīta*. He firmly believed that *rāgas* were capable of expressing certain *bhāvas* and that it was the primary function of a *rāga*, which should be concentrated upon. He said that one should find out what are the inherent emotions expressed by each *rāga*, such as of happiness, seriousness, etc. He explained that when one weeps, the *svaras* sort of roll over gently in a slow tempo over the *komala svaras* (flat notes) without any leap, while in a gay mood or happy situation the *svaras* are used in a sprightly manner in a fast tempo.

In a meeting organised by Bethune Society on 19th April, 1881, Rabindranath delivered a lecture on '*Saṅgīta and Bhāva*'. He commented that *rāga Bhairava* brings to the mind the presence of early dawn, while *Purvī*, suggests the dusk. The same particular *komala svaras* used in both, create two different feelings - while *Bhairava* brings forth the sense of dawn welcoming the day, *Pūrvī/Pūrabī*, with *tīvra madhyama* depicts the gradual fading of the day with a sense of pathos. He believed in the inherent qualities of *rāgas* and *rāgiṇīs* and also the time cycle, season and *rasa* theory of *rāgas*. He used *Pañcama* for summer, *Megha* and *Mallāra* for monsoon, *Bhairava* for autum Śrī for fall, *Naṭa-nārāyaṇa* for winter and *Basant* and *Bāhār* for spring. In later creations, he mixed the *rāgas* to express *bhāva* in a profound manner.

Dhrupada style in Rabīndra-saṅgīta

The songs of the first phase constitute of *Brahma-saṅgīta* which were *dhrupada* based and were of serene nature with slow pace. He used *jhaṭkā, mīnḍ, ās, gamaka* and heavy *tālas* like - *Cautāla, Rūpaka, Dhāmār, Teorā, Jhāptāla, Surfāktā* etc. *Sañcāri* played a very important role in these songs. Tagore's *Sañcāris* were very well defined and brought out the aesthetic value of the *rāga* used in the *bandiś*, in a unique manner. Most of his *Brahma-sangītas* were composed on the basis of *dhrupada* songs of maestros such as Tansen, *bandiśes* of *Bishnupur-gharāna* and songs rendered and composed by Bishnu Chakravarti and Jadu Bhatta. Some examples are as follows:

	Rāga	Tāla
1. *Āji heri sansār amṛtamaya*	*Rāga Bilāvala*	*Cautāla.*
2. *Prathama ādi taba śakti*	*Dīpak Pañcama*	*Surfāktā.*
3. *Ānanda tumi swāmī*	*Bhairavī*	*Surfāktā.*
4. *Devādi deva Mahādeva*	*Devagiri*	*Surfāktā.*
5. *Mahārājā eki sāje*	*Bihāga*	*Jhāptāla.*
6. *Hṛdaya nandana bane*	*Lalitā-gaurī*	*Jhāptāla.*
7. *Śubhra āsane virājo*	*Bhairava*	*Āḍā-cautāla.*
8. *Ke re oi ḍākiche*	*Alhaiyā-bilāvala*	*Dhāmār.*
9. *Tumi phirāle more bāre bāre*	*Naṭa-mallār*	*Ektāla.*

The poet has maintained perfect balance between the *rāga* and the *vāṇī* or lyric of his compositions.

(About 156 songs have been compiled by Indiradevi)

A *dhrupada* example

Rāga - Dīpak Pañcama Tāla - Surfāktā.

प्रथम आदि तब शक्ति,
आदि परमोज्ज्वल ज्योति तोमारि हे गगने गगने ।
तोमार आदि वाणी बहिछे तब आनन्द,
जागिछे नब नब रसे हृदये मने ।
तोमार चिदाकाशे भाते सूरय चन्द्र तारा,
प्राण तरंग उठे पवने ।
तुमि आदि कबि, कबि गुरु तुमि हे,
मन्त्र तोमार मन्द्रित सब भुवने ॥

+				२		३			
							धा	मा	धा
							प्र	थ	म
र्सा	-ा	-ा	ना	धा	धा	मा	-गा	-मा	॥मा
आ	०	०	दि	त	ब	श	०	क्	ति
मा	-ा	-ा	मा	गा	गा	ऋा	-ा	सा	सा
आ	०	०	दि	प	र	मो	ज्	ज्व	ल
(न्)सा	-ा	गा	गा	मा	-ा	धा	धा	मा	धा
ज्यो	०	ति	तो	मा	०	रि	हे	ग	ग
ना	-र्सा	र्सा	र्सा	ऋा॑	-ना	-ा	धा	मा	धा
ने	०	ग	ग	ने	०	०	"प्र	थ	म"
मा	-धा	-ना	र्सा	ऋा॑	-ा	र्सा	र्सना	-र्सा	र्सा
तो	मा	०	र	आ	०	दि	वा०	०	णी

+ न				२		३ न			
सां	सां	सां	-।	सां	सां	सां	ना	-धा	ना }
ब	हि	छे	०	त	ब	आ	न	न्	द
सां	-।	गां	गां	र्रा	र्रा	सां	ना	सां	सां
जा	०	गि	छे	न	ब	न	ब	र	से
ध ना	ना	सां	सां	र्रा	-ना	-।	धा	मा	धा ‖
ह्व	द	थे	म	ने	०	०	"प्र	थ	म"
‖{सा	-।	मा	-।	मा	मा	मा	-।	गा	-।
तो	०	मा	०	र	चि	दा	०	का	०
मा	-धा	धा	-गा	मा	मा	गा	-।	र्रा	सा
शे	०	भा	०	०	ते	सू	०	र	य
सा	-गा	गा	मा	-धा	धा	मा	धा	धा	ना
च	न्	द्र	ता	०	रा	प्रा	ण	त	र
-सां	सां	ध ना	ना	सां	सां	र्रा	-ना	-धा	-। }
ङ	ग	उ	ठे	प	ब	ने	०	०	०
{मा	-।	धा	-।	ना	-।	सां	सां	सां	-।
तु	०	मि	०	आ	०	दि	क	वि	०
सां	-।	गां	गां	र्रा	-।	सां	-ना	सां	सां
म	न्	त्र	तो	मा	र्	म	न्	द्रि	त
ध ना	ना	सां	सां	र्रा	-ना	-।	धा	मा	धा ‖‖
स	ब	भु	व	ने	०	०	"प्र	थ	म"

Ṭappā-aṅg in Rabīndra-saṅgīta

Rabindranath was very much influenced by the *Ṭappā* style of Shori Miya. In *Māyār-khelā* and some other compositions he used this style using fast *tānas* and

Giṭkirī. He also fashioned some of his compositions on North Indian *ṭappā-bandiśes* that attracted him, e.g.

	Original bandiś	Rabīndra-saṅgīta	Rāga	Tāla
1.	*Ve pariyā tāṇḍe*	*Ke basila āji*	*Sindhu*	*Madhyamāna*
2.	*Miyā ve mānula*	*Hṛdaya bāsanā mama*	*Jhinjhiṭ*	
3.	*Āju mana bhāvana*	*Niśidin cāhare*	*Jogiyā*	

Rabindranath was also an admirer of Ndhubabu's *ṭappās,* particularly *Ye (Je) yātanā (Jātanā) Yatane (Jatane) mane mane, man jāne,* - based on Shori Miyā's *O miyā jāne wāle (tānu)*', in *Khamāja rāga.* Tagore followed both the *bandiśes* in his own composition - '*E parabāse rabe ke hāy*', but he set it in *Sindhu rāga* and *Madhyamāna tāla.*

Later, Tagore adopted a style in *ṭappā* which was devoid of fast *tānas.* This unique technique used by him is noticed in: *Āmi rūpe tomāy bholābanā*; *Āji je rajanī jāy*; *Sārthaka janama Mā go,* etc. These songs were set in moderate or slow tempo and consisted of a little *tāna-vistāra* of *ṭappā* style and *bol-tānas.* These were composed mostly on *rāgas* like *Kāfi, Jhīnjhiṭ, Sindhu, Bhairavī, Khamāj* and *tālas* like *Madhyamāna* and *Āḍā-ṭhekā.*

Ṭhumrī and Khayāl-aṅg in Rabīndra-saṅgīta

Khayāl and *Ṭhmrī* styles are not available in abundance in *Rabīndra-saṅgīta,* as he was more in favour of *dhrupada* and *ālāpa* of *rāga-saṅgīta.* Nevertheless there are quite a few songs which fall under *Khayāl-aṅg* but minus the techniques applied in this style. Some examples are as follows:

		Rāga	Tāla
(a)	*Ore bhāi phāgun legeche bane bane*	*Paraj - bāhār*	*Tritāla.*
(b)	*Sīmār mājhe Asīm tumi*	*Kedār-Chāyānaṭ*	*Tritāla.*
(c)	*Mandire mama ke āsile*	*Āḍānā*	*Ektāla.*
(d)	*Amala dhabala pāle legeche*	*Bhairavī*	*Ektāla.*
(e)	*More bāre bāre*	*Naṭ-mallār*	*Ektāla.*

Some examples of Ṭap-khayāl style

(a) *Bandhu raho raho sāthe*
(b) *Ásru bharā bedanā*
(c) *Kār bāśī niśi bhore*

Tagore's compositions on *Ṭhumrī-aṅg* are very few and are not composed on the themes of *śṛṅgāra-rasa* or erotic sentiment which is essential for this style. These songs do not *strictly* conform to the norms of *ṭhumrī*, but have been classified under this style because of their *ṭhumrī* mood. These songs are:

		Rāga	Tāla
(a)	*Tumi kichu diye jāo mor prāṇe*	*Miśra rāga*	*Tritāla*
(b)	*Ki sur bāje āmār prāṇe*	*Pilu Baravā*	*Tritāla*
(c)	*Āmār ekṭi kathā*	*Bhairavī*	*Dādrā*
(d)	*Erā parke āpan kare*	*Pīlu Barvā*	*Khemṭā.*

There is another example which the poet composed on a Hindi ṭhumrī - -

Hindi composition	Rabīndra-saṅgīta
Mahārājā kevadiyā	*Khelār sāthī bidāy dvār kholo*

Kīrtana style in Rabīndra-saṅgīta

Rabindranath paid a great tribute to *kīrtana* as a style which expressed emotions and sentiments of the *padas* through appropriate tunes adapted from *rāgas* and *rāgiṇīs,* yet out of the bondage of strict rules.

His *kīrtana* compositions may be divided into ṭwo categories: a) *anusṛta* or imitation and b) *pravartita,* meaning introduction or innovation of new techniques. Rabindranath adopted the special feature of *Kīrtana,* i.e. changing *rāga, tāla, laya* and *chanda* according to the *bhāva* of the *padas* in the same composition, but he was not in favour of adding too many *ākhars* in a composition that were not complimentary to each other. His *kīrtana* compositions constitute of four *tuks* or stanzas.

In the initial stage, he composed a few *kīrtanāṅga* or *Kīrtana* based songs with *ākhars,* e.g. '*Ohe jīvana vallabha, Ohe sādhana durlabha*'. This song was set in Japa tāla of 12 *mātrās.* He used to sing this song in his melodious voice adding *ākhars,* as follows:

Āmi marmera kathā, antara vyāthā, kichui nāhi kaba,
śudhu jīvana mana caraṇe dinu, bujhiyā laha saba.
Ākhar: 1. *dinu caraṇa tale,*
2. *kathā jā chilo, dinu caraṇa tale,*
3. Pr*āṇer bojhā bujhe lao, dinu caraṇa tale,*
āmi ki ār kabo - - - -

There are a few more examples of *kirtanāṅga* songs with *ākhar:*

(a) *Āmi jene śune tabu bhule āchi*
(c) *Ke jānita tumi ḍākibe āmāy*

(c) *Tumi kāche nāi bole*
(d) *Mājhe mājhe taba dekhā pāi.*

Later, he composed *kīrtanāṅga padas* without any *ākhar.* These fall under the second category of *'pravartita'*, which were novel in character, e.g.

(a) *Āmi praṇami tomāre*
(c) *Āmār man mānenā*
(c) *Āmār nā balā bāṇīr*
(d) *Tomrā jā balo tāi balo, etc.*

Rabindranath was the pioneer in liberating *kīrtana* from its overwhelming *bhakti* element and some times unnecessary expansion of the tune which tends to become monotonous. He composed his *kīrtanas* in three different ways: - the usual style; based on *bāul* tunes; and based on *rāgas.* In the first category the following songs are well known:

(a) *Ābār more pāgal kare dibe ke*
(b) *Khā̃cār pākhī chilo sonār khā̃cāṭite*

The examples of songs under the second category are :

(a) *Ānmanā ānmanā,*
(c) *Āji e nirālā kuñje, etc.*

The songs under the third category are :

(a) *Āmār nayaṇa bhulāno ele,*
(b) *Laho laho tule laho, etc.*

Rabindranath's favourite *kīrtaniyā* was Shibnath Saha of Janipur, (Kushthia, Bangladesh).

A touch of *ḍhap-kīrtana* is noticeable in Tagore's *Citrāṅgadā.* The songs are. a) *Rodana bharā e basanta,* b) *Binā sāje sāji,* etc. The poet has used many *tālas* of Hindusthani classical music for his *kīrtana*-based songs, e.g. :

(a) *Ābār more pāgal kore dibe ke - Jhaptāla,*
(a) *Āmār nā balā bāṇīr ghana yāminīr - Dādrā,*
(c) *Āsana tale māṭīr pare - Thumrītāla.*

Rāmprasādī style in Rabīndra-saṅgīta

The poet applied this style in some of his compositions in *Vālmīki pratibhā* and patriotic songs, e.g.

(a) *Ekbār torā mā baliyā ḍāk*
(b) *Śyāmā ebār cheḍe esechi Mā*

(c) *Āmrā milechi āj māyer ḍāke*
(d) *Āmi i śudhu rainu bākī, etc.*

Bāul and folk tunes of Bhāṭiyāli, Sāri, etc. in Rabīndra-saṅgīta

Bāul faith and *Bāul* music left a deep impression on the very sensitive mind of Kaviguru. He had an estate in East Bengal now in Bengladesh, called Shilaidaha, where he stayed for a few years. This gave him the opportunity to come in close contact with the *Baul* sect of that area. The poet realised his '*Maner mānuṣ*', i.e: 'Inner Being', when he came close to the *Bāuls* of Shilaidaha. They were deep in love with their '*Maner mānuṣ*' whom they wanted to know intimately. Rabindranath called his *Maner mānuṣ*—'*Jīvan Devatā*' and composed many songs on the basis of *Bāul* compositions such as: *Āmi kothāy pābo tāre, āmār maner-mānuṣ jere ....nibhāi keman kore, mari hāy hāy re* . . . . .and *Hari nām diye jagat mātāle* . . . . etc. Kaviguru called himself Rabindra *Bāul* and composed:

(a) *Āmār sonār Bāṅglā - on the model of Āmi kothāy pābo tāre,*
(b) *Jodi tor ḍāk śune keu nā āse - on Hari nām diye jagat mātale,*
(c) *Je tomāy chāḍe chāḍuk - on Man mājhi sāmāl sāmāl, and many more songs.*

Some compositions are called *Ardha Bāul,* e.g.

(a) *Hṛdayer a kul o kul,*
(b) *Tār anta nāi go nai,*
(c) *Ore bhīru tomār hāte*
(d) *Ogo dakhina hāoya, etc.*

Rabindranath's *Bāul* songs were mostly based on *rāga Pīlu* but touches of *rāgas* like *Yaman-Kalyāṇa, Paraja, Deśa, Malhāra* or *Gauḍsāraṅga* are also observed.

There are two *tālas* that are mainly used in *Bāul* songs of Rabindranath, viz: a) *Dādra* of 3 *mātrās* and b) *Kāhārvā* of 4 *mātras.* In a few songs, *Jhaptāla, Ṭhumrītāla, Surfāktā* and *Khemṭā* of 6 *mātrās* have been used. The tempo of his *Bāul* songs are generally medium fast or fast.

The normal *Bāul* songs are of stereotype style but Tagore brought in blended *rāgas* and *rāgiṇīs,* beautiful and sophisticated language, proper *tuks* like *dhrupada* compositions and variety in *tāla* and *chanda.* Some of his compositions are categorised as *Bāuliyā-kīrtana,* viz: a) *Bajre tomār bāje bā̃śī,* b) *Āj dhāner khete roudra chāyāy,* etc. *Sāri* and *Bhāṭiyālī* tunes of the riverine Bengal also has a niche in *Rabīndra-saṅgīta,* but not as much as *Bāul* or *Kīrtana* or *rāga-saṅgīta.* The song examples are:

Bhāṭiyālī	*Grām chāḍā oi rāṅgā māṭir path.*
Sārigāna	(a) *Ebār tor marā gāṅge,* (b) *Tomār kholā hāoyā.*

Rabindranath was influenced by several Bāul*s*, viz. Lalan Faqir/Sai, Faqir Chand, Madan Baul, Padma Lochana, Ishan Yugi, and Jaga Kaivarta. Lalan Sai was a subject of Shilaidaha Zamindari and had a particular rapport with the poet who published many of Lalan's songs. The poet was also very much impressed with *Bāul* Gagan Harkara's phrase — '*Āmār maner mānuṣ*' used in the compositions and *ākhar* of '*Mari hāy hāy re*'.

Pā̃cālī in Rabindra-saṅgīta

Pā̃cālī had influenced the young and tender mind of the poet when he heard Kishori Chattopadhyay, his father's attendant, hum and sing these songs. Earlier on, Kishori was a singer in a *Pā̃cālī* group and Rabindranath learnt from him - (a) *Ore bhāi Jānakīre diye eso dhan,* (b) *Prān to anta holo,* (c) *Bhābo Śrīkānta narakāntakārīre nitānta, kritānta bhayānta habe tabe,* etc. These were compositions of Dasarathi Ray, and Rabindranath composed a few songs on the basis of these, e.g:

(a) *Ore bhāi Jānakīre diye eso ban*
Je lakṣmaṇ kari nirikṣan, re Lakṣmaṇ,
Bipad ghaṭila bilakṣaṇ ———— Rāga Soraṭ, Kavvālī Tāla.

(b) *Prāṇ to anta holo āji āmār kamala ā̃khi,*
Ekbār hṛdaya kamale dā̃ḍāo dekhi ———— Alhaiyā, Ektāla.

Other styles in Rabīndra-saṅgīta

The poet was also influenced by *Maṅgalagīti, Kathakatā, Ākhḍāi, Half Ākhḍāi, Kavigāna* and *Vaiṣṇava-padāvalīs.*

Vālmīki-pratibhā has traces of *Maṅgalagīti* from Biharilal's *Sāradā-Maṅgala.*

Vaiṣṇava *padāvalīs* perhaps had the greatest influence and he composed *Bhānusiṃher-padāvalī* at the age of sixteen under the pseudonym of Bhānu Siṃha, keeping his identity a secret. The choice of the pen-name was also very appropriate, meaning the same as Rabindranath. For a long time the compositions of *Bhānusiṃher-padāvalī* were considered to be of someone as talented as Vidyāpati, till his identity was disclosed. These compositions in Brajabuli are very special creations of the young poet. The famous *padas* are:

(a) *Śāṅana gagane ghora ghana ghaṭā, - in kīrtana style, set on Malhār rāga*
(b) *Maraṇare tuhu mama Śyāma samān - Bhairavī - Ektāla.*
(c) *Śunalo śunalo bālikā - Bhairavī - Khemṭā tāla.*
(d) *Sajanī sajanī Rādhikālo - Mājh - Kavvālī tāla.*
(e) *Āju sakhi muhumuhu - Bihāga - Kavvālī tāla.*

There are 22 *padas* in *Bhānusiṃher-padāvalī* and are compiled in *Gītabitān* part III. Out of these, notated copies of 9 *padas* are available in *Svarabitān* part 21.

Rabindranath composed many songs on various regional styles of India and incorporated some South Indian *rāgas* in his compositions. His eldest brother Dwijedranath first introduced South Indian *rāgas* in composing Bengali songs, e.g: *Bhajare bhajare bhava khaṇḍane,* on the example of the Tamil song — *Namāmi Mahiṣāsura Mardinī (rāga Nārāyaṇī).* Satyendranath and Jyotirindranath also had followed their elder brother's example. Rabindranath composed some songs on *Bhajans* of Mysore, Tamilnadu, Gujarat, Maharashtra, and Punjab. Some of his *padas* based on South Indian *rāgas* and compositions are:

(a) *Āji śubhadine pitāra bhavane —rāga Khamāja, based on Pūrna candrāsane*
(b) *Baḍa āsā kare esechigo kache —Karṇātik Jhījhit.*
(c) *Nilāñjana chāyā—based on Brndāvana lolā.*
(d) *Bāsantī he bhuvana mohinī —based on Mīnākṣī me mudam - raga Pūrvakalyāṇī*
(e) *Bāje karuṇa sure —on Rāga Siṃhendra-madhyama.*

The poet composed a few songs on the basis of Kannada songs, during his stay in Bombay. They are:

(a) *Baḍo āsā kare esechi.*
(b) *Sakātare oi kāndiche.*

Some compositions after Gujrati bhajans:

(a) *Kothā āch prabhu esechi dīna hīna*
(b) *Nami nami Bhāratī , etc.*

Compositions after Sikh bhajans:

(a) *Bāje bāje ramya bīnā—Yaman-kalyāṇa - Teorā*
(b) *Gaganer thāle rabi*—based on Guru Nanak's *dohā—Gaganame thāla baṇi*—Jayjayanti-Jhāptāla.

The poet composed the song '*Je-āmāre eneche ei*' on *tālas* of Candy dance of Ceylon (Srilanka).

Tagore's compositions of patriotic songs or svadeśī-saṅgīta

Around mid 19th century a strong feeling of nationalism was aroused in the minds of the people against the British rule by some noted intellectuals who realised the painful process of slavery they were going through under foreign domination. Jorasanko Thakurbari's contribution in this direction was immense. As has been already mentioned in the article on Jyotirindranath, Hindu Melā was established in 1867 and with it started a new trend of composing songs on nationalistic themes. The first national song or *Jātīya gāna/saṅgīta,* as it was called, was composed by Satyendranath, viz. '*Gāo Bhārater Jai*'. To arouse excitement and enthusiasm, appropriate *chanda* and *laya* were used. Jyotirindranath published a book called *Jātīya-saṅgīta,* compiling the compositions of his brothers and others who took part in the movement.

Influenced by Hindu Melā and later Sañjīvanī Sabhā, Rabindranath composed many songs but one of his earliest compositions '*Eka sūtre bāndhiyāchi sahasra jīvan*' is very famous. It was tuned in *Khamāja* rāga. When sung in fast tempo many *jātīya* songs gave the impression of marching tunes. His songs for patriotism are perhaps the richest in expressing variety of emotive love for the country, greatness of the country and arousing people for the country. Some songs are serene in temperament such as: '*Sārthaka janama āmār*'—(*Bhairavī*), '*Āji Bāṅglā deśer hṛday hote*'—(*Bibhās*), *Āmār somār Bāṅglā*'—(*Bāul*), '*Āmrā milechi āj Māyer ḍāke*'—(*Ramprasādī*), etc.

Some songs express exitement, such as: *Nāi nāi bhay; Saṅkocera bihvalatā; Deśa deśa nandita kari; Sarba kharvatāre dahe,* etc. He preferred and stressed on *rāgas* like *Hamīr* and *Bhupālī* for songs which were more suited for chorus singing.

His patriotic songs may be divided into three sections — a) songs composed before 1906 when *Baṅga-bhaṅga* movement started, b) during the movement, and c) after the movement. The pre-movement songs were mostly *rāga* based, e.g. *Eka sūtre; Ayi viṣādinī vīṇā; Tomāri tare Mā sāpinu; Eki andhakār e Bhāratabhūmi;* etc., while during the movement the songs composed were mostly *kīrtana* or *bāul* based, e.g. *Ebār tor marā gāṅge; Bāṅglār māṭi; Jodi tor ḍāk śune keu; Āji Bāṅglā deśer hṛday hote; Āmār sonār Bāṅglā,* etc. The third group consisted of songs which were of unique nature. In these songs both *vāṇī* and *sur* were distinctive, e.g. *Jana gana mana; He mor citta; Deśa deśa nandita kari; Āmāder jātrā holo śuru,* etc. Rabindranath did not believe that, Western marching songs were the best in expressing or arousing exitement or *viṣama-chandas,* meaning—irregular metrical compositions were necessary to create this mood. He composed many songs in simple *chandas* of *Dādrā, Kahārvā, Tritāla,*etc.to express the sentiment of enthusiasm, e.g.

(a) *Oi mahāmānava āse - Bhairav - Kahārvā.*
(b) *Āmrā nūtan yauvaneri dūt - Khamāj - Dādrā.*
(c) *Khara bāyu boy bege - Kalyāṇ - Kahārvā, etc.*

Rabindranath had set tune to Bankimchandra's '*Vande Mātaram*' and sang the same on 12th Dec, 1896, in the session of Congress. It was sung again in 1917 in Wellington Square. He also sang — '*Kena ceye ācha Mā mukha pāne*' in Town Hall in 1906.

Rabindranath composed '*Jana Gana Mana*' in December 1911, when a friend of his, holding a high post in the government, requested him to compose a poem in honour of George V who was then visiting India. Disgusted with such a degrading request, the poet who was a true nationalist, composed the song — '*Jana gana mana*' in praise of the God Almighty who is the real controller of India's destiny and not the British-raj. However, in certain quarters he was misundrestood which gave great pain to him. Later, this very song was selected as the National Anthem of India (see *svadeśī-saṅgīta*).

Stotras from the Vedas and Upaniṣads:

Rabindranath was a scholar of the ancient scriptures as his father had introduced study of *Upaniṣads* and the *Vedas* in Brahmo Samaj during *upāsanā* (prayer). He was also inspired by *Gāyatrī mantras* after his *upanayana* (sacred thread ceremony). Initially he had tuned a few *stotras* in the same ancient principle of using just a few *svaras.* Later, he tuned these in the style of *rāgālāpa,* giving importance to short and long vowels maintaining proper *chanda.* These were devoid of *tālas.* Some *ślokas* were tuned after Church music and his later creations were in a variety of tuneful *rāgas,* blended according to the meaning of the *ślokas.* The first few *ślokas* that he set to tune were:

(a)	*Tvamīśvarāṇāṃ paramaṃ Maheśvara*	*Upaniṣad.*
(b)	*Śṛṇvantu viśve amṛtasya putrāḥ*	*Ṛgveda.*
(c)	*Saṃ gacchadhvaṃ saṃ vadadhvaṃ*	*Ṛgveda.*

Later, he set to tune some more *ślokas* from *Ṛgveda* for his play - '*Tapatī*' and some *Bauddha mantras* for the dance dramas, viz: *Caṇḍālikā* and *Naṭīr-pūjā.* e.g:

(a)	*Om namo Buddhāya gurave*	*Bauddha mantra*
(b)	*Uttamāṅgena vandehaṃ*	*Bauddha mantra*
(c)	*Namo namo Buddha divākarāya*	*Bauddha mantra*

All these *ślokas, stotras* and *mantras* were tuned so aptly that the sereneness and auspiciousness are revealed to the maximum.

Western tunes in Rabīndra-saṅgīta:

Apart from experimenting with various tunes from Western music, Rabindranath also adapted tunes from Church music in some of his devotional and serious philosophical songs, e.g. *Tomār holo śuru; Satya maṅgala premamaya tumi; Ānandaloke maṅgalāloke; Āji śubha dine pitāra bhavane,* and many others.

During his early life he experimented with Irish melodies in *Vālmīki-pratibhā* and *Kālmṛgayā* but these melodies were given an Indian character. Rabindranath also used the technique of abrupt voice change to enhance beauty of expression, e.g. *Jāgaraṇe jāy bibhāvarī; Ke bale jāo;* etc. He used Western tunes in a few songs of *vīrrasa* and *hāsya rasa.*

Nāṭya-saṅgīta of Rabindranath:

Rabindranath's n*āṭyas* (Dramas) may be divided into the following categories: *Nṛtya-nāṭya, Gīti-nāṭya, Kāvya-nāṭya, Gadya-nāṭya, Vyāṅga/Hāsya-nāṭya, Rūpaka-nāṭya, Ṛtu-nāṭya,* etc. Out of these, *Nṛtya-nāṭya, Gīti-nāṭya* and *Ṛtu-nāṭya* were particularly dominated by music.

(a) *Nṛtya-nāṭya* (Dance-drama):

Tagore was much impressed and inspired by the dance-dramas of Java. He considered dance as an essential part of the curriculum of his university along with music, drama and painting. He himself used to dance and encouraged everyone, even the professors and teachers to participate. He composed *Nṛtya-nāṭyas* specially suited for dancing, acting and singing and thus promoted dancing through Vishwabharati as an art form. Previously dancing was considered to be a profession of the nautch girls only.

His famous *Nṛtya-nāṭyas* are: *Naṭīr-pūjā, Śyāmā, Citrāṅgadā, Caṇḍālikā,* etc.

(b) *Gīti-nāṭyas*

The aim of this type of dramas was to act through songs, like the operas. His famous *gīti-nāṭyas* are: *Vālmīki-pratibhā, Kālmṛgayā, Māyār-khelā, Śāpmocan,* etc. Some of these are '*Gāner sūtre nāṭyer mālā*' meaning — a garland of *nāṭya* strung through the string of *gānas* or songs, viz . *Vālmīki pratibhā* and *Kālmṛgayā,* which can not be enjoyed unless it is staged or acted along with the songs. But *Māyār-khelā* is the opposite, i.e. '*Nāṭyer sūtre gāner mālā*' where songs are more important than acting. He employed various *rāgas* and change of *layas* in such a manner, that the right mood and correct delivery of the dialogue would be expressed.

To express weeping and pathos he used *rāgas* like:

Gārā-Bhairavī	*Hā ki daśā holo āmār.*
Gaurī	*Balba ki ār balba khuḍo.*

To express laughter he used:

Pīlu	*Path bhulechis satyi baṭe*
Kānaḍā	*Hāh hāh bhāyā khāppā, etc.*

To express happiness he used:

Khamāja	*Eka ḍore bāndhā āchi*
Yaman Kalyāṇa	*Ei belā sabe mile calo ho*
Bhāṭiyārī	*Eta śikhecho kothā muṇḍa mālinī.*

To express various moods, *laya* used to be changed adhering to the *mātrās* of *tālas* but not too strictly:

Miśra Bāgeśrī	*Chāḍbanā bhāi*
Naṭa-nārāyaṇa	*Ār nā ār nā*
Bāhār	*Gahane gahane jā re torā*

Some songs were set to tune without *tāla*, to fit the particular dialogue appropriately.

Ṛtu-nāṭyas were *Basanta, Phālgunī, Śeṣ-barṣaṇ, Śāradotsava, Sundar,* etc. The songs of these *nāṭyas* were tuned on *rāgas* that were appropriate for those seasons.

The poet himself classified his innumerable songs under a few main heads. They are: *Pūjā, Prārthanā, Prema, Prakṛti, Vicitra, Ānuṣṭhānik, Gītināṭya, Nṛtyanāṭya, Bhānusiṃher-padāvalī, Nāṭagīti* and *Jātīya/Svadeśī-saṅgita*..

Rāgas in Rabīndra-saṅgīta:

Rabindranath possesed a tuneful voice with a wide range, covering the upper *saptaka* at ease and could grasp the nature of a *rāga* in a short time. That is why, even without formal or rigorous training, he grasped *rāgas* and *tālas* in depth just by listening to the various masters of music who stayed at Jorasanko Thakurbari or came to perform.

At the first stage of his life, his music compositions reflected the *rāga-saṅgīta* that had influenced him by Bishnu Chakravarti, Jadu Bhatta and others. His songs based on *rāga-saṅgīta* may be divided into three categories: a) *Brahma-saṅgīta* - based on pure Hindusthani *bandiśes* b) other *rāga-pradhān gītis,* and c) *gītis* of mixed *rāgas.*

After the first stage, he composed melodies from pure *rāgas,* mixed *rāgas* and *rāgiṇīs* and also innovated new *tālas* to suit the *chandas* of his lyrics. He himself admitted that he depended on classical *rāgas* and *rāgiṇīs,* but his greatest skill was in blending these in a unique manner to yield a melody that would express the emotional content of his lyric.

Intially, Tagore mainly used about eighty *rāgas* but later he made use of twenty *rāgas* and *miśrarāga-rāgiṇīs* in his own creative way. A list of *rāgas* and a few *rāga* based compositions are given below: *Miśra-kāfi, Pūrvī, Bāhār, Bihāga, Hamīr, Śaṅkarā, Kāmoda, Malkauns, Toḍī, Mallāra, Yaman-bhupālī, Paraja-bāhār, Deśkār, Śrī, Sindhu, Miśra-mallāra, Soraṭh, Gauḍ-mallāra, Kānaḍā, Naṭ-mallāra, Bṛndāvanī-sāraṅga, Yaman-kalyāṇā, Kedāra, Āsāvarī, Baḍahaṃsa-sāraṅga, Meghā, Bhairava, Gauḍā, Bāgeśrī, Jhījhiṭ, Sarfardā, Devgiri, Śyāma, Suhā-kānaḍā, Bhupālī, Sohanī, Gurjarī-toḍī, Śaṅkarābharaṇ, Lalitāgaurī, Sindhuvijay, Meghāvalī.* etc.

Varieties of *Toḍī, Kānaḍā, Mallāra, Bhairava* and *Sāraṅga* are found in his compositions and also rare *rāgas* such as *Sindhuvijay* and *Meghāvalī.*

(a)	*Oi dekhā jāy ānanda dhām*	*Sindhuvijay.*
(b)	*Man je āśā laye*	*Meghāvalī.*
(c)	*Din jodi holo abasān*	*Vairāgī-toḍī.*
(d)	*Bimala ānanda jāgo*	*Bāhāadurī-toḍī.*
(e)	*Nūtan prāṇ dāo*	*Lācārī-toḍī.*
(f)	*Prabhāte bimala ānande*	*Gurjarī-toḍī, - and many more.*

Tagore composed some of his songs in various *miśra-rāgas,* some combinations being the outcome of his own experimentation, for example:

Barvā + Bhairava	*Ākula keśe āse.*
Yaman + Pūrvī	*Āmār godhuli lagana.*
Bāhār + Bāgeśrī	*Āmār milana lāgi. - etc.*

Earlier, when the poet mixed the *rāgas,* they maintained their specific identity, but later, he blended them to create a new melody. The following are examples of his early days of experimentation:

Deśa + Sindhu	*Āmār jā āche āmi sakali dite pāri.*
Bihāga + Khamāja	*Sakhi bhāvanā kāhāre bale.*

Rabindranath blended six morning rāgas, viz: *Lalita, Bibhāsa, Rāmkeli, Āsāvarī, Jogiyā, Bhairavī,* and created a melody to set the following:

Āche duḥkha, āche mṛtyu
Āmār jābār samay holo
Ādhār rajanī pohālo
Ālora amala kamala khāni, - etc.

Most of the songs of *Gītāñjali* are composed on tunes blended with more than two *rāgas.*

Like other famous *nāyakas,* such as Tansen, Carju, Surdas, Mirabai and others, Rabindranath also created variety (*vaicitrya*) in *Rāga Mallāra/ Malhāra.*

While blending the *rāgas,* Kaviguru was alert to maintain *rasa* and *svara-saṅgati* that would bring out the beautiful meanings of his *kāvya*: '*Āmār jīvana pātra uchaliyā*' was composed in *Rāmkeli,* but using *komala gāndhāra* a touch of *Bhairavī* was introduced to express the *karuṇa rasa* of the *padas.*

He some times blended more than three *rāgas* in some of his later creations, e.g: *Pīlu + Barvā + Sāhānā + Mallāra — Akāraṇe abelāy mor paḍla; Alhaiyā + Chāyānaṭā + Kedāra + Bihāga + Hamīr + Bhairavī — Arūp tomār bāṇi.*

Rabindranath sometimes changed one or two basic *svaras* of a *rāga,* or added one, to express the correct *rasa* and *bhāva* of a lyric, e.g. *Kedāra* with two *niṣādas*; deleting *tīvra madhyama* in *Rāmkeli* and instead using *komala gāndhāra*; blending

Rāmkeli and *Bhairava* by adding *pañcama* and *gāndhāra*; using both *dhaivatas* in *Purvī* (Tagore called *Pūrvī - Pūrabī*); using *komala ṛsabha* in *Āsāvarī* like the old style, e.g. *Āmār jābār belāy pichu ḍāke, Tomār sur śunāye,* etc.; using different *svara* combinations in *Bhairavī* to bring out unique qualities of the *rāga*. He even used *tīvra-madhyama* and all *śuddha-svaras* in Bhairavi, eg: *Āmār rāt pohālo.* His favourite *rāgas* were *Bhairavī* and *Bihāga* and he used both in various ways.

Though a believer in time cycle (*Samaya cakra*), and *Ṛtu-cakra* (season) of *rāgas*, he sometimes diviated from the prescribed path, e.g. instead of *Mallāra* and *Deśa*, he used *Yaman, Bihāga, Kāfi*, etc. for songs of rain, e.g.

Yaman	*Āji bāri jhare jhara jhara.*
Kāfi	*Āji jhara jhara mukhara bādara dine.*
Bihāga	*Āji tomāy ābār cāi śonābāre.*

Rabindranath was averse to any addition of *rāgālāpa* or *tānas* by individual singers in his song compositions and he expressed this wish very firmly. Two music critics of Bengal, Dilip Kumar Ray and Dhurjati Prasad Mukherji had argued with the poet for his hard-line policy but the poet maintained that his songs were *vānī-pradhān*, expressing certain sentiments which could not be done through *rāgālāpa* or *tānas* of *śāstrīya* techniques. He said that there was something far more important than mere techniques and that was '*Darad*', expressing the inner emotion. This was something—deep within and not an outer show of skill.

Tuks or Kalis in Rabīndra-saṅgīta:

Rabindranath preferred compositions of four *tuks* or stanzas and most of his songs are in *dhrupada* like structure with *sthāyī, antarā, sañcārī* and *ābhoga.* There are however varieties in his compositions having *tuks* numbering (a) 4, (b) 2, (c) 5 to 10, and (d) long narratives. In lyrics of 5 *tuks*, the divisions are: *sthāyī, antarā, second antarā, sañcārī* and *ābhoga.*

In lyrics of 6 *tuks*, the divisions are: *sthāyī, antarā, sañcāri, ābhoga, second sañcārī* and *second ābhoga.* The two *sañcārīs* and the two *ābhogas* are tuned alike. e.g: *Gahana kusuma kuñja mājhe*, a *kīrtana* in *rāga* Jhījhit. The poet has composed many more songs of 6 *tuks*, which do not always follow the same pattern of tuning as mentioned above, e.g: *Nayana tomāke pāyanā dekhite*, in *Miśra Jogiyā.*

There is one song composition consisting of 10 stanzas set in *Bāul* tune of Shilaidaha. The first four stanzas follow the pattern of *dhrupada*, while the last six stanzas are tuned alternately like the *sañcārī* and *ābhoga.*

Some of the compositions of the poet are long and are sung in a unique fashion, as if one is talking to some one. These long narratives are sung by changing *layas* suitably or sometimes without any *tāla*, e.g. *Kṛṣṇakali āmi tārei bali; Tabu mane rekho; Tumi ki kebali chabi,* etc.

There are certain long poems of four or more stanzas set in different *tālas* within the same song, e.g. *He nirupamā,* comprising of four *stavakas* or stanzas of different *chandas.* The first *stavaka* is set to *Miśra Basanta,* the second one is in *Miśra Rāmkeli,* the third one is in *Sindhu* and the fourth is in *Deśa.* Another example is: *Oi āse oi ati Bhairava harase,* consisting of five *stavakas,* set in *Miśra Kānaḍā.* Tagore's *Kṣanikā* and *Mohuā* contain many such *bandiśes.*

Rasa in Rabīndra-saṅgīta:

Rabindranath's songs are predominantly of *karuṇa rasa,* i.e. pathos. To depict pathos he has aptly used *Bhairavī* and other *rāgas,* such as - *Bibhās, Alhaiyā, Devgiri, Kakubha, Jogiyā, Jayjayantī, Sindhu, Deśa, Multānī,* and *Pūrabī.* To depict *vīr-rasa* (braveness) he has used *Sindhuḍā, Naṭa, Mālava, Śaṅkarā, Hamīr, Puriyā,*etc.

One type of song composed by Tagore is called *Ānanda-saṅgīa* in which he has put in abundance of joy. In many songs of *Śarat* and *Basant ṛtu,* this joyful note is clearly perceptible, e.g. *Ore bhāi phāgun legeche bone bone (Paraj Bāhār); Ore gṛhavāsī, khol dvār khol* (Basant).

Tagore chose *Mālkauns* for *gambhīra rasa* or serious mood, eg: *Ānanda dhārā bahiche bhuvane,* etc and *Sāhānā* for *śānta rasa* or serene mood, appropriate for the occasion of a wedding, e.g. *Śubha dine śhubha kṣaṇe,* etc. He considered *Bhairava* as a *rāga* suitable for auspicious occasions and also for *rudra-rasa* or energy. For *śṛṅgāra rasa* the poet selected *Kāliṅgḍā, Paraja, Lalita, Kedāra, Khaṭ, Sohinī* and *Bāhār.*

Rabindranath is often mentioned as '*Varṣār Kavi*' meaning - the poet of the rains. He used *Mallāra* profusely and other *rāgas* also.

Chandas and tālas in Rabīndra - saṅgīta:

Rabindranath's lyrical compositions are rich in varieties of *chanda.* He said - *chanda* is the movement, the motion, and pulsation of a composition. In all his songs, he has maintained the value of *vāṇī,* i.e. the lyric. Thus he has composed his songs using appropriate *chandas* according to the *bhāva* or emotion of the lyrical composition.

The songs that he composed during the early days, modelled after Hindusthani *dhrupadas,* have *rāgas* and *tālas* of that style, such as: *Cautāla, Dhāmār, Surfāktā, Jhāptāla, Teorā,* etc.

During his later days, the poet preferred lighter *tālas* and *chandas,* and composed his songs in *Dādrā, Kāhārvā, Ektāla, Teorā* etc. He even composed some songs in free verse, such as: *He nūtan; Āji kon sure bāndhila,* and many songs in the *Nṛtya-nātyas* which fall under this category.

He always believed in maintaining discipline in *chandas* and *tāla*, but at the same time restraining it, so as not to ruin the essence of music. The traditional *tālas* used extensively by him are: *Cautāla, Dhāmār, Ektāla, Jhāptāla, Teorā, Madhyamāna, Jat, Thumrī-tāla, Tritāla, Āḍā-cautāla, Surfāktā, Pañcamsavārī, Kavvālī, Khemṭā, Āḍā-ṭhekā, Dādrā* and *Kāhārvā.* But he was not satisfied with these *tālas* only, since some of his compositions were of unique *chanda* combinations and could not be categorised under the traditional *tālas.* Therefore, the poet-composer had innovated a few new *tālas* to express the *bhāvas* and *chandas* of his compositions. These new *tālas* are:

(1) *Jhampaka* or *Ardha-Jhāptāla,* consisting of five *mātrās.* In *Jhampaka,* he used *chanda* division in two different ways: (i) 3+2 and (ii) 5. It consists of half the number of *mātrās* of *Jhāptāla,* i.e - 5 and is thus also called *Ardha-Jhāptāla.* The following songs are set in this *tāla, Āji śrāvaṇa ghana gahana māhe; Ei labhinu saṅga taba; Cakṣe āmār tṛṣṇa.*

(2) *Ṣaṣṭhī-tāla* consists of 6 *mātrās.* The *mātrā* divisions are: 2+4 and 3+3. Song examples are: *Śyāmala chāyā nāibā gele; Bidāy niye giye chilem.* Sometimes, the reverse, i.e. 4+2 also has been used to create novelty in *chanda.* Song example: *Hṛday āmār prakāś holo.*

These new *tālas* were formed during the composition of *dhrupadāṅga Brahma saṅgīta* and songs of *Gītāñgali.* Sometimes, he placed the stress on the second letter, thereby creating a speciality in *chanda,* e.g: *Pūrṇa cānder māyā; Dakhina hāoa jāgo,* etc.

(3) *Rupakḍā tāla* consists of 8 *mātrās* and has been formulated by adding one more *mātrā* to *Teoṛā.* The *chanda* is: 4+2+2. Song example is: *Kato ajānāre jānāilo tumi.*

(4) *Nabatāla* consists of 9 *mātrās* and has been formulated in different *chandas,* e.g: 3+2+2+2 ; 4+5; 5+4 ; 3+6; 6+3.

Song example: *Vyākula bakulera phule; Je kā̃dane hiyā kā̃diche; Nibiḍa ghana ā̃dhāre,* etc.

(5) *Ekādaśī* consists of II *mātrās* and has *chanda* variations such as: 3+2+2+4; 3+4+4, etc. It is a mixture of *Teoṛā* and *Kāhārvā.* Song example: *Kā̃piche dehalatā thara thara; Duāre dāo more rākhiyā.*

Rabindranath composed many songs in *Ṭhumrī tāla. Ṭhumrī,* during that period, was more well known as a *tāla* with its 4 *mātrā* divisions having the stress uniquely. The *chanda* of this *tāla* could be compared with *Toṭaka chanda.* At that time, most of the Bengali musicologists maintained that this *tāla* consisted of 8 *mātrās* with one '*sam*' and one '*khālī*', i.e. one beat with stress while the other without. Some even maintained that this *tāla* consisted of 4 *mātrās* only. But the poet used this *tāla* with 8 *mātrās* having 4 divisions consisting of one *sam*, one *khalī* and two *tālis*. This *tāla* was explained in '*Svaralipi-gltimālā*' (1308 B.S.) by Jyotirindranath as follows:

(+ over the first ধা; ० over ने)
| धा धा केटे ताक् | ने धा केटे ताक्, i.e. with two divisions only, *sam* and *khālī*. But Dwijendranath maintained 4 divisions. It is as follows: | 1 2 | 3 4 | 5 6 | 7 8 |
(marks over the numbers: + over 1, २ over 3, ० over 5, ३ over 7)

This was maintained by most musicians.

Rabindranath preferred slow and *madhya layas* with subdued and thoughtful *tāla* accompaniment. In many of his songs, *khol* got preference over *tablā*. Sometimes, instead of the percussion instrument, rhythm was mainained by *mandirā* or accompanying instruments such as piano. He did not specify any special *ṭhekā* for his *tālas* but expected the *tablā* player to maintain the correct *chanda* of the songs. The *ṭhekās* usually played for his *tālas* are:

1. *Jhampaka* - 5 *mātrās*, *Viṣama mātrikā* - 3+2 -

 (+ २)
 | धा धि ना | धि ना ।|

2. *Ṣaṣṭhī tāla* 6- *mātrās*, *Viṣama mātrikā*, - 2+4-

 (+ २)
 | धि ना | धि धि नागे तेटे । |

3. *Rupakḍā tāla* - 8 *mātrās*, *Viṣama mātrikā*, 3+2+3 -

 (+ २ ३)
 | धा देन ता | तिट कत | गदि धेने नाक । |

4. *Naba tāla* - 9 *mātrās*, *Viṣama mātrikā* - 3+2+2+2.

 (+ २ ३ ४)
 | धा देन ता | तिट कत | गदि धेने | धागे तेटे । |

5. *Ekādaśī tāla* - 11 *mātrās*, *Viṣama mātrikā*, 3+2+2+4.

 (+ २ ३ ४)
 | धा देन ता | तिट कत | गदि धेने | धागे तेटे तागे तेटे ।|

6. *Nabapañca tāla* - 18 *mātrās*, *Viṣama mātrikā*, 2+4+4+4+4. -

 (+ २ ३ ४ ५)
 | धा गे | धा गे देन ता | कता धागे देन ता | तिट धा देन ता | तिट कता गदि धेने |

Composer - Rabindranath Tagore - Kālmṛgayā
Rāga - Miśra Kedāra Khemṭā tāla

फुले फुले ढले ढले बहे किबा मृदु बाय ।
तटिनी हिल्लोल तुले कल्लोले चलिया याय ।
पिक किबा कुंजे कुंजे कुहु कुहु कुहु गाय ।
कि जानि किसेर लागि प्राण करे हाय हाय ॥

+			२			०			३		
सं ना	-ा	मा	पा	-धपमा	पा	धा	-सर्नसा	धा	पा	-धपमा	पा
फु	०	ले	फु	०००	ले	ढ	०००	ले	ढ	०००	ले

+			२			०			३		
धा	-णधपा	मा	मा	-रा	सा	सा	-रा	(र) मा	मा	-ा	‖ -ा
ब	०००	हे	कि	०	बा	मृ	०	दु	बा	०	य
सा	-ा	सा	सरमा	-ा	मा	मा	-गमपा	पा	पा	-मपधा	पा
त	०	टि	नी००	०	हिल्	लो	०००	ल	तु	०००	ले
मा	-ा	मगा	मा	-गमधा	पा	मा	-गा	मा	रा	-ा	सा
क	ल्	लो०	ले	०००	च	लि	०	या	या	०	य
(प) र्सा	-ा	नर्सरी	र्सा	-णा	धपध	(ध) णा	न	धणर्सा	णा	-धणा	पा
पि	०	क००	कि	०	वा००	कु	न्	जे००	कु	०न्	जे
र्सा	-धा	मा	र्सा	-धा	मा	र्सा	-णा	णधा	पा	-ा	र्सा
कु	०	हु	कु	०	हु	कु	०	हु	गा	०	य
सा	-मा	मा	पमा	-पमा	पा	धा	-र्सनर्सा	धा	पधपा	-मा	पा
कि	०	जा	नि०	००	कि	से	०००	र	ला००	०	गि
धा	-णधपा	मा	मा	-रा	सा	मा	-रा	सरमा	मा	-ा	-ा
प्रा	०००	ण	क	०	रे	हा	०	००य	हा	०	य

Composer - Rabindranath Tagore , Bhānusiṃherpadāvalī

सजनि सजनि राधिकालो देख अबहुँ चाहिया,
मृदुल गमन श्याम आओये, मृदुल गान गाहिया ।
पिनह झटित कुसुम हार पिनह नील आङ्गिया,
सुन्दरी सिन्दूर देके सीँथि करह राङ्गिया ।
सहचरि सब नाच नाच मृदुल गीत गाओरे,
चन्चल मञ्जीर राव कुञ्ज गगन छाओरे ।
सजनि अब उजार मँदिर कनक दीप ज्वालिया,
सुरभि करह कुञ्ज भवन गन्ध सलिल ढालिया ।
मल्लिका चमेलि बेलि कुसुम तुलह बालिका,
गाँथ यूयि गाँथ जाति गाँथ बकुल मालिका ।
तृषित नयन भानुसिंह कुञ्जपथम चाहिया
मृदुल गमन श्याम आओये मृदुल गान गाहिया ॥

+			२			०			३		
गा	गा	मा	पा	पा	पा	(म)गा	-ा	मा	पा	-धा	पा
स	ज	नि	स	ज	नि	रा	०	धि	का	०	लो
(म)गा	-ा	मा	पा	धा	पा	मा	-ा	गा	(र)सा	-ा	-ा
दे	०	ख	अ	ब	हुँ	चा	०	हि	या	०	०
सा	सा	सा	गा	गा	मा	पा	-ा	पा	(प)ना	-धा	ना
मृ	दु	ल	ग	म	न	श्या	०	म	आ	०	ओये
र्सा	(र्स)र्गा	र्री	र्सा	-ा	र्सा	नधा	-ना	ना	(ध)पा	-ा	-ा
मृ	दु	ल	गा	०	न	गा	०	हि	या	०	०
पा	पा	पा	ना	ना	ना	र्सा	र्सा	र्सा	नर्सा	-धा	ना
पि	न	ह	झ	टि	त	कु	सु	म	हा०	०	र
र्सा	(र्स)र्गा	र्री	र्सा	-ा	र्सा	नर्सा	-धा	ना	र्सा	-ा	-ा
पि	न	ह	नी	०	ल	आ०	०	ङि	या	०	०
(ध)पा	-ा	पा	मा	-गा	मा	पा	-ा	पा	(प)ना	-धा	ना
सु	न्	द	री	०	सिन्	दू	०	र	दे	०	के
र्सा	-र्गा	र्री	र्सा	र्सा	र्सा	नधा	-ना	नधा	(ध)पा	-ा	-ा
सौं	०	थि	क	र	ह	रा०	०	ङि०	या	०	०
सा	सा	सा	सपा	पा	पा	पा	-ा	पा	पा	-ा	धा
स	ह	च	रि०	स	ब	ना	०	च	ना	०	च
धा	णा	णा	धणा	-धर्सा	णधा	पा	-धा	पा	मा	-मा	-ा
मृ	दु	ल	गी०	००	त०	गा	०	ओ	रे	०	०
गा	-ा	गा	गा	गा	-ा	गा	-ा	गा	गमा	पा	पा
च	न्	च	ल	म	न्	जी	०	र	रा०	०	व

मं +			ग २			०			३		
गा	-ा	गा	पा	मा	मा	गरा	-गा	गरा	सा	-ा	-ा
कु	न्	ज	ग	ग	न	छा०	०	ओ०	रे	०	०
			प								
{ पा	पा	पा	ना	धा	ना	र्सा	-ा	र्सा	ना	धा	ना
{ स	ज	नि	अ	ब	उ	जा	०	र	मँ	दि	र
	र्स										
र्सा	र्गा	र्रा	र्सा	-ा	र्सा	नर्सा	-धा	ना	र्सा	-ा	-ा }
क	न	क	दी	०	प	ज्वा०	०	लि	या	०	० }
ध											
पा	पा	पा	मा	गा	मा	पा	-ा	पा	ना	धा	ना
सु	र	भि	क	र	ह	कु	न्	ज	भ	व	न
	र्स								ध		
र्सा	र्गा	र्रा	र्सा	र्सा	र्सा	नधा	-ना	नधा	पा	-ा	-ा ‖
ग	न्	ध	स	लि	ल	ढा०	०	लि०	या	०	० ‖
{ सा	-ा	सा	सपा	-ा	पा	पा	-ा	पा	पा	-ा	धा
{ म	ल्	लि	का०	०	च	मे	०	लि	वे	०	लि
धा	णा	णा	धणा	धर्सा	णधा	पा	-धा	पा	मा	-गा	-ा }
कु	सु	म	तु०	ल०	ह०	वा	०	लि	का	०	० }
गा	-ा	गा	गा	-ा	गा	गा	-ा	गा	गमा	पा	पा
गाँ	०	थ	यू	०	थि	गाँ	०	थ	जा०	०	ति
म			ग								
गा	-ा	गा	पा	मा	मा	गरा	-गा	गरा	स	-ा	-ा }
गाँ	०	थ	ब	कु	ल	मा०	०	लि०	का	०	० }
			प			न					
{ पा	पा	पा	ना	धा	ना	र्सा	-ा	र्सा	नर्सा	-धा	ना
{ तृ	षि	त	न	य	न	भा	०	नु	सि०	ङ	ह
									न		
र्सा	र्गा	र्रा	र्सा	र्सा	र्सा	नर्सा	-धा	ना	र्सा	-ा	-ा }
कु	न्	ज	प	थ	म	चा०	०	हि	या	०	० }

+ ध । २ । ० । ३ प

| पा पा पा | मगा गा मा | पा -ा पा | ना -धा ना |
| मृ दु ल | ग० म न | श्या ० म | आ ० ओये |

र्स । । । ध

| र्सा र्गा र्रा | र्सा -ा र्सा | नधा -ना ना | पा -ा -ा |||
| मृ दु ल | गा ० न | गा० ० हि | या ० ० |||

Composer - Rabindranath Thakur - Ṭappā style
Rāga - Sindhu Tāla - Madhyamāna.

ए परबासे रबे के हाय ।
के रबे ए संशये सन्तापे शोके ॥
हेथा के राखिबे दुखभयसंकटे –
तेमन आपन केह नाहि ए प्रान्तरे हायरे ॥

+ । २ । ० । ३

[सरमा -पधमा -र्सणधा -णा]
|| र्सणधा -णा -ा -ा | णधपा मज्ञा -ा -ा | -रज्ञा -मज्ञरा -ज्ञा -ा | -ाः -रः सन्ा सा |
|| ए०० ० ० ० | प०र बा० ० ० | ०० ००० ० ० | ० ० से० र |

म
| रा ज्ञा रा -ा | -ा रज्ञा -मपमा -ज्ञरा | -ज्ञा -ा -ा -रा | -सन्ा -सा -ा -ा |
| बे ० के ० | ० हा० ००० ०० | ० ० ० ० | ०० ० ० य् |

| सा रा मा मा | पा -ा -ा मगा | मा -णा धा -ा | -ा -णधा -पधणा -र्सणधा |
| के र बे ए | सं ० ० श० | ये ० स ० | ० ०० ००० ००० |

| -णा -ा धा पा | -ा -ा -ा -धपा | मपा -धपमा -पा -ा | रज्ञा -मज्ञा -रसा -रा | [ ] |
| ० न् ता पे | ० ० ० ०० | शो० ००० ० ० | के० ०० ०० ० | [ ] |

[पधा -मा] । । [-र्सर्सा]
{ पा मा -ा पधा | ना -ा -ा -र्सना | -धना -र्सा ना र्सा | -ा -ा -ा -ा |
{ हे था ० के० | रा ० ० ०० | ०० ० खि बे | ० ० ० ० |

| पर्सा -ाः -नः र्सर्रा | र्सर्रर्सा -णधपा -मपधा -णर्सणा | धा पा -ा -ा | -ा -ा -ा -ा }
| दुख ० ० भय | सं०० ००० ००० ००० | क टे ० ० | ० ० ० ० }

| मा पा ना र्सा | र्रा र्रा -ा र्रा | र्रा र्रा -ा -र्ज्ञर्रा | -र्सर्ज्ञा -र्मर्ज्ञर्रा -र्ज्ञा -ा |
| ते म न आ | प न ० के | ह ना ० ०० | ००० ००० ० ० |

+				२				०				३			
र्रा	र्सा	-ा	-ा	-ा	-ा	र्सा	-ा	णर्सा	-र्रसा	-णधा	-पमा	-पधा	-णर्सा	-र्सणा	-धणा
हि	०	०	०	०	०	ए	०	प्रा०	००	००	००	००	००	००	०न्
धा	पा	-ा	-धपा	मपा	-मपधपा	-पमा	-ा	रज्ञा	-मज्ञा	-रसा	-रा	-ा	-ा	-ा	-ा [ ]
त०	रं	०	००	हा०	००००	००	य्	रं०	००	००	०	०	०	०	०

Composer - Rabindranath Thakur - Kīrtana (with ākhar) - Dādrā tāla

माझे माझे तब देखा पाइ, चिर दिन केन पाइना ।
केन मेघ आसे हृदय आकाशे, तोमारे देखिते देयना ॥
[मोह मेघे तोमारे देखिते देयना । अन्धकारे राखे तोमारे, देखिते देयना ।] (आँखर)
क्षणिक आलोके आँखिर पलके तोमाय यबे पाइ देखिते,
(ओहे) हाराइ हाराइ सदा हय भय, हाराइया फेलि चकिते ॥
[आश ना मिटिते हाराइया, पलक ना पड़िते हाराइया,
हृदय ना जुड़ाते हाराइया फेलि चकिते ।] (आँखर)
कि करिले बल पाइब तोमारे राखिब आँखिते आँखिते,
(ओहे) एत प्रेम आमि कोथा पाब नाथ तोमारे हृदये राखिते ॥
[आमार साध्य किबा तोमारे, दया ना करिले के पारे,
तुमि आपनि ना एले के पारे हृदये राखिते ।] (आँखर)
आर कारो पाने चाहिब ना आर करिब हे आमि प्राण पण,
(ओहे) तुमि यदि बल एखनि करिब विषय बासना बिसर्जन दिब ॥
[श्रीचरणे बिषय दिब, अकातरे बिषय दिब,
तोमार लागि बिषय बासना बिसर्जन दिब ॥] (आँखर)

+			०			+			०		
										-ग	
‖{ रा	गमपा	पमा	मगा	गा	गा	रा	गा	रगा	-रगमा	मगा	-रा
मा	झे००	मा०	झे०	त	व	दे	खा	पा०	००	००	इ
									ग		॥
रा	गा	रा	-ा	रा	रा	रगा	-रगमा	-ा	मगा	--रा	-सा }
चि	र	दि	न्	के	न	पा०	०००	इ	ना ०	०	०
											ध
{ पा	धा	धर्सा	-नधा	धा	धा	पा	पर्सा	र्सना	धा	ना	नधपा
के	न	मे०	०घ	आ	से	हृ	दृ	य०	आ	का	शे००

+			०			+			०		
									प		
पा	धा	पा	पा	पा	पमगा	गा	-ा	पा	धपा	-मगा	-रा }
तो	मा	रे	दे	खि	ते००	दे	०	यक्ष्	ना०	००	० }
				न							
{ गपा	पा	-ा	धर्सा	र्सना	-धपा	पा	धा	पा	पा	पा	पमगा
{ मो०	ह	०	मे०	घे०	००	तो	मा	रे	दे	खि	ते००
			प								
गा	-ा	पा	धपा	-मगा	रा) }				-ा	रा	रा
दे	०	य	ना०	००	० }					अन्	ध
गा	पा	-ा	धा	धधा	-नधा	पा	धा	पा	पा	पा	पमगा
क	रे	०	रा	खे०	००	तो	मा	रे	दे	खि	ते००
			प								
गा	-ा	पा	धपा	-मगा	-रसा ‖						
दे	०	य्	ना०	००	०० ‖						
‖{ रा	गमपा	पमा	मगा	गा	गा	रा	गरगा	गा	गा	गमा	मगरा
‖{ क्ष	णि००	क०	आ०	लो	के	आँ	खि००	र	प	ल०	के००
									[रा	-ा	पा]
रा	गा	-रसा	सा	सध्सा	सरा	रा	रगा	-रगमगा	(रा	-ा	ससा) }
तो	मा	०य०	य	वे००	पाइ	दे	खि०	००००	ते	०	ओहे }
											ध
{ पा	धा	-र्सनधा	धा	धा	-ा	पा	र्सा	र्सना	-धा	धना	-नधपा }
{ हा	रा	००इ	हा	रा	इ	स	दा	ह०	य	भ०	००य }
								प			
पा	धा	-पा	पा	पा	पमगा	गपा	पा	धपा	-मगा	रा	-ा
हा	रा	इ	या	फे	लि००	च०	कि	ते०	००	आ	श्
गा	-पा	पा	धा	धर्सना	-धपा	पा	धा	-पा	पा	रा	रा
ना	०	मि	टि	ते००	००	हा	रा	इ	या	प	लक्
गा	-पा	पा	धा	धर्सना	-धपा	पा	धा	-पा	पा	रा	रा
ना	०	प	ड़ि	ते००	००	हा	रा	इ	या	ह	दय
गा	-पा	पा	धा	धर्सना	-धपा	पा	धा	-पा	पा	पा	पमगा
ना	०	जु	ड़ा	ते००	००	हा	रा	इ	या	फे	लि००

\+ ○ + ○

| गा पा धपा | -मगा -रसा -ा || | |

| च कि ते० | ०० ०० ० || | |

|| रा गमपा पमा | मगा गा गा | रा गरगा गा | ग गमा मगरा |

| कि क०० रि० | ले० ब ल | पा इ०० ब | तो मा० रे०० |

[रा -ा पपा]

| रा गा रसा | सा सध्सा सरा | र रगा -रगमगा | (रा -ा ससा) ||

| रा खि ब० | आँ खि०० ते० | आँ खि० ०००० | ते ० ओंहे ||

ध

|| पा धा र्सनधा | -ा धा धा | पा र्सा र्सना | धा धना -नधपा ||

| ए त प्रे०० | म् आ मि | को था पा० | ब ना० ००य ||

प म

| पा धा पा | पा पा पमगा | गा पा धपा | -गा रा रा |

| तो मा रे | हृ द ये०० | रा खि ते० | ० आ मार |

| गा -पा पा | धा धर्सना -धपा | पा धा पा | -ा रा रा |

| सा ० ध्य | कि वा०० ०० | तो मा रे | ० द या |

| गा -पा पा | धा धर्सना -धपा | पा धा पा | -ा रा रा |

| ना ० क | रि ले०० ०० | के पा रे | ० तु मि |

| गा -पा पा | धा धर्सना धपा | पा धा पा | पा पा पमगा |

| आ प् नि | ना ए०० ले० | के पा रे | हृ द ये०० |

प

| गा पा धपा | -मगा -रसा -ा || | |

| रा खि ते० | ०० ०० ० || | |

|| रा -गमपा पमा | मगा गा गा | रा गरगा गा | गा गमा -मगरा |

| आ ००र् का० | रो० पा ने | चा हि०० ब | ना आ० ००र् |

[रा -ा पपा]

| रा गा रसा | सा सध्सा सरा | रा रगा -रगमगा | (रा -ा ससा) |

| क रि ब० | हे आ०० मि० | प्रा ण० ०००० | प ण् ओंहे |

+			०			+			०		
											ध
{पा	धा	र्सनधा	धा	धा	धा	पा	र्सा	र्सना	ध	धना	नधपा}
{तु	मि	य००	दि	ब	ल	ए	ख	नि०	क	रि०	ब००}
								प			
पा	धा	पा	पा	पा	पमग	गा	पा	धपा	–मगा	रा	रा
बि	ष	य	बा	स	ना००	बि	सर्	ज०	०न्	दि	ब
गा	पा	–ा	धा	धर्सना	–धपा	पा	धा	पा	–ा	रा	रा
श्री	च	०	र	णे००	००	बि	ष	य	०	दि	ब
गा	पा	–ा	धा	धर्सना	–धपा	पा	धा	पा	–ा	रा	रा
अ	का	०	त	रे००	००	वि	ष	य	०	दि	ब
गा	पा	–ा	धा	धर्सना	–धपा	पा	धा	पा	पा	पा	पमगा
तो	मा	र्	ला	गि००	००	बि	ष	य	बा	स	ना००
		प									
गा	पा	धपा	–मगा	–रसा	–ा ‖						
बि	सर्	ज०	०न्	दि	ब् ‖						

Composer - Rabindranath Thakur - (Khayāl Aṅg)
Rāga - Meghāvali Tāla - Dhīmā tritāla

मने ये आशा लये एसेछि हलना हलना हे –
ओइ मुख पाने चेये फिरिनु लुकाते आँखि जल,
बेदना रहिल मने मने ।
तुमि केन हेसे चाओ, हेसे याओ हे,
आमि केन कैंदे फिरि ।
केन आनि कम्पित हृदयखानि,
केन याओ दूरे ना देखे ॥

+				२				०				३			
[पर्सा	–नर्सा	धा	पा	ह्मपा	–गा]										
स ‖(न्सा	–ा	रा	गा	गाः	–मः)	–रा	–ा	–ा	–ा	न्सा	–रा	–गा	–ा	रसाः	–न्ः
म०	०	ने	ये	आ	०	०	०	०	०	शा०	०	०	०	लये	०
धन्ा	–धा	–रा	–ा	–ा	न्ा	सरा	–सन्ा	–सा	–ा	–ा	–ा	–ा	–ा	॥ –ा	सा
ए०	०	०	०	०	से	छि०	००	०	०	०	०	०	०	०	ह

+				२				०				३			
सा	-गरा	गा	-ा	-ा	-मगा	-रा	गा	गा	-पा	पा	-ह्मा	पाः	-ह्मः	(ध)-पा	-ह्मपा
ल	००	ना	०	०	००	०	ह	ल	०	ना	०	हे	०	०	००
-गाः	-मः	-रा	गा	गा	-पा	पा	पा	ह्मपा	-धा	पा	-ा	ह्माः	-पः	गा	-ा
०	०	०	ओ	इ	०	मु	ख	पा०	०	ने	०	चे	०	ये	०
रा	गा	रगा	-मा	मगा	रगा	रसा	न्सरा	सन्ा	धन्ा	-धन्साः	-न्ः	-धन्ा	-धह्मा	-धा	-पा
फि	रि	नु०	०	लु०	का०	ते०	आँ००	खि०	ज०	०००	०	००	००	०	ल्
-ा	-ा	सा	सा	न्सा	रा	-ा	-ा	रगा	-सा	रा	रगा	-ा	-ा	(ग)रा	-गा
०	०	वे	द	ना०	०	०	०	र०	०	हि	ल	०	०	म	०
गह्मा	-ा	-ा	-ा	-ा	-ा	(ह्म)गा	-ह्मा	(ह्म)पा	-ा	-ा	-ा	-ा	-ा	(प)-ह्मा	-पा [ ]
ने	०	०	०	०	०	म	०	ने	०	०	०	०	०	०	०
{ गा	-ा	पा	-ा	(प)ना	धा	-ा	-ा	(ध)र्सा	-ा	र्सा	-ना	र्रा	-र्सा	-ा	ना
{ तु	०	मि	०	के	न	०	०	हे	०	से	०	चा	०	०	ओ
(न)धा	-ा	ना	-ा	(न)र्रा	-र्सा	-ा	ना	(ध)नाः	-धः	ह्मधा	-पह्मा	(ह्म)गा	-ा	-ा	-ा }
हे	०	से	०	या	०	०	ओ	हे०	०	००	००	०	०	०	० }
गा	-ा	(गा)ना	-ा	धा	पा	-ा	ह्मा	गा	-ा	मा	-गा	रगा	-मा	गा	-ा
आ	०	मि	०	के	न	०	०	कँ	०	दे	०	फि०	०	रि	०
रगा	-ा	रा	-ा	सा	-ा	न्ा	-ा	(ध्)सा	-ा	न्ा	-ा	(न्)ध्ा	-ा	(ध्)रा	-ा
के	०	न	०	आ	०	नि	०	क	म्	पि	०	त	०	ह	०
सा	-ा	न्ा	-ध्ा	(ध्)न्ा	-ा	ध्ा	-ा	ह्मध्ा	-प्ा	-ा	-ा	-ा	-ा	-ा	-ा
द	०	य	०	खा	०	०	०	नि०	०	०	०	०	०	०	०
गा	-ा	पा	-ा	(प)र्सा	-ा	-ा	-ना	(न)र्रा	-ा	र्सा	-ा	-ा	-ा	-ा	ना
के	०	न	०	या	०	०	ओ	दू	०	रे	०	०	०	०	०
(ध)पा	-ा	-ा	-ह्मा	(ग)मा	-ा	गा	-ा	-ा	-ा	-ा	-मा	-रा	-ा	-ा	-ा ‖ [ ]
ना	०	०	०	दे	०	खे	०	०	०	०	०	०	०	०	०

Composer - Rabindranath Thakur, Rāmprasādī - sur, Ektāla

आमिइ शुधु रइनु बाकी ।
या छिल ता गेल चले,
रइल या ता केबल फाँकि ॥
आमार बले छिल यारा,
आर तो तारा देय ना साड़ा -
कोथाय तारा, कोथाय तारा,
कैंदे कैंदे कारे डाकि ॥
बल् देखि मा, शुधाइ तोरे -
आमार किछु राखलि नेरे,
आमि केबल आमाय निये
कोन प्राणेते बेंचे थाकि ॥

+			२			०			३		
											गा
											आ
गमा	-पमा	-गरा	-सा	सा	रा	गा	-ा	गा	मा	पा	॥ मगा
मि०	००	००	इ	शु	धु	रइ	०	नु	बा	कि	"आ०"
पा	-धर्सा	र्सा	र्सा	र्सा	-ा	प र्सा	र्सा	-ा	ना	ना	-र्सना
या	००	छि	ल	ता	०	गे	ल	०	च	ले	००
धना	-र्सरी	री	र्सा	-ना	र्सना	धना	पा	-धपा	मधा	पा	मगा
र०	०इ	ल	या	०	ता०	के०	ब	०ल्	फाँ०	कि	"आ०"
पा	धा	-ा	-ा	धा	धा	ध[धर्रा] र्सा	र्सा	-ा	ना	ध ना	-धपा
आ	मा	०	र	ब	ले	छि	ल	०	या	रा	००
प र्सा	-ा	ना	र्सा	री	-र्गरी	र्सना	-धनर्सा	र्सा	र्सा	र्सा	-नधा
आ	र्	तो	ता	रा	००	दे०	००य्	ना	सा	ड़ा	००
पा	धा	-र्सा	र्सा	र्सा	-ा	र्स री	र्सा	-ा	ना	ना	-र्सना
को	था	य	ता	रा	०	को	था	य्	ता	रा	००
धा	धना	-र्सरी	-ा	र्सा	ना	धना	पा	-धपा	मधा	पा	मगा
कैं	दे०	००	०	कैं	दे्	का०	रे	००	डा०	कि	"आ०"

+			२			०[र्रा]			३		
-ा	-ा	पा	{धा	धा	धा	धर्सा	र्सा	-ा	ना	ना	-धपा
०	०	बल्	{दे	खि	मा	शु	धा	इ	तो	रे	००
		ध									
पर्सा	र्सना	-ना	र्सा	र्रा	-र्गर्रा	र्सना	-धनर्सा	र्सा	र्सा	र्सा	-ा
आ०	मा०	र्	कि	छु	००	रा०	००ख्	लि	ने	रे	०
[पा	धा	र्सा]									
(-नधा	-पा	पा)}	र्सा	र्सा	-ा	र्रा	र्सा	-ा	ना	ना	-र्सना
००	०	बल}	के	वल्	०	आ	मा	य्	नि	ये	००
									[मधा पा मगा] ‖		
									[था कि "आ०"] ‖		
धना	-र्सर्रा	-र्रा	र्सा	-ना	नर्सना	धना	पा	-धपा	(मधा	पा	-ा) }
को०	०न्	प्रा	णे	०	ते००	बैं०	चे	००	था०	कि	० }

BIBLIOGRAPHY

1. Bhattacharya. Arun. *Rabīndra Saṅgīter Nānādik.* Calcutta, 1968. (Beng.).
2. ———. *Rabīndra Gāner Muktādhārā.* Calcutta, 1982. (Beng.).
3. Bhattacharya, Ashutosh. *Rabīndra-nāṭyadhārā.* Calcutta, 1966. (Beng.).
4. Bhattacharya, *Jayanti. Rabīndranāther Dukhher-gāna.* Calcutta. (Beng.).
5. Chattopadhyay, Basanta Kumar. *Jyotirindranāther Jīvansmṛti.* Calcutta, 1920. (Beng.).
6. Das, P.K. *Rabīndra Saṅgīta Gabeṣaṇā.* Part II & III. Calcutta. 1974. (Beng.).
7. De, Kiran Shashi. *Rabīndra Saṅgīta Suṣamā.* Calcutta, 1975. (Beng.).
8. Ghosh, Mamata. *Jyotirindranath.* Calcutta. (Beng.).
9. Ghosh, Shantideb. *Rabīndra Saṅgīta.* Calcutta, 1949. (Beng.).
10. ———. *Rabīndra Saṅgīta Vicitrā.* Calcutta, 1972. (Beng.).
11. Halder, Asit Kumar. *Rabī Tīrthe.* Calcutta, 1365. B.S. (Beng.).
12. Kundu, Ashok Kumar. *Rabīndra Dinapanjī.* Calcutta, 1986. (Beng.).
13. Mitra, Rajyeshwar. *Bāṅglār Gītikār O Bāṅglā Gāner Nānādik.* 2ṇḍ ed. Calcutta, 1973. (Beng.).
14. Mitra, Suchitra & Chaudhuri, Subhas. *Rabīndra Sangītāyan.* Calcutta, 1990. (Beng.).
15. Mukhopadhyay, Amal. *Rabīndra Saṅgīta Parikramā.* Calcutta, 1971. (Beng.).
16. Mukhopadhyay, Prabhat Kumar. *Rabīndra Jīvanī.* Part I & II. Calcutta, 1353 & 1355. B.S.(Beng.).
17. ———. *Rabīndra Varṣapnji.* Calcutta, 1962. (Beng.).
18. ———. *Rabindra Jīvankathā.* Calcutta, 1959. (Beng.).
19. Nag. Kalidas. *Surer Guru Rabīndranath.* Calcutta. 1986. (Beng.).
20. Pal, Prasanta Kumar. *Rabi Jīvanī.* Part I & II. Calcutta, 1982, 1984. (Beng.).

21. Prajnanananda, Swami. *Saṅgīte Rabīndra Pratibhār dāna.* Calcutta, 1965. (Beng.).
22. *Rabīndra Racanāvalī.* Vols. I to XIV. Centenary Publication. Calcutta, 1961. (Beng.).
23. Ray, Jaydeb. *Rabīndra Gīti.* Calcutta, 1360. B.S. (Beng.).
24. Ray, Sushil. *Jyotirindranath.* Calcutta. 1963. (Beng.).
25. Ray, Sukumar. *Bāṅglā Saṅgīter Rūp.* Calcutta, 1969. (Beng.).
26. Raychaudhury, Sudhakanta. *Dwijendranath Thakur Smṛtikathā.* Calcutta, 1969. (Beng.).
27. Thakur, Abanindranath. *Gharoā.* Calcutta, 1951. (Beng.).
28. Thakur, Rabindranath. *Ghare Baire.* Calcutta, 1951. (Beng.).
29. ———. *Jīvansmṛti.* Calcutta, 1363. B.S. (Beng.).
30. ———. *Saṅgīta-cintā*, Calcutta, 1373. B.S. (Beng.).
31. Thakur, Satyendranath. *Āmār Bālyakathā O Bombāi Pravās.* (Beng.).
32. Thakur, Saumyendranath. *Rabindranāther gāna.* Calcutta, 1966. (Beng.).

Kāvya Saṅgīta

The word *kāvya* means poem, poetry or lyric. If taken literally, most of the vocal styles would come under it. But *Kāvya-saṅgīta* is a modern term, coined during late 19th century meaning those songs which are romantic in theme, free of traditional devotion and rich in literary value. In this style, the lyric plays a more important role than the melody and does not adhere to any strict *śāstrīya* discipline. Sometimes selected musical phrases are set to worded composition in romantic music. The *chanda* of the *padas* determine the *tāla.*

The compositions of many renowned poets, lyricists and litterateurs come under this category, viz. Jyotirindranath Thakur, Rabindranath Thakur, Dwijendralal Ray, Atul Prasad Sen, Rajanikanta Sen, Kaji Nazrul Islam and others. Later lyricists or *gītikars* such as Hemendra Kumar Ray, Subodh Purokayastha, Ajay Bhattacharya and others composed only the lyric of the songs while tunes were set by others who were called *surakārs, sur* meaning tune, i.e. those who specialised in composing tunes for *padas.* This was unlike the pre and contemporary era of Rabindranath when the *surakār* and the *gītikār* (Lyricist) used to be the same person. Some renowned *surakārs* were Dilip Kumar Ray and Himanshu Kumar Datta *Surasāgar.*

Kāvya-saṅgīta was at its peak during the time of Rabindranath and his contemporaries, when tunes were composed mostly on the basis of *rāgas* and yet were free from *ālāpcārī* or *tāna-kartab* and were highly romantic in nature.

It is however of special interest to note that *kāvya-saṅgīta* paved the way for a new creative trend in music from which emerged modern Bengali songs termed as *Ādhunik-Bāṅglā-gāna,* Hindi *Bhāva saṅgīta* and *Sugama saṅgīta* and the later theatre and film music.

(Since Ā*dhunik, Bhāvagīta* and *Filmigītas* are of light nature, these have been excluded from this book.)

Atulprasad Sen

Atulprasad was born on 26th October, 1871 at Dhaka. His father Ramprasad Sen was a Brahmo and a well known doctor but he died when Atulprasad was only thirteen years old. He was then brought up by his maternal grand-father. After completing schooling he joined Presidency College and then went to England to study law. He also studied the arts of painting and acting. After finishing law he came back and practised in Calcutta and Rangpur for a short period He then went away to Lucknow where he settled down as a successful lawyer. He became the President of Oudh Bar Association and Bar Council.

At Lucknow, he had the opportunity to listen to varieties of music styles of U.P and he based his songs on them. He was a keen lover of music and was gifted with a full throated melodious voice.

Atulprasad did a lot of experimentation in composing music for his songs. Although he wrote less than three hundred lyrics, he established a style of his own in the field of *kāvya-saṅgīta.* There has been some influence of Rabindranath but *Atulprasādī* songs stood out because of its unique style. He had applied common, popular and fundamental styles such as *khayāl, ṭhumrī, dādrā,* and the semi-classical styles of Eastern U.P. such as *ghazals, lāvanī, sāwan, kajrī, caiti,* etc. Although he had adopted these styles in his songs, he never allowed to distort the *pada.* That is why, his songs can not be elaborated upon in the same maner with *bol-banāo,* etc, the stress being on the *padas* of the songs.

Unlike Rabindranath, who was partial towards *dhrupadāṅga* style, Atulprasad's creations were more *ṭhumrī* and *dādrā* oriented. There are a few exceptions, like- '*Namo bāṇī bīṇāpāṇī*' which is a perfect *dhrupada.* In his experimentation he has blended *dhrupada* style with *kīrtana* in a unique manner, e.g. '*Jāni jāni tomāre go raṅgarānī*'. He composed some of his songs in *Bāul* tunes and these lyrics are highly romantic, e.g. '*Prakṛtir ghomṭā khāni khol lo badhū*'. '*Ār kato kāl thākbo bose*', '*Megherā dal bẽdhe jāy kon deśe*', etc.

Atulprasad was perhaps the pioneer composer who guided the trend towards *rāga-pradhān gāna,* which was further perfected by Nazrul. Basically, Atulprasad was *rāga* oriented and composed most of his songs in *rāgas* like *Khāmāja,* which was his most favourite *rāga* and its varieties such as *Miśra-khāmāja, Jhījhiṭ-khāmāja, Pīlu-khāmāja, Sindhu-khāmāja, Bihāga-khāmāja,* etc, and also *Bhairavī, Naṭ-malhār, Gauḍ-malhār, Bihāga, Sindhu-kāfī, Āsāvarī, Pīlu, Deś,* etc. Besides, he composed in some serious *rāgas* also, such as - *Megha, Pañcama, Naṭanārāyaṇa, Nāyakī-kānaḍā* and *Karṇāṭī-khaṭ.*

In *dādrā* style his famous song is - '*Ogo niṭhura daradī*'. In *ghazal* style - '*Kato gāna to holo gāoā*', '*Ke go tumi birahinī*', '*Ke tumi ghum bhāṅgāye*', etc. are worth mentioning. He was the first person to introduce *ghazal* in Bengali. His *kīrtanāṅga* songs are: '*Jodi tor hṛd jamunā*', '*Ogo sāthi mama sāthī*', etc. His *svadeśī* songs were set in simple tunes as well as Western tunes, such as: '*Utho go Bhārata Laksmī*', '*Balo balo balo sabe*', '*Hao dharamete dhīr*', '*Moder garab moder āśā*', etc. His fame as a composer spread to Bengal from far away Lucknow. Apart from music, he was instrumental in propagating Bengali culture and literature outside of Bengal through associations such as Nikhil Bhārat Baṅga Sāhitya Sanmelan and Pravāsī Baṅga Sāhitya Samiti and a journal named *Uttarā.* In politics he followed the policy of Gokhle. He was a kind hearted, helpful and most generous person. He gave away most of his property in charity.

He died in 1934 at Lucknow, where he was respected and loved by both Hindus and Muslims and everyone participated in his funeral.

His songs have been published in *Gītaguñja* and *Kākali*. A song example:

Composer: Atulprasad Sen.

Dādrā:

ओगो निठुर दरदी, एकि खेलछ अनुक्षण ।
तोमार काँटाय भरा बन, तोमार प्रेमे भरा मन ॥
मिछे दाओ काँटार व्याथा, सहिते ना पार ता;
आमार आँखि जल तोमाय करे गो चंचल,
ताइ नय बुझि बिफल आमार अश्रु बरिषण ॥
डाकिले कओ ना कथा, कि निठुर नीरबता ।
आबार फिरे चाओ, बल 'ओगो शुने याओ,
तोमार साथे आछे आमार अनेक कथा ॥'

+			०			+			०		
									पा	दपा	-दमा
									ओ	गो०	००
मा	मा	दा	पा	पा	-ा ॥	मज्ञा	-रमा	-ज्ञा	र	सा	-ा
नि	ठु	र	द	र	०	-दी०	००	०	ए	कि	०
									[-ा	पा	दा]
									[०	तो	मार]
रा	मा	मा	पा	मपणा	-दा	पा	-ा	-ा ॥	(पा	दपा	-दमा)
खे	ल	छ	अ	नु००	०	क्ष	०	ण्	(ओ	गो०	००)
(प) र्सा	र्सा	-ा	र्सा	र्सा	-ा	र्सर्रा	-र्सर्रा:	-र्सा:	णधा	णा	-धणपा
काँ	टा	य	भ	रा	०	ब०	०००	न्	तो०	मा	००र्
पा	पा	-दा	णा	(ण) पा	-णदा	पा	-ा	-ा	पा	दपा	-दमा
प्रे	मे	०	भ	रा	००	म	०	न्	ओ	गो०	००
						[मपा	णा	दा]			
		मा	पा	मगा	मा	पा	पा	-ा	दा	पा	-ा
		मि	छे	दा०	ओ	काँ	टा	र	व्य	था	०

+			०			+			०		
-ा	-ा	पा	र्सा	र्सा	-ा	णधा	णा	-णा	दा	पा	-ा
०	०	स	हि	ते	०	ना०	पा	०	र	ता	०
(-दपा	-दा	मा	पा	मगा	-मा)}	पा	पा	-र्सा	र्सा	र्सा	-ा
(००	०	मि	छे	दा०	ओ)}	आ	मा	र्	आँ	खि	०
र्सा	-ा	-ा	र्सरी	र्सर्ग	-र्सा	-ा	णा	णा	णा	णा	धा
ज	०	ल्	तो०	मा ०	य	०	क	रे	गो	च	न्
र्सणा	-धणा	-ा	-ा	पा	-धा	णा	-ा	णा	^{ण}धा	णा	-ा
च०	००	०	ल्	ता	इ	न	य	बु	झि	बि	०
णा	-ा	-ा	णा	^{ध}णा	दपा	पा	-ा	दो	णा	^{ण}पा	-णदा
फ	०	ल्	आ	मा	०र्	अ	श्	श्रु	ब	रि	००
पा	-ा	-ा	पा	दपा	-दमा ॥						
ष	०	ण	"ओ	गो०	००" ॥						
		मा	पा	मगा	-मा	{पा	-ा	पा	दा	पा	-ा
		डा	कि	ले०	०	{क	ओ	ना	क	था	०
-ा	-ा	पा	र्सा	र्सा	-ा	णधा	णा	^{ध}-णा	दा	पा	-ा
०	०	कि	नि	ठु	र	नी०	र	०	ब	ता	०
(-दपा	-दा	मा	पा	मगा	-मा)}	पा	पा	-र्सा	र्सा	र्सा	-ा
(००	०	डा	कि	ले०	०)}	आ	बा	र्	फि	रे	०
र्सा	-ा	-ा	र्सरी	र्सरी	-र्सा	-ा	णा	णा	णा	णा	-धा
चा	०	ओ	ब०	ल०	०	०	ओ	गो	शु	ने	०
र्सणा	-धणा	-ा	-ा	-पा	-धा	णा	णा	-ा	^{ण}-धा	णा	-ा
जा०	००	०	०	०	ओ	तो	मा	र	सा	थे	०

+			०			+			०		
णा	णा	-ा	णा	णा	-दपा	पा	पा	-दा	णा	(ण)पा	णदा
आ	छे	०	आ	मा	०र	अ	ने	०	क	क	था०
-पा	-ा	-ा	पा	दपा	-दमा ‖ ‖						
०	०	०	ओ	गो०	००						

Dwijendralal Ray

Born in 1863, 19th July, in Krishnanagar, Nadia, Dwijendralal was a famous poet, dramatist, playwright, lyricist and composer. He was the son of Dewan Kartikeya Chandra Ray who himself was a learned musician.

Dwijendralal was brought up in an atmosphere of *śāstrīya-saṅgita* from his child hood and showed great promise in literature and music. He wrote the songs of his *Āryagathā* (Part - I) between the age of twelve and seventeen and published them. He passed Bachelor of Arts, from Hoogly College and Master of Arts, from Presidency College with honours. He took up a teaching job, but got a scholarship from the British Government, to go to England to study agriculture for three years.

While in England, he studied Western music which he applied effectively in his songs, particularly in *Hāsir-gāna* and *Kautuk-gāna* (jocular and parodies), which became extremely popular. He translated many English, Irish and Scottish songs in Bengali, using the same tune but these were not so popular.

After his return from England he was offered the post of a settlement officer and then Deputy Magistrateship, although he deserved a higher post. This happened because of his nationalistic attitude which he never compromised with.

He married Surabala Devi, daughter of Pratap Chandra Majumdar, a renowned homeopath.

Dwijendralal's first posting was at Munghyr, where he composed many songs and poems. These were published as *Āryagāthā* (Part - II). The songs written and composed during this time became very popular. While at Munghyr he learnt *śāstrīya-saṅgīta* from *ustāds* and was greatly influenced by Surendranath Majumdar who was the Deputy Magistrate of that place and a well known musician specialising in *ṭap-khayāl*. Dwijendralal composed some of the songs in *ṭap-khayāl* style. This phase of his life was the best and he composed many beautiful songs. After the death of his wife in 1903, when he was only forty, he shunned away from all enjoyments of life. This reflected in his later compositions. Later he started writing dramas and cooperated actively with the National Movement. This created problem for him in his government job and he was harrassed with frequent transfers. However, his posting at Gaya proved another memorable literary phase in his life. He had composed his famous *svadeśī* song — '*Bāṅga āmār, jananī āmār, dhātrī āmār, āmār deś*' at Gaya. Whole of Bengal was influenced by this song. At this time, his national activities were taken note of by the English and he had to take long leave of one and a half years and he came to Calcutta. Most of his famous dramas were written during this period - at Gaya and Calcutta. He took early retirement due to ill health and settled down in Calcutta and started a few clubs for the litterateurs and musicians, viz. India Club, Pūrṇimā Milan, Ḍākāt Club, etc. He kept himself absorbed in various cultural activities till the end. He died in 1913.

Dwijendralal's contribution in music was many fold, e.g.

(a) Being learned in Western music he blended this style beautifully in his songs, particularly *Hāsir-gāna* or *Kautuk-gāna*.
(b) Being brought up and trained in Hindusthānī *śāstrīya-saṅgīta*, most of his songs were *rāga* based. He blended *rāgas* expertly to provide the right emotion to the songs. *Tālas* used by him were *Ektāla, Madhyamāna, Jat, Dādrā* etc.
(c) He composed excellent *kāvya-saṅgīta, svadeśī-saṅgīta* and *nātya-saṅgīta* introducing romanticism, fantasy, contrast and nationalistic temperament. The music he composed for these *padas* was also excellent and appropriate.
(d) He introduced a style of boldness in singing, keeping in mind the emotion and passion expressed in the lyrics.
(e) His *svadeśī-saṅgītas* were most suited for chorus singing.
(f) He organised music mehfils to propagate the then prevalent styles of music.

Dwijendralal however is more well known as a dramatist of historical plays and national songs although he wrote on themes of social, devotional and national importance and themes from the Purāṇas.

Dwijendralal composed his *rāga* based songs in such a manner that the singer had enough opportunity to carry out variations and elaborations of the *rāgas*. Unfortunately, some singers distorted the songs trying to do improvisations that were aesthetically not compatible. He wrote many plays for the professional groups. Among his historical plays: *Sītā, Tārābāi, Pratāp Siṃha, Candragupta, Siṃhala Vijaya, Nurjahan, Shahjahan, Durgādās, Mewār-patan* are famous.

His memorable songs are:

(1) *Kāvya-saṅgīta*: 1. *Āji tomār kāche bhāsiā jāy antara āmar,*
2. *O ke gāna geye geye cale jāy.* etc.

(2) *Svadeśī-saṅgīta*: 1. *Baṅga āmār jananī āmār.*
2. *Dhana dhānye puṣpe bharā.*

(3) *Nāṭya saṅgīta*: 1. *Oi mahā Sindhur opār hote.*
2. *Āy re basanta tor kiraṇ mākhā pākhā tule.*
(4) *Rāga*-based song: *Ekhano tapana oṭheni gagane - Toḍi-bhairavi.*
(5) *Hāsir-gāna*: 1. *Buḍo buḍi dujanāte*
2. *Nandalal - Ekadā ekṭā karila bhīṣaṇ paṇ.*

Dwijendralal expressed national feelings subtly through the satirical songs in his dramas, such as - *Jijiyā-kar, Khusroj, Irāndeśer-kāji,* etc. His son Dilip Kumar Ray is a well known musician (1896-1980) who notated many of his father's songs and published them for posterity.

Svadeśī Saṅgīta: Composer Dwijendralal Ray.

धन धान्ये पुष्पे भरा आमादेर एइ बसुन्धरा,
ताहार माझेआछे देश एक सकल देशेर सेरा ।
ओसे स्वप्न दिये तैरी से देश स्मृति दिये घेरा ।
एमन देशटि कोथाओ खुँजे पाबेनाको तुमि
सकल देशेर राणी सेये आमार जन्म भूमि ॥
चन्द्र सूर्य ग्रह तारा कोथाय उजल एमन धारा
कोथाय एमन खेले तड़ित् एमन कालो मेघे
(तार) पाखीर डाके घुमिये उठि पाखीर डाके जेगे
एमन देशटि कोथाओ खुँजे पाबेनाको तुमि
सकल देशेर राणी सेये आमार जन्मभूमि ॥
एत स्निग्ध नदी काहार कोथाय एमन धुम्र पाहाड़
कोथाय एमन हरित क्षेत्र आकाश तले मेले
(एमन) धानेर उपर ढेड खेले याय बातास काहार देशे ।
एमन देशटि कोथाओ खुँजे पाबे नाको तुमि
सकल देशेर राणी सेये आमार जन्मभूमि ॥
पुष्पे पुष्पे भरा शाखी कुंजे कुंजे गाहे पाखी
गुंजरिया आसे अलि पुंजे पुंजे धेये
(तारा) फुलेर उपर घुमिये पड़े फुलेर मधु खेये ।
एमन देशटि कोथाओ खुँजे पाबे नाको तुमि
सकल देशेर राणी सेये आमार जन्मभूमि ॥
भायेर मायेर एत स्नेह कोथाय गेले पाबे केह
ओमा तोमार चरण तुटि बक्षे आमार धरि
(आमार) एइ देशेते जन्म येन एइ देशेते मरि

एमन देशटि कोथाओ खुँजे पाबे नाको तुमि
सकल देशेर राणी सेये आमार जन्म भूमि ॥

Composer: Dwijendralal Ray: (Composed on Pañcamātrik tāla, i.e. tāla consisting of five mātrās)

पाँचश बछर एमनि करे आसछि सये समुदाय;
एइटि कि आर सइबेनाक – दु'घा बेशी जुतोर घाय ?
सेटा निये मिछे भाबा; दिबि दु'घा देना बाबा ।
दु'घा बेशी दुघा कमे एमनि कि आर आसे याय ।
तबे किना जुतोर गुँतो हये गेछे अनेकबार,
एकटा किछु नूतन रकम कर्ले हत उपकार;
धरना येमन, बेटा बले दिलि नाहय कानटा मले;
जुतोर खोँटा खेये घाँटा पड़े गेछे सकल गाय ।
पड़े आछि चरण तलाय नाकटि गुँजे अनेक काल;
सइबे सबइ, नइत मानुष, आमरा सबाइ भेड़ार पाल;
ये या करिस देखिस चाचा, मोदेर पैत्रिक प्राणटा बाँचा,
शाँसटा खेये आँशटा फेले दिसरे दुटो दुबेलाय ।
तोरा राजा तोराइ मुनिब, मोरा चाकर मोरा पर,
मने करिस चाचा एटा तोदेर बाड़ी तोदेर घर :
मोरा बेटा मोरा पाजि, या बलिस ताइ आछि राजि, –
राजार नन्दिनी प्यारि, या बलिस ताइ शोभा पाय ॥

+					०				ग	+					०				॥
दा	दा	पा	मा	-।	मा	मा	पा	मपमा	-मा	ज्ञा	रा	ज्ञा	मा	-।	ज्ञा	ऋ	सा	-।	-।
पाँच	श	ब	छ	र	एम्	नि	क	रे००	०	आस्	छि	स	ये	०	स	मु	दा	०	य

ण्	ण्	सा	सा	-।	ज्ञा	ज्ञा	ऋ	सा	-।	दा	दा	-पा	मा	मा	ज्ञा	मा	ज्ञऋ	-सण्	सा
-एइ	टि	कि	आ	र	सइ	बे	ना	क	०	दु	घा	०	बे	शी	जु	तोर	घा०	००	य

धा	धा	धा	धा	-।	णा	णा	णधा	णा	-।	णर्सा	णर्सा	णा	दपा	मा	णा	दा	पा	मा	-।
से	टा	नि	ये	०	मि	छे	भा०	बा	०	दि०	बि०	दु	घा०	०	दे	ना	बा	बा	०
धर्	ना	जे	म	न्	बे	टा	ब०	ले	०	दि०	लि०	ना	ह०	य	कान्	टा	म	ले	०
जे	जा	क	रि	स्	दे	खिस्	चा०	चा	०	मो०	देर्	पै	तृ०	क	प्राण	टा	बाँ	चा	०
मो	रा	बे	टा	०	मो	रा	पा०	जि	०	जा०	ब०	लिस्	ता०	इ	आ	छि	रा	जि	०

+					०					+					०				
ण्	ण्	सा	सा	-ा	ज्ञा	ज्ञा	रा	सा	-ा	सा	मा	ज्ञा	मा	-ा	ज्ञा	ऋ्ज्ञ	सा	-ा	-ा
त	बे	कि	ना	०	जु	तोर	गुँ	तो	०	ह	ये	गे	छे	०	अ	नेक	बा	०	र
प	ड़े	आ	छि	०	च	रण्	त	ला	य	नाक्	टि	गुँ	जे	०	अ	नेक्	का	०	ल
तो	राइ	रा	जा	०	तो	राइ	मु	नि	ब	मो	रा	चा	क	र	मो	रा०	प	०	र

ण्	सा	ज्ञा	मा	-ा	पा	दा	पा	णदा	पदा	ह्मा	ह्मा	ह्मा	मा	ह्मा	मा	ह्मा	मा	-ा	-ा
एक्	टा	कि	छु	०	न	तुन	र	क०	म०	क	लें	ह	त	०	उ	प	का	०	र
सइ	बे	सब	इ	०	नइ	त०	मा	नु०	ष०	मो	रा	स	बा	इ	भे	ड़ार्	पा	०	र
म	ने	क	रि	स्	चा	चा	ए	टा०	००	तो	देर्	बा	ड़ी	०	तो	देर्	घ	०	र

णा्	सा	ज्ञा	ज्ञा	-ा	मा	मा	णा	णा	णा	दा	दा	पा	मा	-ा	ज्ञा	मा	ज्ञऋ्ज्ञ	सणा्	सा
दु	घा	बे	शी	०	दु	घा	क	मे	०	ए	म	नि	कि	०	आ	से	जा०	००	य
जु	तोर	खोँ	टा	०	खे	ये	घाँ	टा	०	प	ड़े	गे	छे	०	स	कल्	गा०	००	य
शाँस	टा	खे	ये	०	आँश	टा	फे	ले	०	दिस्	रे	दु	टो	०	दु	बे	ला०	००	य
रा	जा	र	न	०	न्दि	नी	प्या	री	०	जा	ब	लिसता		इ	शो	भा	पा०	००	य

[Hāsir gāna of Dwijendralal Ray]

एखनो तपन ओठेनि गगने पूरब भागे
एखनो धरणी चेये आछे पथ ताहार लागि।
एखनो नीरव तिमिर जड़ित निभृत कुंज,
एखनो घुमाय शाखाय शाखाय मधुप पुंज
आछे शुधु चाहि मेघकुल साजि भूषित अरुण-किरणरागे।
धीरे धीरे ए उठिल गगने दिवसराज,
छड़ाये पड़िल महिमार छटा भुवन माझ,
अमनि उठिल कानने कानने विहग छन्द
अमनि उठिल कुंजे कुंजे कुसुम गन्ध
ढुलिल चामर शीतल समीर परशे भुवन उठिल जागि।

Toḍī-Bhairav - Dādrā (trimātrik chanda tāla)

+			०			+			०		
गा	मा	पा	णा	दा	पदा	मा	पा	दा	पा	मा	मा
ए	ख	नो	त	प	न०	ओ	ठे	नि	ग	ग	ने

गा	मऋ्ज्ञ	ऋ्ज्ञ	गा	-मा	मा	मा	दा	दा	दा	^{प}दा	दा
पू	र०	व	भा	०	गे	ए	ख	नो	ध	र	णी

+			म °			+	प		°		
पा	दा	पा	गा	मा	पा	गा	मा	गा	ऋा	-।	सा }
चे	ये	आ	छे	प	थ	ता	हा	र	ला	०	गि }

{दा	दा	दा	ना	र्सा	र्सा	र्सा	र्सा	र्सा	र्सना	र्ऋा	र्सा
{ए	ख	नो	नी	र	व	ति	मि	र	ज०	ड़ि	त
{अ	म	नि	उ	ठि	ल	का	न	ने	का०	न	ने

ना	र्सना	दा	ना	-र्सा	र्सा						
नि	भृ०	त	कु	०	ज						
वि	ह	ग	छ	०	न्द						

र्सा	र्ज्ञा	र्ज्ञा	र्ऋा	र्सा	र्सा	ना	र्सा	ना	दा	पा	-।
ए	ख	नो	घु	मा	य	शा	खा	य	शा	खा	य
अ	म	नि	उ	ठि	ल	कुं	०	जे	कुं	०	जे

म ज्ञा	मा	णा	दा	-।	पा }						
म	धु	प	पुं	०	ज }						
कु	सु	म	ग	०	न्ध }						

पा	दा	ना	र्सा	र्ऋा	र्सा	ना	र्सा	ना	दा	पा	ममा
आ	छे	शु	धु	चा	हि	मे	घ	कु	ल	सा	जि०
ढु	लि	ल	चा	म	र	शी	त	ल	स	म	र

पा	णा	णा	दा	पा	मा	गा	मा	ऋा	गा	-मा	मा ‖
भू	षि	त	अ	रु	ण	कि	र	ण	रा	०	गे ‖
प	र	शे	भु	ब	न	उ	ठि	ल	जा	०	गि ‖

{मा	मा	मा	मा	र्सा	-।	ना	र्सा	ना	दा	पा	पा
{धी	रे	धी	रे	ए	०	उ	ठि	ल	ग	ग	ने

म ज्ञा	मा	पा	ण दा	-।	दा						
दि	ब	स	रा	०	ज						

+			०			+			०	म	
दा	र्सा	ना	र्सा	ना	ना	पा	दा	मा	पा	ज्ञा	मा
छ	ड़ा	ये	प	ड़ि	ल	म	हि	मा	र	छ	टा
ज्ञसा	ज्ञा	ऋा	सा	-ा	-ा}						
भु०	ब	न	मा	०	झ}						

Rajanikanta Sen

Rajanikanta Sen was born in 1865 in a village called Bhangabari. He is well known as a composer of songs which are of '*Śānta-rasa*'. He was neither a researcher nor did he make any experiment with *rāgas* or Western melodies. He is known as a '*Maramī Kavi*' i.e. a poet whose compositions touched the heart. His lyrics were mostly influenced by Rabindranath. He composed his songs in simple words and tunes and these were *chanda-pradhāna*, using variety in *chanda*, such as - 3+2+3 =8 *mātrās*, e.g. '*Tomāri deoā prāṇe*', '*Kabe tṛṣita e maru chāḍiyā jāiba*', etc. The *rāgas* that he used were straight forward, such as: *Bihāga, Bhairavī, Kānaḍā, Yaman-Kalyāṇa, Khāmāja* etc and were devoid of *ālāpacāri* or *tāna* etc., yet the *rāga-rūpas* were clear.

Some of his songs were on *kīrtana* style in which he used unique *chanda,* e.g. '*Kuṭila kupatha dhariyā*'. One of his famous songs - '*Ṭumi nirmala kara maṅgala kare*' is based on *Bhairavī* and there is scope for simple *ālāpacāri. Bāul-gāna* was his favourite and he composed his famous *svadeśī* song - '*Māyer deoyā moṭā kāpaḍ māthāy tule nere bhāi*', in *Bāul* style.

Rajanikanta's compositions were such that though these were *rāga* based yet there was not much scope for the singer to expand the *rāgas* to make the songs *rāga* dominated. He composed *kāvya-saṅgīta, Hāsir-gāna Bhakti-gīti* and *Svadeśī-saṅgīta.* Though the number of his songs were not many, yet he distinguished himself as a *gītikār* and *surakār.*

Rajanikanta's father Guruprasad was a Sub-Judge and was a musician too. Rajanikanta grew up in the musical atmosphere at home and could sing *Rāmprasādī* songs from his childhood.

He had his schooling from Rajshahi and did his B.A. and B.L. from city college of Calcutta. He started practising law at Rajshahi and side by side he devoted himself in music and composing lyrics. His wife gave him a lot of inspiration in his literary and musical activities.

At Rajshahi, he became known for his lyrics and also as a vocalist with a melodious voice. His songs used to be published in a journal named '*Utsāha*'. He also got encouragement from Akshayay Kumar Maitreya who introduced him to personalities and institutions as a lyricist and singer. He soon took part as a singer in Albert Hall where Rabindranath, and Dwijendralal also sang.

In 1902 his first book *Bāṇī* and in 1905 *Kalyāṇī* were published. These two contain *Bhaktigīti, Prītigīti, Svadeśī-gānas* and *Hāsir-gāna.*

In 1909 he developed cancer of the throat and could sing no more. But he composed some more lyrics which were published as *Amṛta, Abhayā,* and *Ānandamayī.* Some were published in *Sadbhava Śataka* and *Śeṣ-dāna.* Kantakavi, as he was fondly called passed away on 28th Bhādra 1317 B.S. (1910).

Composer - Rajanikanta Sen
Rāga - Bihāg

कबे तृषित ए मरु छाड़िया याइब
तोमारि रसाल नन्दने,
कबे तापित ए चित करिब शीतल
तोमारि करुणा चन्दने ।
कबे तोमाते हये याब आमार आमि हारा,
तोमारि नाम निते नयने बये धारा,
ए देह शिहरिबे व्याकुल रबे प्राण
बिपुल पुलक स्पन्दने ।
कबे भबेर सुख दुख चरणे दलिया,
यात्रा करिब गो श्रीहरि बलिया,
चरण चलिबेना हृदय गलिबेना
काहारो आकुल क्रन्दने ॥

Composer - Rajanikanta Sen

आमि सकल काजेर पाइ हे समय,
तोमारे डाकिते पाइने,
आमि चाहि दारा सुत सुख सन्मिलन,
तब संग सुख चाइने ।
आमि कतइ ये करि बृथा पर्यटन,
तोमार काछे तो याइने,
आमि कत किये खाइ, भस्म आर छाइ
तब प्रेमामृत खाइने ।
आमि कत गान गाहि मनेर हरषे,
तोमार महिमा गाइने,
आमि बाहिरेर दुटो आँखि मेले चाइ
ज्ञान आँखि मेले चाइने ।

आमि कार तरे देइ आपना बिलाये,
ओ पदतले बिकाइने,
आमि सबारे शिखाइ कत नीति कथा,
मनेरे शुधु शिखाइने ॥

+			०			+			०		
										पा	पा
										आ	मि
ध	धर्सा	-धा	पा	ह्मपधपा	पमा	मा	-पधा	पा	मगा	मा	-गरा
स	क०	ल	का	जे०००	र०	पा	०इ	हे	स०	म	०य
रा	सरगा	रसा	सध़्	-सा	सा	सा	-रा	सरा	-गा	पा	पा
तो	मा००	रे०	डा०	०कि	ते	पा	०इ	ने०	०	आ	मि
										गा	गा
										आ	मि
गा	गमा	मगा	रगमा	मगा	रा	गा	गपा	पा	पधा	धा	पधना
चा	हि०	दा०	रा००	सु०	त	सु	ख०	सम्	मि०	ल	न००
पा	धना	धा	ह्म पा	-गा	रगा	सा	-रा	सरा	-गा	पा	पा
त	ब०	सं	ग	सु	ख०	चा	इ	ने०	०	आ	मि
										गा	पा
										आ	मि
पा	पगा	-गपा	पा	पा	धा	धा	धर्सा	र्सा	र्सना	र्रसा	-नधा
क	त०	०इ	जे	क	रि	बृ	था०	पर्	ज०	ट०	०न्
धा	धना	-र्सरी	र्सना	नधा	धपा	पा	-धा	पधा	-ना	-धा	-नधा
तो	मा०	०र्	का०	छे०	तो०	जा	इ	ने०	०	०	००

+			०	पा	पा	+			०	र्	
-पा	-ा	-ा	-ा	(पा	पा)	धा	धर्रा	-र्रा	र्सना	र्सा	-नधा
०	०	०	०	आ	मि	क	त०	की	जे०	खा	०इ
धा	धना	धा	-पा	धा	-पा	गा	पमा	गा	रा	सा	सा
भ	स्म	आ	र्	छा	इ	त	ब०	प्रे	मा	मृ	त
सा	-रा	सरा	-गा	पा	पा ||						
खा	इ	ने०	०	आ	मि						
										गा	गा
										आ	मि
गा	गमा	गा	-रगमा	गा	रा	रगा	गपा	पा	पधा	धना	ना
क	त०	गा	००न्	ग	हि	म०	ने०	र	ह०	र०	षे
पा	धना	धना	ह्मपा	-गा	रगा	सा	रा	सना्	-गा	गा	गा
तो	मा०	०र	म०	०हि	मा०	गा	इ	ने०	०	आ	मि
गा	गमा	मा	-ा	मा	मा	गा	गमा	गरा	रा	गरा	-सा
बा	हि०	रे	र	दु	टो	आँ	खि०	मे०	ले	चा०	०इ
										पा	पा
सा	-ध्सा	सा	सा	सा	सा	सा	रा	ससा	-गा	(गा	गा)
ज्ञा	०न	आँ	खि	मे	ले	चा	इ	ने०	०	आ	मि
पा	ह्मा	पा	पा	पा	-धा	धा	धर्सा	र्सा	र्सा	र्सा	नधा
का	र्	त	रे	दे	इ	आ	प०	ना	बि	ला	ये०
धा	धनर्सर्रा	र्रर्सा	र्सना	नधा	धपा	पा	-धा	पधा	-ना	-धा	-नधा
ओ	प०००	द०	त०	ले०	बि०	का	इ	ने०	०	०	००
-पा	-ा	-ा	-ा	पा	पा	ध	धर्सा	र्रा	र्सना	र्रर्सा	-नधा
०	०	०	०	आ	मि	स	बा०	रे	शि०	खा०	०इ

+			o			+			o		
धा	धना	धा	पा	धा	पा }	गा	गपमा	गरा	रा	रसा	ना
क	त०	नी	ति	क	था }	म	ने००	रे०	शु	धु	शि
सा	–रा	सरा	–गा	पा	पा ‖						
खा	इ	ने०	०	आ	मि ‖						

Kaji Nazrul Islam

Nazrul Islam was born in a poor family in the village of Churulia in the district of Burdwan, on 24th May, 1899. He lost his father at a tender age and had to struggle hard, but his keen interest in music never waned. Since his boyhood, he used to compose songs for the village *mehfils.*

His formal education was limited. When he was a student of tenth class, he joined the army during the First World War and was posted in Karachi, where he had the opportunity to study Persian literature. He sent many articles written in Bengali for publishing in the various journals of Calcutta.

After the end of the war Nazrul came back to his village and thence to Calcutta and absorbed himself in *kāvya* and *saṅgīta.* In 1921, his first sensational poem, '*Vidrohī*' meaning revolutionary, was published in '*Moslem Bhārat*'. It became a hit and Nazrul earned the name of '*Vidrohī Kavi*'. In actual life also, Nazrul had a life of turmoil. He could never accept any bondage and found happiness in diversity. This unique trait of his character marked by cheerfulness, unrestrained delight and happiness, reflected in his compositions. Soon he was an established litterateur and gained experience as a journalist by working in '*Navayuga*' and '*Dhumketu*' papers. Some of his famous works are: *Surbāhār, Biṣer Bā̃śī, Dolan-cā̃pa, Sindhu Hillola, Chāyānaṭ, Sandhyā, Agnivīṇā,* etc.

Nazrul was jailed by the British because of his activities and exciting articles for National Movement. While in the jail, Nazrul took to fast to protest against the atrocities of the jailor. This led to a nationwide movement and Nazrul broke his fast after forty days.

Nazrul married a Hindu lady in 1924. Unfortunately, he went through a number of tragedies: he lost his mother and his son Bulbul, his wife took ill and suffered from paralysis. Later, he himself became ill with an ailment of the brain. By the time he was taken to Europe for treatment, it was too late to recover fully. He suffered for several years and passed away in 1976 at Dhaka.

Nazrul was honoured by the Government of India with the title of *Padma-bhushan* in 1960. In 1972 Bangladesh felicitated him specially by taking him there.

His wealth of compositions are available in notated forms in books compiled by his son Kaji Aniruddha.

Nazrul occupies an important place as a *gītikār* and *surakār* but perhaps more as a *surakār.* He broke away from traditionality by introducing - (1) *rāga-pradhāna* or *rāga* - based songs which could be sung with complete *rāgadāri,* giving more importance to the melody than to the lyric, (2) songs based on folk tunes and rendered also in true folk style, for which he composed extra stanzas, (3) songs adopted from Arabic and other foreign styles, both lyrically and melody wise, (4) *ghazals* in Bengali, with the true *gāyakī* of *ghazal,* (5) *Śyāmā-saṅgīta* and other devotional songs of deep devotional quality, (6) *svadeśī-saṅgīta* with passionate feelings and (7) *ādhunika saṅgīta* with a new trend.

Nazrul's simple and sprightly tunes in love songs; adaptation of language as well as tunes of other lands in his compositions; feel of classical and semi-classical styles such as *khayāl, ṭhumrī, ghazal, kajrī, caiti,* etc. were all his objective contribution. He treated the compositions more from the angle of *saṅgīta* than *kāvya.*

Nazrul's dynamic personality and creativity came at a time when there was a void created by Rabindranath's moving over to Shantiniketan.

Nazrul's popularity was tremendous because of his understanding the popular demands of the time and he experimented accordingly. His compositions of *ghazal* style offered touch of *ṭhumrī, chanda* varieties, sometimes mixed with *dādrā* and the special *gāyakī* of *ghazal,* e.g. '*Keu bhole nā keu bhole*', '*Basiā bijane keno ekā mane*', '*Phāgun rāter phuler neśāy*', etc. He introduced '*Śer*' in *ghazal* and *dādrā,* and his style became known as '*Nazruliyā*'. *Dādrā* was his favourite style and he created variety in it, e.g. '*Mor ghuma ghore ele manohar*', '*Dāḍāle duāre mor*', '*Rumu jhumu rumu jhumu*', etc. Like Atulprasad, Nazrul also excelled in *ṭhumrī* style, e.g. '*Kon kule āj bhiḍla tarī*' in *dādrā tāla.*

Nazrul used *rāgas* and style of classical music perfectly in his compositions. This is clearly observed in his *rāga* based songs rendered by Jñān Goswāmī and Dhirendrachandra Mitra in *khayāl* style, e.g. '*Śūnya e buke pākhī mor*' in *Chāyānaṭ,* '*Jhan jhan jhan jhan pāyelā bāje*' in *Naṭ-bihāga,* '*Kāberī nadī jale*' in *Jogiyā,* etc. Other singers who also have done justice to his *khayāl* and *ṭhumrī* styles, are: K.C. De, Angurbala, Indubala, Sachin Deb Barman and others.

Nazrul's folk based songs are of pure folk style, e.g. '*Āmi bhāi khyāpā bāul*'.

His *svadeśī* songs portray the true sentiment of nationalism, eg. '*Ei śikal parā chal moder*', '*Durgama giri kāntāra maru*', '*Kārār e lauha kapāṭ*', '*Āji rakta niśi bhore*', etc. The first song was composed when he was in jail. Many of his songs have been lost for lack of notation at that time.

Nazrul's songs on Arabic and Persian, Italian and Cuban tunes are: '*Bāgicāy bulbuli*', '*Rumjhum jhum jhum*', '*Śukno pātār nūpur pāye*', '*Dūr dvīpa bāsinī*', '*Momer putul'*, *'Karuṇa keno ā̃khi, dāo go sākī, dāo sarāb'*, *'Musāfir mochore ā̃khijal'*. These have a gay and happy rhythm and depict the sentiments beautifully.

Nazrul's *Śyāmā saṅgīta* compositions also need special mention. He wrote many of them particularly after he lost his eldest son Bulbul. To get mental peace, he very often spent long hours in Dakshineshwar temple in *yogābhyāsa,* and at the alter of the deity his mother-in-law had. Some of his famous *Śyāmā-saṅgītas* are: '*Bal re jabā bal*', '*Tor kālo rūp dekhte Māgo*', '*Mahākāler kole ese*', '*Kālo Māyer pāyer talāy*', etc. Some of his songs on Vaiṣṇava theme are: *Varṇa corā ṭhākur elo*', '*Nāciā nāciā eso Nandadulāl*', '*Ore rākhāl chele*', etc., which are based on *kīrtana* style. Most of Nazrul's *Śyāmā-saṅgītas* were sung by Mrinalkanti Ghosh on gramophone records. During the *Durgā-pujā* festival, demand for *Āgamanī* songs used to be plenty. Nazrul composed a number of them for Gramophone Company, to meet the popular demand. His style of tuning songs of *Śyāmā-saṅgīta* was different from Ramprasad's, although textwise he chose simple word and treated *Umā /Śyāmā* as a close member of the household and also as '*Mā*', the universal Mother, the *Śakti.*

Nazrul experimented with new *chandas* and suitable *tālas* to bring out variety and novelty. Sometimes he composed certain portions without *tālas* and used to create a special *bhāva* by maintaining a pause either at the start of a '*Kali*' or at the end of a '*stavaka*'. For chorus songs his arrangements were perfect to maintain the sentiment of the lyric with the style of singing.

Nazrul's popularity as a *surakār* and *gītikār* was established through Gramophone records and radio with which he was closely associated. He trained many, and composed many songs for these two media. Many of his songs are available today because of the disc records.

Three important achievements of Nazrul are:

(1) to liberate songs from literary burden,
(2) to introduce compositions in Bengali which could be rendered in pure *rāga-saṅgīta* style of *khayāl* and *ṭhumrī*, and
(3) to hail the new style of *ādhunik-gāna.*

He was like a bridge between the traditional and the modern.

A few examples of his variety of song compositions are given below:

Rāga pradhāna - Phuler jalsāy nīrab keno Kavi; Kāberī nadī jale; Meghe meghe andha asīm ākāś; Mahuā bane bane pāpiyā; etc.
Vicitra - Dūr-dvīpa bāsinī; Momer putul; Nurjāhān; Mamtāj; etc.
Ghazal - Hārāno hiyār; Golāp phuler kā̃ṭā; etc.
Ṭhumrī - Paradesi bādhu ghum bhāṅgāyo cumi ā̃khi,
Holī - Āy gopinī khelbo holī,
Kajrī - Kājarī gāhiyā eso gopa lalanā,

Dādrā - Elo oi pūrna śaśī; Kul rākha nā rākha; Campā pārul jūthi,
Jhumur - Ore rākhāl chele; Ore ḍeke de; Cokh gelo cokh gelo,
Folk - Padmār ḍheu re; Meghlā niśi bhore; Dudhe āltāy raṅg jeno tār,
Bāul - Āhār diben jini; Tumi dukher beśe ele bale,
Bhāṭiyālī - Ekul bhāṅge okul gaḍe, Tomāy kule kule bandhu,
Ādhunik - Śāono rāte jadi; Bāsantī raṅg śaḍī paro,
Bhajan - Āmār nayāne Kṛṣṇa nayana tara; Eso Naola Kiśore; Bane cale Bana mālī.
Svadeśī - Gaṅgā Sindhu Narmadā,; Bhārata Laksmī āy Mā phire,
Śyāmā saṅgīta - Āmār Mā je golāp sundarī; Tui kothāy lukāli Mā Kālī,
Kīrtana - Nā miṭite mana sādh jeonā he.
Islāmī - Allah āmār prabhu; E kon madhur śarāb dile; Niśidin jape Khodā.
Hindi bhajan - Sundara ho tuma mana mohana ho; Kṛṣṇa Gopāla.
Hāsir gāna - Tui ulṭā bujhli Rāma; Niye kādā māṭir tāl;

Nazrul used some special *chandas*:

(i) *Caturmātrik ektāla*; this has no *khālī* - |1 2 3 4|5 6 7 8|9 10 11 12| (+ over 1, 2 over 5, 3 over 9)

(ii) *Priyā*: This is of 7 *mātrās* and the *chanda* is - |1 2|3 4 5|6 7 8| (+ over 1, 2 over 3, 3 over 6)

Some of the *rāgas* and *tālas* used by the poet-composer, are:

Rāgas: *Śiva-rañjanī, Mānḍ, Hijāj-bhairavī, Khamāja, Miśra-khamāja, Hindola, Bāgeśrī, Mśra-śivarañjanī, Āsāvarī, Durgā, Dhānī, Miśra-dhānī, Bhairavī, Miśra-bhairavī, Sindhu, Paṭdīpa, Ānanda-bhairava, Pīlu, Darbārī-kānaḍā, Karṇāṭaki-sāmanta, Jogiyā, Jayjayantī, Deśa, Miśra-deśa, Khāmāja-deśa, Miśra-gārā, Sāraṅga,* etc.
Tālas: *Tritāla, Dādrā, Teorā, Ekṭāla, Kahārvā, Gitāṅgī, Kavvālī, Kārfā, Rūpaka, Dhāmār, Addhā-kavvālī, Ṭhumrī tāla, Sādrā, etc.* Some song examples of Nazrul:

Composer: Kaji Nazrul Islam.
Ghazal: Rāga Bageśrī Tāla Karfā.

हारानो हियार निकुंज पथे
कुड़ाइ झरा फुल एकेला आमि ।
तुमि केन हाय ! आसिले हेथाय
सुखेर स्वरग हइते नामि ॥
चारिपाशे मोर उड़िछे केबल
शुकानोपाता मलिन फुलदल
बृथाइ केन हाय ! तब आँखिजल

छिटाओ अबिरल दिबस यामी ।
एले अबेलाय पथिक बे-भुल,
विँधिछे काँटा नाहि यबे फुल
कि दिये बरण करि ओ चरण
निभिछे जीबन जीबनस्वामी ॥

+				०				+				०			
															सा
															हा
		ण											र्स		
सज्ञा	-रसा	धा	णा	सा	-मा	-ा	मज्ञा	मा	धा	धा	धणा	पधा	-णा	-धा	मा
रा०	००	नो	हि	या	०	र	नि०	कु	न्	ज	प०	थे०	०	०	कु
		प						स			म				
मपा	-धा	मा	धपा	मा	-ज्ञा	-ा	ज्ञा	रा	-ा	रा	ज्ञा	रसा	-ा	-ा	सा
ड़ा०	इ	झ	रा०	फु	०	ल	ए	के	०	ला	आ	मि०	०	०	तु
		ण्												प	
सज्ञा	-रसा	धा्	णा्	सा	-गा	मा	मा	धा	पधा	-णर्सा	णा	धणा	-धणा	मा	मा
मि०	००	के	न	हा	०	य	आ	सि	ले०	००	हे	था०	०	थ	सु
		प	ध					स			म				
मपा	-धपा	मा	पा	मा	-ज्ञा	-ा	ज्ञा	रा	-ा	रा	ज्ञा	रा	-सा	-ा	सा
खे०	०	र	स्व	र	०	गे	ह	इ	०	ते	ना	मि	०	०	"हा"
															मज्ञा
															चा०
मा	-णा	धा	धणा	धणा	-र्सा	-ा	र्सरी	र्सा	-ा	णधा	णा	णर्सा	-ा	-ा	र्सा
रि	०	पा	शे०	मो०	०	र	उ०	ड़ि	०	छे०	के	ब०	०	ल्	शु
					र्स र्स							र			
र्सा	-र्सा	णा	धणा	पधा	-णा	-धा	मपा	मज्ञा	-ा	सरा	रज्ञा	सा	-ा	-ा	सा
का	००	नो	पा०	ता०	०	०	म०	लि०	न्	फु०	ल०	द	०	ल्	बृ
		ण्													
सज्ञा	-रसा	धा्	णा्	सा	-गा	मा	मा	धा	पधा	-णर्सा	णा	धणा	-धणा	मा	मा
था०	०इ	के०	न	हा	०	य	त	ब	आँ०	००	खि	ज०	००	ल्	छि
			ध					स			म	र			
मपा	-धा	मा	पा	मज्ञा	-ा	-ा	ज्ञा	रा	-ा	रा	ज्ञा	सा	-ा	-ा	सा
टा०	ओ	अ	बि	र०	ल्	०	दि	ब	०	स	जा	मी	०	०	"हा"
															{सा
															{ए

+		[मपधा	मपा]	०				+				०			
समा	-ा	(मा.	पा)	मज्ञा	-ा	-ा	ज्ञा	सरा	-ा	रा	मज्ञा	रसा	-ा	-ा	मा
ले०	०	अ	बे	ला०	०	य	प	थि०	०	क	बे०	भु	०	ल्	बिं

					र्स र्स			म								
मा	-धा	धा	धणा	पधा	-णा	-धा	मपा	ज्ञा	-ा	रज्ञा	सरा	मा	-ा	-ा }	धणा
धि	०	छे	काँ०	टा०	०	०	ना०	हि	०	ज०	बे०	फु	०	ल् }	कि०

								र्स			र्म	र्र			
र्सा	-र्मा	र्ज्ञा	र्ज्ञा	र्ज्ञा	-ा	-ा	र्ज्ञा	र्री	-ा	र्री	र्ज्ञा	र्सा	-ा	-ा	र्सर्रा
दि	०	ये	ब	र	०	णा	क	रि	०	ओ	च	र	०	ण	नि०

ण					र्स			म		स		र			
सा	-ा	णा	धणा	पधा	-णा	-धा	मपा	ज्ञा	-ा	रा	रज्ञा	सा	-ा	-ा	सा
भि	०	छे	जी०	ब०	०	न	जी०	ब	०	न	स्वा०	मी	०	०	"हा"

Ṭhumrī: Rāga-Mānḍ Tāla-Kavvālī

परदेशी बँधु ! धुम भाडायो चुमि आँखि ।
यदि गो निशीथ जेगे घुमाइया थाकि ॥
यदि दीप नेभेगो कुटीरे,
बातायन पाने चाहि येओ ना फिरे,
निबेछे आँखिर शिखा प्राण आछे बाकी ॥
यदि गान थामे मोर मुखे
फिरिया येओना बीणा रबे तबु बुके,
नाहि गान दुख नीड़े (कुलायेते)
आछे तबु पाखी ॥

+				२				०				३			
-ा	-ा	-ा	{ससा	रमा	मा	पधां	पधा	र्सा	सर्रणा	-धपा:	पधा	मा	-गा	-सा	रगा
०	०	०	{पर	दे०	शी	बँ०	धु०	०	धु००	०म्	भाडा	यो	०	०	चुमि

					स									प	
रगा	-सा	सा }	-ा	-ा	{र्सर्सा	र्सा	र्सा	नर्सा	णधा	धणा	धपा	-ा	पधा	मा	रा
आँ	०	खि }	०	०	{जोदि	गो	नि	शी०	थ०	जे०	गे०	०	घु०	माइ	या

								प		र					
मपा	-पधा	धा	-मपमा	-ा	मपधर्सा	णाः	धपधः	मा	-गा	-सा	रगा	गरसरा	सा	-ा	सरा
था०	००	कि	०००	०	घु०००	म्	भा०डा	यो	०	०	चुमि	आँ०००	खि	०	चुमि

												प		र	
णसधा्	सा	-ा	सस	रमा	मा	मपा	पधा	-मपमा	मपधर्स	णा	धपधा	मा	-गा	सा	रगा
आँ०	खि	०	पर	दे०	शी	बँ	धु०	०००	धु०००	म्	भा:जा०	यो	०	०	चुमि

+	२	०	३
रगा -सा सा -ा	-ा पधा मा -पा	धा धर्सा र्सा पधा	धा -र्सा र्सा -ा
आँ० ० खि ०	० जदि दी प	ने भे० गो कु०	टि ० रे ०
-ा सर्सा -र्सा र्सा	नर्सा नधा धणा धपा	-ा पधा (प)-मा मा	मपा -र्सना धा -ा
० बाता य न	पा० ने० चा० हि०	० जेयो ना गो	फि० ०० रे ०
-ा -ा धनधनध -पधनर्स	-ा र्सर्सा र्सा -ा	ना र्सना (ध)दा धा	धा -र्सा र्सा -ा
० ० ००००० ००००	० जदि दी प	ने भे० गो कु	टि ० रे ०
-ा र्सर्सा -र्स र्सा	नर्सा नधा धणा धपा	-ा पधा (प)-मा पा	पा -ा पा -ा
० बाता य न	पा० ने० चा० हि०	० जेयो ना गो	फि ० रे ०
-ा धर्सा -र्सा र्सा	नर्सा नधा धणा धपा	-ा पधा (प)-मा रा	रमा -मपा पा -धा
० निबे छे आँ	खि० र० शि० खा०	० प्राण आ छे	बा० ०० की ०
-ा -ा -मपा मा	मपधर्सा -नर्सा -णा धपधा	(प)मा (र)-गा -सा रगा	रगा -सा सा ससा
० ० ०० ०	धु००० ००० म भा०डा	यो ० ० चुमि	आँ० ० खि पर
रा मा मा मपा	पधा -ा -मपा -मा	मपधर्सा -नर्सा णा धपधा	(प)मा (र)-गा -सा रगा
दे ० शी बँ०	धु० ० ०० ०	घु००० ००० म भा०डा	यो ० ० चुमि
रगा -सा सा -ा	-ा गपा -घा -र्सा	ना र्सना (ध)पा धर्सा	धर्सा -ा -ा -ा
आँ० ० खि ०	० जदि गा न्	था मे० मोर मु०	खे० ० ० ०
-ा र्सर्सा -र्सा र्सा	नर्सा नधा धणा धपा	-ा पधा (प)-मा मा	मपा -र्सना धनधा -ा
० फिरि या जे	यो० ना० बी० णा०	० रबे त बु	बु० ०० के०० ०
-ा -ा -धनधनपा-पधनर्सा	-ा र्सर्सा र्सा -ा	ना र्सना (ध)पा धर्सा	(ध)र्सा -ा -ा -ा
० ० ००००० ००००	० जदि गा न	था मे० मोर मु०	खे ० ० ०
-ा -पधर्सर्रा -र्गा -ा	-ा र्गर्गा र्गा -ा	र्ज्ञा र्गा र्सर्गर्ज्ञर्पर्गा र्सा	र्सा -ा -ा -ा
आ ०००० ० ०	० जदि गा न	था मे मो०००० मु	खे ० ० ०
-ा र्सर्सा -र्सा र्सा	नर्स नधा धणा धपा	-ा पधा (प)-मा पा	पा -ा पा -ा
० फिरि या जे	यो० ना० बी० णा०	० रबे त बु	बु ० के ०
-ा र्सर्सा र्सा -ा	नर्रा र्सा नध धणा	पधा धपा मा रा	मपा पधा -नधा -पधनर्सा
० नाहि गा न	दु० ख० नी० ड़े०	आ० छे० त बु	पा० खी० ०० ००००
-ा र्सर्सा र्सा -ा	नर्सा नधा धणा धपा	पधा धपा मा रा	रमा -मपा पा धा
० नाहि गा न	दु० ख० नी० ड़े०	आ० छे० त बु	पा० ०० खी ०

+				२				०				३			
-ा	-ा	-मपा	-मा	मपधर्सा	-नर्सा	-णा	धपधा	(प)मा	गा	(र)-सा	रगा	रगा	-सा	सा	सरा
०	०	००	०	घु०००	०००	म	भा०ङा	यो	०	०	चुमि	आँ	०	खि	चुमि
ण्सध्‌ा	सा	-ा	ससा	रमा	मा	पधा	धर्सा	-ा	-र्सरा	-णर्सा	-धा	-र्सा	-ा	-ा	-ा
आँ००	खि	०	पर	दे०	शी	बँ०	धु०	०	००	००	०	०	०	०	०

BIBLIOGRAPHY

1. Aniruddha, Kaji. *Nargis* - Part - IV. Calcutta, 1378. B.S. (Beng.).
2. ———. *Nazrul Sur Paricaya* - Part - II. Calcutta, 1968. (Beng.).
3. Bishi, Prasannakumar. *Dwijendra Racanā Sambhār.* Calcutta, 1372. (Beng.).
4. Das Sharma, Amal. *Saṅgīta Maṇīṣā* - Part I. Calcutta, 1979. (Beng.).
5. Ghatak, Nitai. *Ekśogāner Nazrul Svaralipi.* Calcutta, 1979. (Beng.).
6. Goswami, Utpala. *Kolkātāy Saṅgita Carcā.* Calcutta, 1991. (Beng.).
7. Mitra, Rajyeshwar. *Bāṅglār Gītikār O Bāṅglā Gāner Nānādik,* 2nd ed. Calcutta, 1973 (Beng.).
8. Mukherji, Dilipkumar. *Bāṅgālīr Rāga Saṅgīta Carcā.* Calcutta, 1976. (Beng.).
9. Ray, Dilipkumar. *Dwijendra Gīti.* Calcutta, 1372 B.S. (Beng.).
10. ———. *Gīta Mañjarī.* Calcutta, 1372. B.S. (Beng.).
11. ———. *Naba Mañjarī.* Calcutta, 1934. (Beng.).
12. Ray, Sukumar. *Bāṅglā Saṅgīter Rup.* Calcutta, 1969. (Beng.).
13. Sahanadevi. *Mālikā.* Calcutta, 1926.
14. Sen, Atulprasad. *Gītaguñja.* Calcutta, 1356 B.S. (Beng.).
15. ———. *Kākalī.* Calcutta, 1957. (Beng.).
16. *Surachanda.* (Bengali Journal.) Puja No. Calcutta, Sept. 1984.

Rāga-pradhāna Bāṅglā-gāna

Comparatively modern, *Rāga-pradhāna* style became popular during the 30's of the 20th century. The name was coined by Suresh Chandra Chakravarti and Kaji Nazrul Islam. It may be defined as a style of music which has its lyrics composed in Bengali, set in *rāgas* with norms of *śāstrīya-saṅgīta,* but with moderate *tānas* and *alaṅkāras* that would be complimentary to the literary composition. The lyric or *vāṇī* is elaborated by *rāgālāpa, tānas,* etc. in varieties of *layakārī* of the *tāla* but is never subdued by excessive *tāna-kartab* or *alaṅkāras.* It is a style where *kāvya* as well as *rāga* and *tāla* play an equally important role and is an aesthetic combination of all the three. *Rāgapradhāna* songs are based on *rāgas* and *tālas* yet not bound by rigidity like a *khayāl.* In other words, *Rāgapradhāna* songs are not mere immitation of Hindi *khayāls,* nor any song that is bound by *rāga* and *tāla* is *Rāgapradhāna.*

Bengali *rāga*-based songs were in vogue since the days of the *Caryāgīti.* Various types of Bengali songs such as *Maṅgalagīti, Pā̃cālī, Kaviwālār-gāna, Nāṭya-saṅgīta, Ākhḍāi, Half-ākhḍāi, Ṭappās, Dhrupadas,* etc. were styles based on *rāgas* and *tālas* but were very different from *Rāgapradhāna* which was formed with certain ideas and norms, such as :

1. to uphold the lyrical beauty of the composition which is short, consisting mostly of *sthāyī* and *antarā,*
2. to select appropriate *rāga* for the composition,
3. to choose the right *alaṅkāras* and *tānas* that are complimentary to the lyric,
4. to adopt voice culture of *khayāl* and *ṭhumrīaṅg,*
5. to create artistry in the pre-set song, the singer has enough liberty to show off his individuality and creativity while remaining within the limits of his aesthetic sensibility, and
6. to use *tālas* of madhya *laya* in the nature of *choṭā-khayāl* and not *vilamvita-laya* which is not suited for this style.

Rāgapradhāna style has to maintain a perfect balance between the *rāga* and its development on one hand and the lyrical composition on the other, which is not to be neglected during *rāga* elaboration.

The most eminent composer of *Rāgapradhāna* was Kaji Nazrul Islam. He created variety, diversity and beauty in *rāgas* through *Rāgapradhāna-gāna,* by using certain *svaras* to bring out the subtle meanings of the lyric. He used many *apracalita rāgas,* i.e. *rāgas* rarely used. He also innovated a few *rāgas* for this style of music, e.g.*Dhanakuntalā, Sandhyā-mālatī,* etc. Other composers are : Tulsi Lahiri, Shailen Ray, Pranab Ray, Ajay Bhattacarya, Himanshu Ray, Gauriprasanna Majumdar, Syamal Gupta, Gopal Dasgupta, Himen Naskar, Hasirasi Debi, Subodh Purokayastha, Binoy Mukhopadhyay, Jnanprakash Ghosh and many others.

This style was introduced through All India Radio by Suresh Chandra Chakravarti and popularised through programmes like *Hārāmani, Nabarāgamālikā,* etc.

The most eminent exponents of this style are : Jnanendra Prasad Goswami, Tarapada Chakravarty, K. C. De, Bhismadeb Chattopadhyay, Dhirendra Chandra Mitra, Shachin Deb Barman and Dipali Nag.

BIBLIOGRAPHY

1. Ghosh, Jnanprakash. "*Bāṅglā Rāga-pradhān-gāna*", in *Deshbinodan* (Bengali Journal). Calcutta, 1391. B.S.
2. Mitra, Rajyeshwar. *Bāṅglār Gītikār O Bāṅglā-gāner Nānādik.* 2nd ed. Calcutta, 1973 (Beng.).
3. Nag, Dipali. *Rāgapradhān-gāna.* (Beng.).
4. Ray, Sukumar. *Bāṅglā Saṅgīter Rūp.* Calcutta, 1969. (Beng.).

Bāṅglā Rāgapradhān gāna — an example :

Lyric : Himen Naskar. Tune: Dipali Nag

Rāga - Jayjayantī Tāla - Tritāla.

ताराय ताराय मेघ बरषाय
तोमारे बेसेछि भालो
तोमारि आकाश निखिल भुवन
दियेछे आमारे आलो ॥
आमार गरबेर राशि
हयेछे तोमार पदतले बासि
चरण परश पेयेछे हृदय
एखनो करुणा ढालो ॥

Sthāyī

०				३				+				२			
सा	रगा	पमगमा	रा	सा	सा	रा	ण्ा	मा	-गा	-रा	ज्ञा	रा	-ा	-ा	-ा
ता	रा०	य०००	ता	रा	य	मे	घ	ब	०	०	र	षा	०	०	य
सा	रगा	-गा	गा	गा	मा	पा	-धा	पमगमा	-ा	-गा	-ा	-रा	-ज्ञा	रा	-ा
तो	मा०	०	रे	बे	से	छि	०	भा०००	०	०	०	०	०	लो	०
ना्	ना्	ना्	ना्	सा	-सा	-सा	सा	ना्	सा	न्सरा	-सरा	ण्ा	ण्ा	-ध्ा	प्ा
तो	मा	रि	आ	का	०	०	श	नि	खि	ल००	००	भु	ब	०	न
णा	धपा	मा	-ा	मा	धपा	-णा	धा	मा	-मा	-गा	-मा	-रा	-ज्ञा	रा	-ा
दि	ये०	छे	०	आ	मा०	०	रे	आ	०	०	०	०	०	लो	०

Antarā

मा	पा	ना	ना	सां	सां	ना	सां	धा	-ा	णा	रां	सां	-ा	-ा	-ा
आ	मा	र	स	क	ल	ग	र	बे	०	र	रा	शि	०	०	०
सांरां	सांरां	णा	धा	णधा	पा	गा	मा	गा	-मा	रा	ज्ञा	रा	-ा	-ा	-ा
ह०	ये०	छे	तो	मा०	र	प	द	त	०	ले	बा	सि	०	०	०
सा	सा	रगमा	मा	मा	-ा	-ा	-ा	पधा	पणा	धा	गा	मा	-ा	-ा	-ा
च	र	ण००	प	र	०	०	श	पे०	ये०	छे	हृ	द	०	०	य
रा	गा	मा	-ा	पा	सां	णा	-ा	धणधा	-पधपा	-मपमा	-गमगा	-रा	-ज्ञा	रा	-ा
ए	ख	नो	०	क	रु	णा	०	ढा००	०००	०००	०००	०	०	लो	०

Svadeśī Saṅgīta

Soon after the Battle of Plassey (1757) when the English established their supremacy in Bengal, the people of Bengal realised that it was no ordinary occupation but a domination by such people who were aggressive, and never wanted to merge with India. The British made it a point to rule from distant England, keeping a distance between the ruler and the ruled. Moreover, the Western education made the Bengalis wise in many respects. The educated youth of Bengal started to think freely and a deep sense of national feeling arose in them. The great mutiny of 1857, the movement of the Indigo planters, and various other factors made the intellectuals of Bengal think deeply about achieving freedom of India from the bondage of the British. This national feeling then penetrated into rural Bengal from the urban elites. Dinabandhu Mitra's *Nīladarpaṇa* (1860), Rangalal Bandyopadhyay's *Padminī-Upākhyāna* (1858), Hem chandra Bandyopadhyay's *Vīr vāhu* (1864), Madhusudan Datta's *Meghnādavadha Kāvya* (1861), Bankim Chandra's *Ānandamath* (1892), Jyotirindranath's *Puru-vikrama* (1874)—all were written to arouse national feeling. Not only in the literary front but in various other activities, Bengal expressed her strong objection in accepting any foreign power to rule over India. Thus *Hindumelā/Caitramelā* was founded in 1867 and first national song was composed by Satyendranath Thakur - '*Mile sabe Bhārata santāna------ gāo Bhārater yaśo gāna*' for the second session of Hindúmela in 1868. This song, more well known as '*Gāo Bhārater Jay*' became so popular that the *Hindumelā* sessions used to be inaugarated mostly with this song. The song consisted of seven stanzas describing the past glories of ancient India,—about *ṛṣis,* brave warriors and the great qualities of the ladies of India. This song was orginally tuned and sung by Bishnu Chakravarti, the *saṅgīta-guru* of Jorasanko Ṭhakurbari. Bishnu had set it in *Khāmāja-rāga* and *Āḍā-ṭhekā tāla.* Later, this song was retuned by the authorities of Great National Theatre and this tune became more popular. This song inspired Bankim Chandra to compose his famous poem '*Vande Mātaram*' in *Ānandamath,* and many other poet-composers including Rabindranath. *Vande Mātaram* in turn inspired and influenced the poet-composers of entire India.

The *Hindumelā* gave birth to *Svadeśī-saṅgīta* which were rich in *bhāva, rāga, tāla,* though not set in the formal structure of pure classical music. These musical compositions were those that expressed the love for the motherland, aroused and awakened the minds of the people against the foreign domination and were set to tunes mostly on pure or mixed *rāgas,* folk tunes and sometimes even on Western marching tunes. Later, these stimulating and passionate songs were composed for *Jātīya Mahāsabhā* (1885) or Congress, every session of which used to be inaugarated with these songs.

Svadeśī-saṅgītas were composed in three phases :

(a) Pre-partition of Bāṅglā—1886 -1904.
(b) During the partition period—1905 -1911.
(c) After partition till independence was achieved —1911-1947.

During the first phase, the songs were mostly *rāga* based, set to *tālas* and were composed by intellectuals.

In the second phase, folk tunes, particularly *Bāul,* and simple tunes based on *rāgas* prevalent in Bengal, were used.

In the third phase, the poet composers used mostly *rāga* based tunes.

In 1872, Nabagopal Mitra founded National School where music was also taught along with other subjects. Manomohan Basu, another enthusiast of *Hindumelā* also stressed on *Saṅgīta* section, where musicians used to take part.

Songs of the first phase were mostly set on rāgas like - *Lalita, Bibhāsa, Alhaiyā, Bhairavī, Kāliṅgḍā, Yaman, Mallāra, Gaurī, Sindhu, Kāfī, Jhījhiṭ, Bāhār, Bāgeśrī, Sāhānā, Gārā, Jayjayantī, Multānī, Bihāga, Tilak-kāmoda, Khamāja* and *miśra-rāgas* such as :

Lalita-Bibhāsa, Basanta-Bāhār, Naṭā-Bihāga, Lum-Jhījhiṭ, Paraja-Khāmāja, Sindhu-Kāfī, Sindhu-Bhairavī, Yaman-Kalyāṇa, Jhījhiṭ-Khāmāja and *Kedāra-Hamīr.* Two *rāgas* mentioned for *Svadeśī-gānas,* viz. *Ahaṅg* and *Laganī* are unfamiliar. Some songs were also tuned in *Ramprasādī* and in the style of *jātrā-gānas. Tālas* used were: *Āḍāṭhekā, Dhāmāl, Madhyamāna, Jat, Ṭhumrī,* Kavvālī, Jhāptāla, etc.

Some of the famous songs of this period are :

(a) *Uṭha uṭha sakale Bhārata santān—Rāga Sindhuḍā - Tāla Dhāmāl.*
(b) *Ei dharātale dhanya dhanya kṣatriya lalanā—Rāga Alhaiyā - Tāla Kavvālī.*
(c) *Lajjāy Bhārata yaś gāibo ki—Rāga Bāhār - Tāla Jat.*
(d) *Malina mukha candramā Bhārat—Rāga Naṭa-bihāga - Tāla Jhāptāla.*

The famous composers of the first phase were members of Jorasanko Thakurbari, the pioneers in this field. Others were: Ramnidhi Gupta, Rangalal Bandopadhyay, Nabagopal Mitra, Manomohan Basu, Hemendranath Bandopadhyay, Bishnuram Chattopadhyay, Bankimchandra Chattopadhyay, Kaliprasanna Kāvyaviśārada, Kamini Ray, Shibnath Sastri, Atulprasad Sen, Dwijendralal Ray, Rajanikanta Sen, Saraladevi, Kaji Nazrul, and many others whose names are not known.

It was during *Baṅga Bhaṅga Āndolana,* 1905, that Bengal became most anti-British. Rabindranath composed most of his famous songs during this period, such as: *Ebār tor marā gāṅge, Jodi tor ḍāk śune keu; Āji Bāṅglā deśer hṛday hote; Bāṅglār māṭī Bāṅglār jal; Āmāder jātrā holo śuru; Sārthaka janama āmār; Āmār sonār Bāṅglā ; O āmār deśer māṭī;* and many more which had a great effect on the minds of the people. These songs were mostly set in folk tunes such as *Bāul, Bhāṭiyāli, Jāri* and *Sāri* but *Bāul* was predominant. Among all the poet composers of *svadeśī-saṅgīta* Rabindranath's contribution is the most.

Other composers whose contribution and style are valuable, are:

1. Dwijendralal Ray, who established a unique style of his own. His songs were full of vigour and vitality and he often used Western and marching tunes to express the right mood, although basically these were Indian in sentiment. He was the pioneer in using marching tunes in this style, e.g. *Dhāo dhāo samara kṣetre.* He also introduced comical sentiments in his songs of patriotism, e.g . *Āmi jodi piṭhe tor oi.* A few of his famous songs are: *Dhana dhānye puṣpe bharā; Baṅga āmār jananī āmār; Jedin sunīl Jaladhi hoite;* etc. His songs were most suitable for chorus singing and the poet gave equal importance to Bengal as well as India as a whole in his compositions.
2. Rajanikanta's songs are - *Māyer deoā moṭā kāpad; Āye chuṭe bhāi Hindu Mussalmān; Jay jay janmabhūmi jananī ; Ebār sonār Bāṅglā bhāg kare bhāi* and many more. His songs were set to simple yet impressive tunes.
3. Mukunda Das composed his songs mostly in folk tunes. His memorable songs are : *Āmi daś hājār prāṇ jodi petām; Fuller, ār ki dekhāo bhay; Bhay ki maraṇe rākhite santāne; Rāma Rahim nā judā kar bhāi; Vande mātaram bole nācre sakale;* etc. As a *jātrā* performer he was able to create an enormous impact on the people of rural Bengal.
4. Ashwini Kumar Datta was connected with *Svadeśī jātrā* and composed songs like : *Āy re āy Bhāratvāsī ; Āji maṅgala mohana ; Jananī janmabhūmisca;* etc.
5. Pramathanath Raychaudhuri composed songs such as : *Namah Baṅgabhūmi śyāmaṅginī; He mātah Baṅga;* etc.
6. Kaliprasanna Kāvyaviśārada's compositions are : *Svadeśer dhuli ; Āj Bariśāl punye viśāl;* etc. He based his songs on *rāgas* such as - *Bāhār, Sindhu, Khāmāja, Bhīmpalaśrī,* etc. and tunes from *kīrtana* and *Rāmprasādī.* The *tālas* used by him are *Dhāmār, Ektāla* and *kavvālī.*
7. Atulprasad Sen composed in simple catchy tunes and gave Bengal and India same importance in his songs , such as : *Uthago Bhārata Lakṣmī; Balo balo balo sabe; Hao dharamete dhīr; Moder garab moder āśā; Bhārata bhānu kothā lukāle;* etc.
8. Other important compositions came from composers such as : Bipin Chandra Pal, Rajkrishna Basu and many others.

During the last year of second phase, Rabindranath composed '*Jana gana mana*' in December 1911. This song was declared as the national anthem of India on 24th

January, 1950 by the Constituent Assembly. It also gave '*Vande Mātaram*' the status of national song in the same year. *Jana gana mana* was however played as the Indian National Anthem on September 11th, 1942 in Germany by the Chamber of Orchestra of the then Government Radio Station, Hamburg. The tune of the song was played in a special function held at Hotel Atlantica, Hamburg, and Subhas Chandra Bose had personally selected this song as the National Anthem. *Jana gana mana* was later played as the National Anthem of Azad Hind before a large audience.

During the third phase, that is between 1911 and 1947, there was a change in the compositions of this style both in music and theme, since the circumstances were changing gradually. *Rāgas* and *rāgiṇīs* again became predominant. The poets of this phase were: Rabindranath, Kamini Kumar, Kaji Nazrul, Bijaylal Chattopadhyay, Dilip Kumar Ray, Nishikanta Raychaudhuri, and others while more recent poets are: Hemanga Biswas, Salil Chaudhuri, Binoy Ray and others. Rabindranath's '*Deśa deśa nandita kari'; Saṅkocero bihvalatā; Sarva kharbatāre dahe; Śubha karma pathe* etc are the best songs of this period.

Kaji Nazrul was one of the most wellknown composers of the post *Baṅgabhaṅga* era. He introduced novelty and variety in these '*Muktir gāna*' for which his compositions became instant hits. The range of his compositions included not only songs on the themes of national movement but songs protesting against the British policies, and supporting the causes of the labourers, farmers, students, women and even the soldiers. Some of his famous songs are: *Durgama giri kāntāra maru; Kārār oi lauha kapāṭ; Āj rakta niśi bhore;* etc. Nazrul has used *rāgas* and *ragiṇīs* and their unusual mixed forms to tune his songs appropriately.

BIBLIOGRAPHY

1. Bandopadhyay, Dwarkanath. *Jātīya Saṅgīta.* Calcutta, 1876. (Beng.).
2. Basu, Manomohan. *Manomohan Gītāvalī.* Calcutta, 1887. (Beng.).
3. Chakravarty, Upendranath. *Bāṅgālīr-gāna.* Calcutta, 1905. (Beng.).
4. Chattopadhyay, Gita. *Bāṅglā Svadeśī-gāna.* Delhi University 1983. (Beng.).
5. Chattopadhyay, Nabakanta. *Bhāratīya Saṅgīta Muktāvalī.* Calcutta. (Beng.).
6. Chaudhury, Subhas. "*Muktir-gāna*", in *Deshbinodan.* (Bengali Journal). Calcutta, 1391. B.S.
7. Das, Upendranath. *Jātīya Saṅgīta.* Calcutta, 1906. (Beng.).
8. Sarala.Devi. *Śatagāna.* Calcutta, 1900. (Beng.).
9. Svarnakumari.Devi. *Gītiguccha.* Calcutta, 1922. (Beng.).
10. Goswami, Joyguru. *Cāraṇkavi Mukundadāsa.* Calcutta, 1972. (Beng.).
11. Goswami, Prabhatkumar. *Hājār Bacharer Bāṅglā-gāna.* Calcutta, 1972. (Beng.)
12. Lahiri, Durgadasa. *Bāṅgālīr-gāna.* Calcutta, 1906. (Beng.).

13. Mukhopadhyay, Harimohan. *Saṅgīta-sāra-saṃgraha.* Calcutta, 1901. (Beng.).
14. Mukhopadhyay, Upendranath. *Saṅgitkoṣa.* Calcutta. 1896. (Beng.).
15. Ray, Rajkrishna. *Bhārat-gāna.* Calcutta, 1879. (Beng.).
16. *Saṅgīta Sahasra.* Granthakār Samiti. Calcutta, 1891. (Beng.).
17. Sengupta, Jagadishchandra. *Jātiya gātha.* Dhaka. 1906. (Beng.).
18. Sen, Prabodhchandra. *Bhāratvāsīr Jātīya Saṅgīta.* Calcutta, 1356. B.S. (Beng.).
19. Thakur Jyotirindranath. *Svaralipi Gītikā.* Calcutta, 1897.
20. Thakur, Rabindranath. *Gāna.* Calcutta, 1917. (Beng.).

A few examples of Svadeśī Saṇgīta:

Composer - Satyendranath Thakur
Tuned by - Rabindranath Thakur.

मिले सबे भारत सन्तान, एकतान मनप्राण
गाओ भारतेर, यशोगान ।
भारत भूमिर तुल्य आछे कोन स्थान ?
कोन आद्रि हिमाद्रि समान ?
फलवती, बसुमती, स्रोतस्वती, पुण्यवती
शतखनि रत्नेर निदान ।
होक भारतेर जय ।
जय भारतेर जय, गाओ भारतेर जय,
होक भारतेर जय, कि भय किभय ।
गाओ भारतेर जय ।
रुपवती साध्वीसती भारत ललना,
कोथा दिबे तादेर तुलना ?
शर्मिष्ठा, सावित्री, सीता, दमयन्ती पतिब्रता
अतुलना भारत ललना ।
होक भारतेर जय - - - ।
केन डर भीरु, करो साहस आश्रय
यतो धर्मस्ततो जय ।
छिन्न भिन्न हीनवल, ऐक्येते पाइबे वल,
मायेर मुख उज्जवल करिते कि भय ?
होक भारतेर जय - - - ॥

+						०					
णा	-ा	-धणर्सा	धा	-धा	मा	मा	-ा	-पधा	-पमा	-गरा	-गा
मि	०	०००	ले	०	स	बे	०	००	००	००	०
मा	-ा	-ा	पा	-धपा	मा	पा	-ा	-ा	-ा	-ा	-ा
भा	०	र	त	००	स	न्ता	०	०	०	०	न्
मा	-ा	गा	-ा	-ा	-ा	गमा	-पमा	-गरा	गरा	-सना्	सा
ए	क	ता	०	न्	म	न०	००	००	प्रा०	००	ण

+						०					
सा	-मा	-ा	-गमगा	-रगा	मा	णा	-णा	-धणा	-पधा	-णर्सा	-र्रसा
गा	०	०	०००	ओ०	भा	र	०	००	००	००	००
ना	-ा	-ा	र्सा	-ा	-ा	र्सना	-ना	-ा	र्सा	-ा	-धा
ते	०	०	र	०	०	ज०	०	०	शो	०	०
धणा	-र्सणा	-धपा	पा	-ा	-ा	-ा	-ा	-धपा	-मगा	-रा	-गा
गा०	००	००	न्	०	स	बे	०	००	००	०	०
मा	-ा	-ा	पा	-धपा	मा	पा	-ा	-ा	-ा	-ा	-ा
भा	०	र	त	००	स	न्	ता	०	०	०	न्
सा	-ा	-ा	गा	-ा	-ा	मा	-ा	-ा	पा	-ा	-ा
भा	०	र	त	०	भू	मि	०	र	तु	०	ल्य
मा	-ा	पा	-ा	-धा	-पा	मा	-ा	पा	-ा	-ा	-ा
ता	दे	र	०	०	०	तु	ल	ना	०	०	०
गा	मा	णा	-धा	-पधा	-णर्सा	ना	-ा	र्सर्गा	ना	र्सा	-ा
श	र्म्मि	ष्ठा	०	००	००	सा	वि	त्री०	सी	ता	०
णा	र्री	र्सा	र्री	-ा	-ा	णा	र्सा	-र्रसा	णा	धा	-ा
द	म	य	न्	ती	०	प	ति	००	ब्र	ता	०
-ा	-ा	-ा	-ा	-ा	-ा	पा	र्सा	ना	र्सा	-ा	-ा
०	०	०	०	०	०	अ	तु	ल	वा	०	०
ना	-ा	-ा	र्सा	-ा	-ा	ना	र्सर्री	-र्सणा	धा	-ा	-ा
भा	०	०	र	त	ल	ल	ना०	००	हो	०	क्
मा	-ा	-ा	पा	-ा	-धपा	मा	-ा	-ा	गा	-रा	-गा
भा	०	०	र	०	००	ते	०	०	र	०	०
मा	-ा	-ा	-ा	-ा	-ा						
ज	०	०	०	०	य						

+						०					
र्सा	-ा	णा	धा	पा	मा	र्सा	-ा	-ा	-ा	णा	धा
के	०	न	ड	र	भी	रु	०	०	०	क	र
पा	मा	गा	रसा	-मा	-ा	मा	-ा	-ा	-ा	-ा	सा
सा	ह	स	आ०	०	०	श्र	य	०	०	०	य
गा	-ा	-ा	मा	-ा	-ा	पा	-ा	धा	ना	-ा	-ा
तो	०	०	ध	०	०	र	म	स्त	तो	०	०
-धना	-र्सरी	-र्सना	र्सा	-ा	-ा	-ा	-ा	-ा	-ा	-ा	-ा
००	००	००	ज	०	य	०	०	०	०	०	०
गा	मा	णा	-धा	-पधा	-णर्सा	ना	र्सा	-र्रसा	ना	र्सा	-ा
छि	न्न	भि	०	००	०न्न	ही	न	००	ब	ल	०
णा	-णा	र्री	र्सा	र्री	-ा	णा	र्सा	-र्रसा	णा	धा	-ा
ऐ	०	क्य	ते	पा	०	इ	बे	००	ब	ल	०
-धा	-ा	-ा	-ा	पा	मा	गा	मा	-णधा	-पधा	-णर्सा	ना
०	०	०	मा	ये	र	मु	ख	उ०	००	००	ज्व
र्सा	-ा	-ा	-ा	-ा	-ा	र्गा	-ा	-ा	र्मा	-ा	र्पा
ल	०	०	०	०	०	क	रि	०	ते	०	कि
मा	-ा	-ा	-ा	-ा	-ा	-ा	-ा	-ा	मा	-ा	-ा
भ	०	०	०	०	य	०	०	०	ही	०	क्
मा	-ा	-ा	पा	-ा	-धपा	मा	-ा	-ा	गा	रा	सा
भा	०	०	र	०	००	ते	०	०	र	०	०
मा	-ा	-ा	-ा	-ा	-ा						
ज	०	०	०	०	य						

Śatagāna - P 139.

Composer - Bankimchandra Chattopadhyay.
Tuned by - Rabindranath Thakur.
Rāga - Deśa Tāla - Tālfertā.

वन्दे मातरम्, सुजलां सुफलां
मलयजशीतलां, शस्यश्यामलां मातरम्
वन्दे मातरम् ।
शुभ्रज्योत्स्ना पुलकितयामिनीं,
फुल्लकुसुमितद्रुमदलशोभिनीं,
सुहासिनीं, सुमधुरभाषिणीं,
सुखदां वरदां मातरम्,
वन्दे मातरम् ॥

+				o				+				o			
सा	-ा	सा	-ा	-ा	-ा	-नर्सा	-र्सा	-णधा	-पा	-पा	-ा	पा	-धपा	-मपा	मगा
ब	o	न्दे	o	o	o	oo	oo	oo	o	o	o	मा	oo	oo	तo
रा	-ा	-ा	-ा	-ा	-ा	-ा	-ा	मा	-रा	-मा	-ा	-गमा	-पा	-मपा	-धा
र	o	o	o	o	o	o	म्	मा	o	o	o	oo	o	oo	o
-पधा	-णा	-घपा	र्सा	-नर्सा	-री	-ा	र्सा	र्सरी	-र्सणा	-धपा	-मा	-पा	-ा	-ा	-ा
oo	o	oo	o	oo	o	o	त	रo	oo	oo	o	o	o	o	म्
र्सा	-ा	र्सा	-ा	-ा	-ा	-नर्सा	-र्सा	-णधा	-पा	-ा	-ा	पा	-धपा	-मपा	मगा
ब	o	न्दे	o	o	o	oo	oo	oo	o	o	o	मा	oo	oo	तo
रा	-ा	-ा	-ा	-ा	-ा	-ा	-ा	रा	मा	मा	-ा	-ा	-ा	-ा	-गा
र	o	o	o	o	o	o	म्	सु	ज	ला	o	o	o	o	म्
रा	गा	रसा	-ना	-सा	-ा	-ा	-ा	रा	रा	मा	मा	पा	-ा	-ा	मा
सु	फ	लाo	o	o	o	o	म्	म	ल	य	ज	शी	o	o	त
(म)पा	-ा	-ा	-ा	-ा	-ा	-ा	-ा	मा	-ा	पा	-ा	ना	-ा	-ा	-र्सा
ला	o	o	o	o	o	o	म्	श	o	स्य	o	श्या	o	o	o
(धन)-र्सा	-ा	-ा	ना	र्सा	-ा	-ा	-ा	र्सा	-ा	-ा	-ना	-री	-ा	-ा	र्सा
o	o	o	म	ला	o	o	म्	मा	o	o	o	o	o	o	त
र्सरी	-र्सना	-धपा	मा	-पा	-ा	-ा	-ा	र्सा	-ा	-ा	-ा	नर्सा	-र्सा	-णधा	-पा
रo	oo	oo	o	o	o	o	म्	ब	o	o	o	न्देo	oo	oo	o

\+ ग° + °
| रा -गा -मा गा | रा -ा -ा -ा | मा -ा पा -ा | ना -ा धना -र्सर्रा |
| मा ० ० त | र ० ० म् | शु ० भ्र ० | ज्योत् ० स्ना० ०० |

| र्रा र्सा र्सा र्सा | र्सा: र्स: र्सा -ा | ना -ा ना ना | र्सा र्सा र्सा -ा |
| पु ल कि त | या मि नी म् | फु ० ल्ल कु | सु मि त ० |

| पा ना र्सा र्सा | नसर्रा: र्स: र्रा -ा | र्सा णा -ा धा | णा -ा -धा -णा |
| द्रु म द ल | शो०० भि नी म् | सु हा०० ० सि | नी ० ० म् |

| धा णा र्सा र्रा | र्सा णधा पा -मा | पा पधणा -ा धा | णा -ा -ा -ा |
| सु म धु र | भा षि० णी म् | सु हा०० ० सि | नी ० ० म् |

| णा र्रा र्सा र्रा | र्सा णधा पा -मा | पा पना -र्सा -ा | गा -मा -पा -र्सा |
| सु म धु र | भा षि० णी म् | सु हा०० ० सि | नी ० ० म् |

| णा र्रा र्सा र्रा | र्सा णधा पा -मा | पा ना र्सा -ा | गा मा पा -र्सा |
| सु म धु र | भा षि० णी म् | सु ख दा म् | व र दा म् |

| र्सा -ना -र्रा र्सा | र्सर्रा -र्सणा -धपा -मपा | र्सा -ा -ा -ा | नर्सा -र्रसा -णधा -पा |
| मा ० ० त | र० ०० ०० ०म् | ब ० ० ० | न्दे० ०० ०० ० |

ग
| रा -गा -मा गा | रा -ा -ा -ा | मा -रा -मा -ा | -गमा -पा -मपा -धा |
| मा ० ० त | र ० ० म् | मा ० ० ० | ०० ० ०० ० |

| -पधा -णा -धपा -र्सा | -नर्सा -र्रा -ा र्सा | र्सर्रा -र्सणा -धपा -मा | -पा -ा -ा -ा |
| ०० ० ०० ० | ०० ० ० त | र० ०० ०० ० | ० ० ० म् |

ग
| र्सा -ा -ा -ा | नर्सा -र्रसा -णधा -पा | पा -धपा -मपा मगा | रा -ा -ा -ा ||||
| ब ० ० ० | न्दे० ०० ०० ० | मा ०० ०० त० | र ० ० म् ||||

Jātīya/Svadeśī/Muktir gāna :
Composer - Rabindranath (Notated by Indiradevi Chaudhurani)
(Composed during Baṅgabhaṅga Movement)

बांलार माटी, बांलार जल,
बांलार बायु, बांलार फल
पुण्य हउक, पुण्य हउक,
पुण्य हउक, हे भगवान ।

बांलार घर, बांलार हाट,
बांलार बन, बांलार माठ,
    पूर्ण हउक, पूर्ण हउक
    पूर्ण हउक, हे भगवान ।
बांगालीर पण, बांगालीर आशा,
बांगालीर काज, बागालीर भाषा,
    सत्य हउक, सत्य हउक,
    सत्य हउक, हे भगवान ।
बांगालीर प्राण, बांगालीर मन,
बांगालीर घरे यत भाइ बोन,
    एक हउक, एक हउक, एक हउक
    हे भगवान ।

(Svarabitān - 64th Part, Calcutta 1362 B.S.)

मा	पा	पा	-ा	-ा	पधपा	मा	-पधा	पा	-मगा	गा	-मा
बां	ग	ला	र	मा	टि००	बां	ग०	ला	०र	ज	ल्
मा	-पा	पा	-पा	पा	पमा	पा	-धा	पधा	-ना	ना	-धपा
बां	ग	ला	र	बा	यु०	बां	ग	ला०	र्	फ	०ल
पा	-धर्सा	र्सा	र्सा	र्सा	-ा	नर्सा	-र्रगा	री	र्सा	र्स र्रर्सा	-ना
पु	०न्	न	ह	उ	क	पु०	०न्	न	ह	उ०	क्
धना	र्सा	ना	ना	धनधा	-पा	ह्मा	-पह्मा	गा	ह्मा	पा	-ा
पु०	न्	न	ह	उ००	क्	हे	००	भ	ग	बा	न्
धा	-नर्सा	ना	-धपा	पा	धा	धा	-ना	ना	-ा	ना	-ा
बां	ग०	ला	०र्	घ	र	बां	ग	ला	र्	हा	ट
											[-नधप]
र्सा	-ा	र्सा	-ना	र्सा	-री	र्सा	-र्रगा	री	-र्सा	ना	(-नर्सना)
बा	ग	ला	र्	ब	न्	बा	ग०	ला	र्	मा	००ठ
पा	-धर्सा	र्सा	र्सा	र्सा	-ा	नर्सा	-र्रगा	री	र्सा	र्सर्रर्सा	-ना
पू	०र्	ण	ह	उ	क	पू०	०र	ण	ह	उ००	क

ना	धनर्सा	ना	ना	धनधा	-पा	ह्मा	-पह्मा	गा	ह्मा	पा	-ा ‖
पू	००र्	ण	ह	उ००	क	हे	००	भ	ग	बा	न् ‖
धा	नर्सा	ना	-धपा	पा	-धा	धा	ना	ना	-ा	ना	ना
बां	०गा	लि	०र	प	ण्	बां	गा	लि	र	आ	शा
											[नधप]
र्सा	र्सा	र्सा	-ना	र्सा	-र्रा	र्सा	र्रगा	र्रा	-र्सा	ना	(नर्सना)
बां	गा	लि	र	का	ज	बां	०गा	लि	र्	भा	षा००
पा	-धर्सा	र्सा	र्सा	र्सा	-ा	नर्सा	-र्रगा	र्रा	र्सा	र्सर्रसा	-ना
स	०त्	त	ह	उ	क	सृ	०त्	त	ह	उ००	क
ना	-धनर्सा	ना	ना	धनधा	-पा	ह्मा	-पह्मा	गा	ह्मा	पा	-ा ‖
स	००त्	त	ह	उ	क	हे	००	भ	ग	बा	न् ‖
धा	नर्सा	ना	-धपा	पा	-धा	धा	ना	ना	-ना	ना	-ा
बां	गा०	लि	०र्	प्रा	ण्	बां	गा	लि	र्	म	न्
											[-नधपा]
न र्सा	र्सा	र्सा	-ना	र्सा	र्रा	र्सा	र्रगा	र्रा	-र्सा	ना	(नर्सना)
बां	गा	लि	र्	घ	रे	ज	त०	भा	इ	बो	००न्
पा	-धर्सा	-ा	र्सा	र्सा	-ा	नर्सा	-र्रगा	-र्रा	र्सा	र्सर्रसा	-ना
ए	००	क	ह	उ	क	ए०	००	क्	ह	उ००	क
ना	-धनर्सा	-ना	ना	धनधा	-पा	ह्मा	-पह्मा	गा	ह्मा	पा	-ा ‖‖
ए	०००	क्	ह	उ००	क्	हे	००	भ	ग	बा	न् ‖‖

Composer - Mukunda Das

भय कि मरणे ? राखिते सन्ताने, मातंगी मेतेछे आज समर रंगे ।
ताथै ताथै थै, द्रिमि द्रिमि द्रम द्रम, भूत पिशाच नाचे योगिनी संगे ।
दानव दलनी हय उन्मादिनी, आर कि दानव थाकिबे बंगे ?
साजरे सन्तान, हिन्दु मुसलमान, थाके थाकिबे प्राण, ना हय जाइबे प्राण ।
लइये कृपान हओरे आगुआन, निते हय मुकुन्देरे निओ गो संगे ।

+				०				+				०			
-ा	सा	-ा	सा	रा	रा	रा	-रा	-ा	ज्ञा	ज्ञा	ज्ञा	रा	ज्ञा	रा	ज्ञरसा
०	भ	य	कि	म	र	णे	०	०	रा	खि	ते	स	न्	ता	ने००
-ा	ज्ञा	ज्ञा	ज्ञा	रा	ज्ञा	रा	सा	-ा	णा्	रा	सा	णा्	-धा्	पा्	-पा्
०	मा	तं	गी	मे	ते	छे	आज	०	स	म	र	रं	०	गे	०
-ा	मा	पा	मा	पा	-ा	पा	-ा	मा	पा	मा	मा	ज्ञा	ज्ञा	रा	रा
०	ता	थै	ता	थै	०	थै	०	द्रि	मि	द्रि	मि	द्र	म्	द्र	म्
-ा	मा	ज्ञा	ज्ञा	रा	रा	सा	सा	-ा	णा्	रा	सा	णा्	-धा	पा्	-ा
०	भू	त	पि	शा	च	ना	चे	०	यो	गि	नी	सं	०	गे	०
-ा	णा्	सा	सा	मज्ञा	-ज्ञा	ज्ञा	मा	-ा	मा	पा	मा	पा	-ा	पा	-ा
०	दा	न	ब	द०	०	ल	नी	०	ह	य	उन्	मा	०	दि	नी
-ा	पा	णा	णा	दा	-ा	पा	पा	-ा	मा	मा	पा	मा	-ा	पा	-ा
०	आ	र	कि	दा	०	न	ब	०	था	कौ	बे	बं	०	गे	०
-ा	मा	पा	मा	पा	-ा	पा	-ा	-ा	मा	पा	मा	ज्ञा	ज्ञा	रा	रा
०	सा	जो	रे	स	न्	ता	न्	०	हि	न्दु	मु	स	ल्	मा	न्
-ा	रा	मा	ज्ञा	रा	रा	सा	-ा	-ा	णा्	णा्	सा	णा्	दा्	पा्	-ा
०	था	के	था	कि	बे	प्रा	ण	०	ना	हय	जा	इ	बे	प्रा	णा
-ा	पा	णा	णा	णा	-ा	णा	णा	-ा	णा	र्सा	णा	दा	दा	पा	-ा
०	ल	इ	ये	कृ	०	पा	ण्	०	ह	ओ	रे	आ	गु	आ	न्
-ा	पा	णा	दा-	पा	मा	ज्ञा	रा	-ा	-णा्	रा	सा	णा्	दा्	-पा्	-ा
०	नि	ते	हय	मु	कु	न्	दे	रे	०	नि	ओ	गो	सं	०	गे

[*Bāṅglā gāner vivartan* - Utpala Goswami.]

Evolution of Notation System in Bengal (in comparison to rest of India)

In ancient India the musician, i.e., the *kalākār* and the musicologist i.e., the *śāstravid* used to be the same person who performed as well as wrote *śāstras* on music. He knew his practical and theoretical science well. But during the Madhya yuga, for various reasons the same norm of being a *śāstravid* as well as a *kalākār* was not maintained. Thus gradually arose a rift between the two as the latter deviated from the prescribed path, not knowing the prescription. The problem was that, there being no proper *svaralipi-paddhati* or notation system, the scores by the musicians could not be written down to lay down the same pattern through out the country or at least to refer to. Thus gradually many changes crept into the same *rāga* in different parts of India and there by creating confusion.

The notation systems that existed in ancient India, were not foolproof and even the *śāstras* having them were not easily available. All through the ages, through *guru-śiṣya-paramparā,* a disciple learnt his music and musicology thoroughly from his *guru.* Later, with Muslim occupation, the practice and norms changed radically, particularly towards the latter part of Mughal rule. All *śiṣyas* did not get the same treatment from the *guru*, who was partial to his own *khāndān*— the close family members.

Incourse of time, particularly during the 19th and 20th centuries the necessity of a good notation system became urgently needed and many thinkers and researchers in the field of music, devoted themselves in evolving a good system of notation in Bengal.

A brief account of the ancient systems in India will not be out of place in this context.

Around the 1500 B.C. or earlier (Vedic era), a very simple method of notation was maintained. The signs used were long, and angular lines were drawn over or below the alphabets of the composition to denote *svaras* and the letter 'र' was used with the numbers to mention the length or duration of the *svara.* Later, when *svaras* like *prathama, dvitīya,* etc. came in vogue, only numbers were used to identify the *svaras.* The position of the number over the alphabet or letter of the text or at the side of the alphabet, denoted the duration or the length of time of pronouncing that letter of the text.

Probably during the Vedic era, these three elementary methods were in vogue, as no other system has been found in the documents so far available, to add to the knowledge.

The next text available is, Mataṅga Muni's *Bṛhaddeśī* written around *c* 500 A.D. Mataṅga has used *svaras,* i.e., स र ग म प ध न to notate or explain a *gāna.* But he has not used many signs to notate various nuances of a *gāna,* not even for *Tāra* or

Mandra saptakas, except for one or two *mandra* signs. He has used सा रा गा मा to denote length of time, through *ākāra.*

Around 700 A.D, a notation system is found in Kudumiāmalāi caves chiselled on the stone walls, using स र ग म for denoting *svaras* and adding *ākār, ikār,* etc. to the *sargam* to denote *komala-vikṛta* (flat-sharp) notes. Even this system was incomplete because signs of *tālas* or *mātrās* were not given, but it was perhaps the first step towards evolving a system that was universal in nature.

During the 13th century (1210-1247), Śārṅgadeva evolved a system based on स र ग म and he used the following signs :

Laghu svara - स रि ग म

Guru svara - सा री गा मा

Mandra svara - स़ , i.e. a dot under a svara.

Tāra svara - सं , i.e. a vertical line over a svara.

When सरि,etc. *svaras* were joined together, they meant *laghu-svaras.*

When *svaras* had no words underneath, it meant *vilopa* (विलोप) or extinction or *ṭān* (टान) meaning stretching the *svara.*

For denoting *laghu-mātrā* or *guru-mātrā* , etc. of a *tāla,* signs like I,S,O were used.

Śārṅgadeva however, did not use any special signs for *śuddha* or *vikṛta svaras.*

Rāṇā Kumbha followed the steps of Śārṅgadeva and presented his notation system in his book *Saṅgītarāja* (1456 A.D.).

During early 17th cent. A.D, *Somanātha* introduced a system with a few more signs of *alaṅkāra* or *gamakas,* e.g. स स स स स in his *Rāga-vivoda* (1609 A.D) but it was still far from being perfect.

It was Bengal which became the pioneer and successful in researching, experimenting and evolving various universal type of notation systems during the 19th and 20th centuries, as the acute necessity to document the *rāga-rūpas* properly, and the various *bandiśes* that were becoming rare and extinct, was realised. During this period Bengal produced a galaxy of eminent research oriented musician-musicologists who carried out a thorough research in Hindusthani as well as Western music. They not only wrote treatises on music, got ancient Sanskrit treatises printed but innovated various types of notation systems to bring out the difficult nuances of Indian classical as well as other styles of music prevailing in Bengal at that time. The most prominent among them were: Kshetramohan Goswami, Krishnadhan Banerji, Saurindramohan Thakur, Dwijendranath Thakur and Jyotirindranath Thakur.

1. *Dandamātrik Svaralipi*

The credit of being the first musician in the field of evolving a universal and detailed notation system goes to Kshetramohan Goswami. He formulated a system in Bengali around 1858 A.D. for the orchestra he organised for the drama *Ratnāvalī* that was staged for the first time in Belgāchiā Nāṭyaśālā. Musical scores were written in this notation system, called *Daṇḍa-mātrik,* meant for the players of the orchestra (or concert) team.

During this time there were three great researchers in Pathuriaghata Thakurbari—Kshetramohan Goswami, Saurindramohan Thakur and Krishnadhan Banerji, in the field of evolving a notation system for Hindusthani *saṅgīta.* The last two were disciples of Kshetramohan. While Saurindramohan totally supported his guru, Krishnadhan differed in his opinion and parted company, evolving his own system based on staff notation. Kaliprasanna Banerji, also a disciple of Kshetramohan, helped his *guru* and Saurindramohan constantly in their projects.

Kshetramohan's *Danḍamātrik* became popular and was accepted by the then music society of Bengal as well as outside, although research and experimentation went on in different quarters of Bengal, particularly at Jorasanko Thakurbari.

The success of Kshetramohan's system was possible due to the tireless cooperation of Saurindramohan and Kaliprasanna in all spheres.

At first Danḍa-mātrik svaralipi (1858) used to be written over three lines and was used for his own orchestra team. He published a book with this notation system in 1868 named *Aikatānik-svaralipi* and called the system *Raikhik-danḍamātrik svaralipi.* It is as follows :

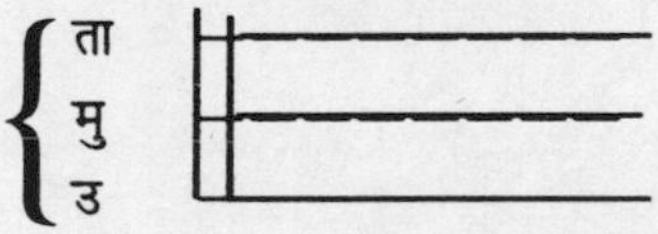

ता = Tārā saptaka
मु = Mudārā/Madhya saptaka
उ = Udārā/Mandra saptaka

The three lines denote three *saptakas,* viz. *Tārā, Mudārā, Udārā,* i.e. *Tāra, madhya* and *Mandra* respectively. A *gat* specimen written and signed by Kshertamohan is given below (copied from Dr. Bimal Roy's library):

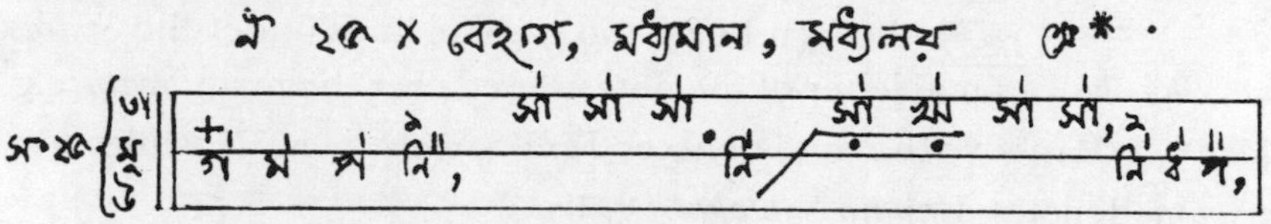

[This notation system of writing *gats* was used in 1858, 31st July for *Ratnāvalī nāṭaka* enacted in Belgāchiā Villa.] (*Initial of Kshetramohan)

Danḍamātrik was the first universal system of Indian notation, evolved by Kshetramohan.

Song example in *Daṇḍamātrik* was also published in *Saṅgīta-sāra* in 1869. In 1876 it was further polished and written in one line, instead of three.

Kshetramohan's initial system lacked the finnese of *mātrā-bibhāga* and sign of three *saptakas*. But these shortcomings were overcome gradually when notation in one line was evolved in *Daṇḍamātrik* and a song was published in 1876 in Saurindramohan's book called *Victoria-sāmrājyam*. This song was notated in one-line-*Daṇḍamātrik* form by introducing a dot over and under a *svara* to denote the *saptakas*. The same song was notated in staff notation also, in the same book.

In 1877, *Victoria-gītimālā* was published (by Saurindramohan) with *svaralipis* of songs in one-line-*Daṇḍamātrik*. The three line system was abandoned totally much later.

Daṇḍamātrik Svaralipi—with details and example:

1. *Seven Śuddha svaras* - स ऋ ग म प ध नि.

2. *Komala svaras* - ऋ̱ ग̱ ध̱ न̱, Δ being the sign of *komala*.

3. *Tīvra svara* - म̃, ⌐ being the sign of *tīvra*.

4. *Ati komala svaras* - ऋ̊, ग̊, ध̊, न̊, Δ̊ being the sign of *ati-komala*.

5. *Mātrā* sign is denoted, by a *daṇḍa* or vertical line or lines, as is required, e.g.:
1. *mātrā* = | = सं ; 2 *mātrās* = || = सं ; 3 *mātrās* = ||| = सं   and so on.

6. When more than one *svara* are sung in one *mātrā*, e.g. संगम are sung or played in one *mātrā* duration, the *daṇḍa* is placed over the first *svara*. The value of the three *svaras* is equal to one *mātrā*.

1/2 *mātrā* = ✓ = सं̌, the sign being = ✓

1/4 *mātrā* = X = सं̽, the sign being = X .

1/8 *mātrā* = (•) = सं̇, the sign being = (•)

7. *Gamaka* = ∿ = सं ; When *gamaka* is required twice, the sign used is—सा

8. *ās* = ————, ऋ ग म प, the sign being a line under the *Svaras*.

9. *Mīnd* = ═══ ऋ म, the sign being two parallel lines under the *Svaras*.

10. *Kaṇ or Bhuṣikā* = a small letter of the note is used over the main *Svara*, e.g. सं̃

11. *Saptaka* = a dot above the note denotes *Tārā Saptaka*, e.g. सं ; while, a dot below the *svara* denotes *Mandra Saptaka*, e.g. सु .

12. *Mūrchaṇā* = a wave like sign, ∿∿∿ is used. But in slow *laya*, the sign is: ....

13. *Double bar lines* mean the end of a song or a *gat*, e.g. ||.

14. *Yati or Virāma* = S, when this sign is applied over a *svara*, one has to pause at that *svara* and then start the next portion, or antarā.

15. *Repeat* sign is = { }. The *svaras* or portion of a song between this bracket sign, has to be repeated once more, e.g. - { स ग म प }

16. *Omit* sign is = ( ). When this bracket sign appears, the *svaras* or portions mentioned inside this bracket sign, has to be omitted, e.g. { स ग (म प) ध प }

17. *Tāla signs* = Originally only three signs were used, viz. *Sam* = +, *Khāli* or *Fā̃k* =O and *Tālī* = I. Later, Tālis with more numbers were introduced to indicate the number of *bihāgas,* e.g. 1 for first *tālī,* 2 for second *tālī,* 3 for third *tāli* and so on. Bar lines were used to mark each *bibhāga* or division. An example of *Tritāla* consisting of 16 *mātrās,* is given below:

| + I I I I | 3 I I I I | 0 I I I I | 1 I I I I ||

18. Kampana = 

19. Ched - vādana = 

A song example :

Rāga - Kāliṅgḍā Tāla - Dādrā

आमि कुंजे कुंजे तोमारे खुँजिया पाइना ।
प्रभु दाओ मोरे दरशन, यातना दियोना ॥
कर्ण कुहरे प्रबेशिल तब मधुर मुरली ध्वनि,
अदूरे थाकिया लुकाये रयेछो तुमि कत जान छलना ॥

		+		o	S	+			o			+			o
मं	ग	मं	मं	पं	पं	पं	धΔ	सं	नि	धΔ	पं	मं	पंधΔ	पं	मं
आ	मि	कुं	जे	कुं	जे	तो	मा	रे	खुँ	जि	या	पा		इ	ना

		+			o			+			o
पं	गं	गंम	पँ	धँΔ	पं	मं	पं	मं	गं	ऋंΔ	सं
प्र	भु	दा			ओ	मो	रे	द	र	श	न

+			o			+			o
नं	सं	गंम	पं	गं	मं	पधΔ	संनि	धंपΔ	मंप
जा	त	ना		दि	ओ	ना			

+ ० + ह्य ० + ०

{ धं धं | निं निं निं | सं सं ऋं | निं सं सं | निं सं गं | ऋं सं सं |

क र्ण | कु ह रे | प्र बे शि | ल त ब | म धु र | मु र ली |

+ ० +

निंसं ऋंसं निंसं | निं धं पं } | पं धं पं | मं पं गं |

ध्व | नि } | अ दू रे | था कि या |

+ ० + ० + ०

मं धं धं | निं सं सं | धं निं सं | ऋं निं सं | निंध निं धं | पं

लु का ये | र ये छ | तु मि क | त जा न | छ ल | ना

[*Gīta Praveśikā* - p. 51. by Gopeshvar Bandopadhyay]

2. ***Kaṣimātrik Svaralipi***—During this same period, the Tagores of Jorasanko were also deeply involved in music and its propagation. The two persons of this family who have become famous in the field of evolving notation systems are Dwijendranath and Jyotirindranath.

Soon after Kshetramohan's 3-line *Danḍamātrik* notation system was formulated for his orchestra, Dwijendranath brought out a system called *Kaṣi-mātrik svaralipi* and published it in the journal named *Tattvabodhinī,* in 1869, (1791 Śaka, Kārtik no. of *Tatvabodhinī*) with the addition of six more pages of notated songs. (Although six pages extra were added to the Kārtika issue of *Tattvabodhinī,* in the Āświna issue, one extra page with a notated song in *Kaṣi -mātrik* was available with Saumyendranath Thakur). This system was also called *Tirjak mātrik svaralipi* and was simpler than the 3-line *Danḍamātrik.* It was written on a single line. In this system, *mātrās* were indicated by a *Kaṣi,*meaning dash; *Mandra saptaka* by a dot under the *svara* and *Tāra-saptaka* by a dot over the *svara.* He worked on it for a few years but did not pursue hard to make it popular among the members of the then music society.

That *Kaṣi-mātrik svaralipi* was formulated by Dwijendranath is substantiated by Brajendranath Bandopadhyay, in his 66th issue of *Sāhitya Sādhaka Caritamālā* and Pratibhādevī in her article *Sahajegāna-sīkṣā,* published in *Bālak* journal of 1292 B.S *Baiśākh* issue.

Kaṣi-mātrik svaralipi —signs and details :

Śuddha svaras : *Ṣadja* = ष, *Rṣabha* = ऋ, *Gāndhāra* =ग, *Madhyama* = म, *Pañcama* = प, *Dhaivata* = ध, *Niṣāda* = न.

Vikṛta svaras : For *Komala-svaras* a dash under the note is used, e.g. ऋ ग ध न.

For *tīvra-svara* a dash is used over the *svara,* e.g. मं .

Saptakas : A dot above the note indicates *Tāra-saptaka,* e.g. सं पं , etc.

A dot below indicates *Mandra-saptaka* , e.g. नि़ ध़ प़, etc.

No special sign is needed for *Madhya saptaka.*

Tāla : Signs for *Khāli* = O, First *tāli* = 1, Second *tāli* = 2, Third *tāli* = 3 and so on.

Bar lines or Cheda : *Tāla-ccheda* or completion = ||,

Tāla divisions are indicated by a single bar line = ।

Continuation or *Āvahamānatā* = ——

Rest or *Virāma* = •/.

Short rest or *Alpa-virāma* = ❟

Repeat signs : To repeat, the portion is written within the bracket sign of - { }

Alaṅkāras :

When this ⌒ sign is used it means that the next higher note is touched: ष॑ = रस

When this ◡• sign is used, it means that the previous lower note is touched: ष॔ = नर्स

When this ⌒⌒ sign is used, it means that the next higher note is touched repeatedly, eg. ष : ऋष ऋष.

When this ◡◡ sign is used it means that the lower note is touched repeatedly, e.g. म = गमगम.

When this ∽ sign is used, it means that the next higher note is touched first then the main note, then the lower note and finally the main note, eg. म = पमगम

This sign ∾ is the reverse of the above one, eg. म = गमपम

Mātrā : Mātrās were maintained by a *Kaṣi* or dash sign, e.g. ष-

In 1880 Dwijendranath experimented with another system, slightly different from *Kaṣi-mātrik.* This system introduced :

1. the *svaras* of *saptakas* as : नि़ स रे ग म प ध नि सं

   i.e. it did away with ष and ऋ and instead introduced स रे,

2. instead of maintaining time factors with *Kaṣi* sign, अ आ letters were used.

The rest of the rules remained the same, as *Kaṣi-mātrik.*

Song example of Kaṣi-mātrik:

Brahma Saṅgīta - Rāga Bihāg - Tāla Kavvālī

० १ २ ३

ष । ग । ग । ग ▮ म । -। प । प ▮ षं । -। षं । षं ▮ नि । -। प । - ▮

{ तु । मि । बि । ना ▮ के । -। प्र । भु ▮ सं । -। कटा।नि ▮ बा । -। रे । - ▮

{ ध । म । ग । ग ▮ पुनरावृत्ति काले ▮ . । . । . । . ▮ . । . । . । . ▮

धा। धप। म । ग॥ म । ग । ग । ग॥ म । पँ । - । म॥ ग । गँ । - । ष॥}

के। •• ।स । हा॥ - । य । भ । व॥ अ । - । - । न्ध॥ का। - । - । रे॥}

[Tattvabodhinī Patrikā - Saptam Kalpa, Tṛtīyabhāga, Āświn- 1791śaka]

3. *Saṅkhyā Svārik Paddhati*

It is to be noted that, before Kshetramohan's one line notation was evolved in 1876, another example of one line notation is available in *Baṅga Darśan* journal of Bankimchandra Chattopadhyay, started in 1872 Baiśākh. This journal published a serial article from Baiśākh to Āṣāḍha on music, which was written by Bankimchandra himself although he did not mention his name. In that article notation system also featured. The author recommended the use of Western system which was already in a very developed form. He took help from an European friend and published the following method of notating an Indian song in *Āṣāḍh* issue. The two redeeming features of this method were: a) no special signs for *komala* or *tīvra* were needed, as each note whether *śuddha* or *vikṛta* were denoted by a number and b) it was written after tablature system i.e. on the basis of a stringed instrument such as violin, where the first string is tuned in *madhyama*. So, the first note is *madhyama,* and the rest of the *svaras* are according to that relationship.

The *svaras* and *svarasthānas* of this system are as follows :

खरज / Mandra			मध्यम /Madhya												सप्तम / Tāra				
$\overline{10}$	$\overline{11}$	$\overline{12}$	1	2	3	4	5	6	7	8	9	10	11	12	$\underline{1}$	$\underline{2}$	$\underline{3}$	$\underline{4}$	$\underline{5}$
र	ज्ञ	ग	म	ह्म	प	द	ध	ण	न	स	ऋ	र	ज्ञ	ग					

A dash overhead denotes *mandra* and underneath means *tāra saptaka,* e.g. र̄ = $\overline{10}$; ग̲ = $\underline{12}$

The signs for *tālas* are : - $(^0)$ = 1, (1^0) = 2, (1^{00}) = 3, (1^{000})= 4 etc.

The sign of *Sam* is = 0. When a note or notes denoted by numbers are placed between 1 or 2 bar lines, that signifies the length of time each note occupies, e.g.

| 5   6 | 5   4   6 | 6   3   8 | 1   5   8   1 | 6   7   8 ||

| 1/2   1/2 | 1/3   1/3   1/3 | 1/2   1/4   1/4 | 1/4   1/4   1/4   1/4 | 1/2   1/4   1/4 ||

A song example of this system called Saṅkhyā Svārik Paddhati : -

Rāga Multānī Gītāvalī - (no. I)

|| 6 8 8 6 4 3 1 1 1 4 6 8 8
|| आ र जा ब ना लो सइ ज मु ना रि ज ले

| 5 5 5 5 8 12 1 1 8 8 8 6 6, 5
| भ रि या ए ने छि कु म्भ न य न स लि ले

| 6 6 6 6 8 12 1 1 1 1 1 1 2
| कि हे रि ला म रुप तार घ रे आ सा ह लो

| 1 1 8 8 8 8 8 8 9 6 6 6 6 7 5
| भा र नाम जे जा नि ने ता र से था के गो कु ले ||

Unfortunately, this system was not explained clearly by the innovator. The *tālas, tāla-bibhāgas, svaras, svara-sthāna* and their signs remained vague and unintelligible. Hence, this system was not further pursued or practised.

4. *Sārgam Paddhati* :

Krishnadhan Banerji was another knowledgeable musician - musicologist who had studied both Hindusthani and Western music in depth and was very much in favour of a notation system for Hindusthani music on the basis of Staff notation, for which he fell apart from his *guru* Kshetramohan and *guru-bhāi* Saurindramohan, as has been mentioned earlier.

An intelligent and keen musician, he evolved a system on the basis of staff notation, and called it *Sāṅketik Svaralipi Paddhati.* This *paddhati* of his was published in 1867, in his book—*Baṅgaikatāna,* a few months ahead of Kshetramohan's *Aikatānik-Svaralipi* and a year earlier than Dwijendranath's *Kaṣi-mātrik svaralipi.* But this was Western style while the other two were Indian. Krishnadhan strived hard to propagate this system but due to printing cost and its alien nature it could not be popularised and he then invented his *Sārgam Paddhati* in 1882-83. The *Sārgam Svaralipi* was publicised through *Gītasūtrasāra,* published in 1885. He applied this new method after 15 years of his first system, which was based on Western principles entirely. For convenience, the details of *Sārgam Paddhati* are furnished first :

Sārgam Svaralipi :

Śuddha svaras—स र ग म प ध न

Vikṛt svaras —*Komala* - रो गो धो नो

Tīvra—मी

Saptakas—*Mandra*: स$_{१}$ र$_{१}$ ग$_{१}$, etc.

Ati-mandra : स$_{२}$ र$_{२}$ ग$_{२}$, etc.

Madhya : स र ग, etc.

Tāra : स^{१} र^{१} ग^{१}, etc.

Ati-tāra :स^{२} र^{२} ग^{२}, etc.

Mātrā : *Hrasva kāla* = *Laghu*, and *Dīrgha kāla* = *Guru*.

1 *mātra kāla* = (सः); 2 *mātrā kāla* =(सः-:); 3 *mātrās*=(सः-:-:) Two 1/2 *mātrās* = (स.सः); i.e. with the *Bindu* sign, I *mātrā kāla* is divided into two halves.

Two 1/4 *mātrās* =(स, स), i.e. the comma sign divides the 1/2 mātrā.

Four 1/4 *mātrās*=(स, स. स, सः)

Two 1/8 *mātrās* =(स स,)

To put it in a simpler way :

I *mātrā* = सः ; 2 mātrās =स :-:, 3 mātrās =स :-:-: and so on.

I *mātrā* may be denoted in many different combinations of *kāla*.

1/3 *mātrā* is shown by a reverted comma, e.g. स‘स‘सः = 1 *mātrā*.

Alaṅkāra signs :

Bal or accent on *svaras* is indicated in the following manner :

(a) *sama-bal* or equal stress ═══

(b) *vardhita-bal* or increased stress <

(c) *hrasva-bal* or less stress >

(d) *sphiti* (s forzando) <>

(e) from *mṛdu* or soft to gradual *vṛddhi* or loud(Crescendo) <

(f) from *vṛddhi* to *mṛdu*(diminuendo) >

(g) *prasvana* or accent > or ∧

(h) an example of the different signs :-

– = < > <> ∧1 >1

| सः रः गः-: मः-: पः-: स स |

Instead of using the signs, letters are also used to convey the same: *mṛdu* (piano) = मृ/*p; Pravala*(forte) = व/*f; vṛddhi* = वृ ; *hrasva* = ह; *madhya-bal* (mezzo) = म/*m;* for very soft/ *mṛdu* = मृमृ *pp;* for very loud/ *pravala/vṛddhi* = वव *ff;* (These signs are common to both the systems i.e. *Sārgam* and *Sāṅketik*)

Ās - When more than one note are sung in one letter of a song, a line is drawn under those notes, e.g. : स. र: ग ग

रा ..... म

Mīṇḍ = When a glide is performed, the following sign is used: ______ , under the *svaras.*

eg.- स. न१: स, स ।

रा . . .. म

Some of the signs of *Sārgam* and *Sāṅketik* are identical, hence these will be given together in *Sāṅketik paddhati.*

5. *Sāṅketik paddhati*

In this system the *svaras* of a *saptaka* rise step by step like a stair-case and when written on a stave paper the position of a *svara* is also visible. The lines that are drawn for this notation system are called *Mañca.* The *svaras* are indicated by drawing a large dot either on the line or between two lines. The *Mañca* consists of 11 lines to accomodate 22 *svaras* of the three *saptakas.* Normally to write songs, only a 5 lined *Mañca* is enough.

Example of a II lined *Mañca* :

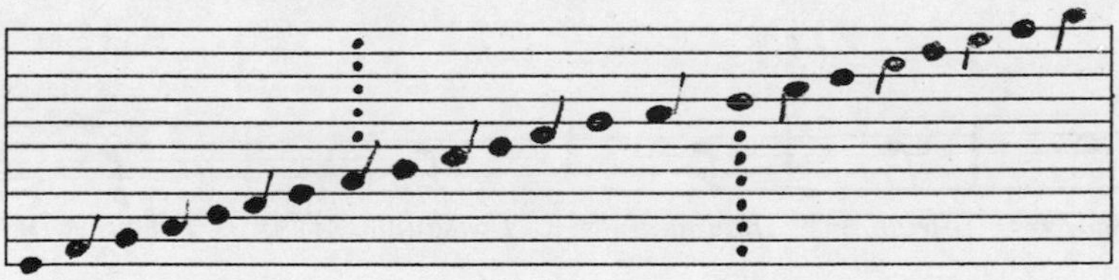

When the middle line of this big *mañca* is taken off, two five - lined *mañcas* remain. The lower part is called *Khād-mañca* and the upper part is called *Ucca-mañca.* To distinguish between the two, they are marked as *Kuñcikās.* The sign 𝄞 - is for *Ucca-kuñcikā* and 𝄢 is called the *Khād-kuñcikā.* For example :

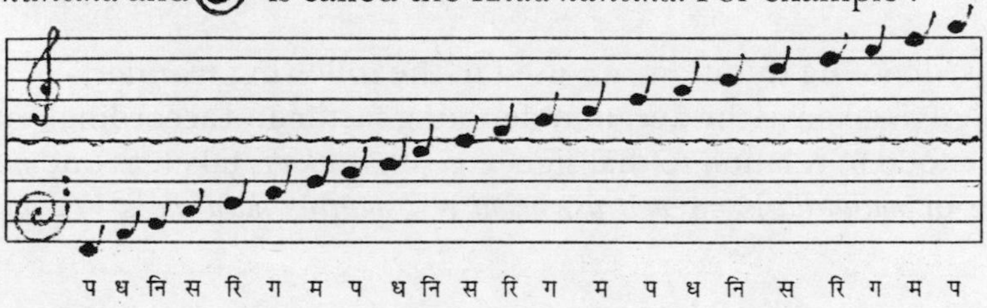

To write Hindusthānī music, one *Kuñcikā* is enough. Both are required only when two octaves are to be shown simultaneously. In Indian music *Ucca-kuñcikā* alone suffice the necessity. For notating Hindusthanī music the following methods have been used :

रेखा (Rekhā) घर (Ghar)

Some times extra lines are drawn in *Ucca-mañca* to accomodate *svaras* of *mandra* or *tāra saptaka*, e.g.

Mandra Saptaka *Madhya Saptaka* *Tāra Saptaka*

The sign for *Tīvra* is - # and *komala* is - ♭

Mātrās in Sāṅketik

The shape of the *bindus* denoting *svaras,* differ according to *mātrās* or their lengths of duration. Normally six situations of length or duration are envisaged and signs are accordingly used. They are as follows :

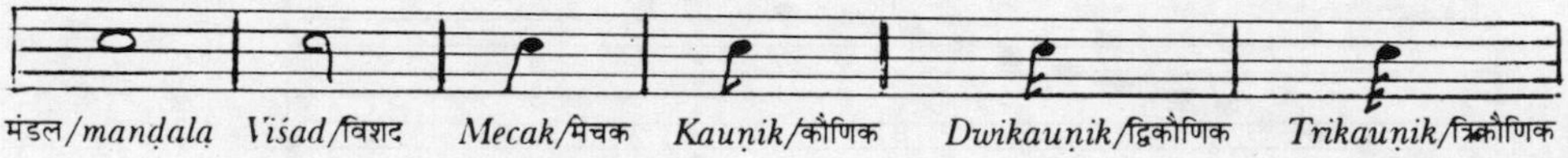

मंडल/*mandala* *Viśad*/विशद *Mecak*/मिचक *Kauṇik*/कौणिक *Dwikauṇik*/द्विकौणिक *Trikauṇik*/त्रिकौणिक

The tails of these *svara*-denoting-*bindus* could be put either way, upward or downward. e.g. 

The six signs, denoting duration, are used in the following manner; -

One of the signs is taken as the duration-denoting-factor and accordingly other signs are understood in relation to that sign, e.g. if *mecaka* is taken as one *mātrā,* then the value of *mandala* is =4 *mātrās, viśad* is 2 *mātrās, kauṇik* is 1/2 *mātrā, dwikauṇik* is 1/4 *mātrā* and so on. If *kauṇik* is taken as I *mātrā*, then the value of the rest will be : *manḍala* = 8 *mātrās, viśad* = 4 *mātrās, mecaka* = 2, *dwikauṇik* = 1/2, etc. When a particular duration is taken as I *mātrā*, the indication is given next to the *Kuñcikā*, e.g. 𝄞 1/2, 3/8 etc.

When a *svara* with '*Koṇ*' —the small angular line attached to the tail of the *svara*-denoting *bindu*, e.g. ♪ is used 3 times or more, then instead of *Koṇ*, straight lines are used joining those *svaras*, e.g.

Number of straight lines denote the number of *Kon.*

When a dot is added after a *varṇa*, the dot denotes 1/2 *mātrā* extra duration to the *varṇa* and therefore the *varṇa* becomes $1\frac{1}{2}$ times in duration. If two dots are added, the second dot gets aded to the 1/2 *mātrā* duration of the first and thus the *varṇa* is of $1\frac{3}{4}$ times duration in length of time, e.g.

: स | - :

Virāma - It implies momentary pause in a musical rendition. *Virāma* is of six types, viz - *manḍala-virāma, viśad-virāma, mecaka-virāma, kauṇik-virāma, dwikauṇik-virāma, trikauṇik-virāma.* The signs are as follows;

Mecaka-virāma for I *mātrā* pause is also expressed as :

To denote 1/3 in this system is to mention the number 3 in the following manner :-

Some comparative examples of a 4 *mātrik* and 2 *mātrik chanda* in *Sārgam* and *Sāṅketik* systems :

Mecaka Mātrā:

	Ek-mātrik	*Dwi-mātrik*	*Tri-mātrik*	*Catur-Mātrik*
Sāṅketik :	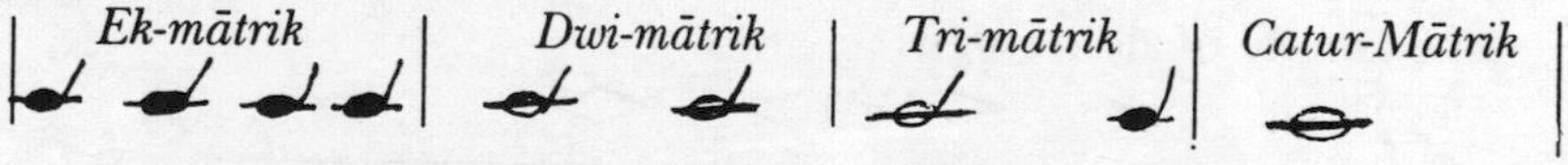			
Sārgam :	स: स: स: स	स :-: स :-	स :-:-: स	स :-:-:-

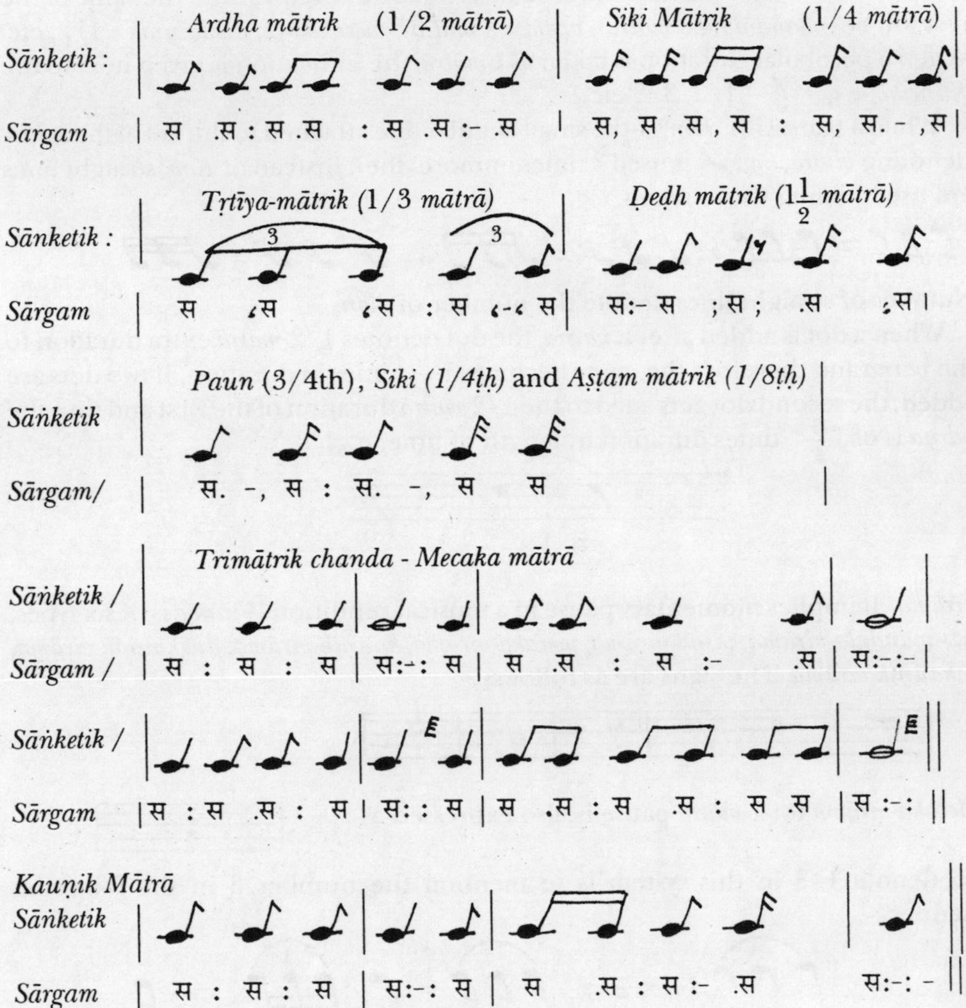

Alaṅkāra—It is the same as *Sārgam* system.
Sama-bal - =; *Vardhita-bal* - < *Hrasva-bal* - > *Sphīti* - <>
Gradual *svara* expansion from *mṛdu* to *vṛddhi* < and the reverse is = >, ie, from loud to soft. Accent or *prasvana* sign is - > or ∧

An example of all the signs :

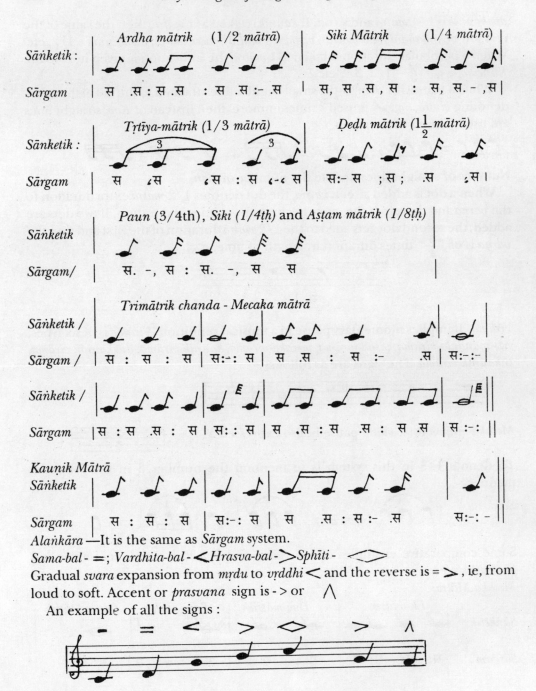

Ās : - This sign is put either below or above the *svaras* which are sung one after the other without a pause meant for one letter of a song. e.g. । स.र : ग. म ।
रा......... म

Alagna - In this *alaṅkāra* a slight pause is also indicated in between *svaras* with sounded rendition. The sign used is = I, which means 1/2 mātrā pause after 1/2 mātrā sound, e.g.

Sārgam = | गं : मं |
Sāṅketik :

Mīnd —When a glide is performed over the *svaras,* the sign used is, ══════ e.g.
। स.र : म .ग ।
रा......... म

Kampan—When one note is sung repeatedly and fast, a) either the sign = ——— like *Ās* is used under the *svaras,* or b) W sign is used, e.g. = *Sārgam* = स = स. स:
Sāṅketik : or स .स .स ,स:
आ...........

Giṭkārī - It is of two types, - plain and with *gamaka.* The sign of *giṭkārī* is a dot on the top of the *svara* and *ās* sign down below, e.g. *Sārgam* = । गं. मं: पं. मं ।
Sāṅketik =

Bhuṣikā - Those *svaras* which are used for a fraction of a second, just before or after the main *svara,* and are written in very small size are sign of *Bhuṣikā.* e.g.

(a) (b) (c)

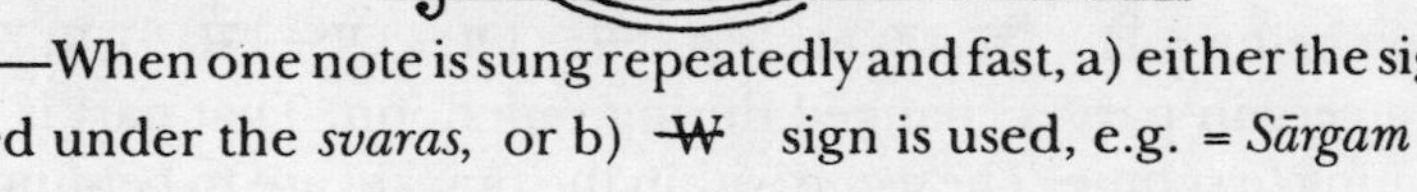

In *sārgam* no special sign is used but the *svara* is written with the main *svara.* e.g । मग :म । the first *svara* म is the *Bhuṣikā.*

Repetition of a certain portion: In *sāṅketik* the following signs are used ⋮ or :: . On whichever side these signs are used, that side is to be repeated. e.g.

Where the first line needs to be repeated after 3-4 lines, :𝄋: - this sign is used. e.g.

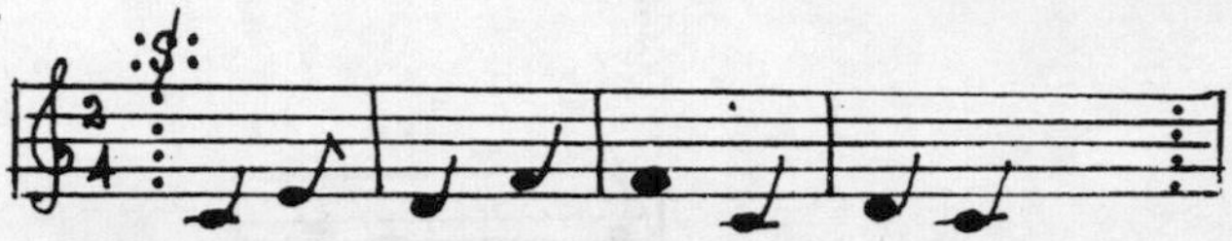

In *Sārgam* these signs can not be used, instead 'प्रथम हइते', meaning 'from the beginning' and in short the abbreviation = प्र: ह: is used.

Other signs of repetitions are - a) 'चिह्न हइते', meaning 'from the sign', the abbreviation being चि.ह. b) 'प्रथम चिह्न हइते', meaning 'from the first sign', the abbreviation being प्र-चि-ह. c) 'द्वितीय चिह्न हइते', meaning 'from the second sign', the abbreviation being = द्वि - चि - ह, etc. e.g. । स:- । ग:- । प:- । सं:- ॥ प्र: ह:

Sometimes a certain part is changed during repetition. That part is marked as, ⌐¬ meaning first time. The*svaras* within the bracket are to be sung for the first time and should be sung with changed notes during the second time. e.g.

प्रथमवार (1st time) द्वितीयवार (2nd time)

As experimentations and researches were going on in different quarters of Calcutta, several systems came up and were published.

Around the sametime Raja Pratap chandra Barua of Gauripur published svaralipis based on Staff Notation.

Notated example of a Thumri - both in Sārgam and Sāṅketik : खमाज (मिश्र)

जानि हमसे बोलो, मैने क्या गुना किया है ।

उलफ्तके वर्छि मार्के जहाँसे खो दिया है ।

मस्‌जिदमें कसम खा के, खोदा दरमेया दिया है ।
उलफतके वर्छि मार्‌के जहाँसे खो दिया है ।

Sthāyī

[*Sāṅketik svaralipi* is on the '*mañca*' and *Sārgam svaralipi* is below each *mañca.*]

A few notated examples of tālas :

1. Jalad Tritāla/Kavvāli :

\+ ३ ० १

। धा .धिन् :धिन् .धा । धा .धिन् :धिन् .धा । धा .तिन् :तिन् .ता । ना .धिन् :धिन् .धा ॥

2. Dhīmā Tritāla :

\+ ३

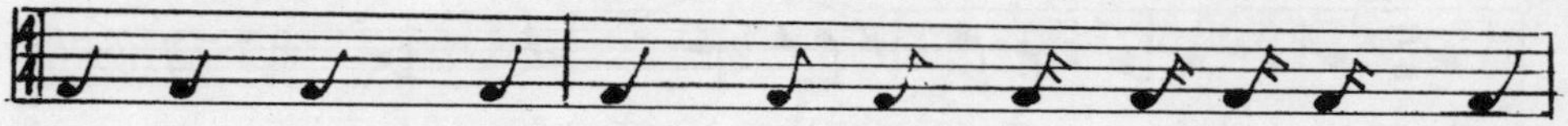

धा : धिन् : धिन् : धा | धिन् : धा .गे : ते, रे .के ,टे : धिन् |

० १

। ता : तिन् : तिन् : ता | धिन् : धा गे : ते ,रे .के ,टे : धिन् ॥

3. Ṭhumrī tāla :

\+ ०

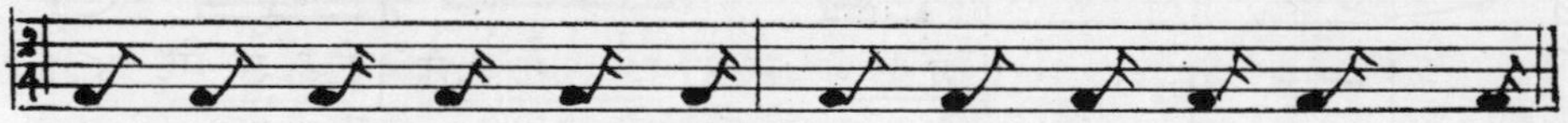

धा धा : के , टे .ता , क । ने . धा : के, टे .ता , क ॥

4. Āḍā ṭhekā - (Āḍi chanda):

१ + ३ ०

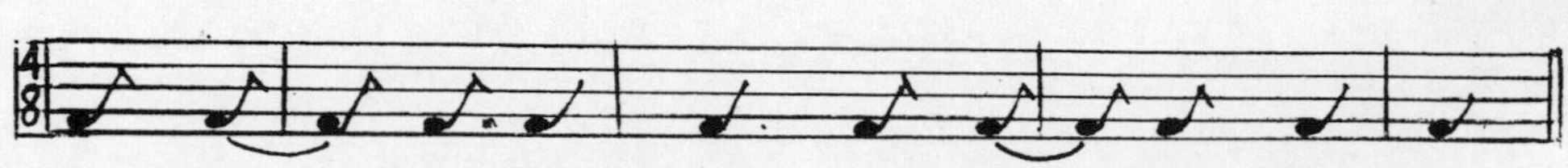

ता : धिन् । -: ता : धिन्:- । धिन् :-: ता : धिन् । -: धिन् : ता :- । तिन् :- ॥

5. Madhyamāna :

१ +

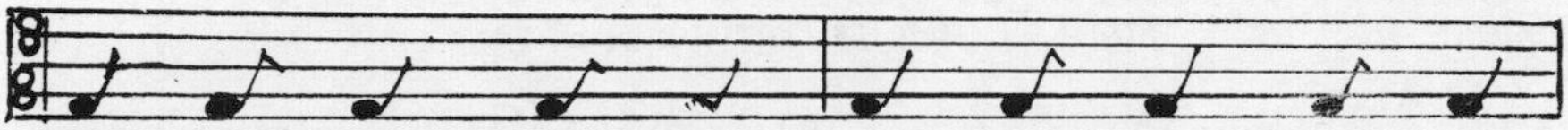

धा :-: धा : धिन् :-: धा : धिन् :- । धा :-: धा : धिन् :-: धा : धिन्:- ।

३ ०

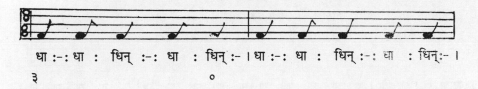

धा :-: धा : धिन् :-: धा : तिन् :- । ता :-: ना : धिन् :-: धा : धिन् :- ॥

6. *Saṅkhyā-mātrik or Sāṅkhya svaralipi:*

Saṅkhyā-mātrik svaralipi was experimented upon by Jyotirindranath Thakur who gave it a good shape in 1888. This system also dealt with the twelve notes (*Śuddha* and *Vikṛta*) in the following manner:

स रो र गो ग म मी प धो ध नो न। रो गो धो नो i.e., ो standing for *komala* and ी for *tīvra svaras, Tīvra madhyama.*=मी.

Mātrās were denoted by a number, e.g. स१ सर१. A horizontal line over the *svara* meant *Tāra-saptaka* and a line under, denoted *Mandra*: e.g स̄, स̱

For repetition, the following signs were used:

(A). आवृत्ति meaning repeat, the first letter आ was used to indicate once.

It was further abbreviated as - आ = -ा = आ ⋮ -ा ⋮

(B). The portion that was to be repeated once, was marked with the sign ८-। little above or below the portion. Similarly, for repeating twice, the sign was ८॥, for thrice=८।।। and so on.

Tāli vibhāga: Tāli vibhāga and starting point of a song were marked by the same sign by writing the abbreviated sign of *sthāyī* (स्थायी), *antarā* (अन्तरा), etc. at the *mātrā* or *tālī* from where the song or *gat* would start, e.g.- तालि । १ (स्था, न्त, भो) ।२।३।
मात्रा । ४

or तालि । १ (स्था, न्त, भो आरम्भ) ।२।३।
मात्रा । ४ ४।४।

Sign of sam is = ꣸

Jyotirindranath published a few notated songs in this style in *Bhāratī* and *Bālak* journals in 1295 B.S. This system was further taken up by his nephew Hitendranath but it did not become very popular. A song example of this system: (Pub. in *Tatvabodhinī*, 1815 *Śaka, Śrāvaṇa issue* - by Hitendranath)

सांख्य स्वरलिपि

अल्हैया - एकताल

तालि । २: (स्था, न्त, आरम्भे) ३। ०। १।

मात्रा ।४ २। २ ।४।

(स्था): ८प्धा धा धा पा । पा पा । मा पा१२ .गा१२। मा गा गा१२ .रे१२ .गा । रे गा गा गा१२ मा१२।

(स्था):- ।दे ह - ज्ञा । - नु् । दि व्य - ।- ज्ञा - - नु् । दे ह - प्री - ।

२...२ २ ।

।पा मा गा गा१२ .मा१२। रे सा सा सा। स्सा सा सा सा । सा सा । नसा नि.।नसा धा धा१२ न१२ -पा।

।- ति शु - - ।द्ध प्री - ति ।तु मि - मं ।- ग । ल आ। - ल - - य।

7. In 1885 Saraladevi formulated a notated system guided by Jyotirindranath.

8. In the same year (1885), Pratibhadevi wrote an article in *Bālak*, named *Sahaje Gana Śikṣā*, in which she had adopted a system different from others. It is as follows: :

Śuddha svaras सा रे गी म पा धा नी

Vikṛt svaras रि ग मा ध नि

Saptaka = *Tāra* - सां, Madhya - सा, Mandra - सा.

Mātrā = for I mātra = सा–, for 1/2 mātrā = सा०

Repeat sign = ॥: :॥. This system was called ***Rekhā mātrik*** or ***Rekhā O Dash Mātrik*** *Svaralipi*. An example -

सा- - नी- - | सा- नी- सा- - | रे- ग- - - | रे- - - - | रे- पा- - -

ब ल् | गो ला प् | मो रे | बल् | तु इ

9. *Ākār-mātrik Svaralipi*

The most effective and successful notation system was evolved by Jyotirindranath in 1891, called *Ākār-mātrik Svaralipi* which was an outcome of years of research and experimentation. To establish and popularise this system he published notated songs and *gats* in books and journals tirelessly for years. But for his notation system it would have been impossible to preserve the wealth of *Rabīndra-Saṅgīta, Brahma-*

Saṅgīta, Kāvya Saṅgīta and other styles that were prevalent at that time and styles that followed later. *Ākārmātrik* became so popular and widely used in Bengal that it soon replaced all other systems.

At the initial stage the system was not perfect. The first initial example is available in *Tattvabodhinī* (1891 A.D. - *Pauṣ* issue) and some more specimens in *Sādhnā* and *Vīṇāvādinī* journals. Jyotirindranath must have had formulated the system earlier than 1891 and perfected it by 1893, when a Vedic hymn was published in *Tatvabodhinī*. At the nascent stage it was different from the finally developed form and was as follows :

1 *mātrā* = -ा, 1/2 *mātrā* = **:** , $1\frac{1}{2}$ mātrās = -ाः,

When the sign I is added to स, र, ग, म, etc. e.g. सा, it become I *mātrā*; सा-ा = 2 *mātrās*.

For fractions, instead of using any sign, it is written as - सना, both 1/2 *mātrā* each.

Ās is denoted by a small dash between *svaras* and *Mīnd* by a big dash under the *svara*.

Śuddha svaras = स, र, ग, म, प, ध, न.

Vikṛt svaras = ल = komal र, ङ्ग = komal ग, द = komal ध, ञ = komal न.

Saptaka = A slanting line over the *svara* for *Tāra* and slanting line under, for *Mandra*, were used, e.g. र्न & न्

Sparśa svara = /·

(In this issue *Tīvra madhyama* was not explained. In *Caitra* issue the sign given for *Tivra madhyama* was = ह्म. Other signs given were - ।। two vertical lines drawn over a *svara* in *Sthāyī*, meaning that the singer had to sing upto that *svara* to start *Antarā*.)

Example of the first initial *Ākārmātrik* notated song :-

ब्रह्म संगीत - नाचारी तोड़ी - धामार, ५-५-४।५; २। ३। १́

२	३	१́
‖ सा - : ल : ञा सा -ा	ङ्गा -। मा -।	पा - म⁄· पा -। मा -ङ्गा ‖
नू - त न -	प्रा - ण -	दा - - - ओ, - ‖

5-5-4 |5 means, the *bibhāgas* of *Dhāmār tāla* consisting of 5,5, and 4 *mātrās* and the number 5 next to the bar means the *laya*, i.e. to count I to 5 quickly it takes a particular length of time which should be the *laya* or speed. २।३।१́ means 2nd *tāli*, 3rd *tāli* and *Sam* respectively.

Gradually the system was perfected by Jyotirindranath to the present form and is still in use exactly the same way with no further change since then.

Details of Ākār-mātrik Svaralipi:

Śuddha svara — स, र, ग, म, प, ध, न

Komala svara — ऋ, ज्ञ, द, ण

Ati komala svara—ऋ१, ज्ञ१, द१, ण१

Anu komala svara — ऋ२, ज्ञ२, द२, ण२

Tīvra/Kaḍi svara — ह्म

Saptaka - Sign of *Tāra* is a slanting line above = '/', र्स, र्, र्ग

Madhya has no special sign - स, र, ग

Mandra sign is = \, स न् ध् प्, i.e..a slanting line under the *svara* .

Mātrā - Sign of *mātrā* is *ākār* = '-ा', e.g. सा = I mātrā.

When two or more *svaras* are sung in one *mātrā* = सरा = 1 *mātrā* ;

सरगा = 1 *mātrā* ; सरगमा = 1 *mātrā.*

When two or more *svaras* are sung in 1/2 *mātrā* duration, the following sign is used = 1/2 *mātrā* = :, therefore स: = 1/2 *mātrā,* सर: = 1/2 *mātrā,* सरग: = 1/2 *mātrā;* सरगम: = 1/2 *mātrā,* and so on.

$1\frac{1}{2}$ *mātrā* is expressed as = सा:. To express स as $1\frac{1}{2}$ *mātrās* and ग as 1/2 *mātrā,* it is written as = सा: ग: = $1\frac{1}{2}$ + 1/2 = 2 *mātrās.*

Kaṇ/Bhuṣikā - The *Kaṇ-svara* is written in small letter above the left side of the main *svara*-eg -मग

Mīnḍ = ‿ This sign is applied under the *svaras,* e.g. सा मा

Virāma = ा. This sign is same as *mātrā* sign but negative the hyphen.

Double vertical lines over a *svara* means either to sing upto that *svara* and then start a new *kali* or stanza or the completion of the song, e.g. पा मा ग र्सा ।.

Repeat sign is denoted by second bracket. e.g. {सा रा}, meaning सा रा is to be repeated once more.

Omit sign is through small bracket sign, e.g. (सा रा)

i.e. while repeating, (सा रा) is to be omitted, e.g. {मा गा (सा रा) ना् सा}

Change of notes during repetition is expressed through third bracket sign [ना् सा], written above the notes which are to be changed, e.g.{सा रा गा [न् सा] मा रा गा सा रा}

After each *āvartana,* one *daṇḍa* = । and after one *kali* or stanza two *daṇḍas* = ॥ are placed, to denote the completion of the stanza.

Note: [Since the notation of songs have been written in Devnagri, the सरगम also have been adapted to Devnagri script. Hence the *komala* and *tīvra svaras* are also in Devnagri equivalent of Bengali letter.]

If *sthāyī* is to be repeated after the *kali* is completed, the sign of double *daṇḍas* || are drawn at that particular position from where the *Sthāyī* repetition is to be done, e.g.

|| ना धा -ा पा | ह्मा पा गा ह्मा | पा -ा -ा -ा | पा ह्मा गा रा |
न्‌ रा गा रा | गा ह्मा पा धा | पा ह्मा गा रा | गा रा सा -ा ||

When the sign of two *daṇḍas* are used for indicating from where the repeat of sthāyī should start, the *svaras* before the sign should not be repeated, e.g.

न्र || सन्‌ ध्‌ न्‌ सा | -ा -ा -ा -ा |

When dots are given over *svaras*, it means that, these *svaras* have to be pronounced with individual stress, e.g.

सां रां गां मां

When the strain of the main *svara* culminates on another *svara*, the other *svara* is written in small letter over the right hand side of the main *svara*, eg - माध

When a *svara* is prolonged for another *mātrā*, a hyphen sign is used while a circle sign = O, is used in the place of the words of a song, e.g.

ना धा -ा पा ह्मा पा गा ह्मा
स दा ० शि व भ ज म

When no letter of the song composition appears under a *svara*, a small hyphen is used in front of the *svara*, e.g.

सा -रा -गा मा
ज ० ० दि

When a letter of the song with a *halant*, i.e. क्‌ ख्‌, etc. appears, a *mātrā* sign is used instead of a *svara*, e.g.

रा -ा -ा सा
क ० न्‌ ठ

Tāla signs :

a) *Sam* sign is a slanting line over the number of *tāli* that plays the most vital role, e.g. १ or २ etc. as the case may be [for convenience, the usual sign of sam, i.e. + has been used for the notated examples, and Devnāgari script instead of Bengali]

b) *Khāli* sign is = O

c) Other *tālis* are denoted by numbers such as 1,2,3,4, etc.

d) *Tāla* divisions are denoted by a vertical line or bar, e.g. | सा रा | गा मा पा |

e) The *sign* of one *daṇḍa* is used when one *āvartana* is completed. The sign ; || || indicates the completion of the whole song or composition. The sign : || is used at the beginning of *sthāyī*, indicating that one has to return there after completing the song.

f) Completion is also indicated by a pair of small vertical lines over the *svara*, e.g. स॑॑ This also means that either one has to stop here or after a pause, start another *kali*.

Song example in Ākār-mātrik Svaralipi (Brahma Saṅgīta)

राग – मुलतान , एकताल
याबे किहे दिन आमार बिफल चलिये ।
आछि नाथ, दिबानिशि आशापथ निरखिये ॥
तुमि त्रिभुवननाथ, आमि भिखारी अनाथ,
केमने बलिब तोमाय एस हे मम हृदये ॥
हृदय कुटीर द्वार, खुले राखि अनिबार ।
कृपा करि एकबार एसे कि जुड़ाबे हिये ॥

– बेचाराम चट्टोपाध्याय ।

०			३			+			२		
ह्मपा	-दा	पा	दना	-र्सा	ना	दपा	ह्मा	ज्ञा	ऋ्ष	सा	सा
जा०	०	बे	कि०	०	हे	दि०	०	न	आ	मा	र

ना्	सा	-ा	ज्ञा	-ा	ह्मा	पा	-ा	-ह्मा	ह्मपा	-दपा	-ह्मज्ञा
बि	फ	०	ले	०	च	लि	०	०	ये०	००	००

पा	ह्मा	-ा	ज्ञा	-ा	ह्मा	पा	ना	-ा	र्सा	र्सा	-ा
आ	छि	०	ना	०	थ	दि	बा	०	नि	शि	०

र्सा	ना	-दा	पा	पा	-ा	ज्ञा	ह्मा	-पा	नर्सा	-नदा	पह्मा
आ	शा	०	प	थ	०	नि	र	०	खि०	००	ये०

०			३			५			२		
पा	पा	-ा	ह्मा	-ज्ञा	ह्मा	पा	ना	-ा	र्सा	-ा	र्सा
तु	मि	०	त्रि	०	भु	व	न	०	ना	०	थ
हृ	द	य	०	०	कु	टी	र	०	द्वा	०	र

ना	र्सा	-ा	र्ज्ञा	र्ऋा	-र्सा	ना	र्सा	-ना	दा	-पा	पा
आ	मि	०	भि	खा	०	री	अ	०	ना	०	थ
खु	ले	०	रा	खि	०	अ	नि	०	बा	०	र

ज्ञा	ह्मा	-ा	पा	-ा	ह्मा	ज्ञा	ज्ञा	-ा	ऋा	ऋा	सा
के	म	०	ने	०	ब	लि	ब	०	तो	मा	य
कृ	पा	०	क	०	रि	ए	क	०	बा	०	र

ना्	सा	ज्ञा	-ह्मा	पा	पा	नदा	पह्मा	ज्ञह्मा	पह्मा	ज्ञऋा	ससा
ए	स	हे	०	म	म	ह्र०	द०	००	ये०	००	००
ए	से	०	कि	०	जु	ड़ा	०	वे	हि०	ये०	००

10. Short-hand Svaralipi

Another notation system was developed and used by the musicians who were involved with stage music. This was a very simple system called *Short-hand Svaralipi Paddhati.* Unfortunately it is not known who was the innovator and exactly when it came about. This much is observed from the various informations that it had some similarity with a few signs of Western system and whosoever invented it, was a musician having knowledge of both Western and Hindusthani music. Initially this method was used by the professional musicians of the stage and then adopted by the music composers of the Gramophone Companies, because at the early stage, the artistes and music directors of Gramophone Companies were mostly stage personalities.

In this system the *śuddha* and *vikṛta rūpas* were denoted by the same sign, but only with smaller and larger versions, e.g. ऋ =/ and र =/; a dot below signifies *Mandra,* while a dot above, is *Tāra.*

An example :

	!	p	/	/	⌢	⌢	(	(	)	(	(	ı	l	p
Svaras -	न्	स	ऋ	र	ज्ञ	ग	म	ह्मा	प	द	ध	ण	न	सं,

i.e. स = P, र =/, ग = ⌢ , म = (, P=), ध = (, न = l.

Komal svsras are: ऋ = /, ज्ञ = ⌢ , द = (, ण = ı

tīvra madhyama is ह्म = (

An example of a notated piece

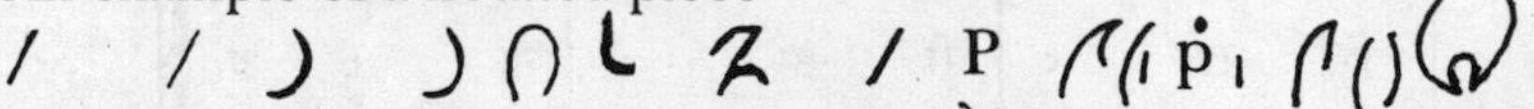

क इ कृ ष्ण ए ल कु ञ्जे प्रा ण सइ

It reads in *Ākār-mātrik* as follows—

।। रा रा | पा प:धप:	मा ग:मग:	रा सा
क इ | कृ ष्ण००	ए ल००	कु ञ्जे

and so on.

This is one of the earliest specimens. Later, some composers introduced more signs to make it more comprehensive. This system is still in use among the stage-musicians and musicians of Gramophone Companies.

Even after the success of *Ākār-mātrik Svaralipi*, efforts were still on to develope new notation systems further. Some more were innovated by musicians/musicologists, such as :

11) ***Svara-daṇḍamātrik Svaralipi*** - around 1932 - by Brajendrakishore Ray Chaudhuri.

12) ***Svara-pada-mātrik Svaralipi*** - around 1933 - by Suresh chandra Chakravarti.

13) ***Rekhā-svārik Svaralipi*** - around 1944/45 - by Satyakinkar Banerji.

14) ***Pratīk Svaralipi*** by Dr. Bimal Roy, published in *Sangita* (Hindi journal), in 1955. The musicologist has envisaged the madhya saptaka as a branch of a tree with a tendril. This tendril is growing gradually higher and higher same as the *svaras* go higher and higher, to reach the *tāra saptaka.* It is depicted in the following manner :

Madhya saptaka : ⊢

स : ⊢•

र : ⊢•

ग : ⊢^

म : ⊢▲ etc. until the tendril of न has almost reached the *Tāra ṣadja, which* is expressed as = ⊬

Signs of Dr. Roy's Pratīk Svaralipi :

Nāda = ।

Saptaka = K, Madhya = ⊢, Mandra = -⊢, Tāra = ⊬

Śuddha and vikṛta svaras -

Madhya Saptaka : स ऋ र ज्ञ ग म ह्म प द ध ण न

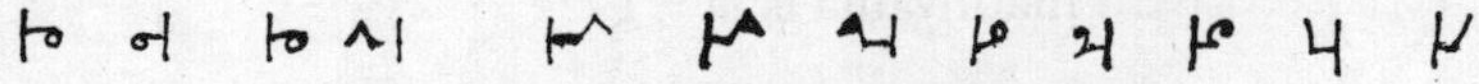

Mandra Saptaka :

Tāra Saptaka : 〔musical notation symbols〕

Tāla-mātrā:

1 mātrā = ḍ, 2 mātrās = 〔symbol〕, 3 mātrās = 〔symbol〕 4 mātrās = 〔symbol〕

1 ½ mātrās = 〔symbol〕, ½ mātrā = ḍ, ⅓ = 〔symbol〕, ¼ = 〔symbol〕 and so on

Svara and mātrā - 〔symbol〕 , 〔symbol〕

combination of svaras in a mātrā - 〔symbols with 2 0 3〕

Bar details - + 2 0 3 or 2 0 3
                    ‖ ⏐ ⏐   ⏐ ⏐ ⏐

or In Roman letters - + II 0 III

Alaṅkāras -

Gamaka - ⊤, 〔symbols〕 , 〔symbol〕

Ākāra (open voice) - 〔symbol〕

Bandhākār (closed lipped) - 〔symbol〕

Pravala (forte) - v = 〔symbol〕

Pravalīkaraṇa (crescendo) - < = 〔symbol〕

Mṛdu (piano) - = ∧ = 〔symbol〕

Mṛdukaraṇa (diminuendo) - > = 〔symbol〕

Samīkaraṇa (normalisation) - z = 〔symbol〕

Sphīti (sforzando) - x = 〔symbol〕

Dam (sostenuto) - 〔symbol〕

Kham (pause) - 〔symbol〕 , or 〔symbol〕 T = 2 mātrā pause, 〔symbol〕 γ = 1/2 mātrā pause
        〔symbol〕 ↑ = 1/4 mātrā.

Chuṭ - 〔symbols〕

Sparś - 〔symbols〕 or 〔symbol〕

Zamzamā - 

Ās - 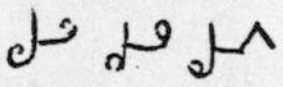

Mīnḍ - 

Murkī - 

Rerak - 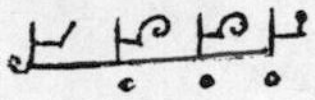

Murak - सरगमगरसर = 

Khaṭka - = गरसन् = 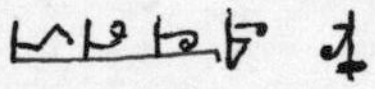

Script of the system :

Vowels : - Silent = 

a - अ
a - आ
A - Same pronunciation of 'a' as that in - *bat* or *barrack.*
i - इ
I - ई
u - उ
e - ऊ
e - ए
E - Prolonged ए of Sanskrit as in and.
O - ओ
(•) - prolonged ओ of Sanskrit.
ai - ऐ
au - औ
R - ऋ
L - (लि)

Consonants : K - क, q - क़, Kh - ख, qh - ख़, g - ग, G - ग़, gh - घ, ng - ङ.
c- च, ch - छ, j - ज, z - ज़, jh - झ, n - ञ.
T - ट, Th - ठ, D - ड, Dh - ढ, N - ण.
t - त, th - थ, d - द, dh - ध, n - न.
p - प, ph - फ, f - फ़, b - ब, bh - भ, v - व, m - म.

y - य but pronounced as ज, eg - यखन = जखन

Y - य but pronounced as य eg - समय

r - र, l - ल, w/B - व,

S - श, & - ष, s - स, h - ह,

Ɗ - ड़, Ɗh - ढ़, M - ṃ, u - :, N - ँ

Laya details :

a.	*Laghu* or *Madhya laya*	- between 96 - 143 -	*mātrās* per minute.		
b.	*Laghu virāma*	- between72 - 95 -	"	"	".
c.	*Guru or Vilamva*	- between 48 - 71 -	"	"	".
d.	*Pluta*	- between 36 - 47 -	"	"	".
e.	*Kākapada/ati-vilamvita*	- between 24 - 35 -	"	"	".
f.	*Miśra kākapada*	- between 18 - 23 -	"	"	".
g.	*Haṅsapada Prati-vilamvita (very slow)*	- between 12 - 17 -	"	"	".
h.	*Miśra-haṅsapada*	- between 9 - 11 -	"	"	".
i.	*Mahā-haṅsapada Nirati-vilamvita*	- between 6 - 8 -	"	"	".
j.	*Druta virāma*	- between 144 - 191 -	"	"	".
k.	*Druta* -	- between 192 - 287	"	"	".
l.	*Miśra Anu druta* -	- between 288 - 383 -	"	"	".
m.	*Anudruta/Atidruta*	- between 384 - 575 -	"	"	".
n.	*Miśra-truṭi*	- between 576 - 767 -	"	"	".
o.	*Truṭi - / Mahādruta* -	768 -	"	"	".

15. ***Major-minor Consonental system*** by Nikhil Ghosh, has been evolved by utilising the signs from the Western notation system and some from various other systems of Bengal. In this system almost every nuance of *rāga-saṅgīta* can be expressed through the various signs adopted suitably. Details of this *paddhati* is available in his book, '*Fundamentals of Rāga and Tāla - with a new system of notation*'.

These systems however, have not gained as much popularity as *Ākār-mātrik,* which has stood the test of time.

Outside Bengal several other systems have come up, such as :

(1). A system based on *Meḷa* in 1873 by Tācur Siṅgār Cārlu: This was very much like Śārṅgadeva's, but was nowhere near perfect. The sign of comma, eg - (,) was used for *laghu-svara.* (History of Indian Music - P. Sambamoorthy)

(2). A system based on number or *saṅkhyā,* in Hindi, was innovated by the descendants of Amṛt Sen, (Senī gharānā) in 1877.

(3). Bīnkār Anna Gharpure introduced a system in 1880, in his book, named *Svara Śāstra.* This was in Marathi language.

(4). Maula Bakhs of Ghisse Khan's *gharānā* formulated a system based on *Danḍamātrik,* in 1886 in his book, *Saṅgītānubhava,* while teaching at Jorasanko Thakurbari. His system had the signs for *śuddha* and *vikṛta svaras* as follows:

न१ सा ऋ∆ ऋ ग∆ ग म म= प ध∆ ध नि∆ नि सा̄

For *komala* - he used the sign ∆ at the right side of the *svara;* for *tīvra*, the sign used was =; for *Mandra saptaka* - १ ; and for *Tāra saptaka* a dash above the *svaras.* Most of the signs of his system were borrowed from others.

(5). In 1900, Subbaram Dikṣitar and Thiruborttiur Thyagyar developed a system for *Karnatik Paddhati.* (History of Indian Music - by P.Sambamoorthy)

(6). In 1905 V. N. Bhatkhande of Maharashtra published his notation system which is very simple and widely used all over India, but it does not express all the nuances.

(7). In 1910, Vishnu Digambar Paluskar brought out his system which was written on three lines and by 1931 this was revised in one line by his disciples, particularly Onkarnath Thakur.

(8). In 1923, Sudarśan Ācārya of Banaras evolved a system called *Saṅkhyā Svārik Svaralipi.* (*Saṅgīta Sudarśana* - by Pt. Sudarśanācārya).

Out of all these systems *Ākārmātrik* svaralipi is most expressive without being complicated, but experimentation to perfect the art of writing a piece of Indian classical music with all its nuances is still on.

BIBLIOGRAPHY

1. *Bālak* (Journal). Calcutta, 1292. B.S. Baiśākh issue (Beng.).
2. Banerji, Gopeshwar. *Gītapraveśikā.* 3rd ed. Calcutta, 1360. B.S. (Beng.).
3. Banerji, Krishnadhan. *Baṅgaikatāna.* Calcutta, 1867. (beng.).
4. ——. *Gītasūtrasāra.* Part I & II. Coochbihar, 1885 & 1886. (Beng.).
5. Bandopadhyay, Nanigopal. *Saṅgīta Darśikā.* 5th ed. Calcutta, 1380. B.S. (Beng.).
6. *Bhāratī.* (Journal). Calcutta, 1287 Śrāvana & 1295. B.S. (Beng.).
7. *Brahma-saṅgīter Svaralipi.* Part I. Calcutta, 1369. B.S. (Beng.).
8. Chattopadhyay, Bankim Chandra. (Ed). *Baṅga Darśan* (Journal). Calcutta, 1872. (Beng.).
9. Das, Prafulla Kumar. *Rāgāṅkur.* Calcutta, 1374. B.S. (Beng.).
10. Ghosh, Laxminarayan. *Gītavādyam.* Calcutta, 1975. (Beng.).
11. Ghosh, Nikhil. *Fundamentals of Rāga and Tāla with a new system of notation.* Bombay. 1968.
12. Goswami, Kshetramohan. *Saṅgītasāra.* 2nd ed. Calcutta, 1879. (Beng.).
13. ——. *Aikatānik Svaralipi.* Calcutta, 1868. (Beng.).

14. Mataṅga Muni. *Bṛhaddeśī.* Tikā in Bengali by Ghosh Pradip Kumar.
15. *Sādhanā* (Journal). Calcutta, 1891. (All issues are important.) (Beng.).
16. *Saṅgīta Praveśikā.* (Journal). Calcutta, 1313. B.S. (Beng.).
17. Sen, Kangalicharan. *Brahma Saṅgīta Svaralipi.* Calcutta, 1362. B.S. (Beng.).
18. *Tattvabodhini* (Journal). Ed. by Dwijendranath Thakur. Calcutta, 1869, 1891, 1893. (Beng.). (All issues are important)
19. *Tauryatrik* (Journal). Ed. by Mitra Sachindranath. Calcutta, all issues of 1965. (Beng.).
20. Thakur, Dinendranath. *Sangīta-vijñāna-praveśikā* (Journal). Calcutta, 1337. B.S. (Beng.).
21. Thakur, Jyotirindranath. *Svaralipi Gītimālā.* Calcutta, 1304. B.S. (Beng.).
22. Thakur, Rabindranath. *Gīta-mālikā.* Part II. Calcutta, 1965. (Beng.).
23. Thakur, Rabindranath. *Svarabitān* (Vols 1-64), Calcutta. (Beng.).
24. *Vīnāvādinī* (Journal). Calcutta, 1891. (All issues are important). (Beng.).

TREATISES OF BENGAL

It is most unfortunate that texts of music of Bengal for the earliest period, are not available, although evidences are plenty in Bharatamuni's *Nāṭya-śāstra* (3rd cent. B.C.), Mataṅga's *Bṛhaddeśī* (5th cent A.D.), Śārṅgadeva's *Saṅgita-ratnākraḥ* (13th cent. A.D), and Kalhaṇa's *Rājatraṅgiṇī* (12th cent. A.D.).

From 10th cent. onwards, some treatises are available to prove the depth of traditional music practised in Prācyadeśa or Greater Bengal. These works are- *Bharatabhāṣya* of *Nānyadeva*, *Gītagovinda* of *Jayadeva*, *Sekśubodyā* and *Pavanadūtam*. During this time, supremacy of Karṇāṭaka over India and their Vaiṣṇvism had dominated the Eastern region very much. *Padāvalīs* of Vidyāpati and Caṇḍīdāsa became extremely popular. Between 12th and 15th cent. A.D., Bengal had the rich traditional music, dance and drama performed extensively. Texts such as Bhuvanānanda's *Viśvapradīpa*, Gaṇeśā's *Saṅgīta-kalpadruma*, and *Saṅgita-kalpavṛkṣa*, Tumburu's *Tumburū-Nāṭaka*, Mammaṭācārya's *Saṅgīta-ratnamāla*, *Saṅgītāvalī*, *Saṅgīta-Śekhara* are available but in these, dramaturgy has been discussed more than music and its techniques. Harināyaka of Orissa (latter part of 15th cent.) has dealt on music in his book named *Saṅgītasāra*, discussing important changes and developments that occurred in the technicalities of music. Harināyaka referred to and discussed in detail, all the chapters of Śārṅgadeva's *Saṅgīta-ratnākara*. Other texts of this period are: *Varṇa-ratnākara* of Jyotirīśvara, *Saṅgīta-sarvasva* of Jagaddhara, *Saṅgīta-dāmodara* of Śubhaṅkara, *Gitaprakāśa* of Kṛṣṇadāsa, dealing with music and its technicalities. There are some more works viz. *Nāradasamhitā* of Nārada, *Saṅgītapārijata* (not of Ahobala), *Bṛhad-saṅgīta-ratnākara* etc., which were written around this time, and dealt with *rāgas* and tālas but not in great detail.

From 16th cent. onwards, with the advent of Śrī Caitanya, Prācyadeśa experienced the taste of a new style of music, that is *Kīrtana*, which got great popularity and importance. During the second half of 16th century *Pañcamasāra-samhitā* was written by one Nārada who followed *Nāradasamhitā* and *Saṅgīta-dāmodara*. He dealt with the *tālas* of *Kīratana* mainly, which points to the fact that *Kīrtana* flourished as a full-fledged style. *Kīrtana* adopted *rāgas* and *tālas* from the *Karṇāṭaka Paddhati* and *Havelī-saṅgita* of Mathurā-Vṛndāvana and Gujarat. It was due to Caitanya's tour of India on religious mission, which covered distant places like Assam and Manipur in the east, Bihar-Orissa as part of Prācyadeśa, Karṇāṭaka in the South, Mathurā-Vṛndavāna in the centre and Gujrat-Maharashtra in the West. There was an exchange and adaptation of *rāgas* and *tālas* of these places in the *Kīrtana* style of music started by Caitanya. As *rāgas* and *tālas* of other regions were incorporated, similarly Bengal's *rāga* system influenced the *rāga* music of

Gujarat, Manipur, Assam and Maharashtra, and the texts of *Kīrtana* were also being compiled, particularly in Assam, Manipur, Karnataka and Gujarat.

During the latter part of 16th cent. another text named *Saṅgīta-dāmodara* by Dāmodara Sena is found.

Both *Pañcama-sāra-saṁhitā* of Nārada and *Saṅgīta-dāmodara* by Dāmodara Sen have some similarities in description of *rāgas*.

Besides the above mentioned treatises, there are many more books which speak of the wealth of music of Bengal. To mention a few periodwise:

	Name of the book	Author	Period
1.	Nātha gītis	—	c 8th to 9th cent.
2.	Caryāpadas	84 Buddhist ācāryas	c 950-1200.
3.	Dohākoṣa	Ācārya Saraha	*c* 1100-1150.
4.	Daśāvatara-carita	Kṣemendra	*c* 1200
5.	Āryā-śaptaśati	Ācārya Govardhana	early 13th cent.
6.	Sadukti-karṇāmṛta	Śrīdharadāsa	early 13th cent.
7.	Gītagovinda	Jayadeva	13th cent.
8.	Pavanadūta	Dhoyī	13th cent.
9.	Bṛhaddharmapurāṇa	—	13th cent.
10.	Varṇaratnākara	Jyotiriśvara	14th cent.
11.	Various Maṅgala Kāvyas:		
a.	Manasā-maṅgala	Vijaya Gupta	15th cent.
b.	—	Vipradāsa	15th cent.
c.	Caitanya maṅgala	Jayānanda	16th cent.
d.	Caitanya Bhāgavata	Bṛndāvanadāsa	16th cent.
e.	Caitanya maṅgala	Locanadāsa	16th cent .
f.	Caitanya-caritāmṛta	Kavi Karṇapūra	16th cent.
g.	Caitanya-candrodaya	Kavi Karṇapūra	16th cent.
h.	Caṇḍī-maṅgala	Kavi Kaṅkana	end 16th cent.
i.	Caṇḍī-maṅgala	Ketakādāsa Kṣemānanda	mid 17th cent.
j.	Dharma-maṅgala	Manikram Ganguli	18th cent.
k.	Annadā-maṅgala	Bhāratcandra	1753
12.	Śrī kṛṣṇa-kīrtana	Baḍu Caṇḍīdāsa	early 15th cent.
13.	Saṅgitasāra	Harināyaka Sūri	15th cent.
14.	Gītaprakāśa	Kṛṣṇadāsa Gosvāmī	16th cent.
15.	Śiva Saṅgīta	Rāmeśvara	15th-16th cent.
16.	Ujjvala Nīlamaṇi	Rūpa Gosvāmī	16th cent.

17.	Gītāvalī	Rupa Gosvāmī	16th cent.
18.	Ananda Bṛndāvana Campū	Kavi Karṇapūr	
19.	Saṅgīta Dāmodara	Śubhaṅkara	mid 16th cent.
20.	Hastamuktāvalī	,,	mid 16th cent.
21.	Pañcamasāra Saṃhitā	Nārada	end 16th cent.
22.	Rāgataraṅgiṇī	Locana Kavi	mid 17th cent.
23.	Rāga Saṅgīta Saṅgraha (not available)	,,	mid 17th cent.
24.	Saṅgīta-saraṇī	Kaviratna Nārāyaṇa Miśra	17th cent.
25.	Saṅgīta-nārayaṇa	Gajapati Nārāyaṇadeva	17th cent.
26.	Saṅgīta-kāmoda	Gopinath Kavibhusaṇa	17th cent.
27.	Saṅgītasāra saṃgraha	Narahari Cakravarti	18th cent.
28.	Kṣaṇadagīta cintāmaṇi	Viśvanāth Cakravarty	18th cent.
29.	Bhaktiratnākara	Narahari Cakravarti	18th cent.
30.	Gīta candrodaya	,,	18th cent.
31.	Kālī-Kīrtana	Ramprasad Sen	early 18th cent.(1720-30)
32.	Padāmṛtasindhu	Radha mohan Sen	end 18th cent.
33.	Saṅgīta-taraṅga		early 18th cent.(1818)
34.	Brahma Saṅgīta	Rammohun Roy	early 19th cent.(1828)
35.	Gitaratna	Ramnidhi Gupta	mid 19th cent.(1838)
36.	Saṅgītarāga Kalpadruma	Krishnananda Vyasā Ragasāgara	mid 19th cent.(1842-47)
37.	Saṅgīta Gaurīśvara	Gaṅgādhara Tarkavāgīśa	mid 19th cent.(1850)
38.	Gopal Uḍer Ṭappā		mid 19th cent.(1862)
39.	Dāśarathi Rāyer Pā̃cālī	Haripada Chakra-varti	mid 19th cent.(1862)
40.	Mūlasaṅgītādarśa	Ramapati Bando-padhyay	mid 19th cent.(1863)
41.	Saṅgīta muktāvali	Becharam Chatto-padhyay	mid 19th cent.(1865)
42.	Baṅgaika tāna	Krishnadhan Bando-padhyay(K.B.)	mid 19th cent.(1867)

43.	Aikatānik Svaralipi	Kshetramohan Goswami	mid 19th cent.(1868)
44.	Saṅgīta Śikṣā	K.B.	mid 19th cent.(1868)
45.	Saṅgīta Sāra	Kshetramohan Goswami	mid 19th cent.(1869)
46.	Yantrakṣetra dīpikā	S.M.Thakur	end 19th cent.(1872)
47.	Saṅgīta Samālocanī (Journal)		(end 19th cent.1872)
48.	Yantra Koṣa	S.M.Thakur	end 19th cent.(1872)
49.	Kaṇṭha Kaumudī	K.Goswami	end 19th cent.(1875)
50.	Six principal rāgas - with a brief view of the Hindu Music	S.M.Thakur	end 19th cent.(1876)
51.	The eight principal rāgas of the Hindus	S.M.Thakur	end 19th cent.(1877)
52.	Gīta Mañjarī	Kartikeya Chandra Ray	end 19th cent.(1878)
53.	Gītapraveśa	Saurindramohan Thakur	end 19th cent.(1882)
54.	Hindu music from various authors (compiled by)	S.M.Thakur	end 19th cent.(1882)
55.	Bhāratīya Saṅgīta muktāvalī	Nabakanta Chatto-padhyay	end 19th cent.(1882)
56.	Saṅgīta Saṅgraha	,,	end 19th cent.(1883)
57.	Saṅgīta Śāstra prakāśikā	S.M.Thakur	end 19th cent.(1884)
58.	Gīta Sūtra Sāra I & II	K.B.	end 19th cent.(1885-86)
59.	Gītagovinder Svaralipi	Kshetramohan Goswami	mid 19th cent.(1278 B.S.)
60.	Saṅgīta Kalpadruma	Narendranath Datta & Vaishnav Charan Basak	end 19th cent.(1887)
61.	Saṅgīta Praveśikā Part I & II	Murarimohan Gupta	end 19th cent.(1889)
62.	Gāndharva Kalā Vyākaranaṃ (Skt) (compiled by)	S.M.Thakur	end 19th cent.(1824 Śaka)
63.	Guptaratnoddhāra	Kedarnath Bando-padhyay	end 19th cent.(1894)

64.	Universal history of Music	S.M.Thakur	end 19th cent.(1896)
65.	Saṅgītakoṣa	Upendranath Mukhopadhyay	end 19th cent.(1896)
66.	Svaralipi gītimālā	Jyotirindranath Thakur	end 19th cent.(1896)
67.	Vinavadini (Music journal)	Jyotirindranath Thakur	end 19th cent.(1896)
68.	Prītigīti	Abinash Chandra Ghosh	end 19th cent.(1898)
69.	Saṅgīta Sāra Saṅgraha	Harimohan Mukho-padhyay	end 19th cent.(1899)
70.	Prācīna dhrupada Svaralipi	,,	end 19th cent.
71.	Saṅgīte parivartana	,,	end 19th cent.
72.	Saṅgīta rasa kallola	Rupchand Pakshi	end 19th cent.
73.	Tattvabodhinī Patrikā (journal)	Dwijendranath Thakur	end 19th cent.
74.	Viśva Saṅgīta	Vaishnava Charan Basak (13th Ed)	end 19th cent.
75.	Bhārati (journal)	Rabindranath Thakur	early 20th cent.
76.	Bālak (journal)	Jorasanko Ṭhākur bāḍī	early 20th cent.
77.	Ananda Saṅgīta Patrika (music journal)	Indiradevi	early 20th cent.
78.	Saṅgīta Vijñān Praveśikā (music journal)	Radhika Prasad Goswami	early 20th cent.
79.	Śatagāna	Saralādevi	early 20th cent.(1900)
80.	Gīta Laharī	Amritalal Bando-padhyay	early 20th cent.(1904)
81.	Bāṅgālīrgāna	Durgādas Lahiri	early 20th cent.(1905)
82.	Saṅgīta Candrikā I & II	Gopeshwar Bando-padhyay(G.B.)	early 20th cent.(1909&1917)
83.	Hajar Bacharer Purano Bāṅglā bhāṣāy Bauddha gāna O dohā	Haraprasad Shastri	early 20th cent.(1916)

84.	Rāger gāthā Śikṣā I & II	Dakshinacharan Sen	early 20th cent.(1925)
85.	Saṅgīta Lahari	G.B.	early 20th cent.(1927)
86.	Saṅgīta vādya ratnāvalī	Rasaraj Mitra Thakur	early 20th cent.(1352 B.S)
87.	Kirtan	Khagendranath Mitra	mid 20th cent.(1352 BS)
88.	Saṅgīta Praveśikā	Murarimohan Gupta	early 20th cent.
89.	Bāṅglār Saṅgīta Paricaya	Rajyeshwar Mitra	mid 20th cent.(1953)
90.	Saṅgīta mañjarī	Ramprasanna Bandopadhyay	early 20th cent.
91.	Rāga O Rūpa I & II	Sw. Prajnanananda	mid 20th cent.(1955 & 57)
92.	Saṅgīta Samīkṣā	Rajyeshwar Mitra	mid 20th cent.(1959)
93.	Bhāratīya vādya yantra O Yantra Sādhaka	Jitendramohan Sengupta	mid 20th cent.(1959)
94.	Rāgas & Rāgiṇīs	Amiyanath Sanyal	mid 20th cent.(1959)
95.	Bhāratīya Saṅgīta prasaṅga	Dr. Bimal Roy	mid 20th cent.(1961)
96.	Rāga rāgiṇīr nāma rahasya	Ardhendu Kumar Ganguli	mid 20th cent.(1961)
97.	Bhāratiya Saṅgīter Itihās I & II	Sw. Prajnanananda	mid 20th cent.(1961)
98.	Hajar bacharer Bāṅglagāna	Prabhat Kumar Goswami	mid 20th cent.(1965)
99.	Bāṅglā nāṭake gāna	,,	mid 20th cent.(1965)
100.	Saṅgīta cinta	Rabindranath Thakur	mid 20th (Beng.)(1966)
101.	Bhāratīya Saṅgīte tāla O chanda	Subodh Nandi	late 20th cent.(1972)
102.	Bāṅglār gītikār O Bāṅglā gāner nānādik	Rajeshwar Mitra	late 20th cent.(1973)
103.	Music of Eastern India	Sukumar Ray	late 20th cent.(1973)
104.	Bāṅgālīr Rāga Saṅgīta Carcā	D.K. Mukherji	late 20th cent.(1976)

105.	Bhāratīya Saṅgītakoṣ	Bimalākanta Ray-chandhuri	mid 20th cent.(1372 BS)
106.	Bhāratīya Saṅgīte gharānār itihās	D.K.Mukherji	late 20th cent.(1384 BS)
107.	Bāṅglā dhrupadmālā	Sw. Prajnananda	mid 20th cent.
108.	Saṅgītī Śabdakoṣ	Dr. Bimal Roy	late 20th cent.(1386 B.S)
109.	Bāṅglā gāner ādiparva	Rajyeshwar mitra	lati 20th cent.(1984)
110.	Rāga O tāhār Prakārbhed I & II	Dr. Bimal Roy	late 20th cent.
111.	Bāṅglā Kīrtaner Itihas	Hitesh Ranjan Sanyal	late 20th cent.(1989)

Annotated bibliography of a few important books are furnished below:

***Gītaprakāśaḥ by Kṛṣṇadāsa Baḍajenā Mohāpātra* (16th cent. A.D.)**

Kṛṣṇadāsa, the author of this treatise perhaps flourished between 1500-1647 A.D.. He was referred to by Haladhara Miśra in his work *Saṅgīta-kalpa-latikā,* another Sanskrit work of Orissa, written between 1623-1647 A.D.. Kṛṣṇadāsa eulogises Gajapati Mukundadeva (1559-1568) the last independent king of Orissa, as he was employed in the royal court of the king.

Abul Fazl mentions in *Ain-i-Akbari* that there were two great singers in the court of Mukundadeva and they were Rāmdāsa and 'Mahāpāter' (Kṛṣṇadāsa), who later entered the services of Emperor Akbar. Mohāpatra was unrivalled in poetry and music in the court of Akbar. Kṛṣṇadāsa composed some of his songs in Brajabuli which points to the fact that he was very much associated with North Indian culture.

Gītaprkāśaḥ consists of seven chapters or *'ullāsas'*-meaning joy. In the first *ullāsa,* the author deals with *Sūḍa-gīta-nirṇaya.* According to him *Suḍa-gīta* is the purest form of *gīta* —

सूड़ गीतमेव प्रवन्ध उच्चते ।
meaning: *Sūḍa* type of *gītas* are called *prabandhas.*

He defines *gīta* the same way as Śārṅgadeva and Harināyaka have, i.e. -
रञ्जक: स्वरसन्दर्भो गीतम्
meaning: *svara* combinations that generate colourfulness constitute a *gīta.*

He also deals with the salient features of *Sūḍagīta* which should be composed of excellent *pada, svara,* and *tāla.* In this chapter he explains a) *Anibaddha-Nibaddha gīta,* b) *Sūḍa, Chāya-laga, Kṣudra-gīta,* c) *dhātu* and its three divisions only, viz. *Udgrāha, Dhruva* and *Ābhoga* :

आद्य उद्ग्राहस्ततो ध्रुवः अन्ते आभोगः,

i.e. *udgrāha* is the beginning, *dhruva* is the middle and *ābhoga* is the end.

(d) *Aṅga*—four in number:

वाक्यं स्वरपाटौ च तेनकः चत्वार्य्यङ्गानि,

meaning: the four aṅgas arē - *vākya, svara, pāṭa* and *tenaka.*

(e) *Śúddha-bheda nirṇaya,* f) Different types of *Prabandhas* and their *jāti* - viz. *Medinī, Dipani, Bhāvanī* and *Tarāvalī.*

The second ullāsa is named as *Sālaga-nirṇaya.*It deals with those *Nibaddha-gitas* which are not so pure as *Sūḍa.*This type of *gītas* is called *Chāyālaga* or *Sālaga.* He also discusses its *lakṣaṇas* and gives definitions. *Lakṣaṇas* of nine *tālas,* viz. *Dhruva, Maṇṭha, Āditāla, Yati, Niḥsāri, Jhampaka, Tripāṭa, Aḍḍa, Rupaka,* and *Ekatāla* are also given. The author mentions that many more *tālas* were in use earlier but they became obsolete later. *Kuḍukka* and *upāḍḍa* were two main tālas used by few. He explains only those that were in vogue and gives examples. He also explains the essential techiques of each *tāla* with its constituents like *virāma, druta, laghu, guru, pluta, mātrā, saśabda,* and *niḥśabda, āvarta, yati, khanḍa* etc.

Third *ullāsa* deals with *Kṣudra-gita-nirṇaya.* This type of *gītas* i..e. *Kṣudra-gītas* were inferior to *Sālaga* types. *Kṣudra* means small but *Kṣudra-gīta* meant those compositions possessing a small part of the characteristics of *Sālaga-sūḍa (Sālaga) prabandhas.* He defines *Kṣudra-gīta* as: लक्ष्मैक देशयुक् क्षुद्रगीतम्. This class consisted of *dhatu* and *tāla only and the other rules of Sālagāsūḍa* were not expected to be observed. The following types belonged to this class:

(i) *Citrapadā,* ii) *Citrakalā,* iii) *Dhruvapadā* of two types: (a) with 3 stanzas, viz. *Udgrāha, Dhruva* and *Ābhoga* and (b) with 2 stanzas, viz. *Dhruva* and *Ābhoga* called *Cuṭkulā* in Pracyadeśa and iv) *Pā̃cālī* which he elaborates as of two kinds, viz. *Sadhruvā* and *Adhruvā.*

He also says that several hybrid *Kṣudragītas* were possible to obtain through proper blending of the four above mentioned types. In *Kṣudragita,* except *Ādi, Niḥsāri* and *Maṇṭha,* all the rest of the *tālas* were used.

The fourth *ullāsa* is called *Guṇa-nirṇaya,* meaning qualities or attributes that contribute to the beauty of *gitas.* These attributes or *guṇas* are: *laya* and *yati* of *tāla*; *gamaka* ; *mātu* or verbal structure; *dhātu* or melodic structure; *rāga*; *punarukti* or avoidance of repetition; usage of *pāṭa, svara* and *tenna*; *padas* composed with proper *alaṅkāra* and *rasa.*

The author also deals with definitions and descriptions of *rāgas* and further explains the terms: *laya, yati, graha, māna* and *gamakas* of 15 kinds.

The fifth *ullāsa* is *Rāga-nirṇaya,* delineating on : *rāga svarūpam*; its *jātis,* viz. *sampūrṇa, ṣāḍava, auḍava* and the *rāgas* falling under these categories; the seasons for singing the specific *rāgas such as Basanta, Paṭha mañjarī,* etc.

About definitions of *rāga,* Kṛṣṇadāsa has the same view as Mataṅga but follows Harināyaka in the treatment of *rāgas.* The changes in the form and content of some *rāgas* prevalent in the 13th century made them confusing during the 16th century, when the *rāga-rūpa* of those *rāgas* could not be interpreted properly. Kṛṣṇadāsa and Harināyaka in their works *Gītāprakāśa* and *Saṅgītasāra,* have tried to revive some of the ancient styles and systems.

The sixth *ullāsa* is *Svara-nirṇaya* which deals with *jāti-lakṣaṇam, svara, grāma, śruti* etc. Krṣṇdāsa says that *svaras* are born out of *śrutis* and the seven *svaras* occupy the number of *śrutis* as follows; *Ṣaḍja, Madhyama* and *Pañcama* have four *śrutis* each and *Gāndhāra* and *Niṣāda* occupy two *śrutis* each while *Ṛsabha* and *Dhaivata* have three *śrutis* each. Both the *svara* and *śruti* together provide *rañjakatva,* meaning charm, colour and pleasing effect to a *rāga. Śrutis* can be experienced on a *vīṇā.*

The author then delineates on *vādī* (sonant), *samavādī* (consonant), *anuvādī* (assonant) and *vivādī* (discordant) *svaras* and explains their relationship. A *svara* is: "रञ्जयन्ति श्रोतृचित्तं स्वयं यस्मात्तत: स्वरा:" ।A *grāma* is: "स्वराणां सुव्यवस्थानां समूहो ग्राम ईष्यते"। meaning: a *svara* is capable of colouring the minds of the listener and a *grāma* is a well structured group of *svaras.*

There are three *grāmas,* viz. *Ṣaḍja, Madhyama* and *Gāndhāra.*He explains the difference between *Ṣaḍja* and *Madhyama grāma* thus: when *Pañcama* stands on its penultimate *śruti* instead of its normal postion in *Ṣadja-grāma,* the *svaras* thus placed and arranged, form *Madhyama-grāma.*

He has named eighteen *jātis* as parent of *rāgas,* and mentions *mūrchanā* as: "मूर्च्छनातानादयश्चाकरेभ्यो ज्ञातव्या:" ।

The seventh *ullāsa* is *Doṣa-nirṇaya,* dealing with the faults in rendering a *gīta.* The author maintains that the verbal structure of *gīta* and its rendition should be faultless, particularly in Sanskrit. In regional varieties however, deviations were permissible.

Gītaprakāśa is not an absolutely original work. The author has referred to the following works of music:

(a) *Saṅgītasāra* of Harināyaka. *Harināyaka* was born in the family of Śrī Raṅga Mohāpatra of Karṇāṭakabāṭaka. Śrī Raṅga ruled over southern region of Orissa near Rājamahendry (*c* 1500 A.D.) and was the grand father of Mukundadeva Gajapati. Probably there was a family tie among Śrī Raṅga,

Harināyaka and Kṛṣṇadāsa. Kṛṣṇdāsa was perhaps sent to Akbar's court on diplomatic mission.

(b) *Saṅgīta-sarvasva* (*c* 1500 A.D.) of Jagaddhara. The author was perhaps the well known *ṭīkākār* (commentator) of Bhavabhūti's *Mālatī-Mādhava* and Biśākhadatta's *Mudrā-rākṣasa*.

(c) *Saṅgīta-dāmodara* of Śubhaṅakara (*c* 1500 A. D.).The author also wrote *Hastamuktāvalī*, a brilliant and comprehensive work on hand poses relating to classical dance.

(d) *Saṅgīta-ratnākaraḥ* of Śārṅgadeva (*c* 1230 A.D.)

(e) *Sāhitya-darpaṇa* of Viśvanātha Kavirāja of Orissa. It is a treatise on *alaṅkāra.*

(f) *Gīta-govinda* of Jayadeva.

(g) *Kāvyadarśa* of Daṇḍī, a book on *alaṅkāra.*

Gītaprakāśa has been published by Orissa Sangeet Natak Akademi, Bhubaneshwar, edited by Nilmadhav Panigrahi.

Pañcamasāra-Saṃhitā- by Nārada

It is estimated that Nārada was born between 1570/72 A.D. and lived till 1630/32 A.D.. Reference of this book is available in *Saṅgīta-Nārāyaṇa* by Gajapati Jagannātha Nārāyaṇadeva of Orissa, *Saṅgīta-Kalpadruma* by Krṣṇānanda Vyāsadeva Rāgasāgara, *Saṅgītasāra-Saṅgraha, Gita-candrodaya* and *Bhaktiratnākara,*

There are two manuscripts under the name *Nārada-Pañcamasāra-Samhitā* in Baṅgīya Sāhitya Pariṣad. These texts have 4 chapters each, while the manuscript with Asiatic Society is named as *Pañcamasāra-Samhitā* and has only one chapter dealing with *rāga.* One more manuscript is in Manipur, copied during the rule of Mahārāj Gambhīra Singh, under the name *Kṛṣṇa-rasa-saṅgita.* There is yet another copy of the original manuscript with Dr. Bimal Roy, the renowed musicologist.

Dr. Roy has given a list of various Nāradas who flourished at different times. They are: "I) Nārada Ṛṣi, 2) Nāradagandharva, 3) Nāradamuni 4) Nārada (author of *Makaranda*), 5) Nārada (writer of *Rāgarāgiṇī-mata-prakāśikā*), 6) Nārada (Writer of *Nāradasaṃhitā*), 7) Nārada (Writer of *Pañcamasārasaṃhitā*), 8) Nārada (writer of *Catvārimsacchata Rāga Nirupaṇa*), 9) if Tyāgarājā's Nārada is counted, then there would be nine Nāradas."

To quote Dr. Roy—"Pañcamasāra-Saṃhitā has followed in many ways *Nārada-Saṃhitā* and *Saṅgīta-dāmodara* and so, languagewise, there is similarity in many instances. But in the field of *tāla,* it has followed the *tālas* used in *kīrtana* .... in this period, *Kīrtana* of Bengal had blossomed out in all its aspects like *Rāga, Tāla, Rīti, Bhāva,* etc. At that time when *Rāga* and *Tāla* of *Kīrtana* followed the old system, it appeared to follow the evaluation of *Kārnāṭik* system of music." (Pañcamasāra-Saṃhitā, edited by Guru Bipin Singh, Manipur Nartanalaya, Cal. 1985).

Pañcamasāra-Saṃhitā of Asiatic Society—This manuscript has only one *adhyāya* dealing with *rāgas* in detail. After a four line *Śloka* offering salutation to Hara-Gaurī, the author takes up *rāgas*. He mentions the following *rāgas*, numbering six, as: *Karṇāṭa, Mālava, Mallāra, Srīrāga, Basanta* and *Hindola*. The *rāgiṇis* or *strī* (wife) of these *rāgas* are:

(1) *Mālava—Dhānasi, Mānasi, Rāmkiri, Sindhuḍā, Āsoārī, Bhairavī.*
(2) *Mallāra—Belāvalī, Purabī, Kānaḍā, Mādhavi, Koḍā, Kedārikā.*
(3) *Śrīrāga—Gāndhārī, Gaurī, Subhagā, Kaumārikā, Beloyārī, Bairāgī.*
(4) *Basanta—Tuḍi, Pañcamī, Lalitā, Paṭhamañjarī, Gurjarī, Bibhāṣā.*
(5) *Hindola—Mādhavī, Dīpikā, Deśakārī, Pāhiḍā, Barāḍī, Mārhāṭi.*
(6) *Karṇāṭa—Nāṭikā, Bhūpāli, Gaḍā, Rāmkelī, Kāmodā, Kalyaṇī.*

The author then gives a time table where particular *rāgas* are to be sung. The periods have been named as *Pūrvokta-kāla, Madhyāhṇakāla, Sāyāhṇa-kāla, Pradoṣa-kāla*, and *Rātri*.

The *Purvokta-kāla* or morning *rāgiṇīs* are:
Āhīrī, Lalitā, Kāmodā, Paṭhamañjarī, Rāmkiri, Beloyārī, Gurjarī, Deśakārī, Subhagā, Pañcamī, Gaḍā, Nuḍī, Bhairavī, Kaumārī.

The *madhyāhṇa-kāla* or noon *rāgiṇis* are:
Barāḍī, Mādhavī, Koḍā, Bairāgi, Dhānasī, Beloyāri, Mārhāṭi.

The *Sāyāhṇa-kāla* or afternoon *rāgiṇis* are:
Gāndhāri, Dīpikā, Kalyāṇī, Pūrabī, Āsoārī, Kānaḍā, Gaurī, Kedār, Pāhiḍā, Mādhvī, Mānasī, Nāṭi, Bhupālī, Sindhuḍā.

During the ten *daṇḍas* of *pradoṣa-kāla* or evening, six *rāgas* are to be sung. After the *daśa-dandas* are over, any *rāga* or *rāgiṇi* may be sung during the night or *Rātri*.

Megha-mallāra rāga is sung any time during monsoon period. *Śrī-pañcamī* starts from *Dūrgā-mahotsava* when *Basanta rāga* is sung. But during a stage performance or by the order of a king any *rāga* may be presented irrespective of any time factor.

Nārada says that as per rule, a *rāga* has to be elaborated first and then the *rāgiṇis* or *bhāryās* (wives) of that *rāga* should follow. He follows the principle of *six rāgas* and *thirty-six rāgiṇis and* gives *rāgā-dhyāna* in detail.

Pañcamasāra-saṃhitā- [with four adhyāyas] (Baṅgīya Sāhitya Patiṣad):

In the first chapter the author describes how *śiṣyas* of Bharatamuni propagated *saṅgīta* in all the three worlds. They were called *naṭas*, - a class of musicinas who were highly qualified in music, dance and drama.The *naṭas* of *Rāḍhadesa* in *Prācyadeśa* were particularly mentioned as great singers, dancers and were also intellectuals: 'राढायां संस्थिता ये च ते नटाः पुनरुत्तमाः । ये गायन्ति सुगीतानि नृत्यन्ति च विचक्षणाः'॥

This indicates that the author might have been of Bengal.

Second chapter deals with *nātya*—bad as well as requisite qualities of a *gāyaka*, a *nāyaka*, a *mṛdaṅga* player (*Vādaka*), dancer, jester (*viduṣaka*), and hiroine (*nāyikā*); definitions of *dhātu, mātu, gīta, abhinaya, saṅgīta,* and *nṛtyas* of *tāṇḍava* and *lāsya* styles; varieties of instruments, their descriptions and examples. *Muraja* has been mentioned as the most important among instruments. Description of *mṛdaṅga* is given with some of its *bols*. A particular *bol* or a *varṇa* represented a deity.

Third chapter depicts Kṛṣṇa as the '*Saṅgīta vilāsa magna*' that is, who enjoys music with his *gopīs.* He is the player of *muralī*- the flute and from his sixteen thousand *gopīs* 16000 *rāgas* evolved. The author mentions that out of these, only the *rāgas* prevalent in Bengal are being discussed.

According to the author, there are six *rāgas* and thirtysix *rāgiṇīs.* The six *rāgas* are: *Mālava, Mallāra, Śrīrāga, Basanta, Hindola* and *Karṇāṭa.* The author also narrates the names of the *rāgiṇīs* of these *rāgas,* followed by *dhyāna-murtis* of *rāgas* and *rāgiṇis.*

There are however some differences between the manuscript of Asiatic Society and the one with four *adhyāyas,* e.g. in the list of six *rāgiṇīs* of *Hindola,* the Asiatic Society copy mentions *Mādhavi rāgiṇī,* while the other manuscript mentions *Māyūrī.* There are some differences in the *dhyāna* portion also.

Fourth chapter devotes itself with *tālas,* its origin, form, number of *tālas* prevalent, names of different *talas* practised in different parts of India, names of eighteen different *tālas* of Bengal and their descripton. How to play these tālas are also given. The author says:

पूर्वभागे चोत्तरे च क्रमेणैव विभाजितम् ।
प्रचरन्ति च ते ताला गौडे त्वष्टादश ध्रुवम् ॥

i.e., in Gauḍadeśa, 18 different *tālas* were practised.

Out of these 18 *tālas* 16 were more in use. The names of these 18 *tālas* were: *Ekatāla, Dharaṇa, Choṭkilā, Gañjana, Viṣama, Yugmaka, Ṣaṭpadī, Viṣama-sandhiḥ, Rūpakam, Daśakuśī, Kundaśekhara, Yati, Vasu, Āṭanī, Yamakam, Haragaurī Jhampakam, Apūrvakāla.*

एकतालस्तु धरणं छोटकिला गञ्जनं तथा ।
विषम युग्मञ्चैव षटपदीस्तदनन्तरम् ॥
विख्यातं विषमसन्धिः रूपकं प्रेमवर्धनम् ।
ततोऽपूर्वकला चैव हरगौरी च झम्पकम् ॥
यमकं दशकुशीञ्चैव कुन्दशेखरमेव च ।
यति वसुं दासगीतम् आटनी च विसर्जनम् ॥

The author also gives details about the method of playing these tālas, e.g.

वाद्याचतस्त्रस्तु कलालये तु कलाद्वयं पूरणके च वाद्यम् ।
कलाद्वयं स्यादथ घातिनीषु पूर्वाक्षरं स्यादगुरुरेव तस्मात् ॥,

This is followed by some *ślokas* dealing with the details of playing the *tālas.* It ends with

इति श्रीनारदकृतपञ्चमसारसंहितायां चतुर्थोऽध्याय: ॥

(These original treatises were studied, researched, compiled and translated in Bengali by Deepa Das Gupta and scrutinised by Dr. Bimal Roy)

Nāradakṛta Pañcamasāra-Saṃhitā is now available under this name along with *DāmodarSen Kṛta Saṅgītadāmodara,* published and edited by Guru Bipin Singh, from Manipur Nartanālaya, Cal, 1984.

***Saṅgīta Dāmodara- by Dāmodara Sen* (late 16th & early 17th century A.D.)**

This work is different from *Saṅgīta-dāmodara* of Śubhaṅkara. Dāmodara Sen who lived during the end of 16th century A.D. and early 17th, same time as the author of *Pañcama-sāra-Saṃhitā,* was a Vaiṣṇava and was perhaps the author of both *Saṅgīta-dāmodara* and *Pañcama-sāra-Saṃhitā.* Some findings point to this assumption by scholars, e.g.

1. Narahari Cakravarti mentions in *Gītacandrodaya* -

दामोदर श्री पञ्चमसारसंहिताते ।
ध्रुवकादि निरुपिल सालगसूड़ेते ॥

meaning: Dāmodara categorises *dhruvaka* etc. under *Sālaga-sūḍa* in *Pañcamasāra-Saṃhita.* This means- Dāmodara is the author of *Pañcamasāra-Saṃhitā.* (*Vaiṣṇava-Saṅgīta-Śastra* p. 974).

Narahari also mentions in *Bhaktiratnakara,* that Dāmodara was the maternal grandfather of Govindadāsa Kavirāja.

2. In the handwritten manuscript of *Sangita-dāmodara* (in the collection of treatises with Dr. Bimal Roy), the first chapter begins with - ''शिवनारदसंवादे रागमाला नाम प्रथमोऽध्याय:,'', while the second chapter ends with ''इति श्रीशिवनारदसंवादे संगीतदामोदरमाश्रित्य गौडदेशीयताल: ।'' Dāmodara Sen has used the word ''शिवनारद'' instead of ''नारद उवाच''

It is surmised that Nārada of *Pañcamasāra-Saṃhitā* and the Nārada of 'Śivānārada' may be the same persoṇ The *rāga-mālā* portion of both the works also tally.

The treatise *Saṅgīta-dāmodara* is divided into three chapterṣ The first deals with *rāgas* and their descriptions, the second describes tālas and the third gives *ślokas* on *Daśāvatāra prabandha* and *Nitya-nāṭya prabandha vādyam.*

1st chapter - The first four *ślokas* of this chapter are on Gaṇeśa *vandanā* and from fifth onwards starts *rāga* description, which is similar to those of *Pañcama-Sāra-Saṃhitā* (3rd chapter, *ślokas* 8 to 67)

2nd chapter - This chapter starts with names of *tālas* prevalent in Gauḍadeśa. The *tālas* are: *Aṣṭatāla, Rudratāla, Brahma-tāla, Indra tāla,* and *Caturdaśa tāla.* The description of the *tālas* are oriented on the views of the *mṛdaṅga* players of Bengal.

3rd chapter - This chapter begins with *Dasāvatāra prabandhas* and ends with *nitya-nātya-prabandham.* The first part is devoted to the ten *avatāras* (incarnations) and the description of *prabandha nṛtya* of Lord kṛṣṇa and Śrīmatī Rādhā.

[This treatise is available in the *Nāradakṛta Pañcama-sāra-Saṃhita tathā Dāmodara Sen Kṛta Saṅgīta-dāmodara* - Ed by Guru Bipin Singh, Calcutta 1985.]

Rāgataraṅgiṇī- Locanakavi (Jhā) of Mithila
(end 17th cent. - beginning of 18th cent.)

Scholars opine that there had been two musicologists of the name Locana. The first Locana was a contemporary of Emperor Jahangir. His work *Rāgataraṅgiṇī* on music was written in Sanskrit and had *gītas, rāga-rāgiṇī bibhāgas* and their explanations which had been referred by Hṛdaya Nārāyaṇa Deva, in his work *Hṛdaya-kautuka* (mid 17th cent.) which also has *rāga-rāgiṇī* explanations as per Locana. The second Locana or Locana Kavi of Mithila was of a later date, i.e. during the end of 17th cent. A.D and early 18th cent. He did not describe the *rāgas* in his work but gave *gāna* examples, although he based his work on the treatise of the first Locana.

Rāgataraṅgiṇī of Locanakavi of Mithila, is a work on music and is also valuable as a book of Maithilī literature. This treatise was written and compiled by Locana by the request of Śrī Narapati Ṭhākur, the younger brother of Rājā Mahīnāth Ṭhākur of Mithila.

The treatise is an important document for understanding the music culture that prevailed in Greater Bengal at that time.

The author has used three languages viz. Sanskrit, Braja, and Maithili. The enumeration and definition portions are in Sanskrit, the *dohās* to explain the facts are in Braja, so that these could be understood by even a layman, which was his aim, and the examples of *gītas* are in Maithili. 103 *gitas* written by 29 poets of Mithila are compiled in this book. Out of these 103 *gītas,* 53 are of Vidyāpati, 5 are of unknown poets, while the rest are by poets such as Purānamalla, Gaja Siṃha, Kavi Kumudī, Kavi Śekhara and others. Some are his own compositions.

This treatise is divided into five *taraṅgas* or chapters, each one having valuable information about music. Besides, he has given some details about the ruling dynasty of Mithila in the first chapter and the musical tradition practised in Mithila in the third chapter. He has given an analytical account of the *Padāvalīs* of different poets along with the descriptions of the *rāga-rāgiṇī mūrti,* technical terms, specialised *rāgas* and *tālas* practised at that time in Mithila. He also gives a short account of *Kathakatā,* that was in practise in Mithila. He says that Vidyāpati trained one Jayat,—a *Kathak,* in *rāga-saṅgīta* of Mithila. He also mentions that Vidyāpati had introduced a special style of music and some *rāgas* unique to Mithilādeśa.

A Sanskrit scholar and poet, Locanakavi was also a musician and musicologist who practised *Prācīna* and *Arvācīna* i.e. ancient and regional music methodically and studied treatises of music thoroughly to have the balanced knowledge of theory and practice. He had even studied Amir Khusrau's system or *mokām-paddhati.* His patron Mahārājā Narapati Ṭhākur was an expert himself in regional *Maithilī-saṅgīta* and was referred to by Locana as *Dhvani-gāna-sindhu.*

Locana has mentioned the following *ācāryas* and works in his book, viz. Muni Bharata, Hanumāna, Kohala, *Saṅgīta-dāmodara, Gīta-govinda,* and *Tumburunāṭaka.*

The first chapter of *Rāgataraṅgiṇī* contains *Maṅgalācāraṇa, Prastāvanā,* and description of *puruṣa-rāgas,* viz. *Bhairava, Kauśika, Hindola, Dīpaka, Śrīrāga,* and *Megha-rāga.*He has enumerated the technical portions in Sanskrit while the *dhyāna-rūpa* and *gītas* are in Braja and Maithili.

In the second chapter, Locana describes *strī-rāgas* (*rāgiṇīs*) of *puruṣa-rāgas.* The list of *rāgas* and *rāgiṇīs* is as follows:

Rāgas	Rāgiṇīs
1. *Bhairava*	*Baṅgālī, Madhu-mādhavī, Barāḍī, Sindhu, Bhairavī.*
2. *Kauśika*	*Toḍī, Khambhāvatī, Gaurī, Kakubhā, Guṇḍakarī.*
3. *Hindolaka*	*Belāvalī, Deśākha, Rāmkarī, Lalitā , Paṭamañjarī.*
4. *Dīpaka*	*Kedāra, Kānaḍā, Deśī, Kāmoda, Bihāgḍā.*
5. *Śrīrāga* -	*Basanta, Mālava, Āsāvarī, Mālaśrī, Dhanāśrī.*
6. *Megha*	*Mallārī, Deśkārī, Bhūpālī, Ṭaṅka, Dakṣiṇa-gurjarī.*

Each of these *rāgiṇīs* has been described in Brajabhāṣā.

The third chapter contains: *Nāda-nirūpaṇa, Gītotpatti, Gīta, Dhātu-mātu,* the origin and historical development of *Maithil-saṅgīta-paramparā,* the 36 *rāgas* practised in Mithila, *Chanda-lakṣaṇa/Rāga-lakṣaṇa, Laghu-guru vicāra,* etc., which are important topics of music. He has defined *rāga* as :

नादमय - स्वरमूर्च्छनाऽधीना च रागोत्पत्तिः ।
तदुक्तम्स्वरः सम्मूर्च्छते यत्र रागतां प्रतिपद्यते ॥

He also defines *Mārga* and *Desī-saṅgīta, Nibaddha-anibaddha gītas, chandas,* and *Laghu-guru vicāra.*

Locana has given a list of *rāgas* with their variants. Each of these has short *lakṣaṇam* or description in Sanskrit, followed by examples of *gīta* or *dohā* in Maithili.

In the 4th chapter, *Saṇkīrṇa rāgas* practised in Mithila are enumerated with *Chandas. Gītas* composed in Maithili are given as examples. The *Sankīrṇa rāgas* famous in Mithila are:

1. *Vibhāsī*
2. *Āhirānī (Bhīmpalāsī)—Āhirānī - Bhīmpalāsikā, Ramyā - Bhīmplāsikā, Dhanyā-Bhīmpalāśikā, Vitatā-Bhīmpalāśikā.*
3. *Gopīvallabha.*
4. *Sāraṅgī—Śuddha-Sāraṅgī, Deśī-Sāraṅgī, Abhirāmā-Sāraṅgī, Śobhanā-Sāraṅgī, Anupa-Sāraṅgī.*
5. *Suhaba—Śuddha-suhaba, Kāma-suhaba, Karunā-suhaba, Sundar-suhaba.*
6. *Koḍāra—Viyogī-koḍār, Moraṅgīa-koḍāra, Dandaka-koḍāra, Śuddha-koḍāra, Vitatā-koḍāra, Smara-sandīpana-koḍāra.*
7. *Dhanachī—Maṅgalī-dhanachī, Pahaḍiyā-dhanachī, Pañcamasvara-dhanachī, Śrivimiśra-dhanachī, Jogiyā-dhanachī, Śambhavī-dhanachī, Śobhanā-dhanachī.*
8. *Gauḍa-mālava—Gauḍīya-mālava, Maithil-malava.*
9. *Raja-Vijaya—Deb-rājāvijaya, Alān-vimiśra, (Aḍānā) Deś-raja-vijaya, Kānaḍā-miśra-rājā-vijay, Maṅgala-rāja-vijaya, Manmod-rāja-vijaya, Bhāṭhiāl-rāja-vijaya.*
10. *Nāṭa-Śuddha-nāṭa, Malārī-nāṭa, Śaṅkuka-nāṭa, Kāmodā-nāṭa, Uttama-nāṭa.*

Locana calls these *rāgas* as *Tirbhukti-deśīya saṃkīrṇa rāgas.*
In the 5th chapter, Locana deals with:

a. *Svara-prakaraṇa* or *svara-sañjā,*
b. Position of the *svaras* on 22 *śrutis,*
c. *Svara-śruti vibhāga* on *viṇā,*
d. *Rāga -saṃsthiti,*
e. *Svara-jāti,*
f. *Svara-nirūpaṇa,*
g. *Rāga-saṅkara,*
h. *Rāga-gāna-kāla,*
i. *Nāyaka-nāyikā-bheda* descriptions.

Locana maintains that there were 12 *saṃsthānas* or *thāṭas* (on *viṇā*) prevalent in Prācyadeśa, under which all other *rāgas* were placed. These *rāga-saṃsthānas* were: *Bhairavī, Toḍī, Gaurī, Karṇāṭa, Kedāra, Iman, Sāraṅga, Megharāga, Dhanāśrī, Pūrvā, Mukhārī and Dīpaka.*

He accepts the principle of classifying *rāgas* under the frame of *Janaka-janya paddhati* or *Mela paddhati,* i.e. Parental scales and their derivative *rāgas.* He has also dealt with the *rāga-paricaya* (description) of the twelve *janaka-rāgas,* giving details of *svaras* and *śrutis* used; time factor; and *lakṣaṇas* (spcial attributes). He maintains *Bhairava* as the *śuddha-rāga.*

(*Locanakṛta Rāgataraṅgiṇī* - Ed. by Śaśīnāth Jhā, Maithili Academi, Patna, 1989).

Bhakti-ratnākara (B.R.), Saṅgītasāra-saṃgraha (S.S.S.), Gītacandrodaya (G.C.)—(Gītacandrodaya-Maṅglācaraṇaputhi)—Narahari Cakravartī 18th cent. A. D.

Narahari Cakravartī also known as Ghanaśyāmadāsa, wrote these books on music which are very valuable. Out of these, *Bhakti-ratnākara* is the best and *Gitacandrodaya* is the shortest. Narahari most probably wrote these books while in Brindavana and covered all aspects of music. He has tackled the origin of music from the time of the *Vedas* in *Bhakti-ratnākra* and *Saṅgītasāra-samgraha* and has referred to books such as-*Saṇgīta-pārijāta, Saṅgīta-śiromaṇi, Saṅgītasāra, Saṅgīta-dāmodara, Saṅgīta-muktāvalī, Pañcamasāra-saṃhitā, Gītaprakāśa* and *Saṅgīta-ratnamālā.* Authors mentioned by him are: *Kohala, Śārṅgadeva* and *Harināyaka.*

Narahari has defined the following subjects in his book:

1. *Saṅgīta,*
2. *Mārga* and *Deśī-saṅgīta,*
3. Origin of *gīta,* i.e.-*Nāda,*
3. *Lakṣaṇas* of *gīta,* i.e. *Dhātu, Mātu* etc.,
5. *Śrutis* and their names. However, the names vary slightly in *S.S.S.* from *B.R.*

Svara: Narahari was conscious of the fact that the *svaras* were born out of *śrutis* and writes in *S.S.S.* : स्वराणामित्यत्र पुत्राणां पिता इतिवत् जन्यजनक सम्बन्धे षष्ठी । स्वराणां जनिका इत्यर्थ:।।

i.e. *Śruti* is the father and *svara* is the son. The relationship between *Śruti* and *Svara* is that of father and son. He has followed *Saṅgīta-dāmodara* to explain about *svaras.*

Sthāna: Narahari elaborates on *Mandra, Madhya* and *Tāra sthānas* and their positions.

Grāma: In his view *grāmas* are- स्वराणां सुव्यावस्थानां समूहो ग्राम इष्यते ।
and that *Ṣaḍja grāma* is most important.

Mūrchanā: Out of the three books, *S. S. S* has more details about *Mūrchanā.* In *B.R* he says:

मूर्च्छना आधार ग्राम

and - ग्रामत्रये सप्तस्वर मूर्च्छना प्रचार ।

षड्ज ग्रामे स-रि-ग-म-प-ध-नि निर्धार ॥
ग-म-प-ध-नि-स-रि गान्धार सुनिच्चय ॥ [भ. र. २४०]

In *S.S.S.* he says that in *Ṣadja-grāma* the *mūrchanās* start with स and end with स. Similarly, in *Madhyama grāma* and *Gāndhāra grāma,* the *mūrchanās* start and end with म and ग respectively. He has named the 21 *Mūrchanās* as: *Lalitā, Madhyamā, Citrā, Rohinī, Mataṅgajā, Sauvirī, Varṇamadhyā, Ṣadjamadhyā, Pañcamī, Matsyarī, Mṛdumadhyā, Śuddhāntā, Kalāvatī, Tīvrā, Raudrī, Brāhmī, Vaiṣṇavī, Khecarī, Varā, Nādavatī, Viśālā.*

Tāna: He follows the principle of *tānas* of *Saṅgīta-dāmodara.* He says that there are 49 *tānas* born out of 7 *svaras. Kūṭa-tānas* are further born out of these *tānas* and number 5033.

Varṇa and Alaṅkāra: He has referred to *Saṅgīta-pārijāta* and has mentioned the four *varṇas.* He says that there are 26 *alaṅkāras* of *Sthāyī varṇa,* and 12 each of *Ārohī, Avrohī and Sañcārī varṇas* and to achieve perfection in practical music, it is essential to practise these *alaṅkāras.* He has detailed discussion on *alaṅkara* in *B.R.*

Graha-Aṃśa-Nyāsa : Narahari explains these three as the most important ones out of the ten *Rāga-lakṣaṇas. Graha* is the *svara* to start a *rāga* with. *Aṃśa-svara* expresses *anurāga* and *nyāsa* is the *svara* to end the *rāga* on.

Jāti: Narahari explains *jāti* as a *gīta* which originates from *śruti, svara,* and *grāma* and that *rāgas* originate from *jātis.* He refers to Harināyaka and opines that, to experience perfectly from *śruti* to *jāti,* it is possible only through *vīṇā.*

Rāga: Narahari was conversant with the different *matas* of *Rāga-rāgiṇī paddhati.* He says:

षट्त्रिंशते राग छय रागिनी त्रिंशत्
प्रति रागे पंच भार्या एहो सुसम्मत ॥ (भ. र. २४४)

i.e. there are six *rāgas* having five *rāgiṇīs* or *bhāryās* (भार्या) each.

He has named them as follows:

	Ragā	Rāgiṇī
1.	*Bhairava -*	*Bhairavī, Kauśkī, Bibhāsa, Megha, Naṭanārāyaṇa.*
2.	*Basanta -*	*Āndolitā, Deśākhyā, Lolā, Prathama-mañjarī, Mallārī.*
3.	*Mālava-kauśika-*	*Gaurī, Guṇakarī, Barāḍī, Kṣamāvatī, Karṇāṭī.*
4.	*Śrī -*	*Gāndharī, Devagāndhārī, Mālavaśrī, Āsāvarī, Rāmkirī.*
5.	*Megha -*	*Lalitā, Mālasī, Gaurī, Nāṭī, Devakirī.*
6.	*Naṭanārāyaṇa-*	*Tārāmaṇi, Stathābhirī (Ābhirī), Kāmodī, Guñjarī, Kakubhā.*

Narahari comments that *rāgas* vary from region to region-

देशे देशे राग गण नाम भिन्न हय ।

केह ना करिते पारे रागेर निर्णय ॥

In *B.R.* there are three *sreṇīs* (class) of *rāgas*:

1. *Sampūrṇa,* i.e. *rāgas* with all the seven *svaras,* e.g. *Śrī, Naṭa, Gupta-basanta, Śuddha-bhairava,* etc.
2. *Ṣāḍava-rāga,* i.e. *Rāgas* with six *svaras,* e.g. *Gauḍa, Karṇāṭa-gauḍa, Deśi, Dhannāsikā,* etc.
3. *Auḍava-rāga,* i.e. - *rāgas* with five *svaras,* e.g. *Madhyamādi, Mallāra, Deśpāla,* etc.

Narahari mentions a separate category as *Saṅkīrṇa rāgas,* which are achieved when the above mentioned three categories are mixed together, e.g. *Pauravī, Kalyāṇī, Sāraṅga, Rāmkelī,* etc.

Narahari also specifies time and season for singing these *rāgas* and says if a *rāga* is sung out of time or season, it is due to the wish of the king or on the stage, as per the situation of the drama.

Saṅgīta: *Saṅgīta* is mentioned by Narhari as *Nibadha* and *Anibaddha* and defined as:

अनिबद्ध रागालापरुपी निरुपय ॥

बद्धहीन ये गीत से अनिबद्ध हन ।

रागालापे कहि राग प्रकटीकरण ॥ (भ. र - २५४)

Definition of *anibadda* and *nibaddha* are the same in *B.R* and *S.S.S.* but in *G.C.* he adds:

वर्णादि नियम नाइ अनिबद्धगीते ।

केबल आलाप राग प्रकट याहाते ॥ (गी. च. पुँथि पत्र २२ ख)

meaning, any *ālāpa* of a *rāga* is *anibaddha* and it is a *gīta* with no bondage of words or *pada,* neither any time cycle or *tāla* and no hard and fast rule of *varṇa,* etc. He says there are two types of *ālāpa*: a) with meaningless *huṅkāra* (syllables) and with b) *svaras,* recommended by *śāstras.* He then further explains *ālāpa/ ālapti* by referring to Harināyaka. He elaborates on the *ālāpa* rendered in *Kīrtana* in *B.R* and *Narottamavilāsa.*

He defines *nibaddha* as a style that is bound by *dhātu, aṅga,* etc. and is also called *Prabandha-Saṅgīta.* It is of three kinds: *Śuddha, Chāyālaga* and *Kṣudra.* He says that these three names are mentioned differently by other musicologists, e.g. Harināyaka mentions them as *Prabandha, Vastu* and *Rūpaka.*

Narahari maintains that *Śuddha* or *Prabandha* is made up of *ālāpa, dhātu* and *aṅga*. It consists of four *dhātus* and six *aṅgas* while *Vastu* consists of three *dhātus* and five *aṅgas* and *Rūpaka* has two *dhātus* and two *aṅgas*.

Dhātu: *Dhātus* are the *avayava* or parts of the lyrical composition of a *prabandha*. These are normally four in number and are called—*Udgrāha, Melāpaka, Dhruva* and *Ābhoga*. Narahari says that different musicologists have maintained different views on the names, numbers and positions of *dhātus*, e.g.

1. *Saṅgīta-dāmodara* maintains —*Udgrāha, Dhruva, Antarā,* and *Ābhoga.*
2. *Saṅgītā-Śiromaṇi* —*Udgrāha, Dhruva* and *Ābhoga.*
3. *Harināyaka—Udgrāha, Melāpaka, Dhruva, Antarā* and *Ābhoga.*

Harināyaka uses *antarā* as the joiner between *Dhruva* and *Ābhoga*. Narahari does not stress on any particular opinion but gives examples by composing *padas* on each one. These are available in *B.R.* and *G.C.*

Aṅgas: He also mentions the ancient six *aṅgas* as - *Svara, Viruda,Pada, Pāṭha, Tenaka,* and *Tāla*.

Jātis of *prabandhas*: Giving reference to *Saṅgīta-Pārijāta,* Narahari mentions the five *jātis* of *prabandhas* as—*Medinī* with six *aṅgas, Nandinī* with five *aṅgas, Dīpanī* with four *aṅgas, Pāvanī* with three and *Tārāvalī* with two. He gives examples in *B.R.* and *G.C.*

Rules and divisions of *Prabandhas*: *Prabandhas* are divided or categorised into 26 types, and he names them in *B.R* and *S.S.S.* In *B.R* he has given some descriptions of *Svarārtha prabandha* and has defined some more in *S.S.S.* He has speficied the order in which these are to be sung. In all the three books he has explained *Svarārtha-Mātṛkā* as two separate *prabandhas,* i.e. *Svarārtha* and *Mātṛkā.* In *S.S.S.* he has explained ten types of *Prabandas.* He defines *Chāyalaga* and names nine kinds of *Chāyālaga/ Sālaga* as per *Saṅgīta-dāmodara* and *Pañcamasāra-saṃhitā,* and their further kinds.

Narahari defines *Kṣudra* or *Saṃkīrṇa-gīti* which is of four kinds, viz. *Citrapadā, Citrakalā, Dhruvapadā,* and *Pā̃cālī*. He says that the variety of *Dhrupadā* with two *kalis* was called *Chaṭikīlā*. Historians believe that this *Chaṭikilā* was most proably the *Cuṭkulā* of Husein Shah Śarkī who stayed in Bengal as a refugee king. During that period *Cuṭkulā* was very popular in Bengal.

Narahari has given examples of *Dhruvapadās* consisting of two, three and four *kalis*.

Narahari explains *Pā̃cālī*.as a *gīta-prakāra* of a very long narrative type, composed of many *padas* and are of two types: *Sadhruva* or *dhruva sahita* (with *dhruva*) and *Adhruva* or *dhruva rahita* (without *dhruva*).

He also divides *gītas*— 1) According to the language these were composed in.

These were(a). *Divya,* composed in Sanskrit, (b). *Mānusa/mānuṣi* composed in local colloquial languages and (c). *Divya-mānuṣa/ Divya-mānuṣi* composed in a mixed language of Sanskrit and *Prākṛta. Mānuṣa gītas* were composed in the regional languages of *Aṅga, Baṅga, Kaliṅga* and other places.

2) The second category of division is: according to the number of *mātrās.* These are: *Sama, Visama* and *Ardhasama. Samas* were composed of four *caraṇas* (foot). *Ardhasama-gītas* were composed in a manner where the first and third and second and fourth lines consisted of same number of *mātrās. Visama-gītas* were of uneven *mātrās* in all the *caraṇas* and were called *Miśra gīta* in *S.S.S.*

In *B.R.* and *S.S.S.* Narahari defines nine *guṇas* or attributes of *saṅgita.* These are: *Graha; Laya; Yati; Māna; Dhātu-punaruktatā,* meaning repetition *dhātus* in which of certain portions of a *gīta* are repreated over and over again in a novel manner, creating novelty every time; *Mātur-anekārthatā,* meaning a process of presenting one single phrase of the *pada* in a variety of ways; *Rāga -suramyatā* or aesthetic presentation of *rāgas; Gamakas* of fifteen varieties; *Artha-nairmalya,* i.e. to express the meaning of the *pada* perfectly with good pronunciation and suitable *rasa.*

Narahari then elaborates on the *gīta-doṣa* or adverse qualities of a singer and also the good qualities.

Narahari describes varieites of instruments in his three books but the best descriptions are in *S.S.S.* He divides the instruments in the traditional categories of *tata, ānaddha, suṣira* and *ghana.* Apart from the usual varieties of *vīṇās* and other percussion, wind and idiophonic instruments, he names some unusual ones, such as - *Brahma, Triśarī, Gadāvāraṇahasta, Madhusyandrī, Ghonā* (stringed varieites); *Śṛṅgikā, Svaranābhi* and *Lāpika-baṃśa* (wind variety); *Śuktikā* and *Aṅkur* (idiophonic variety).

The instruments Narahari describes in details are *Alāvanī vīṇā* (in S.S.S) *Mardala, Mṛdaṅga,* and *Bāśī.* He says that *mardala* and *mṛdaṅga* were very similar and explains the ways of playing *mṛdaṅga.* He gives details about its making and the required measurements, etc.

In *S.S.S.* he has categorised *ghana-vādya* into two, viz- a) *Anurakta,* that goes with *gīta* and b) *Birakta,* that goes with *Tāla.*

Narahari has discussed the various aspects of *nṛtya, nṛtta* and *naṭya* in great details in his treatise. *Saṅgītasāra-Saṅgraha* is divided into six chapters, viz. *Gīta-prakaraṇa, Vādya-prakaraṇa. Nṛtya-nātya-prakaraṇa, Āṅgikābhinaya-prakaraṇa, Bhāṣādi-prakaraṇa,* and *Chanda-prakaraṇa.*

Rāga-ratnākara*—*by Ghanaśyāmadāsa/Narahari Cakravartī

This is a small work written in Sanskrit and consists of five chapters or *Prakaraṇas.* The treatise deals with the traditional classification of *rāgas* with their corresponding *dhyāna-mūrtis* which explain the *rāga-rūpa* clearly.

Prathama Prakaraṇa is the longest and consists of *maṅgalācaraṇa* and *rāga-svarūpa* of a great number of *rāgas*. The author refers to Nārada's *Pañcamasāra-Saṃhitā, Saṅgīta-dāmodara, Saṅgīta-kaumudī, Saṅgitasāra* , *Ratnamāla* (also called *Saṅgīta-ratnamālā/ Saṅgīta-mālā* written by Mammaṭācārya), *Gītaprakāśa*, etc. to establish the *rāga svarūpas*. He gives definition of *rāga* and then elaborates on the various aspects of *rāgas* such as:

1. *Rāga-rāginī* relationship, i.e. six *rāgas* and their *rāginīs*.
2. Detailed description of *rāga-rāginīs* with their *lakṣaṇas*, viz. *jāti*, etc.,
3. *Śruti*, 4. *Grāma*, 5. *Mūrchaṇā*, 6. *Graha, Aṃśa, Nyāsa*, 7. Nine *rasas*, 8. *Gamaka* and 9. *rāga-mūrti* of different *rāgas*.

Ghanaśyāmdāsa refers to the above mentioned authors and works throughout the book.

Dvitīya prakaraṇa deals with *rāgas* of *ṣāḍava jāti* referring to other scholars/ and their works. *Ṣāḍava-rāgas* are depicted with essential *lakṣaṇas* and *dhyāna-mūrtis*.

Tṛtīya prakaraṇa consists of detailed description of *ragas* belonging to *Auḍava-jāti*.

Caturtha prakaraṇa deals with *Saṃkīrṇa-rāgas*, first defining what a *Saṃkīrṇa rāga* is, quoting from Harināyaka. Number of *Saṃkīrṇa-rāgas* discussed are only ten.

Pañcama Prakaraṇa, the last chapter is devoted to the time and season that is appropriate for singing a *rāga*. The author says that *gāna-samaya* i.e. presenting a *rāga* at a particular time may vary from one country to another. He refers to other scholars and treatises, to substantiate the theory of time and season and also points out that one should adhere to the prescribed formula for each *rāga*.

Rāga-ratnākara by Ghanaśyāmdāsa is a comparatively recent discovery by Sri G. Surchand Sharma of Manipur and had not been mentioned earlier by other scholars. It is edited by Mr. Sharma and published by Manipur State Kalā Academi in 1971.

Annadā-maṅgala—Bhāratchandra Rāyaguṇākara

Bharatchandra completed his *Annadā-maṅgala* in 1752 A.D.

He divided this *kāvya* in three parts: *Annadā-maṅgala, Vidyā Sundara* and *Bhavānanda Majumdār-pālā*. All the three, are independent of each other. The poet wrote this *kāvya* under the patronage and request of Raja Krishnachandra of Nadia - Krishnanagar.

There are 96 poems in *Annadā-maṅgala*. At the beginning the poet maintained the *maṅgala-kāvya* tradition and composed poems in praise of different gods and goddesses such as: Ganeśa, Śiva, Sūrya, Viṣṇu and others. He also gave the reason for composing this *kāvya.* Raja Krishnachandra was taken a captive by Alivardi Khan because the Raja could not pay the *nazrānā* sum of 12 lakhs of rupees. The Raja was a devotee of Goddess Durgā who appeared before him and told him to get a *maṅgala-kāvya* written on her divine power and qualities by Bharatchandra, and that, this would free him from all problems.

The speciality of this *kāvya* is that, though it is a *maṅgalakāvya* yet it has risen above the stereotype level and is an excellent composition which is rich in literary value. The poet has introduced some novel techniques in the style of writing. Many new *chandas, alaṅkāras* and *rasas* have been incorporated. Bhāratchandra stressed on life styles that were down to earth. His excellent *kāvya* became the herbinger of modern Bengali literature.

Although during Bharat's life time Bengal was full of historical upheaval and turmoil, he did not mention any of these in his *kāvya.* He restricted himself to the descriptions and details of Krishnanagar, its court and about the main story of the *kāvya.* He concentrated more on the beauty of the lyrics although he maintained some of the laid down norms of *maṅgala kāvyas.* He said: नूतन मंगल आशे भारत सरस भाषे, राजा कृष्णाचन्द्रेर आज्ञाय ।

He brought varieties in *chanda* and used them selectively for depicting different *rasas* appropriately at the proper places. He even used some non-Bengali words to add to the charm and beauty of the lyrics. His applications of *alaṅkāras* are commendable.

Informations about music are available in the *kāvya,* among the various *vandanās* and *pālās.* In *Sarasvatī Vandanā* he says:

"वेद विद्या तन्त्र मन्त्र वेणुवीणा आदिमन्त्र
नृत्य गीत वाद्येर इश्वरी ।
छत्रिश रागिणी मेले छय राग सदा खेले
अनुराग ये सब रागिणी ।
सप्तस्वर तिन ग्राम मूर्छना एकुश नाम
श्रुति कला सतत सङ्गिनी ॥
तान मान वाद्य ताल नृत्य गीत क्रियाकाल
तोमा हैते सकल निर्णय ।

While describing the court of Krishnachandra, he says:

कालोयात गायन विश्राम खाँ प्रभृति ।
मृदंगी समझखेल किन्नर आकृति ॥
नर्तक प्रधान शेर मामुद सभाय ।
मोहन खोषाल चन्द्र विद्याधर प्राय ॥

In *Siddhighotan palā*, he says:

शंखघन्टारव महामहोत्सव
त्रिभुवने जय जय
नाचिछे नाटक गाइछे गायक
राग ताल मान लय ॥

In Śibe annadāna :

ताधिया ताधिया बाजये ताल ।
ताता थेइ थेइ बले बेताल ॥
बबम बबम बाजये ताल ।
डिमि डिमि बाजे डमरु ताल ।
भभम भभम बाजये शिंगा
मृदंग बाजये ताधिंगा धिंगा ॥
पंच मुखे गेये पंचम ताले
नाचेन शंकर बाजाये गाले ॥

In *Annapurnār Adhiṣṭhāna:*

वसन्तराजा आनि छय रागिणी राणी ......
घरे घरे नाना यन्त्रे वसन्तेर गान
संगे छय रागिणी वसन्त मूर्तिमान ॥

Music was the way to worship and he has repeated this time and again:

एकमने मोर गीत ये करे मानना ।
आमि पूर्ण करि तार मनेर कामना
चैत्र मासे शुक्ल पक्षे अष्टमी पाइया ।
गाइबे संगीत मोर संकल्प करिया ॥

In *Vyāser Vārānasī Praveśa:*

संहति वैष्णवगण हरिनाम संकीर्तन
नाना रसे नाचिया गाइया ॥
कीर्तनीयागण संगे गान करे नाना रंगे
वाल्य गोष्ठदान बेश रास ।
पूर्वरंग रसोद्गार माथुर विरह आर
हरि भक्ति याहाते प्रकाश ॥

वाजे खोल करताल केह वले भाल भाल
केह काँदि भावे गदगद ।
वीणा बाँशी आदि यन्त्रे वेद पुराणादि तन्त्रे
नानामते गान विष्णुपद ॥

Bharatcandra himself was well versed in music and possessed a good voice, as he has mentioned at many places in the *kāvya* . Although no *rāga* names have been mentioned above the *padas,* it is surmised that this *kāvya* was presented in *raga* music, because of his knowledge in *Śāstrīya saṅgita* and being a good singer.

Saṅgīta-taraṅga* — *Rādhāmohan Sen Dās

This book on musicology is written fully in verse form and is in Bengali language, with a sprinkling of Persian, Sanskrit and even a few English words.

Radhamohan Sen was born at the end of 18th century and wrote this treatise in 1818 A.D. He wrote another book named *Rasasāra-saṅgīta* which is not easily available. Radhamohan was a resident of Kansaripara in Calcutta, and composed many *ṭappās.* He was a learned pundit in Sanskrit and Persian. He has used bits of both these languages with Bengali while composing *Saṅgīta-taraṅga.* That he had a vast knowledge of music and had read music treatises, is evident from the list of books and '*matas*' he has referrd to and mentioned in his book. Some of the books mentioned by him are: *Saṅgīta-darpaṇa, Saṅgīta-dāmodara, Saṅgīta-ratnākaraḥ, Saṅgīta-Makaranda, Mānkutuhala, Saṅgīta-pārijāta, Tohfat-ul-Hind* and many more. He is the first in India who has explained all the '*matas*' described in Sanskrit and Persian works. These are: *Someśvara-mata, Hanumān-mata, Bharat-mata* and *Kallinātha-mata.*

Saṅgīta-taraṅga is particularly valuable from the point of view of theoretical information about musicology, which has been dealt with in great detail. Various '*matas*' and a huge number of *rāgas* have been explained thoroughly with their *lakṣaṇas, dhārā* and *dhyāna-mūrtis,* i.e. with all essential qualities required for each *rāga.*

From the theoretical side, the following subjects have been dealt with methodically, mostly with diagrams for easy understanding, viz:

1. *Nāḍi nirṇaya, Svara sthāna-Svara-nāma-nirṇaya, Śruti-yantra, Murchanādi-yantra, Varṇa, Vādī-svara-nirṇaya, Alaṅkāra* with its detailed varities and how to practise them, *Svara-prastāra, Gamaka* and its varieties.

A few diagrams are given as examples:
Alaṅkāra-Prasta-parasāda variety-

सासा	रिरि	गग	मग	रिगरिसा |	रिरि	गग	मम	पम	गमगरि |
गग	मम	पप	धप	मपमग |	मम	पप	धध	निध	पधपम |
पप	धध	निनि	सांनि	धनधप |					

Śruti-yantra-

	नि-२			नि-४	
क्षोभ		नी	अभ		ङ्गी
उ	ध-३	ग्रा	ध्रि		ङ्गी
रमे		या	पर		छना
रोहि		नी	ले	ध-३	प्ता
मद	प-४	न्ती	सु		प्ता
आला		पनी	त्रिभ		ङ्गी
सन्दि		पनी	सोर	प-३	ङ्का
र		क्ता	ए		ङ्का
य	म-४	ती	वयं		का
मार्ज्ज		नी	मंग	म-३	ला
पार्व		ती	सोके		ला
प्रसा		रिणी	कोके		ला
बीज	ग-२	रेखा	कम	ग-३	ला
क्रो		धा	मोह		नी
रु	रि-३	द्रा	शोभ		नी
रति		का	प्रवी	रि-३	णा
रंज		नी	नवी		ना
दया	सा-४	वती	वा		णा
छन्दो		वती	म	सा-३	ध्या
म		न्दा	मृ		दु
कमो		दत	अ		त्या
तव		रवा	दी		प्ता

In this *yantra*, the centre line of the column shows the number of *śrutis* each *svara* has, while the two side lines together give the names of *srutis,* e.g. प्रसारिणी, बीजरेखा etc.

Mūrchanādi-yantra—		सुर	मन्द्रस्थान	मध्यस्थान	तारस्थान
नि	गोपी				
ध	विस्तारिणी	नि	लज्जा	संकोची	गोपी
प	जमली	ध	आधारिणी	विहारिणी	विस्तारिणी
म	आरामिणी	प	कोमली	निर्मली	जमली
ग	आलापी	म	विश्रामिणी	कामिनी	आरामिणी
रि	वयंका	ग	आनन्दी	प्रलापी	आलापी
सा	प्रमोदिनी	रि	दीर्घा	शिखरा	वयंका
नि	संकोची	सा	आमोदिनी	विनोदिनी	प्रमोदिनी
ध	विहारिणी				
प	निर्मली				
म	कामिनी				
ग	प्रलापी				
रि	शिखरा				
सा	विनोदिनी				
नि	लज्जा				
ध	आधारिणी				
प	कोमली				
म	विश्रामिणी				
ग	आनन्दी				
रि	दीर्घा				
सा	आमोदिनी				

Radhamohan has also included certain *alaṅkāras* practised in the *Senī-gharānā.* The names mentioned by him however, have defective pronunciation, e.g. *vyāmī-vāyami* (व्यामी - वायमि).

2. *Rāga*: (a) *Jātis* of *rāgas*, viz. *Sampūrṇa, Sāḍava , Auḍava.* He has named all *rāgas* under these categories with detailed information of each *rāga.*

(b) *Varṇas* of *rāgas*-viz. *Śuddha, Sālaṅka* and *Saṃkīrṇa.* Definition of each of these and how to determine them, have been furnished. Two more varieties have been named, viz. i) *Guru sārasā,* a mixture of *Sālaṅka* and *Saṃkīrṇa rāgas* and ii) *Laghu sārasā,* a mixture of two *Samkīrṇa rāgas.*

(c) Six *rāgas* and their families consisting of six *bhāryās* (wives), six *putras* (sons), six *putra-badhūs* (daughters-in-law), one *sakhā* (friend), and one *sakhī* (girl friend).

3. *Mata:* -Hanumān, Bharata, Someśvara, Kallinātha and theories from *Nāda Purāṇa.*

4. *Rāga:- Samaya* (time theory of *rāgas*).

5. *Miśra rāgas.*

6. *Rāga rāginī dhyāna.*

Out of the huge number of *rāgas* mentioned and elaborated, some are rare and unique, e.g. *Rājdhānī, Sālaṅgopākṣaṇa* (सालंगोपाक्षण) *Nīlāśrī, Mukunda, Prāṇa, Kampana, Kalpataru* and many more.

The *rāgas* have been treated in this book with great details, such as: their origin, *svara* combination, *jāti, vādī-samavādī, calan,* etc. which he calls *dhārā,* meaning system. Besides, timē-cycle, season and song example of each *rāga* have been furnisheḍ.

7. The author has given details, a) from *Tohfā-tul-Hind,* b) the music duel between Gopāla Nāyaka and Āmīr Khusrau and how the latter cunningly learnt Gopāl's knowledge of *rāgās* and formulated his own by combining Persian and Hindusthānī *rāgas* such as-*Moher, Sājgiri, Jilf,* etc.

c) Husein Shāh Śarki's *rāgas.*

8. Other technicalities dealt with by the author are: *Śabda-vivaraṇa, Tānaprakaraṇa, Grāma-yantra, Ālāpaṇa-prakaraṇa,* definition and difference between *gāyaka* and *nāyaka, kalāvanta-kavvāl,* good and bad qualities of a musician, etc.

In *Prabandhādhyāya* Radhamohan defines *prabandha, dhruvapada, khayāl, tāppā* and other styles. He gives details of different kinds of *prabandha* and *dhruvapada.* He informs that *dhruvapada* used to be called by different names such as *dhorpad* (धोरपद्) and *dhrupada.* He defines *dhruvapada* and its varities like, *phulabandha, yugalbandha, rāgasāgara, viṣhupada,* etc. From the descriptions he has given, it is easy to understand, how *dhrupada* evolved through various stageṣ.

In *Rāgādhyāya,* the author describes various categories of *rāgas* viz. *Rāgāṅga, Bhāṣāṅga, Kriyāṅga, Upāṅga,* as per the four *matas* of Someśvara, Hanumān, Kallinātha, and Bharata. Number of possible *rāgas* along with *deśī* ones are given as 540606606.

Thāṭas, avarjita-svara and *dhun* have been discussed and defined.

In *Hastādhyāya, vādyas* (instruments) have been classified under the four usual categories, viz-*tata, ghana,ānaddha* and *suṣira.* Many instruments have been enlisted with elaborations.

In *Tālādhyāya,* origin and definition of *tāla, kāla-nirṇya, mārga, kriyā, aṅga, girā, viṣama, atīta, anāghāta, jāta, paya, jit* and *praśna* have been discussed.

Ektāla, Dhīma-tintāla, Jalad-tintāla, Teorā, Jhāptāla, Rūpaka, Dhāmār, Āḍā-cautāla, Baḍa-cautāla, Surfāktā, Sawārī and Farodast tālas have been enumerated with thier *bol, mātra, bibhāga, tālī and khāli.*

Radhamohan has explained how to perform *ālāpa* step by step at different stage, through *bols* like"*Anārinā nā dārete rom*" , etc. and has recommended four stages of *alāpa* to establish a *rāga* perfectly. He does not approve of *ālapa* with *sargam.*

Saṅgītā Rāga Kalpadruma-Kṛṣṇānanda Vyāsa Deva Rāgasāgara

It is a rare anthology compiled by the author Kṛṣṇānanada Vyāsa Deva and has 13,900 bandiśes in 45 different languages, including English, Burmese, Chinese etc. apart from Indian languages such as: Sanskrit, Brajabhāṣā, Marathi, Gujarati, Bengali, Oriya, Telegu, Karnati. It also contains theoretical music.

This book was printed and published by *Rāgasāgara* in four parts originally, the first in 1842 and the last in 1849. (in 1842 A.D a part of *Saṅgīta-rāga-kalpadruma* was published under the name *Raṅgina gāna-majmuyā*). These four parts were priced at Rs 25- each and Rs. 100/- for the whole set. Rāgasāgara's attempt to publish his extraordinary collection and compilation of thirty-two years, from his primitive press in Calcutta, in the model of *Śabda-kalpadruma* of Rājā Rādhākānta Deb, was remarkable. These were more like first proof, hence some portions were not legible.

Rāja Jogindra Nārāyaṇa Rao Bahadur of Lālgolā had a complete set and presented the set to Baṅgīya Sāhitya Pariṣat and expressed a desire to publish the set before 1912 and that he would bear all the expenses for printing and publication. When these were reprinted, efforts were made to correct the errors as much as was possible but some portions had to be abandoned.

Rāgasāgara mentions that number of songs compiled by him were 12,25000 (which seems to be abnormally high) and in 45 languages, but mainly *bandiśes* in Hindi, Urdu, different dialects of Rajasthan, Brajabhāṣā, Bengali, Sanskrit, Marathi, Gujarati are found. Songs of other languages are very few. Some languages like Chinese, Burmese, Balkh, etc. could not be deciphered and hence were not published.

In the first part, Rāgasāgara has mentioned names of many treatises-, a total of 116 books. This gives an idea as to the wealth of information he collected. Many books from this list are not available today.

This anthology is immensely valuable for the following reasons:

1. The long list of treatises mentioned,
2. innumerable number of compositions,
3. many of which bear the *bhaṇitā,* i.e. the pen name of the composers, some of whom were ancient, famous and their compositions were hard to find,
4. huge number of *rāgas* and *rāgiṇīs* mentioned,
5. varieties of styles of *gītis,*
6. names of ancient singers and

7. their patrons, some of whom were musicians,
8. and many historical, social and religious informations through the compositions, are available.

During the 18th, 19th and early 20th century the rich class of people in India including Bengal and particularly Calcutta were great patrons and connoisseurs of music. Many of them were highly knowledgeable musicians and composers. Their compositions would have been lost, but for Rāgasāgara who collected, compiled, printed and published them single handedly.

The book mentions the names of the initial members who wanted to purhcase the book. It enlists not only the name of Queen Victoria but many rajas, maharajas,amirs and umrahs of that time.

Part of *Saṅgīta-raga-kalpadruma* is written in Bengali and a part in *Devnāgri* print. The copy that was under the possession of Rāja Bāhādur of Lālgolā, consisted of the following chapters:

1. *Sucanikā O Svākṣara Nāmāni*
2. *Svarādhyāya, Tālādhyāya, Nṛtyādhyāya, Rāga-rāginī-vivekādhyāya,*
3. *Dhruvapada-Khayālādigāna*
4. *Raṅgīnagāna majmuyā*
5. *Kīrtana or Nitya-kīrtana*
6. *Holi-raṅgīnagāna*
7. *Adhyātma O jñāna tattva sāgara*
8. Hindi *Bhaktamāla-dhṛta Kabīrer Bījaka*
9. Some pages from the parts that are missing in this book are:
   a. *Surdāsjīkṛta Surasāgara Sārāvalī*
   b. *Surasāgara Badhāi, Surasāgara Bālalīlā, Yamalārjuna, Aghāsura-vadha, Rādhā Kṛṣṇajīke prathama milana līlā, Govardhanalīlā, Gocāraṇalīlā, Kālīya-damanalīlā, Dāvānala-pānalīlā, Vastraharaṇalīlā, Panghaṭki līlā, Khanḍtā etc.*
   c. *Surasāgara Muralīlīlā, Rāslīlā O Mānlīlā*
   d. *Surasāgara Mathurālīlā, Surasāgara Bhramaragīta (Rāgasāgara Saṅgraha)*
   e. *Apno dīnatā Prabhujīko māhātmya, tathā vinaya patrikā*
   f. *Kalāvatī Horigāna*
   g. *Rājā Bharatari gīta O Rāja Gopīcandra gīta*
   h. *Raṅgīna gāna* (*Ghazal Rekhtā Śāyar Rubāi,* etc. in Hindi and Persian language).

(*Saṅgīta-rāga-kalpadruma*-KṛṣṇānandaVyāsa Deva, III Parts, printed under the patronage of Rājā Rāo Śrī Jogīndra Nārāyaṇa Rāy Bāhādur of Lālgolā, Ed. by Nagendranath Basu- Cal-1973).

Mūla Saṅgītādarśa-Ramāpati Bandopādhyay

This book was published by the author in 1269 B.S. It contains some rare original *bandiśés* in Hindi/Brajabhasa and his own Bengali compositions based on these *bandiśes*. Sometimes there are more than one Bengali compositions based on a particular *bandiś*.At the begining of the book there are 42 original songs in Hindi/Brajabhasa along with Bengali compositions by Ramapati, based on the same *rāgas* and *tālas* of the Hindi versions, followed by 90 more compositions by him, with the mention of *rāgas* and *tālas* over them. In the concluding part there are 17 *Āgamanī* songs. The book also includes one song by his father *Gaṅgābiṣṇu* and some by his wife *Karuṇāmayī* who was a musician. The first composition in the book is of Tānsen, set in *Bhairavarāga* and *Cautāla*.The other *rāgas* and *tālas* on which *Ramāpati* has based his Bengali compositions are as follows:

	Rāga		Tāla
1.	*Megha*	—	*Cautāla*
2.	*Meghmallāra*	—	*Kavvālī*
3.	*Sāraṅga*	—	*Cautāla.*
4.	*Sāraṅga*	—	*Kavvālī*
5.	*Gauḍa-sāraṅga*	—	*Madhyamānā.*
6.	*Yamana*	—	*Ektāla.*
7.	*Khambāvatī*	—	*Kavvālī.*
8.	*Deś-mallāra*	—	*Dhīmā-tintāla.*
9.	*Bhaktāvalī-kānaḍā*	—	*Kavvālī.*
10.	*Khāmāja*	—	*Cautāla.*
11.	*Khāmāja*	—	*Kavvālī.*
12.	*Kedārā-bahār*	—	*Ektāla.*
13.	*Dhur-mallāra*	—	*Kavvālī.*
14.	*Lalit*	—	*Ektāla.*
15.	*Putracandrabimba*	—	*Āḍā.*
16.	*Jayeta*	—	*Ektāla.*
17.	*Himāl*	—	*Kavvālī.*
18.	*Toḍī*	—	*Dhāmār.*
19.	*Bihāga*	—	*Tritāla.*
20.	*Bihāga*	—	*Ektāla.*
21.	*Alhaiyā*	—	*Kavvālī.*
22.	*Aḍānā*	—	*Cautāla.*
23.	*Jayetśrī*	—	*Madhyamāna.*
24.	*Gārā-bhairavī*	—	*Postā.*

25. *Lāvani-pīlu* — *Thumrītāla*
26. *Rāmkelī* — *Savārī.*
27. *Sorat* — *Postā.*

There is one *bandiś* which is mentioned as *Nakśgol* and set in *Tālafertā* in which various *tālas* are used such as -*Teoṭ, Kavvalī, Postā* and *Jat.*

Besides the above mentioned *rāgas* of the original Hindi songs, Ramāpati's own independent compostions were set on many *rāgas* such as *Paraja, Jhījhiṭ, Barvā, Kaliṅgḍā, Gārā-bhairavi, Bhaktāvalī-kānaḍā, etc.* while his wife's compostions were set on *rāgas* like *Bihāga, Suraṭā mallāra, Deśa mallāra, Bhairavī, Kāliṅgḍā, Lalit* etc.

Saṅgīta-sāra : Kshetramohan Goswami.

During the 16th, 17th, 18th, and 19th centuries, the same *rāga* used to be practised differently in different parts of India. Kshetramohan, felt the need to thrash out differences of opinion amongst *ustāds* of different *gharānās* regarding the following points:

1. *Rāga - rūpa,* 2. *Rāga - jāti,* 3. *Thāṭa,* 4. other essential qualities of a *rāga* and 5. various theoretical matters practised differently by the *ustāds.* For this purpose he organised an "All India Music Conference" for the first time, in 1867 in Calcutta, under the guidance of Laxmiprasad Misra. Saurindramohan and Jotindramohan Thākur gave him financial and all other support. This conference was a meet of the then great *ustāds* who discussed their views on *rāgas* and other musical queries which were considered from *śāstrīya* angles and later compiled by Kshetramohan with his own views, in his book named *Saṅgīta-sāra.*

The first edition of this book was published in 1869 consisting of 318 + 10 pages. The second edition consisting of 409 + 24 pages was published in 1879 by Kaliprasanna Bandyopadhyay and was dedicated to Jotindramohan Thakur.

This book is divided into two parts, first part containing *gīta, vādya* and *nṛtya-kāṇḍas* or chapters, while the second part consists of notated forms for practical music (क्रियासिद्ध तौर्यत्रिक).

The first part deals with *nāda, śruti, mūrchanā, gamaka, tāna, laya,* etc; origin, time cycle, various *lakṣaṇas* of *rāgas*; names of famous musicians; *tālas*; description of Indian instruments, their history of origin; and dance.

The second part mainly consists of notation system and its necessity; notated *gats* and *ālāpas* of different *rāgas*; how to play the *tablā* and *sitār*, comparison with Western music, etc. *Daṇḍamātrik* notation system innovated by him, has been used to illustrate the *rāgas.*

According to him, there was a notation system in ancient India, written with the first letters of the *svaras.* Pythagorus learnt this method from India and taught the Greek and that was the beginning of notation system in Europe.

Kshetramohan's other valuable books are : *Aikatānik Svaralipi,* - pub. in 1868; *Gītagobinder Svaralipi* - pub. in 1871; *Kanṭha Kaumudī* - pub. in 1875; *Āśurañjanī Tattva,* pub. in 1885.

Gītasūtra-sāra : Krishnadhan Banerji

Gītasūtra-sāra is the result of studies and research in both Indian and Western classical music in depth, by the author. He has dealt with notation system in great length and evolved two systems - 1. *Sāṅketik* and 2. *Sārgam.* The first one is based on Universal Staff Notation of Western music while the second is based on Tonic Solfa with the basic seven Indian *svaras,* their *vikṛta rūpas* and other details of various signs. Some signs are common to both the systems.

Gītasūtra-sāra is one of the most valuable treatises of music of 19th cent. Pt. Bhatkhande specially learnt Bengali to understand the theories enumerated in this book and included it in the syllabus of Lucknow Marris College of Music.

Gītasūtra-sāra consists of two parts. The first part of the book was first published by the author in 1885 from Cooch Bihar, sponsored by Maharaj Nṛpendranārāyaṇa Bhūp Bāhādur of Cooch Bihar, followed by the second part in 1886.

The salient features of part I of this book (apart from detailed notation systems), are:

Kanṭha-mārjanā or voice culture; *Svarasādhan* i.e. practice of singing the *svaras* methodically; *Svara prakaraṇa; Svara grāma* and *Svarāntara* dealing with the seven notes and their positions and other details; *Rāgas* and *rāgiṇis,* their origin, *jāti, matas,* time of singing, how to determine *thāṭas* (with charts), their *graha* and *nyāsa-svaras, vādī-samvādī svaras,* various openions regarding *rāgas; Ālāpa* of a *rāga* and its step by step presentation; the various styles of *rāga-saṅgīta,* viz. *Dhrupada, Khayāl, Ṭappā, Prabandha gāna, Horī, Telenā* (*Tarānā*), *Trivaṭa, Caturaṅga, Gulnakś, Qaul - Qaulbanā, Sargam, Rāgamālā, Yugalbandh, Ṭap-khayāl, Ṭhumrī* and *Ghazal;* the various steps observed in presenting a *Khayāl,* e.g. *tāna, bānṭ, bol-bānī,* etc. The author also explains how to create *rasa* through music; the ancient *Śāstras* of Hindu music dealing with subjects of theoretical music, such as : *svaras, saptaka, śruti, grāma, svara* position (with charts), *mūrchanā, tāna, graha-nyāsa, vādī-vivādī, gamaka,* short descriptions of *rāga-rāgiṇīs* and *tālas.* Accompaniments with vocal music, good and bad points of tānpurā, have also been discussed in length. Other topics dealt with are: details of *mātrā, chanda* and *tālas* with diagrams and notation signs; how to determine *grāmas* of *rāgas; Ṣadja-parivartana* and *Ṣadja-saṅkrāmaṇa.*

There are 17 *paricchedas* or chapters in the first part dealing with the theoretical aspects of music mentioned above and are as follows:

1. *Upakramaṇikā* (introductory Chapter)	dealing with origin of music, music of India, necessity and usefulness of notation system, etc.

2. 1st *Parriccheda*	*Kanṭha mārjanā.*
3. 2nd *Parriccheda*	*Svara Prakaraṇa O Svara - Sādhan.*
4. 3rd *Parriccheda*	*Svara-grāma O Svarāntarer niyama Sāṅketik svaralipite surer saṅketa.*
5. 4th *Parriccheda*	*Komala O kaḍi surer vivaraṇ.*
6. 5th *Parriccheda*	*Svaralipite surer sthāyīkāla jñāpak saṅket.*
7. 6th *Parriccheda*	*Gāner alaṅkāra.*
8. 7th *Parriccheda*	*Rāga-rāginīr utpatti viṣayak yukti vicāra.*
9. 8th *Parriccheda*	*Rāga-rāginīr vivaraṇa.*
10. 9th *Parriccheda*	*Rāga-rāginīr gāoyār-samaya o thāṭa-prabhṛti nirupaṇa.*
11. 10th *Pariccheda*	*Ālāpa o gāner rīti.*
12. 11th *Parriccheda*	*Saṅgīta dvārā raser uddīpanā.*
13. 12th *Parriccheda*	*Hindu Saṅgīter prācīna śāstra.*
14. 13th *Parriccheda*	*Kanṭher sahita yantrer saṅgata.*
15. 14th *Parriccheda*	*Mātrā, chanda, o tālādir vivaraṇa; Svaralipite chander padavibhāga; Chander prakāra o jāti Svaralipite paunaruktir saṅketa.*
16. 15th *Parriccheda*	*Pracalita tālasamūher mātrā o chanda niraṇaya; Caturmātrika - jāti: Kavvālī tāla, Dhimā-tetālā, Ṭhumrītāla, Chepkā o Kāhārvātāla, Āḍāṭhekā, Madhyamāna. Trimātrika-jāti : Khemṭā, Āḍ-khemṭā, Ektāla, Cautāla, Viṣamapadī-jāti : Jhaptāla, Surfāktāla, Jat, Dhāmār, Postā, Teot, Rūpaka, Cautāla, Teorā, Pañcamasavārī. Tāler cāri graha, Layer gatibheda o tāhār uddeśya, Vilamvita laya (dhimā) Mātrāmān-yantra.*
17. 16th *Parriccheda*	*Rāgādir grāma nirupaṇa*
18. 17th *Parriccheda*	*Ṣaḍja parivartana o Ṣaḍja saṅkrāmaṇa.*
19. *Nirghanṭa* (Index)	

Second part of this book contains mainly notated examples which are mostly written in *Sāṅketik-paddhati* and some in *Sārgam-paddhati.*

At the end, the author has provided with an index, an important feature introduced by him at that early period.

This book was published again in 1934 by his son Nīrendranāth, combining both the parts. This edition was also translated in English by Himanshu

Bandopadhyay of Behrampur. Another edition of the first part only, was published by Nibha Mukhopadhyay in 1332 B.S.

Other valuable books written by the author are: *Baṅgaikatāna*, -1867, *Hindusthani Airs arranged for the Piano Forte* - 1868, *Saṅgīta - śikṣā* - 1868, *Gīta-śikṣā* - 1873, and Harmonium-*śikṣā* - 1899.

Saṅgīta-praveśikā, (arthāt Hindu Tauryatrika Samvandhīya Sandarbha Grantha) — Murarimohan Gupta

Published in two parts, first part (154 pages) deals with short history of Indian music, *Mṛdaṅga,* different *tālas* with details, *ṭhekās* and bols of *mṛdaṅga.* Later in 1889, (consisting of another 85 pages) second part was published. This part specially deals with *tablā,* or *Tala-mṛdaṅga,* its *bols* and techniques of playing.

Saṅgīta-praveśikā is the second publication on *mṛdaṅga,* the first one being Saurīndramohan Thakur's '*Mṛdaṅga-Manjurī*' published in 1873, but it is perhaps the first on *tablā.*

Index

Corrigendum Volume II

Sr.no.	Page	Line	For	Read/Remarks
1.	298	13	सुशेभित	सुशोभित
2.	331	Last line of notation		In place of the first four vertical lines, there should be only one
3.	454	Ist line of the song	धुम	घुम
4.	454	Ist & 4th lines of notation	धुम	घुम
5.	455	6th line of notation	धुम	घुम
6.	478	8	Tatvabodhinī	Tattvabodhinī
7.	510	2	Chandhuri	Chaudhuri
8.	511	9	Dipani	Dīpanī
9.	511	13	Rupaka	Rūpaka
10.	511	23	Gita	Gīta
11.	511	23	Dhatu	Dhātu
12.	511	27	Pracyadeśa	Prācyadeśa
13.	512	36	Mohāpatra	Mohāpātra
14.	513	19	Gita	Gīta
15.	521	29	Ragā	Rāga
16.	526	23	pālas	pālās
17.	537	1-30	Parriccheda	Pariccheda